United States
Marine Reconnaissance
in the Vietnam War

ALSO BY LEO J. DAUGHERTY III
AND FROM McFARLAND

*Counterinsurgency and the United States Marine Corps:
Volume 1, The First Counterinsurgency Era, 1899–1945* (2015)

*The Marine Corps and the State Department:
Enduring Partners in United States Foreign Policy, 1798–2007* (2009)

*Pioneers of Amphibious Warfare, 1898–1945:
Profiles of Fourteen American Military Strategists* (2009)

*The Allied Resupply Effort in the China-Burma-India
Theater During World War II* (2008)

BY LEO J. DAUGHERTY III AND RHONDA L. SMITH-DAUGHERTY

*Counterinsurgency and the United States Marine Corps:
Volume 2, An Era of Persistent Warfare, 1945–2016* (2018)

United States Marine Reconnaissance in the Vietnam War

Ghost Soldiers and Sea Commandos, 1963–1971

Leo J. Daugherty III

McFarland & Company, Inc., Publishers
Jefferson, North Carolina

LIBRARY OF CONGRESS CATALOGUING-IN-PUBLICATION DATA

Names: Daugherty, Leo J., author.
Title: United States Marine reconnaissance in the Vietnam War : ghost soldiers and sea commandos, 1963–1971 / Leo J. Daugherty III.
Other titles: Ghost soldiers and sea commandos, 1963–1971
Description: Jefferson, North Carolina : McFarland & Company, Inc., Publishers, 2024 | Includes bibliographical references and index.
Identifiers: LCCN 2023054553 | ISBN 9781476690964 (print) ∞
ISBN 9781476650135 (ebook)
Subjects: LCSH: United States. Marine Corps. Force Reconnaissance—History. | Vietnam War, 1961–1975—Reconnaissance operations. | Military reconnaissance—History—20th century. | BISAC: HISTORY / Wars & Conflicts / Vietnam War
Classification: LCC DS559.8.R43 D38 2024 | DDC 959.704/345—dc23/eng/20231222
LC record available at https://lccn.loc.gov/2023054553

BRITISH LIBRARY CATALOGUING DATA ARE AVAILABLE

**ISBN (print) 978-1-4766-9096-4
ISBN (ebook) 978-1-4766-5013-5**

© 2024 Leo J. Daugherty III. All rights reserved

*No part of this book may be reproduced or transmitted in any form
or by any means, electronic or mechanical, including photocopying
or recording, or by any information storage and retrieval system,
without permission in writing from the publisher.*

Front cover: A 3rd Force Reconnaissance team led by Staff Sergeant Livingston before patrol in the summer of 1968 (photograph courtesy of LtCol Berwick Babin, USMC Ret.)

Printed in the United States of America

*McFarland & Company, Inc., Publishers
Box 611, Jefferson, North Carolina 28640
www.mcfarlandpub.com*

To all Reconnaissance Marines, Army Special Forces,
LRRPs and Rangers, Navy Underwater Demolition Teams,
SEALS, and U.S. Air Force Air Commandos
who served in the Republic of Vietnam, 1958–1973—
you all were part of the most successful and finest field army
the United States ever sent into battle

In Memoriam
To the late Major Christopher K. Ives, U.S. Army, PhD
"My Friend, Colleague, and Fellow Warrior"
FOR
"JOHNNY and JAGDTIGER"

Table of Contents

Acknowledgments — ix
Glossary of Terms — xiii
Preface — 1
Introduction — 3

1. Birth of a Concept: The Origins of Marine Force Reconnaissance (1898–1943) — 5
2. Amphibious Reconnaissance Company Goes to War (1943–1945) — 41
3. Reconstitution and Expansion: Marine Corps Amphibious Reconnaissance (1946–1963) — 64
4. Vietnam: The Early Years (1963–1964) — 86
5. "Land the Landing Force": Recon Goes to War (1965–1967) — 93
6. "The Year of the Offensive": 1st Marine Reconnaissance Battalion in Action (1966–1967) — 126
7. "Anatomy of a Reconnaissance Patrol" — 137
8. The Year of the Offensive: Recon and the Fight for the Hills (1967) — 149
9. "Some Hard Fighting": Marine Reconnaissance and the Year of Tet (1968) — 190
10. The Eyes and Ears of the 1st and 3rd Marine Divisions: Reconnaissance from the Air — 215
11. High Mobility and Standdown: Recon's War (1969–1970) — 220
12. Redeployment and Deactivation (1969–1970) — 241
13. "A War by Detachments": U.S. Army Long-Range Reconnaissance Patrols in Vietnam (1966–1973) — 253
14. "Ghost Soldiers" and "Sea Commandos": Marine Recon's War in Vietnam (1963–1971) — 275

Appendix A: Marine Reconnaissance Equipment — 279
Appendix B: The Medal of Honor Citation for 1st Lieutenant Frank Reasoner, USMC — 281

Appendix C: Summary of Event Concerning VC Contact 21–22, 1966   282

Appendix D: The Strategic Importance of An Hoa Combat Base   284

Appendix E: "A Reconnaissance Patrol in 'Happy Valley' by 'Killer Kane' 1st Force Reconnaissance Company by 2nd Lieutenant Andrew R. Finlayson, USMC, Commander, 5th Platoon, 1st Force Reconnaissance Company, III MAF"   288

Appendix F: Lessons from Marine Recon's War in Vietnam: Colonel Andrew R. Finlayson, USMC (Ret.)   292

Appendix G: Weapons of the Viet Cong and North Vietnamese Army   296

Appendix H: Reflections of a Reconnaissance Marine—Lieutenant Colonel Berwick Babin, USMC (Ret.), 3rd Force Reconnaissance Company (1967–1969)   298

Appendix I: "My Story": One Reconnaissance Marine's War in Vietnam—Sergeant William Moss and Team Atlas   300

Chapter Notes   303

Bibliography   319

Index   327

Acknowledgments

This book has undoubtedly been one of the more challenging projects this author has ever undertaken. Having started out as a pamphlet for the Marine Corps Historical Foundation and ending up as a book title for McFarland, it has been a "long journey" from conception to reality.

In 2014, Mr. Charles D. Melson, then chief historian for the Marine Corps History Division, asked whether I would be willing to take on this project for a series that was in the works on the U.S. Marine Corps in the Vietnam War. Without any hesitation, I gave an enthusiastic "yes," as it would be the perfect follow-up to my published work with History Division on the British Royal Marines and South Korean Marine Corps during the Korean War (1950–1953).

Work commenced full time after completing two other writing projects. My first step was to contact the Third Force Reconnaissance Association, receiving an invitation to their reunion in Asheville, North Carolina. Here, I had the honor of meeting members of Third Force Reconnaissance, especially Sergeants "Butch" Menning and William Moss, Corporal Lou Kern, Major Bruce D. "Doc" Norton, and Lieutenant Colonel Berwick Babin. After interviewing team members over two days and holding lengthy discussions with Colonel Babin (who has become not only a friend but also a mentor in my understanding of the differences between "Force" and "Division" Marine Reconnaissance), I came to understand the important role Marine and Army Reconnaissance played in Vietnam. Barry and Colonel Andrew R. Finlayson (whom I contacted after reading his superb *Killer Kane*, about his exploits with 1st Force Reconnaissance Company) have also become true "mentors," schooling me in the methods and techniques of Marine Force Reconnaissance and their experiences in Vietnam from 1967 to 1970. Sergeant "Butch" Menning has likewise become a trusted friend and fellow Marine over these years. To all of you, as Bette Midler sings, "you … are my heroes…. You are the wind beneath my wings."

To my professors at John Carroll University in Cleveland, Ohio, where I received my BA (1979) and MA (1985) in history, I could never have mastered such a project without the training, mentoring and guidance with which you all provided me. A special mention goes to the best of the best, the late Reverend Donald W. Smythe, Jr., S.J., PhD; William J. Ulrich, PhD; George J. Prpic, PhD; Michael S. Pap, PhD; Reverend Howard Kerner, S.J., PhD; and Walter Kosinski, PhD. While you all have passed on to a better life, you live on in my work as a military historian and scholar. I could never repay the patience, mentorship, and time you spent working with me. This book is for you all.

To my professors at The Ohio State University, especially my mentor and a fellow Marine, Colonel Allan R. Millett, USMC, PhD. To Williamson Murray, PhD—"Wick," you were tough, but you taught me how to write. I enjoyed your classes on World War II, especially our Eastern Front course. To the late John F. Guilmartin, PhD, a true hero, who as a U.S Air Force search and rescue pilot flew missions in Vietnam; Michael Hogan, my diplomatic historian; Alam Payind, PhD, my Middle East and Central Asian professor—you all finished what my professors at John Carroll University started.

To my drill instructors at Marine Corps Recruit Depot, Parris Island, South Carolina: Staff Sergeant Howard, Staff Sergeant Derig, and Sergeants Parham and Western. You were the best teachers I ever had.

To my late friend and colleague, Major Christopher K. Ives, PhD—in our many discussions at The Ohio State University on Special Forces and counterinsurgency, Chris taught me much about special operations and Special Forces doctrine. His untimely death has left a void in all of those who knew him.

To Mrs. Stephanie Peters of the Barr Library, Fort Knox, Kentucky, for helping locate the article on Colonel James Logan Jones, Sr.; to Dr. Steven R. Wise, director of the Command Museum at Marine Corps Recruit Depot (MCRD), Parris Island, South Carolina, and his very able assistants—Mrs. Cheryl Huff, Mrs. Kim Zawicki, and Ms. Emily May—for allowing me unlimited access to the Major General Oscar F. Peatross, USMC, papers; to Dr. Eugene Alvarez, PhD, a friend, and fellow Marine and historian of MCRD Parris Island, South Carolina, and his sidekick and companion, "Taco."

To Ms. Genoa Stanford at the Donovan Library, the U.S. Army Maneuver Center of Excellence at Fort Benning, Georgia, who has been a friend and colleague over the years and helped me in my research regarding Army training in the 1960s and provided me with a copy of the Haines Report. To Ms. (Dr.) Stephanie Lang, the editor of the *Registrar, Journal of Kentucky History,* who has allowed me to quote from my forthcoming article on ROTC training during the 1960s, and to Mr. Steven Coode at the Marine Corps History Division Reference Section, whose quick response in filling a last-minute request for photos was much appreciated.

To my late parents: Leo J. Daugherty, Jr., a Marine, and Frances H. Daugherty. I thank you both for the education you provided and sacrificed to give me. I succeeded because you had faith in me, and I never wanted to let you down.

To my friend and fellow Marine, Lieutenant Colonel Thomas Crecca, USMC (Ret.), at the U.S. Army Center of Military History—the discussions we have had on special operations over the years inspired me to move forward on this project.

To my wife and academic partner for life, Dr. Rhonda L. Smith-Daugherty. I know that I have been absent many nights working in my study on this project, in addition to dragging you to a Third Force Reconnaissance reunion of "old" Marines when you would rather have been on a beach in the Caribbean. Hopefully, you will understand and forgive. You are a fine scholar in your own right. Also, to my faithful companion Paris, our "Alpha" cat and one who kept me company while I put the finishing touches on this book.

Special thanks go out also to Colonel John Vogel, (USMC), (RET.), who gave me permission to include the photos of SCUBA 1 during the Battle for Hue City, and Major Barry Broman USMC (Ret.), who provided the photo of the "Simmons Ladder" in operation.

Finally, this book goes out to all the young men mentioned in these pages and those who are not—you were all part of the finest field army the United States ever sent into battle. You won your war in Vietnam; it was a forgetful nation that will never acknowledge this latter fact. You were victors—then ... now ... and always.

Glossary of Terms

AK-47—Soviet/Chinese-supplied "Kalashnikov" assault rifle
AO—Aerial Observer
ARVN—Army of the Republic of Vietnam
CAP—Combined Arms Platoon
CCTs—U.S. Air Force Combat Controller Teams
CHICOM—Chinese Communist
CIA—Central Intelligence Agency
CIDG—Civilian Irregular Defense Group
CORDS—Civil Operations and Revolutionary Development Support
COSVN—Central Office for South Vietnam (served as headquarters for the Lao Dong Party)
DA—Department of the U.S. Army
DMZ—Demilitarized Zone
DRV—Democratic Republic of Vietnam (North Vietnam)
DZ—Drop Zone
FA—Field Artillery
"Firecracker"—M-33 fragmentation grenade introduced in 1968 and used by Marine Recon teams
FMF—Fleet Marine Force
FMFLant—Fleet Marine Force, Atlantic
FMFPac—Fleet Marine Force, Pacific
H&I—Harassment and Interdiction
Harbor Site—The position established by Recon teams as a base of operations and security for the team prior to and after a mission
HLZ—Helicopter Landing Zone
HQMC—Headquarters Marine Corps
KACHINS—Burmese natives who assisted American and Allied forces in Burma during World War II
KEYHOLE—A four-man Marine Recon team inserted for observation and surveillance
KIA—Killed in Action
LRRP—Long-Range Reconnaissance Patrol
LZ—"Ladder Zone" used for extraction of Recon teams via the "Ladder" device; also used to describe a landing zone
M-79—Hand-held shotgun-like weapon (commonly known as the "blooper")
MAB—Marine Amphibious Brigade
MACV—Military Assistance Command Vietnam
MAF—Marine Amphibious Force
MAGIS—Marine Air-Ground Intelligence System
MAW—Marine Air Wing
MR—Military Region
NAD—Naval Advisory Detachment
"NASTIES"—Norwegian patrol boats used by Recon Marines

Glossary of Terms

NLF—National Liberation Front (official name of the "Viet Cong," South Vietnamese Communists)
NKPA—North Korean People's Army
NUNGS—Chinese mercenaries in service of the CIA
NVA—North Vietnamese Army
OP—Observation Post
PAVN—People's Army of Vietnam (North)
PBR—Patrol Boat, River
PF—Popular Forces (lightly armed South Vietnamese militia trained by U.S. advisors)
Phoenix—Program established by the CIA to root out South Vietnamese Communists
PLA—People's Liberation Army (Communist China)
POSREP—Position Report
PRG—Provisional Reconnaissance Group
PRU—Provincial Reconnaissance Unit (action arm of the CIA's Phoenix Program, manned primarily by South Vietnamese Special Forces and a U.S. advisor)
PSID—Patrol Science Intrusion Device
Radio—Location on a prominent terrain feature, usually atop a hill or mountain and used by Relay Site Marine Reconnaissance teams for the transmission and re-transmission of radio traffic
RECONDO—"Reconnaissance, Commando, Doughboy" (a school established in 1965 to train Army, Marine and Navy personnel in long-range reconnaissance techniques)
ROAR—Reconnaissance Area of Responsibility
ROK—Republic of Korea
RZ—Reconnaissance Zone
SAF—Small Arms Fire
SCAMP—Sensor Control and Management Platoon
SEAL—Sea, Air, and Land (Navy Special Forces evolved from Underwater Demolition Teams)
SERE—Survival, Evasion, Resistance, and Escape
SITREP—Situation Report
SLF—Special Landing Force
SOE—Special Operations Executive (established by the British during World War II to train commandos, paratroopers and Royal Marines)
SOG—Studies and Observations Group
SPIE—Special Personnel Insertion and Extraction Rig
"Spooky"—A converted C-47 Air Force gunship mounted with 90mm cannons or mini-guns
SRC—Surveillance and Reconnaissance Center
SRG—Strategic Reconnaissance Group
STA—Surveillance and Target Acquisition
STABO Rig—A special rig consisting of two straps on the Recon team member's backpack, which are then brought through his legs and securely snapped in front with a climber's snap link called a carabiner; a hundred-foot nylon cord is dropped by the encircling helicopter with two "D" rings, which the team member snaps in before being pulled upward into the helicopter
STINGRAY—A Marine Corp Reconnaissance tactic or technique that employed small reconnaissance teams to call in supporting arms on the enemy distant from friendly lines
TAOR—Tactical Area of Responsibility
UDT—Underwater Demolition Teams (forerunners of the Navy SEALs)
USAF—United States Air Force
USN—United States Navy
USSF—United States Special Forces (U.S. Army)
VC—Viet Cong
VCI—Viet Cong Infrastructure
VNMC—South Vietnamese Marine Corps
WIA—Wounded in Action

Preface

In 1906, Major Dion Williams, while a student at the Naval War College, wrote what was perhaps the first treatise on amphibious reconnaissance. In his study, *Naval Reconnaissance: Instructions for the Reconnaissance of Bays, Harbors, and Adjacent Country*, the Marine major, who can be considered the "Father of Marine Corps Reconnaissance," outlined the reasons for and missions of Marine amphibious reconnaissance.

Over the next six decades, the term "amphibious reconnaissance" became more defined as a method of gathering, analyzing and disseminating intelligence of an enemy beachhead before, during and after an amphibious or (to use the language of the time) "advanced base" landing. Furthermore, it is important to stress that the development of amphibious reconnaissance doctrine from 1907 paralleled the evolving Marine Corps' advanced base doctrine, which, over time, grew into that service's amphibious warfare doctrine.[1] From mid–1938, during the fleet exercises on Culebra, Puerto Rico, to the time when the first Marine "amphibious reconnaissance" units stood up under the command of Captain (later Colonel) James Logan Jones, Sr., in December 1940, Marine amphibious reconnaissance found itself (with one exception on Saipan in June 1944) engaged in every major American landing in the Pacific Ocean area during World War II. Subsequently deactivated, and then reactivated after a very brief period at the end of World War II, Marine Reconnaissance, now defined by land and sea missions, continued its evolution as a major component in Marine (and Navy) planning during the next three decades.[2]

When American advisors deployed to the Republic of Vietnam in 1963–1964, Marine ground reconnaissance units, based primarily in Okinawa, Japan, were there as part of what was then called the Studies and Observations Group (or SOG), which conducted hydrographic soundings and terrain and enemy analysis along South Vietnam's lengthy coastline. This activity soon became relevant when the first Marine conventional forces came ashore at Da Nang in March 1965. For the next six years (1965–1971), Marine Reconnaissance units, both Division and Force Reconnaissance, played an essential role in scouting out, fighting and defeating large bodies of enemy troops in northern South Vietnam (or I Corps) and in the Mekong Delta. A true measure of their success can be found in the fact that Marine Force and

Division Reconnaissance forced the North Vietnamese Army to commit large forces to hunt down and destroy these reconnaissance teams.

This book, *United States Marine Reconnaissance in the Vietnam War*, discusses the evolution of Marine and Army reconnaissance doctrine and forces from their earliest origins in 1898 through the end of ground involvement the Vietnam War in March 1971. This evolution was one of trial and error and resulted in the formulation of one of the most effective war-fighting doctrines ever devised by the U.S. military, which is to this day still used by Marine, Navy, Air Force, and Army Special Forces. Many of the techniques, procedures, force structure, and technological developments originated in the jungle of Vietnam. As such, the Vietnam War, like any other conflict, served as a laboratory for the tactics, technologies, doctrine, and force structure employed by today's special operating forces. This latter point is reflected in the fact that this author, as a young Marine corporal, was schooled in the concept of MAGIS (Marine Air-Ground Intelligence Systems) devised after the TET offensive in 1968, as well as the employment of SCAMP (Sensor Control and Management Platoons), used by Marine and Army reconnaissance teams along the Demilitarized Zone in Vietnam. Little did I realize at the time that these same systems were first thought of during 1968 to monitor and measure infiltration by NVA units infiltrating into the south. As this book will demonstrate, Marine Reconnaissance was at the forefront of the technological revolution that enhanced the capabilities of Special Operating Forces—much like that of the British Special Operations Executive (or SOE) of World War II fame.

Finally, this book is about the young men who faced danger day in and day out, fighting in all types of weather, food and sleep deprived, against a wily, determined enemy. The record of these reconnaissance teams speaks for itself—they were, in fact, the most effective means of detecting and defeating the NVA over eight years of employment in the jungles and hills of Vietnam. This book tells the story of how they accomplished this feat within a few short years, becoming known by a respectful adversary as "Ghost Soldiers ... and Sea Commandos."

Introduction

During the Marine Corps' long involvement in Vietnam, Reconnaissance Marines played an integral role in the war against the National Liberation Front (Viet Cong or "VC") and the North Vietnamese Army (NVA). Many of the tactics, techniques, and procedures used by reconnaissance units in Vietnam were established before, during and after World War II and remained the core operating principles guiding reconnaissance operations in the post–Vietnam years. Reconnaissance Marines fought and died in Vietnam with resolve, courage and distinction. Their battlefield legacy continues to inspire doctrine and training, echoing throughout today's technologically enriched Marine Reconnaissance and special operation units. The Marines of 1st and 3rd Force Reconnaissance Companies, and their brothers-in-arms from 1st and 3rd Reconnaissance Battalions, faithfully served as the "eyes and ears" of Marine battalion, regimental, and division-level commanders who directed the war in their respective tactical areas of responsibility (TAORs) against enemy forces infiltrating across the Demilitarized Zone (DMZ) and along the Vietnamese/Laotian border. From 1963 until their withdrawal in 1971, Marine Reconnaissance teams maintained an active presence in I Corps, where they conducted deep reconnaissance missions despite a determined, resourceful enemy and harsh conditions of a pernicious war.

Their record of unit and personal valorous awards, enemy attrition ratio and captured enemy war material points a sure finger toward that which is difficult to quantify. Notwithstanding non-doctrinal missions, periods of underutilization, poor personnel rotation and the adversities of war, Marine Reconnaissance patrols returned with critical information that shaped the battlefield and enabled the 1st and 3rd Marine Divisions to attrite the enemy to an unprecedented degree in modern warfare. Together with their Army and Navy counterparts, Marine Reconnaissance teams forged an incredible rate of success, despite adverse weather, a hostile enemy, and at times an indifferent command. What follows is how Marine Reconnaissance came about, as well as the evolution of its doctrinal and operational techniques, all of which began at the dawn of the twentieth century and culminated in the jungles of Vietnam.

1

Birth of a Concept

The Origins of Marine Force Reconnaissance (1898–1943)

The origins of Marine Reconnaissance—both Force and Division—are rooted in the development of the Advanced Base Force, the predecessor to the Marine Corps' doctrine of amphibious warfare refined in the two decades following World War I (1920–1941). The concept of the Advanced Base Force, conceptualized with the birth of the "New Steel Navy" during the 1890s and developed in the aftermath of the War with Spain (1898), brought with it the requirement of a force dedicated to scouting, reporting and analyzing enemy beachhead defenses and ports, in addition to providing hydrographic information to Navy and Marine officers aboard ship as they prepared to conduct an amphibious landing. Such would be the initial missions of Marine Reconnaissance up to 1945.[1]

"Birth of a Mission": The War with Spain (1898)

The "birth" of Marine Reconnaissance coincided with the initial landing of Marines at Guantanamo Bay, Cuba, during the War with Spain in June 1898, coming on the heels of an aborted mission by the U.S. Army to funnel arms and ammunition to Cuban *insurrectos* then fighting the Spanish Army on May 10, 1898. In a follow-up mission the next day, sailors and Marines assigned to the USS *Marblehead* were ordered to cut the transoceanic cables that connected the Spanish leaders in Cuba with Spain. On May 11, 1898, "a handful of sailors and Marines from the *Marblehead* piled into cutters" and, after rowing closer to the shoreline, began to drag the ocean floor for the transoceanic cable. Working with chisels, axes, hacksaws and wire cutters, these early forerunners of the Navy's famed Underwater Demolition Teams (UDTs) managed to cut two of the three cables.[2] The Spanish troops ashore watching the Americans work did not attack immediately. When the cables were cut, however, the Spaniards opened up on the Americans with machine gun and rifle fire. As the sailors and Marines completed their mission and gathered their casualties, the boats pulled anchor and moved out of range, carrying with them seven wounded (two of whom subsequently died of their wounds). This mission by the

An artist's rendition of the Marines and sailors cutting the cable at Cienfuegos during the War with Spain in 1898 (courtesy of U.S. Navy History and Heritage Command).

Marines and sailors, while more successful than that of the Army, nonetheless failed to cut all three of the cables, leaving one in operation.[3]

This would not be the only use of a pre-assault force during the War with Spain. In the pre-dawn hours of June 10, 1898, prior to the landing of a battalion of Marines at Guantanamo Bay commanded by Lieutenant Colonel Robert W. Huntington, USMC, Captain Bowman H. McCalla of the U.S. Navy, commanding officer of the task force assigned to seize and fortify Guantanamo Bay as a naval coaling station, ordered the landing of a detachment of sixty Marines commanded by Captain Mancil C. Goodrell, USMC, the Fleet Marine officer aboard the USS *New York*, "to reconnoiter Fisherman's Point, the proposed landing site of Huntington's Marine Battalion, and to destroy a Spanish cable station and a few huts."[4] With forty Marines

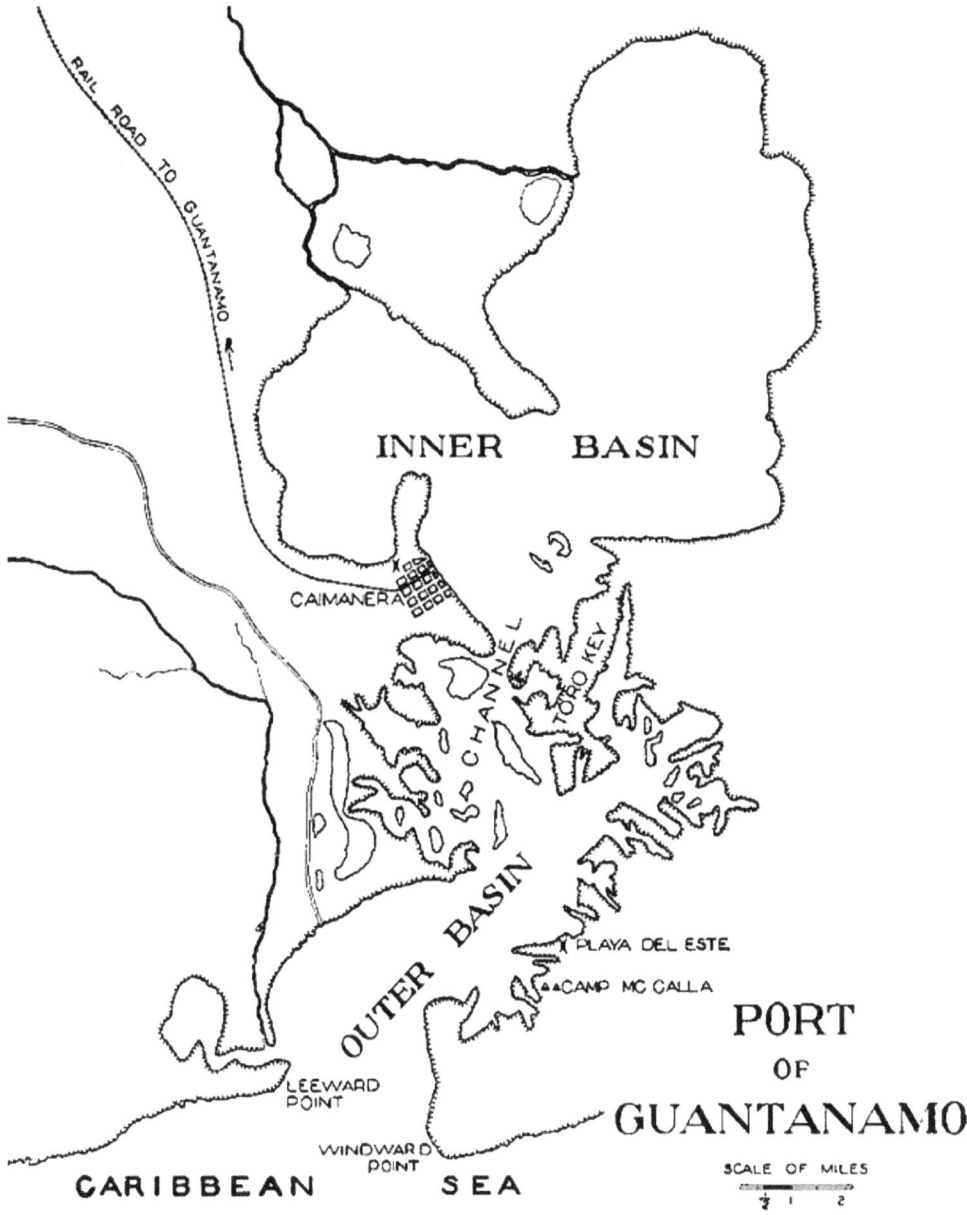

Map 1: Map of Guantanamo Bay, Cuba, during the War with Spain, 1898 (USMC History & Museums Division).

from the USS *Oregon* and twenty Marines from the USS *Marblehead*, Goodrell and his company of leathernecks conducted a reconnaissance ashore; afterward, they reembarked their respective vessels and awaited the arrival of Huntington's Marine battalion, which was to execute the first advanced base landing by Marines that same afternoon.[5] As a result of Captain Goodrell's reconnaissance, Commander McCalla decided to land Huntington's battalion at Fisherman's Point.

Even before Goodrell's reconnaissance off Guantanamo Bay, on May 1, 1898,

First Lieutenant Dion Williams, a native of Williamsburg, Ohio, and graduate of the U.S. Naval Academy (Class of 1891), landed with a detachment of Marines and Navy bluejackets from the USS *Baltimore* and took control of the Spanish naval base in Subic Bay in the Philippines. While not a "reconnaissance" mission in the classic sense, the experience nonetheless highlighted the need for pre-assault surveying and hydrographic information, points that Lieutenant (later Brigadier General) Dion Williams incorporated in his treatise on pre-assault reconnaissance and the need for a dedicated reconnaissance force as early as 1909.

"Recon Marine": Major Dion Williams and the Doctrine of Amphibious Reconnaissance (1906–1927)

The concept of amphibious reconnaissance developed almost simultaneously with the Advanced Base Force concept and the doctrine of amphibious warfare. In 1906, Major Dion Williams wrote what is considered the "first American doctrine for amphibious reconnaissance."[6] Participating in the pacification campaign in the Philippines from 1898 to 1900, Williams returned to command the Marine Barracks, Boston Navy Yard, from 1900 to 1902, where he commanded a company of Marines sent to the Isthmus of Panama as part of an expeditionary force to protect American lives and property against Panamanian insurgents during the Colombian revolution. Captain Williams' mission was to "seize the guns and ammunition [of the insurgents], and replace a Colombian battalion that had occupied the wharf." At first, the Colombians refused to obey when Williams and twelve enlisted Marines, in a show of force, ordered them to vacate the wharf. During the showdown, Williams informed the Colombian officer that "in case the Colombian troops loaded their rifles the Marines would be compelled to open fire." Not willing to test Williams' determination, the Colombians "desisted and withdrew from the wharf."[7]

Leaving Panama, Williams resumed his duties afloat until ordered to shore duty. After a brief tour of duty at the Marine Barracks in Washington, D.C., Williams reported to the commanding officer of the USS *Maine* (December 1902–September 1903) as the commanding officer of the Marine detachment aboard that vessel. He then became Fleet Marine Officer for the North Atlantic Fleet (September 1903–January 1905). During his tour of duty with the North Atlantic Fleet, Williams participated in the annual fleet exercises, including the first Advanced Base Force exercise off Culebra Island, Puerto Rico.[8]

Promoted to the rank of major (February 28, 1905), Williams remained with the Atlantic Fleet until Headquarters Marine Corps (HQMC) ordered him to report to the U.S. Naval War College, Newport, Rhode Island, in March 1905. While at the Naval War College, Major Williams lectured on the concept of the Advanced Base Force in addition to authoring the first major treatise on the importance of amphibious reconnaissance in 1906.

"Father of Amphibious Reconnaissance"

Major Williams' study, *Naval Reconnaissance: Instructions for the Reconnaissance of Bays, Harbors, and Adjacent Country* (1906), was the first systemic study of the need for reconnaissance of an enemy beachhead and shoreline. In addition to establishing the guiding principles for conducting reconnaissance prior to an amphibious landing, Williams laid out the prerequisites for the creation of a specialized force dedicated to carrying out amphibious reconnaissance prior to (as well as during) an assault on an enemy beachhead. In the study, Williams wrote that "only specially talented and experienced men should be assigned to this work." According to him, among the requirements for those Marines assigned to amphibious reconnaissance were the following: (1) thorough technical knowledge, to include surveying, mapping, recording observations, and map reading; (2) a quick and energetic nature to ensure that the work was accomplished without unnecessary delay; (3) sufficient resourcefulness to overcome unexpected obstacles; (4) a reticence to ensure that results were kept confidential; and, finally, (5) exactitude of work.[9]

Besides setting out the requirements for amphibious reconnaissance, Williams was the first Marine officer to delineate the responsibilities for the Navy and Marine Corps as well as dividing reconnaissance between those "concerned with the sea up to the shore and those concerned with the beach and adjacent land."[10] In his study, Williams outlined the responsibilities of both Navy and Marine Corps officers assigned to amphibious reconnaissance duty. First and foremost was the

First Lieutenant Dion Williams, USMC, and the Marine detachment that ran up the first American flag to fly over the Philippines render military courtesies to Commodore George Dewey on his first visit ashore on May 3, 1898 (USMC photograph).

requirement that both officers were well qualified for the task of conducting reconnaissance during the pre- and post-assault phases of an amphibious landing:

> A naval officer who has had experience in surveying and intelligence work should be assigned to cover the sea and shore line and all that pertains to ships, boats, and naval resources, and a marine officer who has had practical experience in topographic work, the construction of semi-permanent fortifications and fieldworks and in camping in the field should be assigned to cover that part of the work.[11]

In Williams' *Naval Reconnaissance*, the "exactness" and scope of pre-assault reconnaissance were requirements in the successful execution of an amphibious landing. This exactness included technical expertise in both sea and shore lines and topographic work.[12]

This scope of a pre-assault reconnaissance effort was later expounded on by Lieutenant Colonel Earl H. Ellis, who wrote in his *Advanced Base Operations in Micronesia* that in any pre-assault planning reconnaissance was necessary and that "the best troops and facilities should be assigned to special objectives and the forces should proceed direct and attack at all necessary points in force." Colonel Ellis added, "The occupation forces should be assigned sub-sectors (or groups) and proceed to occupy and search out the various islands; not necessarily simultaneously, except that they should begin operations in their respective areas at the same time."[13] Ellis emphasized that reconnaissance was essential in determining such missions and "might be carried by small parties of men, going ashore at night for the purpose of seizing positions preparatory to landing in force."[14]

Both Williams and Ellis agreed in their respective studies that reconnaissance work required Marines (and sailors) trained in reconnoitering an enemy shoreline and beachhead prior to a landing. Yet, whereas Ellis' concern lay in the actual landing, Williams' treatises on naval reconnaissance focused on the pre-assault phase of a landing. Williams likewise went one step further in outlining in detail the types

The "Father of Marine Corps Amphibious Reconnaissance," Brigadier General Dion Williams, USMC (1869–1952), shown here as a colonel (USMC photograph).

of missions Marine (and Navy) reconnaissance teams were to carry out prior to, during, and after a landing. These included:

1. Hydrographic reconnaissance
2. Determination of directions and distances
3. Configuration of the ground, cities, towns, roads, trails, railroads, telegraph cables, telephone lines, wireless telegraphy, rivers, canals, resources (coal, repair facilities, land transportation, electric plants, food supplies, water supply, and hospitals)
4. Conditions of harbor and harbor steamers, wharves, docks, and other adjacent facilities
5. Naval and military forces
6. Existing defenses (location, form, adaptability, and description thereof; garrisons and forces available)[15]

It was in these enumerated missions that Williams' and Ellis' work converged, as both Marine officers wrote that prior to any assault, hydrographic data, terrain analysis, and, as developed during World War II, soil and beach composition all became important tasks of Marine and Navy reconnaissance teams.

For both Williams and Ellis, hydrographic reconnaissance was the single most important mission of prior to a landing of Marine Reconnaissance teams:

> In order to prepare intelligent plans for the attack or defense of a harbor or bay, it is necessary to have at hand a comprehensive description of the hydrographic features and accurate charts, showing the depths of water at all points, the reefs, rocks, shoals, and peculiar currents, which constitute dangers to navigation, and the tributary streams and channels which may form avenues of attack or furnish anchorages for a portion of the floating defenses or auxiliaries of the defender.[16]

One last point regarding the importance of Williams' and Ellis' doctrine on reconnaissance and advanced base operations and their impact on the development of amphibious warfare lies in technological innovations such as the use of the submarine and airplanes in military operations. Williams' second edition of *Naval Reconnaissance*, published in 1917 (the year the United States entered World War I), "included discussion of additional capabilities of observation from airplanes and submarines, and [placed increased] emphasis on information acquired [by reconnaissance] for long term planning."[17] Indeed, as early as 1912, the use of submarines for purposes other than directly in the attack role began to slowly find its way into the doctrinal development for use with or in support of the Marine Corps' Advanced Base Force. In a 1912 lecture at the Naval War College, in clear reference to what he called "Advanced Base Auxiliaries," Major Williams stated, "Certain classes of vessels not required to remain with the active fleet in it search for the enemy, or which on account of their size or speed are not able to keep the sea with the battleship, may be used to great advantage in assisting [in] the defense of the base."[18] In this case, according to Williams, the "auxiliary class of vessels" he had in mind was the submarine.

Williams' emphasis in the second edition of *Naval Reconnaissance* on the importance of reconnaissance in assisting long-term planning was paramount in the development of Marine Force Reconnaissance doctrine in the 1930s and 1940s. In fact, "it was this latter emphasis on obtaining information long before hostilities that was perhaps of greatest significance."[19] Whereas naval reconnaissance in the past supported operations already underway, the continued evolution of the Advanced Base Force concept, coupled with the technological evolution of and need for intelligence gathering, placed greater emphasis on pre-assault reconnaissance. Williams wrote:

> The object of the naval reconnaissance of any given locality is to acquire all of the information concerning the sea, land, air, and material resources of that locality, with a view to its use by the Navy in peace and war, and to record this information that it may be most readily available for; the preparation of plans for the occupation of the locality as a temporary or permanent naval base … the preparation of plans for the attack of the locality by sea and land should it be in possession of an enemy.[20]

Evolution of Marine Reconnaissance's Mission

Part of Williams' emphasis on pre-assault reconnaissance centered on the need for hydrographic reconnaissance, a theme that he, Ellis, and Navy and Marine planners in the late 1920s and 1930s continually stressed. During World War II, Marine and Navy reconnaissance teams surveyed enemy beachheads and took soundings to determine the depth of the waters and, on Tarawa, tidal readings. Later, in March 1965, Marine Reconnaissance teams conducted hydrographic surveys on Red Beach prior to the landing of elements of the 9th Marine Expeditionary Brigade. Likewise, Navy SEAL teams carried out hydrographic soundings south of Saigon in the Mekong Delta in IV Corps to determine accessibility for an amphibious landing.

In fact, in the Navy's *Fleet Training Publication 167* (*FTP 167*), which incorporated the Marine Corps' *Tentative Manual 1934* (which in essence was the blueprint for the conduct of amphibious operations during World War II and beyond), the authors stressed the need for "human observation" versus observation by submarines, aircraft, surface craft, or photography, in order to "gain information regarding the enemy's strength and dispositions on shore." To carry out the reconnaissance missions ashore, *FTP 167* stated that such missions were to be undertaken by "agents, patrols, or reconnaissance in force."[21]

FTP 167's importance cannot be overstated. The authors of the manual further divided the reconnaissance effort, differentiating "naval" and "military" reconnaissance.[22] "Naval" reconnaissance, the manual stated, consisted of scouting and reporting on an enemy's naval dispositions, hydrographic and meteorological data, suitability of beaches and those areas designated as potential landing sites "from a navigational standpoint, the location of mines and underwater obstacles, suitable routes to landing areas, and establishing necessary navigational aids."[23] For

Williams (and the authors of *FTP 167*), "Amphibious Reconnaissance could determine whether or not the beaches were in fact held by enemy forces thereby conserving naval ammunition as well as enabling concentration of fire on positions that were actually manned."[24] By contrast, "Military reconnaissance included the nature of terrain in proposed zones of operation, enemy dispositions ashore, defensive works, strongpoints, machine gun and artillery emplacements and positions, location and intensity of defensive barrages (known later as Bomb Damage Assessment or BDA), landing fields, location of reserves and their routes of advance, and supply and ammunition facilities." In short, these were all missions that Marine Reconnaissance teams would carry out ashore during World War II and through the Vietnam War.

The "types" of information to be gathered by amphibious reconnaissance teams included:

1. Identification of "fixes" on the beach and possible establishment of navigational aids
2. Determination of enemy naval dispositions within and in the vicinity of the landing area
3. Determination of suitability of beaches and sea areas required for the conduct of the operation
4. Location of underwater obstacles and other obstructions
5. Ascertainment if beaches were gassed
6. Location of mined areas
7. Determination of enemy dispositions on shore and selection of suitable targets, landmarks, and aiming points for fire support ships
8. Determination of the enemy air forces[25]

One last doctrinal point was the fact that, in order to maintain their secrecy, reconnaissance patrols were to land silently, in fog and/or darkness, without the benefit of fire support or aviation, which might inadvertently alert the enemy to the presence of these reconnaissance teams. With the increased use of the submarine and suitable boats to carry them ashore, Marine amphibious reconnaissance teams set out to test the doctrine as established by the 1927 Joint Action of the Army and the Navy, which laid the foundation for joint landing doctrine developed in the 1930s and practiced in the 1940s. Indeed, in this joint action, amphibious reconnaissance prior to a landing was stressed, a practice that the Navy and Marines had been carrying out since the beginning of the century.[26]

The basic doctrinal foundation of amphibious reconnaissance as carried out by the Marines and Navy Underwater Demolition Teams (UDTs) during World War II had, in fact, been established by the Army and Navy during the 1920s even as students at the Marine Corps Schools wrestled with the problems associated with amphibious operations.[27] The principles of amphibious reconnaissance formulated by the Joint Board in the 1920s, in fact, remained in place through the Second World

War. With the continued evolution of amphibious warfare doctrine during the 1920s and 1930s at the Marine Corps Schools at Quantico, Virginia, "naval doctrine of 1927 continued to emphasize reconnaissance for advanced planning as well as reconnaissance to verify the soundness of formulated plans and reconnaissance during the last phases ... of planning ... and execution."[28] More important was the division of reconnaissance into two components: a sea component and a land component. As Marine Reconnaissance (and more specifically "Force" Reconnaissance) developed, both components merged to form the basis of Marine Force Reconnaissance's mission during World War II and after.

The Fleet Exercises of the 1930s

With the doctrinal foundation of amphibious reconnaissance before and after World War I, the next phase in the evolution of Marine Force Reconnaissance was through practical application in exercises with the fleet. During Fleet Exercise Number 4 (FLEX-4), the basic tenets of amphibious reconnaissance were carried out in accordance with *FTP 167*. During this exercise, Rear Admiral A.W. Johnson (the commanding officer of the Attack Force) carried out a series of reconnaissance missions on the island of Vieques, and on Puerto Rico. The objectives of the reconnaissance teams included "method of operation of inshore water patrols, location of general reserve, nature of and location of beach defenses, location and extent suitable landing beaches and conditions of the surf, entrenchments, and the extent of beach defenses at certain locations."[29] FLEX-4 was broken up into two phases, with the first phase conducted off the island of Vieques, and the second phase held off of Puerto Rico, east of Ponce Playa.

The first phase of the exercise, conducted by Marines, soldiers, and sailors, witnessed the first use of submarines by a Marine Reconnaissance team from Company F, 5th Marine Regiment, consisting of Second Lieutenant Kenneth D. Bailey, Corporal Courson, Private Currie, and Private Olson of F Company, 1st Marine Brigade Headquarters Company, all of whom reported aboard the submarine S-47. The Marines, who were to row ashore in inflatable rafts, were instructed to land on the "enemy" shoreline under the cover of darkness and reconnoiter the defenses ashore, conduct hydrographic readings and beach surveys, and return to their respective submarines (S-45, S-46, and S-47) the next night. Unfortunately, the surf did not cooperate with the plan, with the result that the mission was aborted.

During the Puerto Rican phase (February 28–March 1, 1938) of FLEX-4, Lieutenant Bailey and Privates Olson, Macinni, and Meniere reported to the submarine S-47, which transported them to the objective area. After coming within 100–1,200 yards of the beach, the submerged submarine discharged its Marine passengers in an air-cushion boat; they subsequently rowed about 1.2 miles due north in the early evening hours of February 28. Forty-five minutes later, the Marines came ashore, hid their rafts, and proceeded to carry out their mission. Taking cover until the next morning, Lieutenant Bailey's reconnaissance team began its mission at 0700. While the entire team was eventually "captured" by the defending force, the umpires ruled Bailey's mission a "success." Lieutenant Bailey later wrote, "I believe a reconnaissance of this type can be successful against a normally alert enemy."[30]

One very important lesson that emerged from FLEX-4 and the use of Marine Reconnaissance teams ashore, and one that impacted the development of Marine Reconnaissance doctrine in general, was the requirement of timely communications. While Bailey's team was able to land undetected from the submarine, they encountered a problem with the transmission (or lack thereof) of intelligence back to the planners aboard ship. As historian Ray Stubbe noted, "reliance on technological development was made apparent by the discovery of a problem that was to concern reconnaissance patrols until the present—communications." Lieutenant Bailey noted that reconnaissance teams "should be provided some means of communications that enable a patrol to transmit information immediately: not waiting until ['friendly'] troops land in order to make their findings available to those that could use them." Bailey wrote that while gathering "very significant information was easy," it was ultimately useless, as his teams were unable to transmit it back to the ship or submarine in a timely manner.[31]

Despite the shortcomings on these first two reconnaissance missions on a hostile shore, Major Lee H. Brown, the 1st Marine Brigade intelligence officer, was optimistic and saw a definite future for the use of reconnaissance teams prior to and during an amphibious operation: "While neither of the patrols were successful in either reporting or transmitting any information to the Attack Fore, it was established, that, where darkness prevails and moderately smooth water exists which will permit launching of life rafts, it is feasible and practical to land patrols from submarines for shore reconnaissance." Major Brown added, "With greater care, and with more experience in operations within enemy lines, it is believed that invaluable information can be obtained by landing shore patrols in the method outlined above."[32]

During both Fleet Exercise Number Five (FLEX-5) (January 13–March 19, 1939) and Fleet Exercise Number Six (FLEX-6) (January 11–March 13, 1940), the principle of landing reconnaissance teams via submarines and rubber rafts was well established.[33] More important is the fact that by March 1940, Europe had been at war for nearly seven months, with the British experimenting with the concept of landing commando teams ashore via submarines and small boats in order to conduct raids and gather intelligence. While commando raids per say fell outside the range of mission or scope of Marine Reconnaissance teams, the further use of submarines and development of a fleet of small boats specifically designed for use by Royal Marine Commandos was not lost on Marine planners as HQMC organized its first permanent reconnaissance teams.[34]

Small Boat Developments and the Marine Corps (1938–1940)

Lieutenant Bailey's use of rubber rafts and air-cushion vehicles to land his reconnaissance team during FLEX-4 pointed to the next step in the development of Marine Reconnaissance during World War II: finding the right type of boat to transport reconnaissance teams ashore. While the bulk of the Marine Corps' efforts during the 1930s concentrated on finding and developing the right type of assault boat or landing craft, some of the findings had an indirect impact on the development of suitable landing craft for Marine Reconnaissance teams during and after World War II.

Lieutenant Colonel David L. Brewster, the executive officer for the 5th Marine Regiment, in a training memorandum from October 1939, outlined several principles that directly affected not only the development of the boats themselves but also landing and disembarkation procedures as teams neared an enemy's shoreline. While most of Lieutenant Colonel Brewster's memorandum concentrated on the disembarkation and cover of infantry platoons landing on a hostile shore, two salient points remained fundamental to a successful insertion by a Marine Reconnaissance team: speed and the clearing of the beach once ashore.[35] According to Brewster:

> Speed in disembarking and clearing the beach is absolutely essential. Not only is the beach the most dangerous place but it is essential to close with the enemy in the fewest possible number of seconds after the gunfire lifts and the aircraft attack ceases. Also remember the safest place is inside the enemy's position. Upon clearing the beach, leading men may pause and open firer, from a kneeling or prone position, or take up assault fire, long enough for the rear of the squad to catch up. There must be no appreciable delay in bringing fire on the enemy or in charging positions within assault distances.[36]

In a follow-up to Lieutenant Colonel Brewster's training memorandum on the disembarkation of boats, Marine First Lieutenant C.P. Van Ness wrote in a paper, "The Development and Procurement of Special Landing Boats for the Marine Corps," at the Marine Corps Schools at Quantico, Virginia, that due to the Advance Base mission and its close working relationship with the Navy, the requirements of the Marine Corps called for the development and procurement of a full range of landing boats, each suited to a different supporting mission for the Fleet Marine Force (FMF). One of these "supporting missions," of course, was reconnaissance. Prior to the advent of the submarine in the first decade of the twentieth century, Marine and Navy landing teams depended on either ships' boats or whale boats converted to military use. According to Lieutenant Van Ness, "Since the organization of the Fleet Marine Force (December 1933), as a part of the Fleet and the recognition of the important part that Force will play in any Fleet operation involving the seizure of Advance Bases, the Marine Corps has become increasingly aware of the necessity for developing landing boats with special characteristics suitable and necessary for this specialized type of operation."[37]

Van Ness stated that "Navy small boats, while ideally suited to Navy requirements, fell short in many respects, of those desired by the Marine Corps, chief among their short comings are; lack of speed, poor surf characteristics, lack of adaptability of different beaching conditions and the difficulty to arm and armor them."[38] He added that various ideas for different types of boats, "ranging from the Beetle Boat (an armored and covered whaleboat) to small, two-man, outboard motor boats," had run the gamut of the various service journals, and though boards composed of Navy and Marine officers met from time to time to consider new boat designs and ideas, the end result was that "nothing really constructive was done until comparatively recently."[39]

The bulk of Van Ness' paper dealt with the exhaustive effort by the Navy's Bureaus of Construction & Repairs and Engineering to test and evaluate different types of boats that could carry and land troops ashore. During the late 1930s, the Navy tested four specific designs (the Red Bank Boat, the Bay Head Boat, the Freeport Boat, and the Greenport Boat), which were respectively used by the fishermen off Cape May, New Jersey, and New York, as well as a Sea Sled, and had important troop-landing qualities that called for further testing and evaluation. The Marine lieutenant wrote that by adopting and testing various types of boats for consideration of adoption for troop usage, "we are well on our way toward the fulfillment of one our outstanding needs; a suitable landing boat for assault combat units."[40] Van Ness admitted that this step alone could not meet all the requirements incident to landing operations and that "we must consider the landing of Reserve units, supplies, tanks and artillery, and for them we also need a distinct type of craft especially designed for its purpose."[41] This would also include developing a boat specifically for landing Marine Reconnaissance teams.

Van Ness' paper and Brewster's memorandum pointed to the fact that that the technology already existed in terms of boat design and armament. Indeed, both Brewster and Van Ness called for the adoption of what today is called utilizing "off-the-shelf technology," with the idea that these boats were multifunctional and could be used by amphibious reconnaissance teams. This leads to an important point in that, since the formulation of the first amphibious reconnaissance doctrine as laid out by Brigadier General Williams, Marine Reconnaissance has been able to remain innovative through the use of off-the-shelf technology, whether that be in the realm of means of delivery, landing craft, weapons, or communications. In fact, Colonel Bruce Meyers, a pioneer of Marine amphibious and Force Reconnaissance during the 1950s and 1960s, wrote that this has been one of the most enduring and unique characteristics (and strengths) of Marine Force Reconnaissance doctrine: the ability to innovate through the use of off-the-shelf technology and its application to the reconnaissance mission.[42] In fact, off-the-shelf technology, insofar as the reconnaissance mission was concerned, came to play an ever-increasing role in the development of Marine (and later Army) Force Reconnaissance during the late 1930s. The organization and employment of Marine Reconnaissance teams prior to and during

In the 1930s, the Marine Corps and U.S. Navy experimented with a variety of small boats during fleet exercises. Here, Marines disembark from a whaleboat unloading supplies during an exercise (USMC photograph).

amphibious landing missions immediately before and during World War II coincided with the technological innovations that would have implications into the 1950s and 1960s in connection with the development of Marine Force Reconnaissance.

Formation of the "Teams": Organization and Development of the Observer Group (1940–1942)

"By 1940, the U.S. Marine Corps had developed a comprehensive amphibious reconnaissance doctrine that had been tested and found valid for planning purposes to include aerial reconnaissance and photography, submarine reconnaissance, and amphibious reconnaissance conducted via rubber boats."[43] The next step in the development of amphibious reconnaissance was the organization of a dedicated unit that specialized in "reconnoitering enemy shore lines," defenses and troop dispositions.[44] Shortly after the Japanese attack on Pearl Harbor in December 1941, HQMC organized what can be considered the first permanent organization dedicated to conducting amphibious reconnaissance and intelligence gathering in January 1942 at Quantico, Virginia. Composed of two officers and twenty enlisted Marines and officially designated "Observer Group," this unit "is believed to have been the first unit in the Marine Corps to be organized and trained specifically for amphibious reconnaissance."[45]

Selected to command this new unit was Captain James Logan Jones, Sr., who had originally been commissioned an Army Reserve second lieutenant on

September 13, 1933, though he "did not perform any active duty at this time" and focused instead on his job with the International Harvester Corporation (IHC), where, as a salesman, he traveled extensively in North Africa, the Middle East, and Europe and was fluent in French. When World War II broke out, the IHC recalled Jones from Europe. At this time, due mainly to the influence of his brother William K. Jones, a Marine second lieutenant, he applied for and at first was "turned down," due to his age (he was twenty-seven), for a direct commission in the Marine Corps. After the intercession of "some high-ranking officials," and with war clouds on the horizon, the Marine Corps commissioned James Logan Jones a second lieutenant in the Marine Corps on February 3, 1941. After attending the Reserve Officers Course at Marine Barracks, Quantico, Virginia, in May 1941, HQMC assigned Second Lieutenant Jones to the 1st Marine Division, Fleet Marine Force, before ordering him back to Quantico, where he served as Commanding Officer, Headquarters Company, Task Force 18, which at the time had been engaged in planning for the invasion of Vichy-controlled North Africa.[46] Attached to the staff of Colonel Graves B. Erskine, the chief of staff to Major General Holland M. Smith, Jones' French fluency and knowledge of North Africa made him the ideal candidate to lead this first amphibious reconnaissance unit known as Observer Group.[47]

During the early days following the United States' entrance into World War II, the Marine Corps organized series of "special" units designed for specific missions. These units included Raider battalions, Glider Troops, Paratroopers, and Anti-Aircraft Defense Battalions. Each of these units played an important role in the Marine Corps' amphibious warfare mission and the conduct of operations in the Pacific theater of operations.[48]

Major James Logan Jones, Observer Group and Amphibious Reconnaissance Company (1941–1943)

Captain Jones' selection as the first commanding officer of Observer Group was significant due not only to his foreign language skills and wide travel throughout Africa, the Middle East, and Europe but also to his background and familiarity with machinery and mechanized vehicles. Coinciding with the organization of Observer Group, Fleet Marine Force (and the selection of Captain James Jones as its first commanding officer), were developments taking place in the United Kingdom connected with special or commando operations and their application in the gathering of intelligence and conducting raids on enemy installations. Captain Jones was not, however, the first Marine officer to be aware of these developments, as progress in Great Britain was observed by several other Marine officers, along with the training of a select group of Marines, taken from the U.S. embassies in Ireland and Great Britain for commando training by the Royal Marine Commandos in preparation for the proposed landings in Northwest Africa.

Indeed, prior to the United States' entry into World War II, all three services (Navy, Marine Corps and Army) expressed an interest in the experiments being conducted by the British in the use of commando and raiding forces. After the United States entered the war on December 7, 1941, both the U.S. Marine Corps and the U.S. Army sent representatives to England to observe the Royal Marine Commandos and British Airborne forces then engaged in such operations against German forces in Norway and the western coast of France, as well as British commando operations against the Vichy French fleet based at Toulon.

After observing and talking with British military personnel engaged in such operations, the American naval and military attachés filed reports on their findings, which in turn found their way into the organization and training of such "special forces" before and after war was declared on Japan and Germany in December 1941. Two such Marine Corps observers were Captains Samuel B. Griffith and Wallace M. Greene, who, on orders from General Thomas Holcomb, served with several British commando units in order to observe and report on their amphibious warfare techniques. Later, Major Greene (he was promoted during his time overseas) submitted a detailed report that the Marine Corps later incorporated into its amphibious doctrine. Captain Griffith later became executive officer and subsequently commanding officer of a company in the 1st Marine Raider Battalion under Lieutenant Colonel Merritt A. "Red Mike" Edson, commanding officer of the 1st Marine Raider Battalion on Tulagi and Guadalcanal.[49]

Upon the return of the Marine observers from England, and based on their observations of the Royal Marine Commandos and Special Operative Executive, Headquarters United States Marine Corps organized the first of two Raider Battalions, parachute troops, and glider troops. Marine reconnaissance doctrine had, in fact, already been established during the interwar era and particularly during the fleet landing exercises from 1938 onward. The developments taking place at home and in the United Kingdom had an indirect influence on the development of Marine Reconnaissance teams, particularly in the fields of small boat development, communications, and delivery by submarine.

Captain James Logan Jones, USMCR (shown here as a colonel), the first commanding officer of Observer Group, V Amphibious Corps, 1942–1945 (USMC photograph).

Working with the G-2 (intelligence)

of General Smith's Amphibious Corps, Atlantic Fleet, Lieutenant Colonel Louis Ely and Brigadier General Erskine organized a combined Army-Marine Reconnaissance force composed of some thirty Marines and soldiers who began conducting squad-level amphibious reconnaissance missions along the Chesapeake Bay area; in Norfolk, Virginia; and off St. Mary's and Solomon Island, scouting each other's "defensive" positions.[50]

The officers and men of Observer Group continued to experiment with different types of small boats, folding canvas boats, kayaks, outboard motors, lightweight radios and other communications equipment, signal lights, and clothing. As the men practiced their reconnaissance techniques, the G-2 section of the 1st Marine Division and the U.S. Army's 1st Infantry Division continued to refine the doctrine for the conduct and employment of amphibious reconnaissance patrols. In its final pre-combat employment format, both G-2 staffs wrote:

Major Wallace M. Greene, USMC (shown here as a brigadier general), observed the British Commandos and wrote a detailed report on their operations against the Germans. He would become commandant of the Marine Corps in 1964 (USMC History Division photograph).

> Since the capabilities and limitations of amphibious reconnaissance had not at the time been determined by actual combat experience, it was difficult to prescribe specifically what missions would and not come within the scope of amphibious reconnaissance. It was tentatively decided that patrols, properly trained, could accomplish a variety of intelligence missions. These ranged from a hydrographic reconnaissance of the sea floor near the shoreline to an inland reconnaissance to determine practicability of the terrain for air landings. Incidental missions of a non-intelligence nature could include diversions, minor night raids, and disruptions of enemy communications.[51]

After the division of the Atlantic and Pacific Oceans between the Army and the Navy, the soldiers assigned to Amphibious Corps, Atlantic Fleet, came under the command of the Western Task Force, then preparing for the invasion of North Africa. Captain Jones and his leathernecks likewise transferred with Major General Smith's headquarters to Camp Elliott, San Diego, California, in January 1943, where they began to prepare for the reconquest of the Pacific islands controlled by the Japanese.[52]

"Incidental Missions of a Non-Intelligence Nature": British Commandos, the SOE and Marine Force Reconnaissance Doctrine (1939–1942)

Cooperation between the three services (U.S. Army, Navy, and Marine Corps) during the preceding years (1938–1941) was, in fact, paramount to the continued development of the Marine Corps' amphibious reconnaissance doctrine. Lieutenant Colonel William S. Riddle, who was assistant military attaché to the U.S. Embassy in London and, along with Marine and Navy officers assigned to the U.S. Embassy in England, observed the training of British Commandos and Special Operative Executive troops in Scotland, wrote a detailed report on the activities of these special troops titled "Planning and Execution of a Seaborne Raid," much of which the Army and, to a greater extent, the Marine Corps incorporated into their raider, parachute, and amphibious reconnaissance during World War II.[53]

In his report, Lieutenant Colonel Riddle listed fourteen considerations when planning for and executing a raid against an enemy coastline. Riddle's list had a direct impact on the development of amphibious reconnaissance doctrine later adopted by Captain Jones' Amphibious Reconnaissance Company. These "considerations" were as follows: (1) choice of target; (2) choice of landing places; (3) reconnaissance; (4) size of the landing forces and means of sea transport; (5) selection of date and timing of the raid; (6) the naval plan; (7) the air plan; (8) the military plan; (9) special training; (10) security arrangements; (11) sea passages; (12) actions after landing; (13) arrival at home; and (14) publicity.[54]

Several of Riddle's points correspond directly to the development of Marine amphibious reconnaissance doctrine during and after World War II. Regarding "choice of target," Riddle wrote that it was important to "select an area of the enemy's coastline with respect to which one had good information as to hostile strength and dispositions." He added that insofar as selection of the landing site was concerned, it should be "within an area which has the best facilities for an undetected approach from the sea and which is not obviously impossible for a landing." Riddle said that it was important to avoid those areas that were well defended by the enemy or located near a large concentration of enemy troops.[55]

As for the "choice of landing place," the Army lieutenant colonel emphasized that cooperation with naval officials was important in order to ensure that the chosen landing site offered the most in surprise and a safe approach for the force coming ashore. Insofar as "reconnaissance" was concerned, Riddle's report echoed the views of both Brigadier General Dion Williams and Lieutenant Colonel Pete Ellis in that prior to an actual landing, reconnaissance was necessary for advanced planning and verifying "the soundness of formulated plans."[56]

Riddle's report validated Williams' view that amphibious reconnaissance had three distinct phases, which were later made permanent in a directive issued by V Amphibious Corps (VAC). These phases included:

PHASE I: Prior to completion of operation plans for landing, information is sought for preparation of plans in sufficient time prior to the operation to avoid the loss of secrecy which may incurred by reconnaissance shortly prior to an attack.

PHASE II: Between completion of plans for the landing and the actual embarkation of a landing force, further information is necessary for the execution of the plan, such as later data on the enemy's strength and dispositions.

PHASE III: During the last days prior to D-Day further information is sought of the enemy's disposition and strength as well as the movement of hid reserves.[57]

Riddle's views likewise echoed the Navy's *Fleet Training Publication 167* (1938), which discussed at great length the use of units such as Marine paratroopers or the four Raider Battalions organized after 1940 to conduct preliminary operations besides reconnaissance operations. As *FTP 167* stated, "The advisability of having an actual human observation vice 'machine' observation was emphasized since information obtained by surface craft or submarine, aerial observation and photograph, might be able to disclose if emplacements were manned or reveal carefully camouflaged machinegun positions. Against an alert enemy ... the attacker will have to depend upon landing parties ... to gain information regarding the enemy's strength and dispositions on shore. The landing parties may consist of agents, patrols, or reconnaissance-in-force."[58]

As for "the size of the raiding force and means of transport," Lieutenant Colonel Riddle stated that there had to be a compromise between the precise number of troops required to achieve the objective and the Navy's ability to transport them to the intended target area. Riddle added that "the soldier must, of course, estimate the smallest number of troops which can do the job, but the upper limit will usually be set by the carrying capacity of the available boats."[59] He continued:

> The method of transport at sea offers two alternatives. Either the whole operation can be carried out in ocean-going motor boats, starting from a shore base or from a parent ship well outside the coastal zone, or the ship must be brought close inshore and troops transferred to landing craft carried in the ships, either row-boats, motor-boats, or specially designed landing craft. The distance of the target from the nearest shore-base will settle the choice.[60]

The U.S. Army's military attaché to the United Kingdom further elaborated in this report that

> If the target is within range of motor-boats, and suitable craft of this type are available there are many advantages in using them. They are fast and unobtrusive, and they offer possible targets for aircraft, guns, or mines. Furthermore, they reduce to a minimum the time taken to disembark and re-embark, and enable simultaneous landing to be made at wisely-separated points.[61]

Colonel Riddle noted that the disadvantages of using the above-mentioned type of boats were that they made too much noise and required a calm ocean in crossing from island to island. Instead, he proposed that either the "Eureka" or the "Higgins" boats then under construction be used in transporting a raiding force to the shore. Finally, Riddle wrote that if the distances were too great for ordinary small boats (rowboats, rafts, etc.), then the solution lay in finding a fast ship whose davits could be adapted to carry either motorboats or the "Eureka"-type boats.[62]

One specific area of interest to Captain Jones and his Observer Group was Riddle's introduction of the idea that the moon or illumination (known as "Elint") as well as tidal conditions were critical factors to be considered when planning a raid or landing. Riddle wrote that the object was to land the force in almost complete darkness, with the ships proceeding ashore virtually undetected and the force landing against the moon's illumination as the ships pulled out to sea. He added that it was imperative that the raiding force land during high tide, "to ensure that the Navy would be able to land the raiding force (or reconnaissance team) onto the beach."[63]

As for both the "Military Plan," and the "Navy Plan," Riddle wrote that the former plan established the objectives and laid out the number of troops to be used, estimates of the enemy force, and the plan of maneuver while the latter plan "decides the types of boats to be used by the raiding force or reconnaissance team in order to disembark or re-embark once the mission ashore is complete." Riddle added that "'The Navy Plan' likewise established the types of signals to be used by both the raiding force and personnel between ship and shore." Both plans required naval charts, maps, signals, and other important data to ensure that the Navy and land forces (Army or Marines) were operating on the same page.[64]

Riddle added two final points that were critical to the success of a raiding mission, a landing, or a reconnaissance mission. These were categorized as "Special Training and Preliminary Rehearsals" and "Sea Passages and Landings." For the first point, Riddle emphasized that rehearsal was the key to success or failure, as "the sole object of the training period is to rehearse the operation under conditions approximate as nearly as possible [to] those which will be met during the raid." He added, "Every effort should be made to rehearse the landing on a piece of coast which is like the one chosen for the attack. To prepare for the landing action, the chief aim will be to get the raiding troops thoroughly familiar with the ground over which they are to operate." This latter point was, in fact, critical, as "the success or failure of the raid [or reconnaissance mission] will oftentimes depend on how many times the raiding [or reconnaissance force] conducts dress rehearsals over terrain that is similar to the area where the intended raid [or landing] will take place." Rehearsals, Riddle added, "identified any special equipment such as scaling ladders, demolitions equipment, etc., required for the successful completion of the raid."[65] He wrote that pre-planning was paramount in the success of such missions. Pre-planning included the use of full-scale models, intelligence photographs, and other firsthand reports or observations of the intended target area in order to ensure success of the mission.

As for "Sea Passages and Landings," Riddle wrote in his report that each member of the landing or raiding force should be trained in the use of passwords so as to ensure recognition and easy identification by friendly forces during re-embarkation. Also, the landing or raiding force should be issued inflatable lifebelts to prevent accidental drowning. Finally, the troops going ashore should wear recognizable pieces of equipment such as helmets, helmet covers, and other items on their uniforms. This last point is important, as during the landings beginning with Apamama Island on

November 19–20, 1943, in the Tarawa landings in the Gilbert Islands, Reconnaissance Marines were among the first Marine units to wear camouflaged utilities. Shortly thereafter, Marine paratroop and Raider units and, by 1943, ground units adopted camouflaged utilities.[66]

Colonel Riddle's report is important, as it outlined the specific requirements for the execution of a successful reconnaissance or raiding mission. In fact, as Observer Group was integrated into Amphibious Reconnaissance Company, V Amphibious Corps, the Marine Corps adopted many of the Army colonel's recommendations. Riddle's careful and detailed observations of the work being carried out in England by the Royal Marines and Commandos of the SOE soon found their way across the Atlantic Ocean and were employed with deadly effect against the Japanese in the Pacific theater of operations.[67]

"Commando" vs. "Raiding" During Pre-Assault Operations (1940–1942)

Colonel Riddle's report brought to the fore an important issue regarding the concepts of amphibious reconnaissance and raiding. In early 1942, there was no clear delineation between the two totally different force structures and missions. Each contained elements of the other with no clear definition, as the two forces had yet to be employed under wartime conditions. Furthermore, the differences between "amphibious" reconnaissance and "raids" that occurred in the Pacific during World War II were prevalent even before the United States entered the war, for the use of "Commandos," "Rangers," airborne and Marine ships' detachments in operations prior to an amphibious landing differed among the Allied leaders as well as among the respective heads of the services involved (i.e., Navy, Army, and U.S. Marine Corps) in terms of mission statement and purpose. In the aftermath of the evacuation from Dunkirk, the British turned to the idea of using "Commandos" or small raiding parties in May–June 1940.[68] Both the Admiralty and the Defense Ministry then set out to outline the differences among raiding forces, paratroops, and Royal Marines. The "differences" of forces, in fact, lay in terms of definition and types of missions, which affected the development of Special Forces across the ocean in the United States.

Only weeks after the evacuation from the continent (Operation "Dynamo"), Prime Minister Winston S. Churchill and General Sir John Dill, chief of the Imperial General Staff, along with Lieutenant Colonel D.W. Clarke of the Royal Artillery, drafted a plan to "use small bands of trained soldiers up and down the length [of the French coast—from Bordeaux and along the Norwegian coast and fjords into Narvik] to demonstrate on small bodies of the enemy that offensive spirit," until such time that more conventional forces could be employed in full-scale operations.[69]

On June 4, 1940, only days after the successful evacuation of British forces from

Dunkirk, Churchill declared in the House of Commons, "We shall not be content with a defensive war." That same afternoon, following his speech, the prime minister wrote General Sir Hastings L. Ismay, his right-hand man in the War Cabinet, saying, "We should immediately set to work to organize self-contained, thoroughly equipped raiding units."[70] In a follow-up letter two days later, Churchill again urged the formation of commando-type units: "Enterprises must be prepared with specially-trained troops of the hunter class who can develop a reign of terror down the enemy coasts. I look to the Joint Chiefs of Staff to propose measures for vigorous enterprises and ceaseless offensives against the whole German occupied coast-line, leaving a trail of German corpses behind them."

After intense pressure from Churchill, the heads of the British Army and Admiralty, while voicing opposition to such a plan (much like their American Marine counterpart, Major General Thomas Holcomb, commandant of the Marine Corps, who saw such special units as a drain on resources and men), set about organizing forces for what the prime minister labeled "special service of a hazardous nature." Under orders from Churchill, Generals Ismay and Dill instructed Lieutenant Colonel Dudley Clarke in June 1940 to "prepare a scheme" for such operations. It must be noted that Clarke—like his contemporary, Orde Wingate of Chindit fame—had conducted guerrilla-type operations in Palestine and was thus very familiar with organizing such forces. After only a few days at work, Clarke came up with a plan whereby the men selected for such "irregular warfare should ... be formed into units [that were] to be known as 'Commandos,' a name he derived from Britain's war in South Africa against the Dutch settlers known as Boers."[71] Clarke selected this term from the tactics employed by Arab bands against a whole army corps of regular troops. After some initial hesitation on the part of Admiralty and Army officials, the term "Commando" was accepted.

The idea of forming what was essentially a "raiding" force was built on two premises. First, after the withdrawal from the continent, the British Army could not spare manpower, as it became clear that the primary forces might be needed to repel a German invasion. The second idea governing the formation of "commandos" was the fact that "the most stringent economy in weapons had to be exercised." Arms being produced in British factories were earmarked primarily for the main army. Thus, only a few weapons of modern design could be placed at the disposal of the troops engaged in raiding.[72] In fact, during the raids carried out in Norway, British commandos could draw only weapons such as Thompson sub-machine guns ("Tommy Guns") for that specific mission, and the arms had to be returned forthwith at the conclusion of the operation.

The shortage of arms inevitably affected the number of troops organized. During the first three years of the war (1940–1942), the first troops specifically chosen for raiding were the Independent Companies. These were raised in a hurry to meet the need for the planned offensives against German installations in Norway. As Brigadier John Durnford-Slater recalled, the commandos were all volunteers "taken from every regiment in the British Army and placed under specially selected officers."[73] In line with Churchill's directive, ten "Commando" units, of five hundred men each, were to be formed.[74]

The formation of these ten semi-independent units was, in fact, deliberate. More than just an economy-of-force, the "Commandos" formed after Dunkirk were self-contained units designed to take on specific missions, such as the landings at Largs and Vaagso in the fall and winter of 1940 in Norway. As the official history of the Combined Operations office stated:

> The Independent Companies had been formed and special training was given to them that they might be available as a force to supplement the Royal Marines, in whom reposes the tradition of amphibious warfare. Such a course was necessary, for the rapidly growing strength of the Royal Navy imposed a considerable strain on the resources in men of the Royal Marines, most of whom at the outbreak of the war went to sea in His Majesty's ships.[75]

More to the point is the fact that up to Operation "Overlord" in June 1944, the independent Commando units were to be used for specific operations throughout the European and Mediterranean theaters of operations. "The Independent Companies or Commandos were [organized and] designed to be complete units in themselves, and to be contained in a ship [or, in some cases, a submarine] which was to be their home and or floating base. They could be thus moved almost anywhere at very short notice and in comparatively short time. They were trained to dispense with the normal methods of supply. They were not to depend on the Quartermaster, but were to be, as far as possible, self-contained."[76]

Later in the war, and in time for the Normandy landings, "when the Independent Companies gave way to the Special Service Battalions which later were transformed into the Commandos, the original conception of their tactical use was preserved."[77] This point, of course, implied that the Commandos were to work closely with the Royal Navy in not only conducting actual operations but also training. Schools, organized largely through the efforts of Admiral Sir Roger Keyes and later Lord Louis Mountbatten as head of Combined Operations, and conducted along the British and Scottish coastlines (most notably at Argyle, Dundee, and Inveraray, in western Scotland), trained Commandos, Special Operations Executive (SOE) agents, Office of Strategic Services (OSS) agents, U.S. Marines, and Army Rangers (Darby's Rangers) in demolitions, hand-to-hand fighting, small boat operations, and scaling mountains and cliffs and rock climbing.[78]

"To the Shores of Tripoli": U.S. Marines and Operation "Torch"

With the Allied decision to invade Northwestern Africa set for November 8, 1942 (Operation "Torch"), the mission of Admiral Bennett's group of Americans became neutralizing the fortresses and bunkers manned by Vichy French and German troops prior to the landing of Major General George S. Patton's Western Task

Force near Oran and the port of Casablanca.[79] Admiral Bennett's mission was to train a select group of sailors and Marines to act as landing detachments in the use of small arms and basic tactics. Bennett's force consisted of 82 U.S. Navy, 3 U.S. Marine, and 9 U.S. Army officers, along with an enlisted force composed of 520 Navy enlisted men, 30 Marines, and 209 soldiers who came from the Army's 1st Engineer Amphibious Brigade.[80] The U.S. Army's main combat force was to be the 1st Battalion, U.S. Army Rangers, led by their famed commander, Lieutenant Colonel William O'Darby.[81]

At Inverness, Royal Marines and SOE instructors conducted "plenty of practice with explosives. The principal one used was a Woolwich (home of the Royal Ordnance Corps) invention, one in which was hard to come by, plastic explosive (PE)." Plastic explosives "consist of cyclonite mixed with a plasticising medium; it is considered to be one of the safest explosives and will not detonate if struck by a rifle bullet or when subject to the ordinary shock of transit; it requires a detonator well-embedded in the mask of the explosive [and can be] moulded into shape like dough. Agents who got to know and handle it as familiarity as if it were butter; which the best types resembled in colour and consistency [and were] quite odourless."[82]

Other preparation consisted of parachute training and using codes and ciphers. Parachute training was conducted at nearby Ringway airfield in Manchester, with each SOE and Commando making five jumps. Parachute training consisted of jumping with "many pounds of equipment in a bag strapped to his leg, and tied to his ankle by a cord." The trainee at Inverness was taught to loosen the cord on opening the parachute, with the bag spreading out so as not to impede the parachutist while landing.[83]

Assigned to train the sailors were forty U.S. Marines selected from the detachments garrisoned in Londonderry, Ireland, as well as the Marine detachment stationed at the U.S. Embassy in London. These Marines, all skilled marksmen and experts in hand-to-hand combat, shortly thereafter set about teaching the bluejackets the principles of marksmanship, hand-to-hand combat techniques, and bayonet training from their base located at Base Two, Roseneath, Scotland. After two months of rigorous training, Admiral Bennett's special force of Marines, sailors, and soldiers reported on October 25, 1942, to their rendezvous points in preparation to set sail on what was to be the first joint Allied amphibious landing of the Second World War, code-named Operation "Torch."

The U.S. Marines, under the command of Lieutenant Colonel Louis C. Plain, USMC, who were scattered aboard the various ships of the convoy, continued to train and familiarize themselves with various Commando techniques as they sailed for the northwest African coastline. Some of the leathernecks, placed aboard British ships, found themselves in company with Britain's famed seagoing soldiers—the Royal Marine Commandos, who were also to take part in the "Torch" landings. The U.S. Marines provided classes to their British counterparts on the .45 caliber pistol and Thompson sub-machine gun.[84] During the subsequent actions on shore,

Marines likewise conducted reconnaissance of the enemy's defensive positions prior to the main landings on November 8, 1942.[85]

The assignment and training of Marines in Commando techniques was not deliberate, as the Marine Corps (specifically the Raider Battalions and Amphibious Reconnaissance Company) absorbed many lessons from their association with British and special warfare techniques. These same techniques were later used by Captain Jones' Amphibious Reconnaissance Company and the Marine Raiders in the amphibious campaigns against the Japanese as early as August 1942.

As for the eagerness and professionalism of the Marines who trained at Inverness at the Commando Depot, Lieutenant Colonel L.E. Vaughan, the British commandant of the school, had nothing but praise for the Leathernecks. In a report to Lord Mountbatten later forwarded to General Holcomb, Lieutenant Colonel Vaughan wrote:

> The whole of the detachment were a credit to the United States Marine Corps, from the start they were all keen and entered into an arduous training with enthusiasm and cheerfulness.... They have undergone an arduous Commando training with an exceptionally unconquerable spirit which never wavered during the course. I am sure that they have benefited by the course and are fit to take their place in a Commando.[86]

The head of the Commando Depot concluded his report to Lord Mountbatten by saying, "It was a pleasure to be associated with such an excellent detachment."

The Special Operations Executive

Marine familiarity with British special warfare techniques did not end with the observation of the training of Royal Marines and Commandos in Inverness, Scotland. During the first two years of World War II in Europe, the British Special Operations Executive (SOE), which had been organized to carry out Prime Minister Churchill's directive "to set Europe ablaze" through the waging of irregular warfare along the European coastline and engaging in subversive activities under a single minister, worked in coordination with the British Admiralty and Political Warfare Executive (which was later subsumed by the SOE) and the Royal Marine Commandos in order to operate primarily behind enemy lines in occupied Europe to disrupt and or destroy German lines of communication, installations, and submarine and naval bases along the length of the French coastline, in addition to assisting local resistance movements in harassing the enemy. The SOE agreed, in an informal agreement with Combined Operations on December 14, 1940, that it would "handle small raids, say up to thirty men, and all the raids far behind the coastline (using foreign nationals or locals of the country concerned) as far as possible, to make escape more easy, while Combined Operations Headquarters would handle the rest."[87]

The SOE's "main contribution to combined operations was to be, however, technical. It provided, for instance, notes on the kind of minor damages which might be wrought by forces who have time on their hands," to be used when training Commandos. SOE's Research and Device Section, in fact, developed techniques in small boat handling, demolitions, and communications, as well as weapons employed not only by SOE agents but also by the commanders of such outfits as the Special Service Brigade, the Small Boat Squadron (SBS), the Royal Marine Commandos, and the first parachute units, all of whom visited SOE's workshops and training facilities and took back ideas that they later incorporated into the training of their own forces.[88]

The work done by the SOE, in fact, indirectly impacted the work of both U.S. Marine Raider Battalions and Captain Jones' Observer Group (and later the Amphibious Reconnaissance Company). This "influence" extended to the fields of communications, use of submarines, small boats, torpedo boats, and finally "Commando" raids.[89]

Communications

As for communications during World War II, Marine and Army special units encountered the usual problems associated with communications with higher headquarters, the relaying of critical data for operational employment, and transmission of timely intelligence to higher headquarters. The SOE trainers at Inverness and elsewhere considered "the wireless as the most valuable link in the whole ... chain of operations," which consisted "of single-short-wave Morse WT transmitters, communicating from the field to stations in the home countries in cipher." As the official history of the Special Operations Executive stated, "Without these links ... we would have been groping in the dark."[90] Nevertheless, and as was the case with the development of all special forces during World War II, "Communications were perhaps the most important problem [they] faced" as they figured out the best methods for conducting operations behind enemy lines and passing on important information regarding the enemy's position, troop strength and dispositions.[91] The challenge most common to all Allied special forces was equipment, specifically the size, weight, and range of communications equipment necessary for field operations.

The radio-receiver set most frequently used by SOE teams was the short-wave Morse transmitter (or, as it was often called, "transceiver"), which was a transmitter and receiver combined. The type generally used by SOE teams (as well as American OSS teams) was the B Mark II, which weighed thirty pounds and fit into an ordinary small suitcase measuring two feet in length. Its frequency was quite wide—some 3.5–16 megacycles a second. One disadvantage was that it was too weak, "for a set so small could not produce more than 20 watts at best."[92] Additionally, the B Mark II required some seventy feet of aerial or an antenna, impractical for Marine reconnaissance (or any Commando) teams, which required a much smaller, more compact means of communicating with a submarine or torpedo boat. Each radio operator carried two crystals that determined the frequency used during day or night. Crystals were very fragile and oftentimes were damaged on hitting the ground after a parachute drop or, in the case of a seaborne raid, became waterlogged and thus rendered useless.

One solution to the weight and size of the B Mark II was the introduction of the smaller A Mark III transceiver (which measured ten inches by seven inches by five inches); unfortunately, it was still too bulky to be "simply hidden" or carried from ship to shore. The other remedy was the development of a set of "jerry-rigged" radios (locally produced) that weighed three pounds each. These radios were developed by the teams of Detachment 101 of the OSS, though they were never adopted by Marine Raider or Reconnaissance teams. These radios, essentially scratch built, were light, easily carried and operated, and able to withstand the harsh conditions of the Burmese jungle.[93]

One problem Commando teams, SOE agents, OSS teams, Raiders, Marine Reconnaissance teams never overcame was the use and transportation of a sufficient number of batteries. Batteries often were heavy, bulky, and (as Marine Reconnaissance teams discovered two decades later in Vietnam) an addition to the individual weight carried by team members. Indeed, the three-pound radio developed by Detachment 101 in Burma required a cumbersome thirty-five-pound battery and constant air resupply. However, batteries were not the only hindrance to effective communication.[94] Crystals, like batteries, often became waterlogged from the rain or surf, as well as the humidity that permeated most jungle-heavy Pacific islands, rendering them useless.[95]

Encoding and enciphering wireless traffic in the field was difficult and oftentimes dangerous, as it was very time consuming and exposed the operator to enemy fire. Nevertheless, both enciphering and encoding were vital to the mission of intelligence gathering and required skill, patience, and secrecy while in the field.[96] During the initial organization of Marine Observer Group, Captain Jones' Marines experimented with lightweight radio and signals equipment, though the problem of communications equipment was never sufficiently resolved.

Submarines, Small Boats, and Torpedo Boats

During the fleet exercises of the late 1930s, Marine Reconnaissance teams practiced landing on an "enemy" shore, being first transported via submarines or motorboats and then transferred to rubber boats. These rubber boats, sometimes tethered together with a light line or cable, then proceeded ashore, paddled by their Marine crews and accompanied by a "lightly equipped patrol" that swam ashore on its side.[97]

As mentioned previously, the U.S. Marine Corps and Navy experimented during the 1930s with a number of boat designs, small outboard power boats and speedboats, "Rum Runners" (the type used by smugglers bringing illegal alcohol across the Great Lakes from Canada into the United States during the Prohibition era), kayaks, rubber boats, and other makeshift craft used by Marines in Nicaragua. As U.S. and British officials discovered, "Suitable craft were harder to find than suitable beaches."98

During the early stages of the war, the British Admiralty was reluctant to commit to using large ships or boats due to the size and vulnerability of such vessels to enemy shore observation or shore batteries. As such, "the use of submarines" was envisaged from an early stage, though, unlike their American counterparts, Royal Navy officials hesitated at first in committing their submarines for carrying SOE and Royal Marine Commando teams and would use these silent craft only in such high-risk missions such as the extraction of Free French officials (including General Henri H. Giraud) prior to the landing during Operation "Torch" in Northwest Africa in November 1942.

Unlike the British, both U.S. Marine and Navy officials from the start contemplated the use of submarines in the insertion of reconnaissance teams on a hostile shore. As pronounced by Brigadier General Dion Williams as early as 1912, the use of submarines "and special craft" was paramount in inserting reconnaissance teams.99

"When amphibious reconnaissance was first developed, submarines were the first vehicle of choice." They had the advantage of stealth in approach and could surface at night to launch their Reconnaissance, Raider, or Commando teams.100 The first two submarines used by Marine Reconnaissance and Raider teams were the USS *Nautilus* (SS-168) and USS *Argonne* (SM-1). Both were former mine-laying submarines and displaced approximately 2,700 tons each. Both vessels had large after-spaces, "normally used for storing and dropping mines," which made them ideal for carrying Marine Reconnaissance and Raider outfits, their gear, and rubber rafts.

The first combat missions of *Nautilus* and *Argonaut*101 took place in August 1942 off Makin Island when 228 Marines of the 2nd Raider Battalion, commanded by Lieutenant Colonel Evans Fordyce Carlson, USMC, raided a Japanese-held atoll in the Gilbert Islands. The *Nautilus* (now designated APS-1) later participated in landing Marines from Major Jones' Amphibious Reconnaissance Company on Apamama Island on November 19–20, 1943, during Operation "Galvanic" (the landings on the Tarawa atoll).102

As the war in the Pacific progressed, Marine Reconnaissance teams utilized the smaller *Guppy* class of submarines when conducting their missions. One such mission was conducted by the USS *Grayling* (SS-209), which landed a Marine Raider Battalion's reconnaissance teams on the Shortland and Treasury Islands in August 1943. Toward the end of World War II, the Navy converted USS *Perch* (APSS-313) and USS *Sea Lion* (APSS-315) to transport submarines. These latter two submarines remained in service during the 1950s.

While submarines remained the primary method of transporting reconnaissance and raider teams, both American and British officials agreed that fast, small

The USS *Nautilus* (SS-168), a former submarine minelayer, weighed 2,730 tons and was one of two submarines used by Marine Reconnaissance teams as well as Marine Raiders during World War II (courtesy Major General Oscar F. Peatross, USMC, Papers, Marine Corps Recruit Depot, Parris Island, South Carolina).

surface craft were most desirable in landing reconnaissance and Commando teams. Indeed, Captain Jones' Observer Group "experimented with many types of small landing craft including rubber boats, folding canvas boats, kayaks, [and] outboard motors." As the war in the Pacific unfolded, it became obvious that "all the various parties of men we are now training, had to be landed from the sea" in suitable (though imperfect) landing craft.[103]

Over time, rubber boats became the primary means of transport used by Marine Reconnaissance teams to reach the enemy shore. They were readily transportable, easy to inflate, and could carry a sufficient number of Marines (depending on the type used) ashore. "This included the two-man Navy Life Raft, Mark II, used mostly from seaplanes such as the PBYs; the four-man Mark IV rubber raft; seven-man LCR [M] and ten-man LCR [L] inflatable boats."[104]

As noted by Colonel Bruce F. Meyers, a veteran Marine Reconnaissance officer, rubber boats, while imperfect, became the preferred method of insertion by Marine Reconnaissance teams during World War II and after. Meyers noted there were two ways the Navy launched a Marine Reconnaissance team in rubber boats:

> The main advantage of rubber boats was that they could be deflated and rolled up for carrying aboard the particular vessel used to transport the recon teams to a position seaward of their assigned objective. Normally, rubber boats would be deflated aboard the APDs[105] or subs until a determined distance out from the objective. If the landing was to be from APD, the boats would be inflated by air hoses on the fantail and lowered over the sides. Marines would then clamber down ropes, cargo nets, or ladders, board their craft, then lower their weapons, radios, and other gear to be used on the particular mission.[106]

When landing from a submarine,

the rubber boats would be deflated and rolled into a diameter small enough to allow them to be transported and passed up through the hatch to the weather deck. There, the submarine crew would use air hoses to inflate them and they would be lowered over the sloping sides of the sub. Marines, using lines, would more or less "rappel" or walk down the curving and slippery sides (usually covered with green algae) of the submarine (many slipped or fell into the boats or the sea at one time or another during these walk-downs). Then the ships company would pass all weapons, radios, and other equipment to the rubber boats, where they would be secured by line to cross member/seats.[107]

Colonel Meyers noted that securing the boats was important "in the event of the boat turning over or flipping in going through the surf to the beach"; doing so also prevented the loss of valuable gear during the movement from ship to shore.[108] In order to keep the gear from becoming waterlogged, "waterproofing … was a must."

There were, of course, disadvantages when landing a reconnaissance team from a rubber boat: The boats were slow, difficult to handle in the rough surf, and often tired out their crews before "the actual insertion ashore." They were also difficult to launch from the shore in the heavy surf once the reconnaissance team completed its mission. As Meyers noted, "We lost some Marines in rubber boats going through the surf zone."[109]

Submarine Weight Designation Type

SS *Nautilus*, 2,730 tons, SS-168, Mine-layer/Transport*
SS *Argonaut*, 2,710 tons, SM-1, Mine-layer/Transport†
SS *Narwhal*, 2,730 tons, SSN-671, Attack Submarine
SS *Grayling*, 2,391 tons, SS-209, *Guppy*-Class Transport
APSS *Perch*, 1,526 tons, APSS-313, *Guppy*-Class Transport
APSS *Sea Lion*, 1,526 tons, APSS-315, *Balao*-Class/Transport§

* The SS *Nautilus* was later designated AP-1.
† The *Argonaut* was sunk during a patrol in January 1943. A second *Argonaut* was commissioned in 1944 and served in its traditional role as an attack submarine.
§ During the 1950s, the *Sea Lion* was converted to a helicopter-pad submarine and remained in service until 1977.

One last technique with which the SOE experimented, though it was never adopted by either the OSS nor the Marine Corps, was the one-man submarine. Known as the "Welman," and designed specifically to penetrate German U-boat pens, "there were," as the official history of SOE stated, "many discussions where and how it could be used" in carrying out clandestine operations against the German Navy. In the end, however, the "Welman" was never adopted by SOE, and the idea was "laid to rest."[110]

Commando Raids

One final doctrinal development in the employment of Marine amphibious reconnaissance teams during World War II was connected to their role as a raiding force or as "Commandos" and the carrying out of "Commando raids." Here, the indirect impact of SOE and development of special Marine Corps units during World War II was most noticeable.

Late in 1940, an informal arrangement between SOE and Combined Operations, the two British agencies responsible for carrying out operations against German forces in France and the Mediterranean area, "proposed that SOE would handle small raids" of up to thirty men, who would carry out operations "far behind the coastline [of France and Northwest Africa]," while Combined Operations would execute raids of "all sizes."[111]

Special Operations Executive's "research laboratories research and devices sections were far ahead of anyone else's, for the special purposes of raiding techniques, and commando parties were often equipped with snowshoes, silenced weapons, delay fuses, and so on of SOE's design."[112] SOE's laboratories and workshops produced a variety of "devices" and techniques used by the Special Service Brigade, the Small Boat Squadron (the forerunner of the Special Air Services), the Royal Marine Commandos, and British Airborne Forces or "Paras." Indeed, due to its "gathering" of vital intelligence about French dockyards, naval gates, and navy yards in general, SOE became a conduit of knowledge that enabled British Commandos to cripple or hinder German and Vichy French shipping and submarine pens. One such raid, in fact, severely damaged the only dry dock capable of handling the German battleship *Tirpitz*.[113]

While Americans and British Commandos continued to train in the conduct of special operations, HQMC debated the need for "special troops" (or units trained in Commando techniques) for the war against Japan. As noted earlier, Major

SS *Narwhal,* used by the Alaska scouts during the invasion of the Aleutian Islands (U.S. Navy photograph).

USS *Sea Lion* (APSS-315) was of the *Guppy* class and used by Marine Reconnaissance teams during World War II and through the Vietnam War. Its unique helicopter pad assisted in launching reconnaissance missions (U.S. Navy photograph).

USS *Perch* (APSS-313) submarine, used extensively by Marine Reconnaissance starting in 1944 and continuing through the Vietnam War (U.S. Navy photograph).

General Commandant Thomas Holcomb resisted the creation of special units, as, in his eyes, it served only to draw qualified officers and noncommissioned officers from the Fleet Marine Force just as the Corps began its expansion for service overseas. Pressure to create "special units" or "Commando-type" outfits came primarily from inside the Corps (Lieutenant Colonel Evans Ford Carlson and Captain James Roosevelt—the president's youngest son) as well as from William J. "Wild Bill" Donovan, the head of the Office of Strategic Services. Donovan, in a letter to

President Franklin D. Roosevelt, dated December 22, 1941, urged the president to set up "small groups" working under "definite leaders" to organize and establish "guerrilla forces" that were military in nature, "to strike the enemy where he least expects it and yet where he is most vulnerable."[114] General Holcomb, after consulting Major Generals Holland M. Smith, Commanding General Fleet Marine Force Atlantic, and Charles F.B. Price, Commanding General, Department of the Pacific, on the appointment of Donovan as a reserve Marine brigadier general in charge of a Marine Raider-type unit, rejected the idea based on the latter's inexperience in amphibious warfare and the drain such units would create on the Marine Corps as a whole.[115]

Inside the Marine Corps, efforts on the part of Lieutenant Colonel Evans F. Carlson had more successful results. As a result of his observation of the Chinese Communist 8th Route Army, Carlson influenced the organization of two Marine Raider Battalions—the first organized at Quantico, Virginia, and placed under the command of Lieutenant Colonel Merritt "Red Mike" Edson, and the second organized at Camp Elliott, San Diego, California, with Carlson as commanding officer, with the provision that the men (officers and enlisted) came from Marines recruited directly for such duty.[116] It might be added that Carlson's efforts were aided by FDR's son, James, who was a captain in the Marine Corps Reserve and a strong proponent of the organization of such a Raider force.

Captain Roosevelt, in a letter to General Holcomb, urged the creation of a unit based on the British Commandos with the "spirit" of the 8th Route Army: "The purpose of this group of especially trained and equipped fighters is to inflict on the enemy surprise and swiftly moving blows." Then, echoing his commanding officer (Lieutenant Colonel Carlson), Roosevelt added, "Similarly, the Eighth Route Army in China has proven an invaluable obstacle to any continued Japanese offensive in the North China, or Border District." The younger Roosevelt emphasized that such "raids" and such a force would keep the Japanese off balance, forcing them to extend their already vulnerable supply lines throughout the Pacific.[117]

While the debate continued as to the merits of both the mission and the organization of a Marine force along the lines of the British Commandos, it is important to note that the evolution of Marine Amphibious Reconnaissance doctrine continued with its traditional "reconnaissance" missions and the inclusion of what were classified as "non-intelligence" gathering missions of sabotage and demolition of enemy installations and strong points. These "non-intelligence" missions included:

1. To create a diversion from proposed landing point[s]
2. Minor night attacks
3. To assist a landing by executing light demolitions
4. To disrupt enemy communications by wire cutting and jamming radios
5. To set flares for naval gunfire at night, or to smoke a beach in order to screen a landing wave, or to otherwise mislead the enemy[118]

While Captain Jones' Observer Group trained along lines similar to those used by Marine Raider Battalions, such as swimming, demolitions, scouting, patrolling, and marksmanship, this is where the similarity ended. Jones' "Recon" Marines also studied terrain features, hydrography, sketching, concealment, communications techniques, signals intelligence, how to properly mark beaches, and reporting procedures.[119]

Much in line with their British Marine counterparts, Marines who were part of both the Raiders and amphibious reconnaissance units received rigorous physical and military training. To ensure that they were prepared to successfully carry out their assigned missions under all types of adverse weather and wartime conditions, exceptionally high physical condition and agility were required of both officers and enlisted men. In short, "All individuals should have confidence in their ability to handle themselves in water 'and on land,' or they will lose interest."[120]

The impact of the Marine Corps' informal contacts with both SOE and British Combined Operations training, while "peripheral," nonetheless became embedded in the formation of the two Raider Battalions, a parachute battalion, and the Amphibious Reconnaissance Company. The work by SOE and the training and techniques developed by Combined Operations, coupled with the observation by Marine officers at Inverness and Roseneath, Scotland, indirectly impacted the work of Jones' Amphibious Reconnaissance Company. With the exception of several units formed by the Australians and New Zealanders in the Southwest Pacific during World War II, SOE and Combined Operations Command laid the foundation for all special operations carried out by the Allies during World War II on both sides of the Atlantic and those employed in the Pacific against the Japanese. Recent scholarship likewise asserts that SOE and Combined Operations Command laid the doctrinal foundation for today's Special Forces.[121]

General Holland M. Smith, in his post–World War II analysis of the development of amphibious warfare doctrine, stated that "Marine raider battalions," as well as other special units (such as the Para-Marines), "were formed because of the notable success of British commando-type organizations at a time when everything else was going badly for the Allies."[122] Unlike the Raider Battalions and Para-Marines formed in the early part of the Marine Corps' mobilization for World War II, amphibious reconnaissance had been well established as a vital component of a successful amphibious landing.

From Observer Group to Amphibious Reconnaissance Company (1942–1943)

While Jones' Observer Group continued to train for operations against German forces in Northwest Africa, the division of theaters between the Army and the Navy that resulted in the latter's primary responsibility for operations against the

1. Birth of a Concept 39

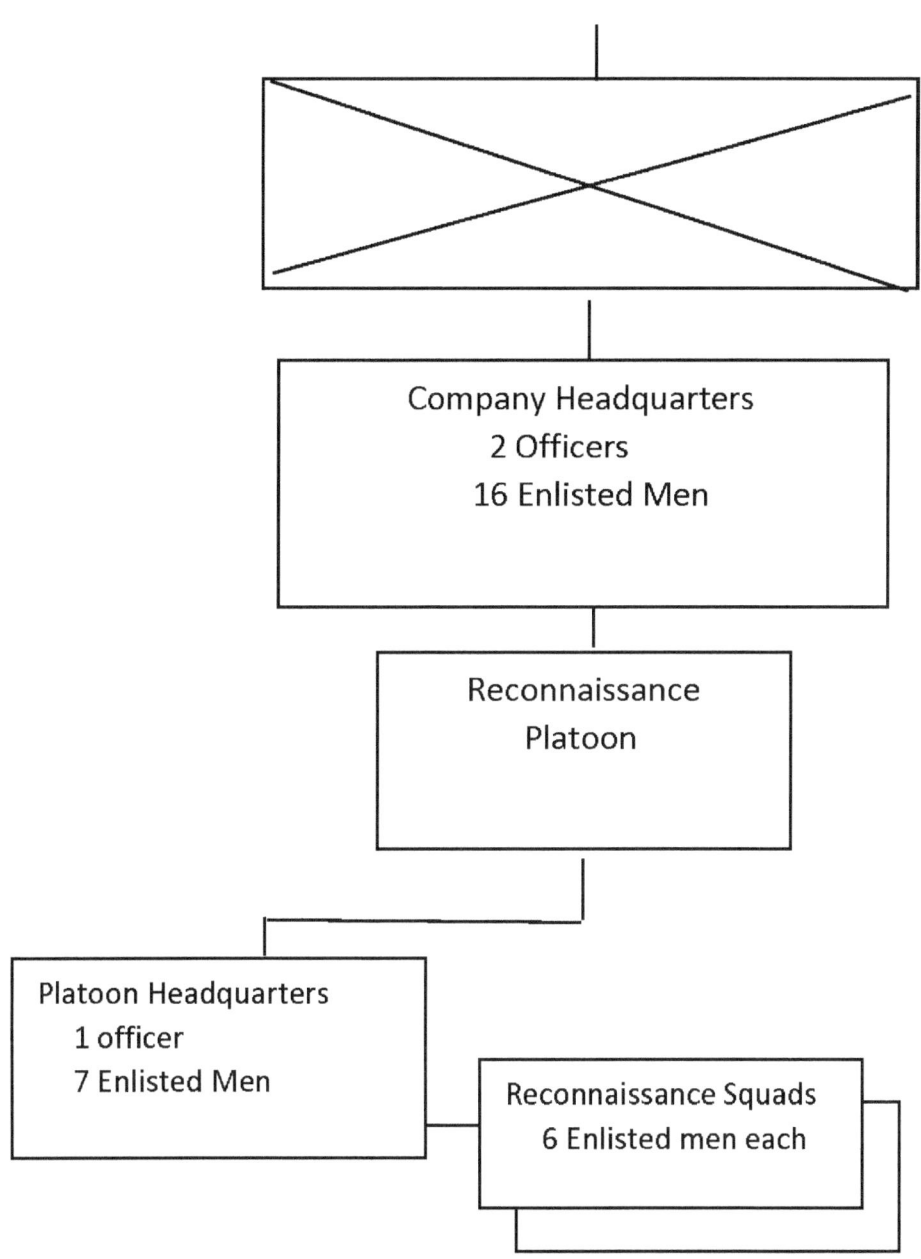

Diagram 1: V Amphibious Corps (VAC) Amphibious Reconnaissance Company 1942 (Stubbe, *Aarugha!*, 17–18).

Japanese in the Pacific impacted Jones' Observer Group, which officially became, on January 7, 1942, Amphibious Reconnaissance Company.

The new organization consisted of a headquarters of two officers and sixteen enlisted Marines, as well as a reconnaissance platoon consisting of a platoon headquarters of one officer and seven enlisted Marines, further broken down into two reconnaissance squads of six enlisted Marines each.[123]

For the next nine months, Jones' Amphibious Reconnaissance Company trained at Camp Elliott, California, near the San Diego Marine Corps Base, on the same site used to train Carlson's 2nd Marine Raider Battalion. While there, those in the Amphibious Reconnaissance Company perfected the techniques that they had learned over the past twenty-four months. In addition to their own training, the Marines assigned to Amphibious Reconnaissance Company trained two Army units for "reconnaissance missions," one of which "was later cited for its performance in the campaigns of Attu, Alaska, and Kwajalein, in the Marshall Islands." In July 1943, VAC Reconnaissance Company departed its base in California for duty in Adak, Alaska, and Kiska, in the Aleutians, on August 1–23, 1943. For Captain Jones' Marines, the campaign in the Aleutians set the stage for its first major mission as a team in the Marine Corps' long trek across the Central Pacific that commenced in November 1943.

Evolution of a Mission—A Summary

By November 1943, Marine Reconnaissance had evolved from the detachments sent ashore from the USS *Oregon* and *Marblehead* during the War with Spain through their indoctrination in the techniques of special operations as taught by British Commandos and SOE. As both Brigadier General Dion Williams and Lieutenant Colonel Earl H. "Pete" Ellis wrote in their respective studies, reconnaissance (specifically, amphibious reconnaissance) would play an important part in the evolution of amphibious warfare and, indirectly, in the field of special operations. More important was the fact that during this evolutionary period of experimentation, organization, and doctrinal development, techniques emerged that would remain characteristic of Marine amphibious reconnaissance as it prepared for its first major test as an organization during World War II.

While General Holcomb disdained the creation of "Special Units," Marine Reconnaissance teams demonstrated their usefulness and importance to the success of amphibious landings during the fleet exercises of the late 1930s and early 1940s. The necessity of pre-assault reconnaissance prior to a landing came to the fore as U.S. Army and Navy leaders sought to integrate amphibious reconnaissance as a necessary element in planning and executing an amphibious assault in the build-up to the landings in Northwest Africa in November 1942 and later during the retaking of the Aleutians in August 1943.[124] The stage was now set for Amphibious Reconnaissance Company's first war, which began in November 1943 during Operation "Galvanic" during the landings on Tarawa.

2

Amphibious Reconnaissance Company Goes to War (1943–1945)

With the division of theater responsibilities established by the Joint Chiefs of Staff, Captain Jones' Reconnaissance Marines continued to train and prepare for employment as the "eyes and ears" of Marine and Navy commanders in the Pacific Ocean. On September 10, 1943, V Amphibious Corps (VAC) headquarters issued Jones a package of sealed orders with instructions to prepare for its first major employment as a reconnaissance company—the invasion of the Gilbert Islands, codenamed Operation "Galvanic," with the target being the Tarawa atoll.

Prior to VAC Amphibious Reconnaissance Company's first major action against the Japanese, Marines and soldiers continued to hone their reconnaissance skills in the Aleutians; on the Solomon islands of Tulagi, New Georgia, Choiseul and Guadalcanal; and in the Southwest Pacific on islands such as Bougainville. As Colonel Bruce Meyers later wrote, examination of these campaigns and Amphibious Reconnaissance Company's activities in the Central Pacific is crucial, as it provides "better insight" into the reasoning behind the activation of 1st Force Reconnaissance Company in 1957 and the importance reconnaissance played during the Marine Corps' involvement in Vietnam a decade later.[1]

Operations in the Aleutians Islands, May 1943

As VAC Amphibious Reconnaissance Company continued to train and prepare for its role in Admiral Chester Nimitz's Central Pacific drive against the heart of the Japanese Army's string of island fortresses, the U.S. Army launched the second major assault against enemy forces that had occupied the Aleutian islands of Kiska and Attu during the early Japanese conquests. In the course of this assault, the two Army units that had trained with VAC Amphibious Reconnaissance Company—the U.S. Army's 7th Scout Company and Reconnaissance Troop from the 7th Infantry Division—conducted a pre-assault reconnaissance that established how Marines from Amphibious Reconnaissance Company would operate prior to an amphibious assault beginning in November 1943.[2] More important is the fact that the reconnaissance operations conducted by the 7th Scout Company and Reconnaissance Troop, 7th Division, confirmed the joint nature Marine Reconnaissance operations during World War II and into the post–World War II era.

As Admiral Nimitz and his associates planned the next move against Japan, a joint Army-Navy staff assembled in San Diego, California, under Rear Admiral Francis W. Rockwell, commander of Amphibious Force, North Pacific, who had been designated as Commander, Amphibious Task Force (CATF), and Major General Albert E. Brown, U.S. Army, Commanding General, 7th Infantry Division, in order to plan for retaking the islands of Attu and Kiska.[3]

Grappling with the heavy fog that blanketed the target area, and outside of aerial photographs and a Coast and Geodetic survey of Attu that "showed the terrain back to approximately one thousand yards from the shore" and "warned all shipping not to approach closer than two and one-half miles to three miles," as well as "very little knowledge of the harbors," planners on Admiral Rockwell's and General Brown's staff could only estimate the type of terrain the landing force could expect to find as they came ashore.[4] More important was the "scant information concerning Japanese defenses and enemy's strength on the island." Prior to the American invasion of Attu, the Japanese garrison commanded by Colonel Yasuyo Yamazaki numbered 2,400 men, which included "one and half battalions of infantry, three antiaircraft batteries armed with 75-mm dual-purpose guns and lighter weapons, two platoons of a mountain gun batteries armed with 75-mm pack howitzers, medical units, as well as several engineer units whose mission had been to construct an airfield at the head of East Arm of Holtz Bay."[5]

"The lack of information on topography and offshore hazards, as well as enemy strength and disposition," necessitated the formulation of several plans to seize Attu by the time the assault force set sail from San Francisco on April 24, 1943.[6] It was during the landings on Attu and later Kiska that the amphibious reconnaissance doctrine was first employed during wartime conditions.

From a doctrinal standpoint, Army, Navy, and Marine planners agreed that amphibious reconnaissance "patrols are landed on hostile shores in order to secure information on the enemy, the terrain and hydrography, and for the purpose of effecting a deception."[7] During the landings on Attu, known as Operation "Land Crab" (May 11–30, 1943), the lack of information on the landing beaches, the weather, and hydrographic conditions on and near the shoreline called for reconnaissance prior to the full-scale landing of the 2nd and 3rd Battalions of the 17th Regiment, as well as the 1st and 2nd Battalions of the 32nd Infantry Regiment on BEACH BLUE and BEACH YELLOW at Massacre Bay.

The assault commenced with the landing of the 7th Scout Company during the pre-dawn hours of May 11, 1943, on BEACH SCARLET, about four miles northwest of BEACH RED, on the north shore of the island. The 7th Scout Company was part of "a provisional battalion commanded by Captain William H. Willoughby, the remainder of the 7th Division's Reconnaissance Troop (minus one platoon),"[8] which was scheduled to land immediately after the 7th Scout Company had made its initial reconnaissance of the shoreline and enemy dispositions. [MAP # 2] The remainder of Reconnaissance Troop was scheduled to land immediately after the 7th Scout Company, whose landing was temporarily delayed due to a thick blanket of fog that had descended over the entire eastern end of the island. Meanwhile, 7th Scout Company had moved inland, "well up a steep valley that led south from the beach. At the head of the valley was a pass which gave access to one of the valleys leading back from Holtz Bay, and from which it was hoped Scout Company could attack the enemy from the rear."

Another reconnaissance force, composed of Alaska Scouts and Company A, 17th Infantry, landed on BEACH RED in order to determine the feasibility of landing the entire northern force (RCT-17–1), which consisted of the 1st Battalion, 17th Infantry. The Alaska Scouts and soldiers from Company A, who came ashore in rubber rafts from the submarines *Nautilus* and *Narwhal*, reported back to General Brown that the rock-studded shoreline prevented a full-scale landing by the assault force, as it could handle no more than three boats at a time. Despite the scouts' report of a steep escarpment that began 75 feet from the water's edge and rose to a height of 250 feet above the beach, as well as cliffs that overlooked the proposed landing site, Colonel Frank L. Cullen, commanding officer of the 32nd Infantry, as well as a Navy beachmaster who accompanied the reconnaissance force ashore, determined that the beach was capable of handling the landing force. At 1530 that afternoon, BCT-17–1, commanded by Lieutenant Colonel Albert E. Hard, landed on BEACH RED. Meanwhile, the 2nd and 3rd Battalion of the 17th Infantry conducted simultaneous landings on BEACHES BLUE and YELLOW.[9]

During the subsequent landing on Kiska, both Major General Simon Bolivar Buckner, U.S. Army (commanding the Kiska operation), and Major General Holland M. Smith, USMC (who was sent to observe the follow-up landing in the Aleutians), urged Admiral Kinkaid, overall commander of the landing, to put ashore a force of Alaska Scouts to determine enemy strength on the island. Kinkaid, not wanting to risk either lives or ships, preferred to land the entire assault force. Instead of finding a well-entrenched enemy, however, the assault force discovered that the Japanese garrison on Kiska had been evacuated undetected by Kinkaid's task force, under the cover of a heavy fog, by the Imperial Japanese Navy, a fact that remained unknown until after the war.[10] Nonetheless, the landings on Attu and later Kiska by the 7th Scout Company and Alaska Scouts validated the Marine Corps' amphibious reconnaissance doctrine just as planners began laying the groundwork for Admiral Nimitz's Central Pacific Drive and VAC Amphibious Company's landing on Apamama Island in the Gilberts as part of the Tarawa landings in November 1943.

The landings in the Aleutian Islands, in fact, codified the core tents of amphibious reconnaissance, which served as the basis for Marine amphibious reconnaissance after World War II. These tenets included the following points:

1. To determine the characteristics of beaches available for landing, and report the same to commander at sea;
    a. By hydrographic reconnaissance of water near the shore line.
    b. By examining terrain in immediate vicinity of beach.
    c. By noting beach defenses—wire, mines, and other obstacles; troops in immediate vicinity.
2. To report landmarks for assisting in locating landing beaches.
3. To mark beaches and landing points during a landing.
4. To determine location, strength, and composition of troops in landing area.
5. To take and hold in concealment a prisoner or prisoners and be prepared to turn them over to Headquarters Landing Force.
6. To spot observers to report enemy activity by radio or by panel.
7. To determine road net and be prepared to meet and guide elements of the landing force.
8. To determine practicability of terrain for air landings.
9. After the beachhead has been established, to contour the sea floor beginning at the ten foot line and using a two front contour interval in order to expedite the unloading of supplies by locating most advantageous channels and beaches.[11]

During the landings in the Aleutian Islands, the 7th Scout Company, Alaska Scouts, and Reconnaissance Troop, 7th Infantry Division, both trained and indoctrinated in the tenets of amphibious reconnaissance prior to their commitment to the Attu and Kiska operations, laid the foundation for the success of Major Jones' VAC Amphibious Reconnaissance Company in the forthcoming drive across the Central and Southwest Pacific theaters of operation.

Guadalcanal to Bougainville (August 1942–November 1943)

The first major land offensive against the Japanese after the victory at Midway in June 1942 occurred in the Solomon Islands on the island of Guadalcanal on August 7, 1942. It was during this campaign that the Marine Corps successfully employed the technique of reconnaissance against enemy positions by dedicated ground assets.

There were several instances during the Guadalcanal campaign when Marine commanders employed Marines in the reconnaissance role or as scouts. The first example was carried out on the night of August 12, 1942, by Lieutenant Colonel Frank B. Goettge, the intelligence officer (G-2) of the 1st Marine Division. Goettge, acting on reports of a group of Japanese wishing to surrender, organized a "beach-to-beach" amphibious reconnaissance patrol that "was to go west down the north coast [of Guadalcanal] to a point west of the Matanikau River, where the alleged surrendering enemy were located." The Marine lieutenant colonel, who led

2. Amphibious Reconnaissance Company Goes to War (1943–1945)

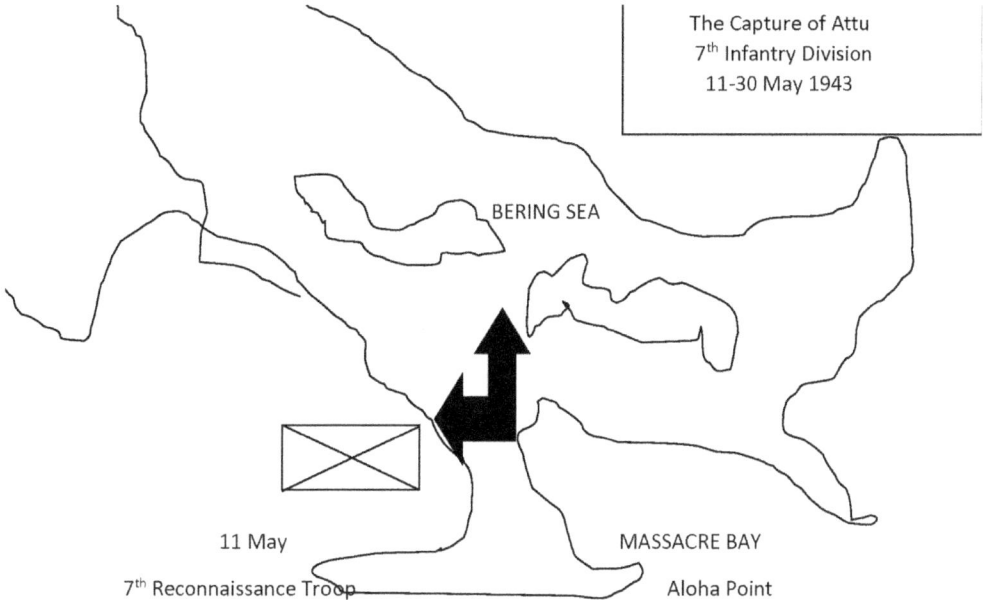

Map 2: The 7th Reconnaissance Troop's Landing on Attu on May 11, 1943 (Conn et al., *Guarding the United States and Its Outposts*, 280).

the patrol himself, landed with his team at 2200 on the evening of August 12 and came under immediate enemy fire in what turned out to be well-planned ambush. In the ensuing action, Goettge, Lieutenant Commander Malcolm Pratt, USN (the assistant division surgeon), and Lieutenant Ralph Corey (a Japanese Army linguist), along with the bulk of the patrol, were killed. Only three patrol members managed to survive the ambush, swimming back to the Marine lines to report what had occurred.[12]

A more successful reconnaissance on Guadalcanal led by 1st Marine Raider Battalion Platoon Sergeant Francis C. Petrus, the intelligence chief/scout, and three Marine Raiders, along with two scouts, two radio operators, and two natives, got underway on September 27. The mission was to scout out and report on two Japanese encampments said to be near Aola, some thirty miles from the Marine positions at Henderson Field, as well the condition and morale of the Japanese troops they encountered.[13] Initially transported by Higgins boats, Sergeant Petrus' patrol moved inland once ashore and began their reconnaissance of Aola as well as the villages of Gurabusa and Gegende. Here, the Marine patrol observed and later reported to Division G-2 the presence of some one hundred Japanese soldiers. After observing the enemy encampments, Petrus' patrol made its way back to the original landing site through the swamps; they then boarded the Higgins boats to take them back to friendly lines. "All of the intelligence gathered on this recon mission [by Sergeant Petrus' team] was of great benefit to the division, which now had a much better idea of the locations and the strengths, physical condition, and morale of the Japanese troops" on Guadalcanal.[14]

Gathering information on Guadalcanal regarding the enemy's troop dispositions, strength, and possible courses of action initially proved difficult. Almost from the time of the landings on Guadalcanal, Marine commanders, due to their unfamiliarity with jungle warfare, were hesitant to initiate an aggressive, if somewhat overcautious, patrolling of known (and, in some cases, unknown) avenues of approach used by the Japanese, in what soon became a stock in trade for Marine (and Army) reconnaissance teams. As the campaign on Guadalcanal intensified, "each regiment in the perimeter, including the 11th Marines [Artillery,] was assigned certain areas outside the perimeter for such operations." Patrols, varying in size from squads to companies, "were sent out daily and in general operated between the hours of 0700 and 1800." "While the patrols were limited in mission and duration and in general were at best a mixed success," they nonetheless provided information on the nearest enemy force regarding the defensive perimeter around Henderson Field. However, the patrols often demonstrated that the length and scope of the mission required them to operate far from the perimeter in all directions and in territory occupied by the enemy.[15]

One last innovation regarding the use of reconnaissance teams on Guadalcanal and initiation of a more aggressive patrolling schedule was the Scout/Snipers formed by Lieutenant Colonel William J. Whaling, the executive officer of the 5th Marine Regiment (given the nickname "Daniel Boone" by his fellow Marine officers). Colonel Whaling's Scout/Snipers acted as the "eyes and ears" of the 1st Marine Division. The Scout/Snipers, composed of "the best field craft Marines" from each of the rifle companies of the 1st Marine Division (and who were, for the most part, individuals who were skilled outdoorsmen and "received additional training"), became the division's primary reconnaissance asset, acting as guides, scouts, and, on occasion, carrying out long-range patrols.[16]

New Georgia to Bougainville (July–December 1943)

Prior to the assault on New Georgia, toward the end of February 1943, elements of the 1st Raider Battalion conducted a series of reconnaissance patrols in order to determine potential landing beaches. The reconnaissance patrol, led by Captains Clay A. Boyd and Edward Wheeler, and wearing the newly issued camouflaged utilities, soft covers, and soft canvas-sneaker-like jungle boots, remained on the island until evacuated by a Navy PBY seaplane off the eastern end of the island, having conducted a three-week recon of New Georgia and nearby Rendova Island. For the next three months, coast watchers and Marine Raiders conducted additional reconnaissance missions on both islands to determine their suitability as airfields. On the island of Kolombangara, the reconnaissance teams reported the unsuitability of its terrain and "intense" Japanese activity on the island, which caused Admiral William Halsey to eliminate that island as an objective.[17]

In late July 1943, a Marine Reconnaissance team conducted an extensive patrol of Vella Lavella and reported that the terrain located at the "southern end of the island near Barakoma" was suitable for the construction of an airfield. New Zealand and Australian coast watchers, as well as natives, informed Halsey's staff that the Japanese garrison on Vella Lavella numbered only 250 officers and men and was located primarily on the northern tip of the island.[18] Admiral Halsey, after rejecting Kolombangara as the site of an airfield, ordered the seizure of Vella Lavella, which began in the pre-dawn hours of August 15, 1943.

Prior to the seizure of Choiseul by elements of the 2nd Marine Parachute Battalion, commanded by Lieutenant Colonel Victor H. Krulak, a Marine-Navy patrol conducted several reconnaissance missions on the island. "One group, landed from a patrol boat (PT) on the southwest coast of Choiseul, moved northward along the 'Slot' side of the island toward the coastwatcher station at Kanaga. After crossing the island thee patrol was evacuated by a Navy patrol bomber on September 12th after six days on the island."[19] Two subsequent patrols made up of Marines, U.S. Navy sailors, and New Zealanders scouted the northern end of Choiseul and Choiseul Bay for eight days (September 22–30, 1943) before being withdrawn by Navy patrol boats. "Their reports indicated that the main enemy strength was at Kakasa where nearly 1,000 Japanese were stationed and Choiseul Bay where another 300 enemy troops maintained a barge anchorage." In keeping with the main tenets of amphibious reconnaissance doctrine, the patrols likewise reported the sites of several potential airfields as well as "good beaches suitable for landing purposes." The reconnaissance teams informed I Marine Amphibious Corps (IMAC) headquarters that "Japanese activity ... was generally restricted to Kakasa and Choiseul Bay."[20]

Prior to the assault on Cape Gloucester, First Lieutenant John D. Bradbeer, along with elements of the Alamo Scouts, conducted three reconnaissance patrols on New Britain starting on September 23, 1943, to determine the hydrographic conditions, enemy beach defenses and troop strength prior to the full-scale landing, which took place on December 26, 1943. During the first of these patrols, Lieutenant Bradbeer and his team paddled ashore in rubber rafts launched by Navy PT Boats 110, 325, and 327 in order to conduct an extensive reconnaissance of the proposed landing site. Upon reaching the shore and evading Japanese patrols, Bradbeer's team made extensive sketches of enemy coastal fortifications and the shoreline. Lieutenant Bradbeer made two subsequent landings prior to the assault at Cape Gloucester that confirmed the suitability of the beaches elected for the main assault by Marines from the 1st Division.[21]

The reconnaissance missions conducted from Guadalcanal to Cape Gloucester validated the pre–World War II principles of amphibious reconnaissance. As the official Marine history of the landings at Cape Gloucester stated, "Personal reconnaissance by trained observers was required to accumulate the necessary detailed geographic and hydrographic information upon which to base a decision," insofar as selection of objectives was concerned. Moreover, the work of Lieutenant Colonel Whaling's Scout/Snipers confirmed the necessity of a dedicated reconnaissance force to scout, report on and, if necessary, raid enemy activities and positions once ashore. The reconnaissance missions undertaken by Marines, sailors, and New Zealand and native scouts in the southwest and northern Solomon Islands served as the testing ground for the doctrine of amphibious reconnaissance and its ultimate trial in the Central Pacific starting in November 1943.

Apamama Island (November 19–20, 1943)

The baptism of fire for Captain Jones' and the Marines of VAC Amphibious Company occurred during the initiation of Admiral Nimitz's Central Pacific drive during Operation "Galvanic"—that is, the landings on Tarawa atoll in the Gilbert Islands on November 20, 1943. In fact, "the amphibious reconnaissance in the Gilbert Islands in November 1943 was the first performed by the Amphibious Reconnaissance Company."[22] Colonel Bruce Meyers, whose career in Marine Reconnaissance began during World War II, later wrote that to meet the ever-growing need for amphibious reconnaissance, VAC Amphibious Reconnaissance Company was expanded to battalion strength and redesignated Amphibious Reconnaissance Battalion. From November 1943 until the end of World War II in the Pacific, "The company/battalion performed more amphib[ious] recon[naissance] (over 150) than any other single recon unit in the Pacific during World War II."[23]

The islands of Tarawa, Makin and Apamama were strategically situated to support the forthcoming invasion of the Marshall Islands (set for February 1944) as advance air and naval bases. Later, Army planners viewed Apamama, located some seventy miles from Makin, as an ideal location to construct an airfield for its heavy bombers to be used later during the invasion of the Marshall Islands. The mission of Captain Jones' VAC Amphibious was to scout by periscope as well as through the insertion of reconnaissance teams on several atolls in order to determine the strength of the enemy's garrison and defenses on the island. Specifically, Jones was instructed to "reconnoiter the atoll in order to determine whether there was any sizable Japanese force ashore, and to select and mark suitable to be used later by other forces."[24] Should the Marines encounter any opposition, they were to return to the submarine. Jones' mission had been conceived by General Holland M. Smith, commanding general of V Amphibious Corps, who had "reasoned that it would be best to land scouts on the main island of Apamama Atoll by submarine to reconnoiter enemy positions before committing sizeable forces."[25]

Reconnaissance and War Plan Orange in the 1920s and 1930s

The emphasis placed on the Gilberts and the Central Pacific Ocean area insofar as Navy and Marine Corps strategic planning was concerned had its origins in the war plans formulated during the interwar era and, in fact, dated as far as back as the mid-nineteenth century. Accelerated by the advent of the modern U.S. Navy and its need for coaling stations or "advance naval bases," as well as the expanding U.S. commercial interests in the Pacific, the various island chains in the Pacific Ocean, because of their proximity to the Asian mainland and China market, became the focal point of naval planning for a war in that region. The rise of Japan as a Pacific economic and military power and its growing naval strength in the first two decades of the twentieth century made possession of and/or access to the area vital to the U.S. Navy's ability to project power some 12,000 miles from the continental United States. Given the importance of this region to the U.S. Navy, it became the focus of Navy and Marine officers assigned to the Office of Naval Intelligence (ONI). Multiple Marine officers, including Colonel Richard M. Cutts; Lieutenant Colonels Earl H. "Pete" Ellis, Pedro A. Del Valle, and Evans Fordyce Carlson; and Captain Charles C. Brown, conducted clandestine reconnaissance missions in the Pacific Ocean area and on the Asian mainland during the 1920s and 1930s.[26]

Of the above-mentioned Marines, perhaps the most important was Lieutenant Colonel Earl H. "Pete" Ellis. Ellis' mission and work on what would be the Marine Corps' contribution to War Plan Orange remains one of single most important "reconnaissance" missions conducted by Marines during the interwar era.[27] Ellis' *Advanced Base Operations in Micronesia* and his quixotic mission to Micronesia (and, more specifically, the Palau group of islands) was the first major reconnaissance mission conducted by a Marine officer since Captain Goodrell's mission ashore at Fisherman's Point, Cuba, during the War with Spain in 1898. The bulk of Ellis' study "consisted of detailed discussions of the sea, air and climate, land types, native populations, economic conditions, and the enemy, concluding with an outline of our strategy of seizing key islands as bases to project our forces, a discussion of material requirements such as planes capable of dropping torpedoes in the water … against ships and for carrying large automatic or quick fire guns for employment against the ships." Despite what the Marine Corps' official history referred to the "crudeness of his plan" insofar as an amphibious assault was concerned, Ellis' plan "broke with tradition" regarding his call for Marines to be used in an offensive role (i.e., "seizing") instead of a defensive role in protecting what then were called "advanced bases."[28]

The Importance attached to Ellis' *Advanced Base Operations in Micronesia* cannot be overemphasized. Indeed, as War Plan Orange evolved during the 1920s and 1930s, and as the Marine Corps' mission evolved from base defense to seizure of enemy-held islands, Marine planners built on the foundation Ellis laid with his study. His "time-tables, mobilization projections, and predictions of numbers of men necessary to seize certain targets such as Eniwetok, Woje-Mille, Jaluit, Elmo, and Likeib, in the Marshall Islands, were so accurate … that the American drive across the Central Pacific followed … every essential detail of the Ellis' plan, if not its precise schedule, in detail."[29] Lieutenant Colonel Ellis' reconnaissance mission and his death on May 12, 1923, on Palau remain today shrouded in mystery. While historians will never know what occurred during Ellis' last days on the island of Koror and what he may or may not have found in Micronesia, Lieutenant Colonel Pete Ellis was the first Marine to conduct a land reconnaissance on the same islands where other Marines, twenty years later, would establish the principles of land and amphibious reconnaissance.

Ellis' reconnaissance of Micronesia was followed up by Colonel Richard M. Cutts, USMC, who, on a mission to revise *Advanced Base Operations in Micronesia*, "investigated the Philippine island of Tawitawa, located in the Sulu Archipelago between the Sulu Sea and Celebes Sea, about 40 miles east of Borne in the Marshalls, [and] prescribed measures to seize and defend two atolls in the Marshalls as subsidiary bases from which U.S. forces could defend lines of communications to the Philippines."[30] Colonel Cutts' revised study of Ellis' plan, which relied on aerial reconnaissance and outdated information, concluded that "there is at the present no known Orange [i.e., Japanese] force in the Marshall Islands."[31]

Assigned to the Office of Naval Intelligence, Major William A. Worton and Captain Charles C. Brown, both Chinese language officers, were assigned by Major General Commandant John H. Russell to ONI for "certain urgent work … in the Far East in 1935, specifically in northern China." Worton, who retired in 1945 as a brigadier general, briefly left the Marine Corps in order to undertake his clandestine mission. Much like Ellis' mission to Micronesia, only Major General Russell, Captain William Dilworth Puleston, the head of ONI, and Admiral William H. Standley, chief of naval operations, knew of Worton and Brown's secret mission, which remained "classified" as late as the early 1980s.[32]

During World War II, First Lieutenant (later General) Robert H. Barrow, USMC, observed the situation in China as part of the U.S. Navy–led Naval Group China, headed by Captain Milton Edward "Mary" Miles, USN, which, as part of the Sino-American Cooperative Organization (SACO), had been assigned to collect operational intelligence on the military operations in China as well as maintain contact with the Nationalist Armies of Chiang Kai-shek along the eastern seaboard of China near Hong Kong.[33] Barrow later recalled that his mission was to conduct hydrographic surveys and conduct terrain reconnaissance as well as report on Japanese military activities in the area.[34] Interestingly, during the latter stages of the Korean War (1952–1953), Barrow conducted a similar mission along the Formosan (Taiwanese) Pescadore Islands, in addition to working with Nationalist Chinese Army and Navy officials and bands of mercenaries (essentially pirates) who collected intelligence on the People's Liberation Army of Mao Zedong on the Chinese mainland.[35]

Two other individuals who merit mention are Captain (later Brigadier General) Evans Fordyce Carson, USMC, and Major Edward Hagen, USMC, and their mission to China in 1937. Carlson, who would later form the 2nd Marine Raider Battalion during World War II, "gained permission to observe" Mao Zedong's 8th Route

Army. Carlson, a controversial figure whose later exploits in China gained the attention of President Franklin D. Roosevelt, accompanied elements of the 8th Route Army between December 1937 and February 1938 during their long retreat into the mountains of Yunnan Province, known as the "Long March," and met Mao Zedong and his lieutenant, Chou En-Lai.[36]

Finally, there was Lieutenant Colonel Pedro A. Del Valle, USMC, who, as a member of ONI, served as a neutral observer with the Italian Army during its war in Ethiopia in 1935 and aboard vessels of the Italian Navy.[37] Del Valle, who retired as a lieutenant general, was, in fact, personally decorated by the Italian dictator Benito Mussolini for his bravery under fire.[38] It might be added that both Carlson and del Valle caused something of a stir in Marine Corps circles during and after World War II as being sympathetic to opposing forces—in Carlson's case, to Mao Zedong's 8th Route Army, as opposed to Del Valle's expressed sympathy to Mussolini and unfounded accusations that he was pro–Fascist.[39]

Much like Captain Jones, who led VAC Amphibious Company during World War II, Marine officers from Earl Ellis to Pedro Del Valle performed what were essentially clandestine reconnaissance missions that gave war planners at HQMC and within the operations section of the Chief of Naval Operations (CNO) information on hydrographic soundings, terrain analysis, and operational data on foreign armies and military operations starting in 1923 until the end of World War II.

It was Captain Jones and Marines of VAC Reconnaissance Company who took amphibious reconnaissance to the next level of development as they carried out numerous reconnaissance missions against the Japanese throughout the Central Pacific area of operations.

Reconnaissance Operations in the Gilbert Islands (September–November 1943)

Reconnaissance of the Gilberts began in earnest on September 16, 1943, when Captains Jones of the Marines and D.L. Newman of the U.S. Army boarded the USS *Nautilus* at Pearl Harbor, where they were to accompany Commander William D. Irwin, the *Nautilus*' commander, on its sixth patrol. The mission of Jones and Irwin was to make a photo reconnaissance of Tarawa, Kuma, Butaritari Makin, and Apamama in the Gilberts. Admiral Richmond Kelly Turner, USN, who commanded the amphibious assault task force, "wanted detailed photographic coverage of all the beaches to be involved in retaking the Gilbert[s]."[40] Army, Navy, and Marine planners at Pearl Harbor wanted "detailed information" regarding the location of enemy defenses, gun and troop positions, and hydrographic and terrain data in order to form a more accurate picture of the landing conditions the assault force might encounter.

Captain Jones and Irwin's reconnaissance was, in fact, a "first," as "periscope photography" was still, as Colonel Bruce Meyers noted, "in its infancy." As such, the technology they used was still developing in order to provide a more accurate picture of the objects being photographed from afar. As was the case with the Special Operations Executive and its technological contributions to special operations, the U.S. Navy developed "specially fabricated brackets (mechanical 'shelves' attached to the periscope to hold the cameras) and three types of cameras which included: (1) a large view camera; (2) a camera that used medium-sized roll film, and; (3) a miniature 35-mm camera."[41] In order to process the film quickly, the lower sonar room on the *Nautilus* was converted to a temporary darkroom. Unfortunately, during Jones' mission, the Navy's cameras were unable to provide the detail required to ensure an accurate description of the target area. Moreover, the periscope-mounted camera tended to vibrate and did not allow sufficient light in to take an accurate picture. The *Nautilus*' executive officer, Lieutenant Commander Richard Lynch (who was, as Meyers wrote, "an avid amateur photographer"), suggested the use of his German-made Primaflex camera, which took 2.25-by-2.25-inch negatives that were "far superior to the Navy's cameras." The Primaflex camera "was overlapped by 50 percent which as the photos were taken, was coordinated carefully with a chart of the target island, giving the submarine the exact distance from each beach."[42]

In time, all submarine periscopes were outfitted with the special brackets, and Primaflex cameras became standard use when conducting periscope photography. The photos taken by Jones and Irwin proved to be a "boon to the intelligence officers and were quickly reproduced and distributed" to all troop leaders prior to Operation "Galvanic."

Landing on Apamama Island (November 19–20, 1943)

On the evening of November 7–8, 1943, Captain Jones and forty Marines boarded the USS *Nautilus* at Pearl Harbor. Along with the Reconnaissance Marines were eight other officers, including Australian George Hard, who had lived on the island before the war; Lieutenant E.F. "Bing" Crosby, a Navy Civil Engineering Corps officer from the 95th Construction Battalion (Seabees); and Major Wilson Hunt from the 8th Base Defense Battalion. Lieutenant Crosby's mission was to conduct a survey of the island's suitability for an airfield while Major Hunt was to select gun positions once the island had been secured. In the pre-dawn hours of November 8, 1943, the *Nautilus* set sail for the objective area. Marine Reconnaissance was going to war.

Arriving off Tarawa before the main invasion fleet, the *Nautilus* conducted an extensive patrol to determine the presence of enemy shipping. The targets of VAC Reconnaissance Company on Apamama were the islands code-named JOE, JOHN, ORSON, and OTTO.

On the afternoon of November 20, as the 2nd Marine Division launched the

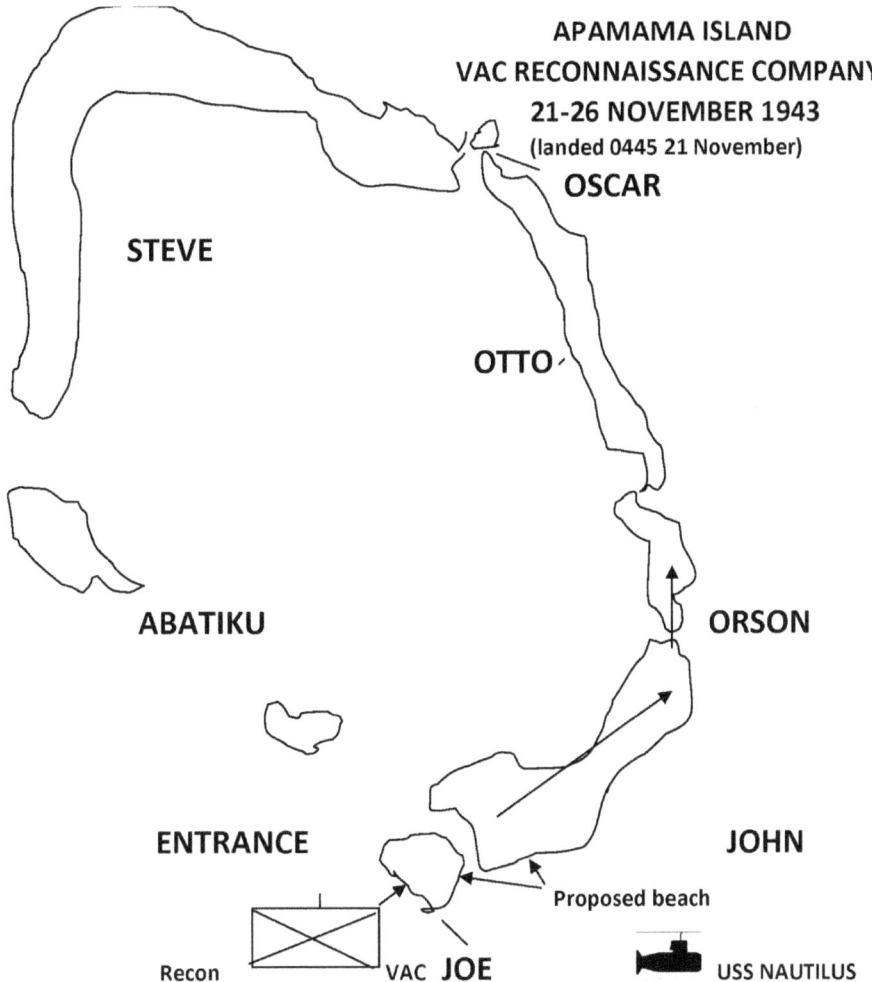

Map 3: VAC Amphibious Reconnaissance Company Landing, November 21, 1943 (Shaw et al., *Central Pacific Drive*, 101).

main invasion of Tarawa, Jones' men embarked in rubber boats and paddled for the target island known as JOHN. An unexpectedly strong current, however, forced them to land on JOE just to the west. Jones' Marines shortly thereafter paddled their rafts over to JOHN. Upon landing on JOHN, the leathernecks encountered a three-man Japanese patrol. After a brief firefight in which they killed one Japanese soldier, the reconnaissance team proceeded to its next objective—ORSON. Securing the rafts on ORSON, Captain Jones came on a group of natives, who informed him that there were some twenty-five Japanese troops "entrenched at the southern tip of neighboring OTTO."[43]

On November 23, 1943, the company "attempted to move across the sand spit connecting ORSON and OTTO Islands," though it was halted in its tracks by the Japanese defenders, whose fire proved so intense that Jones "decided to break off action and attempt to outflank the defenders."[44] In the meantime, First and Third

Platoons reconnoitered JOHN and STEVE islands on November 23 from 0700 to 1615 in the afternoon. As Jones' men proceeded to move out across ORSON, the Japanese defenders once again opened up with an unrelenting fusillade of machine guns and mortar fire toward the advancing Marines. Captain Jones' plan was to "neutralize the enemy's fire by spotting the ship's gunfire."

Moving out at 0330 in the pre-dawn hours of November 24, 1943, Jones' positioned his third platoon with light machine guns some two hundred yards to the enemy's front with orders to fire at targets of opportunity and provide a base of fire while the First and Second Platoons assaulted the right flank, "in an attempt to outflank the entrenched enemy." The attack, however, did not go as planned, as Japanese fire was unrelenting despite the arrival of the *Nautilus*, which provided fire support for Jones' men with its five-inch gun.[45] Later that day, the arrival of a friendly destroyer provided fire support to Jones' Marines as it shelled the Japanese emplacements, which abruptly ended enemy resistance. On November 25, friendly natives reported to Jones that "all the Japanese were dead." Marine patrols later confirmed this news after discovering the bodies of eighteen Japanese soldiers—all of whom had committed ritual suicide. Four of the enemy dead had been killed by naval gunfire. In their first action against an enemy-held island, Jones' Marines suffered two dead and one injured. On that same afternoon, Brigadier General Leo D. Hermle, assistant division commander, arrived with the 3rd Battalion, 6th Marine Regiment, to "assume responsibility for the defense of the atoll."[46] Its mission complete, VAC Amphibious Reconnaissance Company received orders to re-embark aboard the USS *Harris*, which it did the next morning on November 26, 1943.

The U.S. Navy's Underwater Demolition Teams (1942–1945)

One last element of amphibious reconnaissance that came into being in the aftermath of the Tarawa landings was the formation of Navy underwater demolition teams (UDTs), or simply "frogmen." The failure to detect the shallow reefs prompted the Navy and VAC to organize a specialized unit whose sole mission was to scout out and destroy enemy underwater obstacles planted to obstruct or prevent an amphibious landing. With the recognized need for "underwater scouts," the Navy organized the first underwater demolition teams at Fort Pierce, Florida, under the command of Lieutenant Command Draper Kauffman USN. The "frogmen" were tasked with handling and planting explosives in obstacles obstructing landing craft or ships from going ashore or ships entering narrow waterways or harbors. Navy frogmen were superb swimmers and were trained to handle small rubber boats in both daytime and nighttime operations. Over time, the UDT men became the forerunners to the Navy's SEAL teams and had as their motto "that the right man with the right training can only be stopped by total disablement or death."[47]

"Flintlock"—Operation "Sundance"—Majuro Atoll (January 30–February 2, 1944)

The next phase of Admiral Nimitz's Central Pacific Drive was seizure of the Marshall Islands (code-named Operation "Flintlock"), with the capture of Kwajalein Atoll being the first objective. VAC Amphibious Reconnaissance /Company's mission was to seize, in conjunction with the Army's 2nd Battalion, 106th Infantry Regiment, the Majuro Atoll, which American planners believed was the least defended of the three atolls in the Kwajalein group.[48]

On the evening of January 30, 1944, the USS *Kane* (APD) entered Majuro Lagoon. Coming ashore in rubber rafts, a small detachment of VAC Reconnaissance Company landed on the atolls of Eroi and Calalin, which were discovered to contain no enemy troops, though later a native disclosed that a lone Japanese warrant officer and a few civilians were the only enemy personnel on the atoll.[49] However, Jones' men were informed that some three hundred to four hundred Japanese were located on nearby Darrit.

On the morning of January 3, 1944, the remainder of VAC Amphibious Reconnaissance company landed on Dalap. Fanning out across the island, the reconnaissance patrols found no enemy troops. On nearby Uliga, natives told the Marines that the Japanese garrison there had been evacuated before they arrived. In the evening hours of the same day, "a platoon from Jones' company landed on Majuro Island and captured the Japanese naval warrant officer responsible for Japanese property left on the island."[50] The civilians who assisted him had fled into the jungle prior to the Marines' arrival.

At midnight on February 1, 1944, a detachment from VAC Amphibious Reconnaissance Company landed on Arno Atoll, located some ten miles from Majuro Island, in order to investigate the whereabouts of the crew of a downed American airplane. The natives informed the leathernecks that the Japanese had removed the crew to nearby Maloelap Island. Re-embarking aboard the *Kane*, the reconnaissance detachment returned to Majuro the next morning.

Operation "Catchpole": Eniewetok (February 17, 1944)

VAC Amphibious Reconnaissance Company's next assignment was the capture of a series of small islands in the Eniwetok Atoll. Specifically, VAC Amphibious Company was "On Dog-Day at How-Hour," to land on and seize CAMELLA, CANNA, CAERNATION, COLUMBINE, and BUTTERCUP islands and cover the landings of the 2nd Separate Pack Howitzer Battalion and 104th Field Artillery Battalion. The initial landing was to be made on CANNA and CAMELLA.

Landing from Landing Ship "Tank" (LST) 272 in amphibious tractors (LVTs), Captain Jones, two other officers and fifty-seven enlisted men landed on CAMELLA at 1320 on the afternoon of February 17, 1944, and shortly thereafter reported back to the ship that the island was uninhabited with no sign of the enemy. Ten minutes after Jones' party landed, another group of four officers and fifty-seven men landed on CANNA and discovered twenty-five natives but no Japanese.[51] The natives, however, did inform Jones of the presence of some one thousand Japanese troops guarding "each of the three objectives of Tactical Group 1." The natives likewise reported the presence of some 1,000 Japanese laborers on the island of Engebi.[52] Captain Jones' Reconnaissance Company made five subsequent landings on the other islands southeast of Engebi, though they were found to be devoid of any Japanese troops.

Meanwhile, to better assess the presence of any enemy troops on ZINNIA, just west of Engebi, Brigadier General Thomas E. Watson, USMC, commanding officer of Tactical Group 1, ordered Scout Company, 4th Marine Division, to seize the island. By 0327, ZINNIA was in the Marines' hands. With the seizure of CAMELLA, CANNA, and ZINNIA, the Japanese had been deprived of the ability to send reinforcements to oppose the landing.

A Model Operation for Special and Joint Operations

The capture of Eniwetok, and the Marshalls campaign in general, served as a model operation for amphibious reconnaissance. Moreover, the landings on Eniwetok served as a laboratory of sorts for reconnaissance operations. Besides the landings on CANNA, CAMELLA, and ZINNIA, U.S. Navy underwater demolition teams (UDTs) were used to scout out and report on the presence of any underwater obstacles. Finding the shoreline free of any obstacles, the landings proceeded and objectives were met. Use of Scout Company, 4th Marine Division, complemented the work of Jones' VAC Reconnaissance Company. In short, the pre-war doctrine of combined and joint operations ashore prior to and during a landing proved successful and established the pattern of cooperation between the services that ensured the successful landings during operations on Kwajalein, the Tinian landing during the Marianas Campaign, and assaults on Iwo Jima and Okinawa. Finally, the landings in the Marshalls represented the first time VAC Reconnaissance Company was brought ashore by LVTs instead of rubber boats or submarines.[53]

Its missions complete, and having suffered fourteen killed in action, VAC Amphibious Company boarded ship and set sail for Pearl Harbor on February 24, 1944.[54] After its arrival in Hawaii, the company began preparations for the next major phase of Admiral Nimitz's Central Pacific campaign—seizure of the Mariana Islands. Upon arrival in Hawaii, the company quickly replaced the men killed and wounded with fresh team members and implemented a rigorous training schedule. Successful in its first three campaigns, the company was expanded to battalion size with the addition of firepower and better communications equipment. Amphibious reconnaissance had come of age, its place in the execution of an amphibious assault established, its men, tactics, doctrine and material battle tested.

Reorganization and Expansion of Amphibious Reconnaissance Company (March–April 1944)

With the increased tempo of offensive operations in the Pacific Ocean area of operations, and notwithstanding the success of VAC Amphibious Company during the first phase of the Central Pacific drive, Lieutenant General Holland M. Smith recommended to the commandant of the Marine Corps, Lieutenant General Alexander A. Vandegrift, that Amphibious Reconnaissance Company be expanded to a full battalion with the addition of a second amphibious reconnaissance company, to include the addition of a weapons company. General Vandegrift approved the request on April 28, 1944, with a new table of organization that included two reconnaissance companies, a headquarters company and a weapons platoon to consist of mortars and machine guns. The strength of the reconnaissance battalion was set at 23 officers and 292 enlisted men, including 13 Navy corpsmen. The official designation of Amphibious Reconnaissance Battalion occurred several months later, after the Marianas campaign, on August 26, 1944, when it became Amphibious Reconnaissance Battalion, Fleet Marine Force, Pacific.[55]

With the reorganization of Amphibious Reconnaissance Company, Captain Jones was promoted to major while the company's executive officer, Captain Merwyn Silverthorn, Jr., was given command of Company "A," with First Lieutenant Russell Corey assuming command of Company "B." First Lieutenant Leo B. Shinn assumed command of the small headquarters company.[56]

Given the Marine commanders' recognition of the need for "dedicated reconnaissance assets," HQMC redesignated Marine Scout companies as Division Reconnaissance companies and brought them into the division's headquarters battalion. This redesignation of Scout companies as Division Reconnaissance companies gave the commanding general of each division an important intelligence-gathering asset. More to the point, this move created a division of effort—that is, amphibious reconnaissance would evolve after World War II into "Force Reconnaissance," with its command and control at corps level (later Marine Amphibious Force, or MAF, level), while Division Reconnaissance companies would remain solely a "division or operational asset."[57] In short, the reorganization and redesignation of both amphibious reconnaissance battalions and division-strength reconnaissance companies established the foundation and concept of employment for the post–World War II Marine Corps Tables of Organization regarding Force and Division Reconnaissance Battalions. This arrangement, in fact, created two very distinct forms of

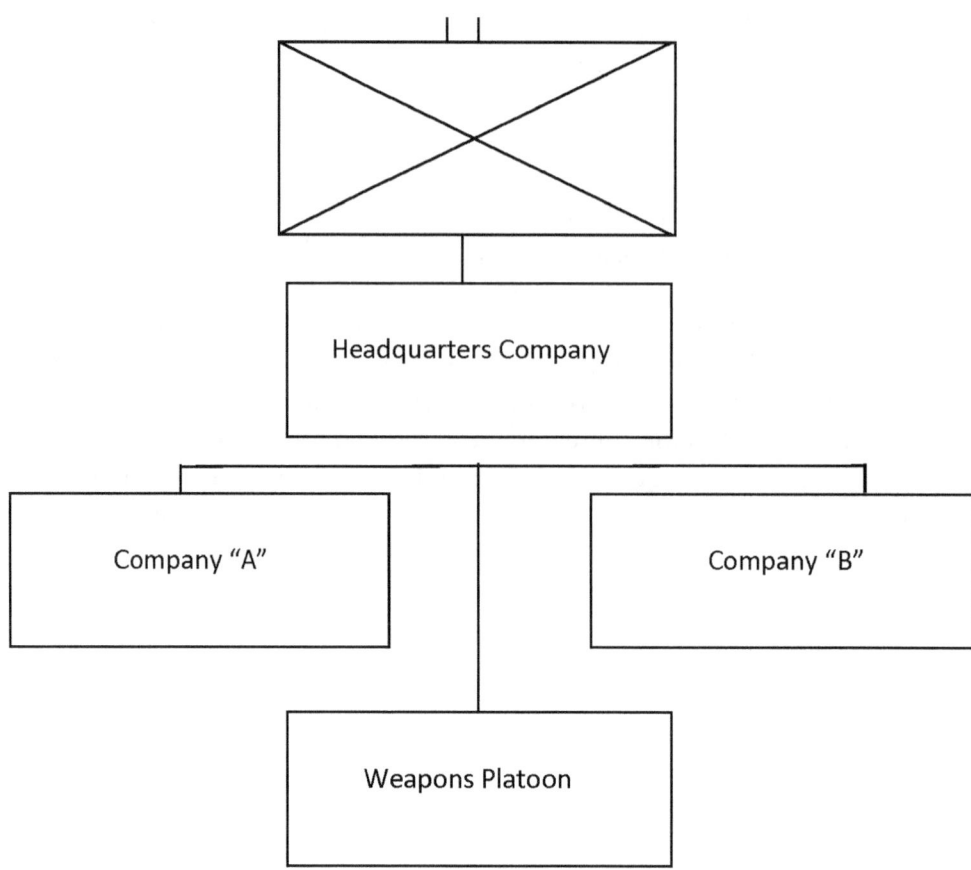

Diagram 2: Reconnaissance Battalion, V Amphibious Corps, April 28, 1944.

reconnaissance assets that Marine commanders would have at their disposal during the Vietnam War.[58]

Operation "Forager"—Landings in the Mariana Islands (July 1944)

The next phase of Admiral Nimitz's Central Pacific drive took aim at the strategically located Mariana Islands of Saipan, Tinian and Guam. Seizing these islands would give the U.S. Army Air Forces airfields capable of launching heavy bombers against the Japanese homeland. The islands likewise made up the so-called "inner ring" of the Japanese defenses. Capturing these islands would essentially pave the way for a full-scale invasion of the Japanese home islands.[59]

The mission for Captain Merwin Silverthorn's Company A, VAC Reconnaissance Battalion, was to conduct a landing on D-1 on the night of June 14, 1944, and seize 1,554-foot Mount Tapotchau, located in the center of the island. However, Vice Admiral Richmond Kelly Turner, USN, the amphibious task force commander, cancelled the operation on D-3, due to the lack of concrete intelligence as to the strength of the Japanese garrison on the island.[60] Instead, reconnaissance of the assault beaches was carried out by Navy UDTs, under the command of Lieutenant Commander Draper Kaufman, which conducted pre-assault beach surveys and searches for alternate beach landing sites.[61]

Tinian (July 9–10, 1944)

As was the case with the island of Saipan, the Joint Chiefs of Staff considered Tinian ideal for the construction of airfields to be used in the strategic bombing of Japan. The least mountainous of the Marianas, Tinian was seen as "most suited for the new American long-range bombers," particularly the B-29. In fact, "it was from Tinian that the B-29s rose to bomb Hiroshima and Nagasaki in August 1945."[62] The Japanese commander on Tinian, Colonel Keishi Ogata, realizing the value of Tinian and its airfields, knew that sooner or later the Americans would invade; thus, he divided the island into three defensive sectors, with the bulk of his strength centered at Ushi Point and Tinian Town.[63]

The mission of Major Jones' Amphibious Reconnaissance Battalion was to

> investigate the beaches, measure the cliffs, and note the area just beyond, including the exits. They were to report the trafficability of the beaches for LVTs and DUKWs in particular. The naval UDT-men were to do the hydrographic reconnaissance—measuring the height of the surf and the depth of the water, observing the nature of the waves, checking the reefs and beach approaches, and looking for underwater obstacles.[64]

After conducting a rehearsal on the night of July 9–10, 1944, off the beaches of Magicienne Bay, Saipan, VAC Amphibious Battalion and UDTs boarded their respective ships, USS *Gilmer* and USS *Stringham*, for the short journey to positions off northern Tinian. Company A, commanded by Captain Silverthorn, was to land at Yellow Beach, while Company B, led by First Lieutenant Leo B. Shinn, undertook a reconnaissance of the White Beaches.[65]

Embarking in their rubber rafts around 2030, the Marines of Company A had the advantage that moonrise would not occur until 2232, in addition to a cloudy sky that would conceal their movement to the objective area until midnight, when the moon would be at its brightest. "Thus, the final 500-yard swim to the beaches could be made under the cover of darkness."[66]

The twenty Marines and eight Navy UDT men of Captain Silverthorn's Company A landed on Yellow Beach and quickly set out to reconnoiter the proposed landing site. After conducting a thorough reconnaissance, Silverthorn's team returned to the ship and reported to Admiral Turner's staff. Their findings were, however, disappointing, as Yellow Beach was surrounded by a series of forbidding cliffs, thus making a landing impracticable and potentially dangerous. The UDTs likewise informed Admiral Turner that a high surf and double-apron barbed wire on the beach, as well as the fact that the approaches to the beach were heavily mined and contained numerous potholes, boulders, and other natural obstacles, made an amphibious assault too risky.[67]

Reconnaissance of White Beach 1 and White Beach 2, by contrast, "got off to a bad start," as a strong tidal surf pushed the rubber rafts off course, forcing the team assigned to land on and scout White Beach 1 instead of White Beach 2. Despite being blown off course, the Marines of Company B landed and quickly conducted a thorough reconnaissance of White Beach 1. Major Jones, disappointed by the failure to reach White Beach 2, ordered another reconnaissance mission for the next night. This time, radar from the USS *Stringham* as well as radio communications using SCR-300 radios successfully guided the Marines and UDTs ashore.

Once ashore on White Beach 2, the Marines and UDTs reported that while surrounded by cliffs, both White Beach 1 and White Beach 2 were suitable for an amphibious landing. More important, the Recon Marines and frogmen reported that the cliffs surrounding both beaches were not as steep (six to ten feet high) as those off Yellow Beach, which were as high as twenty-five feet, and that "LVTs, DUKWs[68] and tanks could negotiate the reef and land. Moreover, it showed that LCMs and LCTVs could unload on the generally smooth reef which extended about 100 yards offshore."[69] Finally, the reconnaissance teams reported that the landing area was wide enough to land a sizeable force abreast. Major Jones and his two company commanders reported to Admiral Turner that the landings could be made on the White Beaches, and "successful exists were possible inland."

During the Tinian operation, amphibious reconnaissance had more than proven its worth, as Admirals Turner and Harry Hill, as well as Major General Harry Schmidt, the Marine commander, concluded that White Beaches 1 and 2 were the most suitable for conducting the landing.[70]

Guam (July 21, 1944)

The last part of the Mariana Islands campaign (Operation "Forager") was the recapture of Guam, which been an American outpost since it was surrendered by Spain in 1899. Tasked with its seizure was the 3rd Marine Division under Major General Allen Turnage and the 1st Provisional Marine Brigade under Brigadier General Lemuel C. Shepherd. During the Guam campaign (July 21–26, 1944), Major Jones' VAC Amphibious Battalion would not be used, although UDTs conducted a pre-assault reconnaissance of the proposed landing beaches.[71]

Operation "Detachment"—Iwo Jima (February 19–March 26, 1945)

During Operation "Detachment" (the seizure of Iwo Jima), Marines from Company B, Amphibious Reconnaissance Battalion conducted a reconnaissance of both

Kama and Kangoku Rocks, situated northwest of Iwo Jima, to determine the presence of enemy forces. Both Kama and Kangoku Rocks had been of major concern, as Marines advancing along the west coast of Iwo Jima had received intermittent Japanese fire situated on both islands.[72]

Landing in twelve amphibious tractors supplied by the 2nd Armored Amphibian Battalion, the reconnaissance teams set out on their mission. The first target of the reconnaissance teams was Kama Rock, where the reconnaissance teams from Company B encountered only silence. "It was therefore decided that a landing by the entire company could take place." Subsequently, six officers and ninety-four men from Company B came ashore "without incident." Finding no enemy or signs of enemy presence on Kama Rock, the reconnaissance teams set out for the next target—Kangoku Rock, the larger of the two islands. Here the Marines found abandoned Japanese emplacements and caves that had been inhabited by enemy soldiers. "Having completed its mission, the reconnaissance company withdrew from the islands."[73]

Operation "Iceberg"—Okinawa (April 1–June 22, 1945)

During Operation "Iceberg," Company A, VAC Amphibious Battalion, led by Major Jones, beginning on March 26, 1945, a week before the full-scale assault on Okinawa, conducted a series of reconnaissance patrols of the surrounding islands. The first target of Jones' Marines was Keise Shima (March 26–27), where "no enemy were found."[74] On March 27–28, the Recon Marines conducted similar patrols on Aware Shima and Kure Shima, once again encountering no enemy. Subsequently, Jones' two companies ("A" and "B") conducted a series of patrols on six other islands. It was on April 6, 1945 (five days after the landing by the 1st Marine Division on the main island of Okinawa), on the island of Tsugen Shima, that the Reconnaissance Marines encountered stiff enemy resistance, necessitating a withdrawal, though, as a result of the enemy resistance, the Japanese "had been forced to show their hand," insofar as their strength on the island was concerned.[75]

Subsequent landings by Company B on Ike Shima and Takabanara Shima, as well as Haenza Shima and Hamaskia Shima, throughout the day of April 7 uncovered some 1,700 "frightened civilians." Later, Major Jones' Amphibious Reconnaissance Battalion participated in the Ie Shima operation and "assisted the 6th Marine Division in securing the northern section of Okinawa by seizing and occupying the small islands lying off the Motobu Peninsula." VAC Amphibious Battalion, having conducted some thirteen night patrols and actions during the Okinawa campaign, participated in the final "mopping up" operations, landing on June 26, 1945, at Kume Shima, fifty-five miles west of Naha, Okinawa's main city, though they discovered no enemy activity.[76]

In a personal letter of commendation to Major Jones, General Joseph W.

"Vinegar Joe" Stilwell, Commanding General, 10th U.S. Army, praised not only Jones' efforts but also to the efforts of the officers and men of VAC Amphibious Reconnaissance Battalion. Stilwell wrote in his commendation:

> For your superior performance under the capable leadership of Major James Jones in carrying out your assigned missions in the Ryukus Campaign. The Fleet Marine Force may well be proud of the development of amphibious reconnaissance as exemplified by your activities. Use of your battalion as the *only ground reconnaissance Agency held under TENTH Army* Headquarters expedited the accomplishment of all phases of the recent campaign [Stilwell's emphasis]. Your aggressive action made unnecessary the use of large forces in the seizure of the eastern islands of Okinawa, the islands off Motobu Peninsula and Kume Shima.[77]

For his leadership during the Ryukus campaign, Major Jones received the Silver Star for actions on March 26–29 and April 6–7, 1945.[78]

War's End (August–September 1945)

By the end of Operation "Iceberg," VAC Amphibious Reconnaissance Battalion numbered some 252 men and had participated in every major campaign in the drive across the Pacific. Operation "Iceberg" marked VAC Amphibious Reconnaissance's last campaign of the war. Aboard the USS *Elkhart*, the battalion had made it as far as Ulithi Atoll when news broke regarding the dropping of the atomic bomb and Japan's subsequent surrender. The battalion arrived at Pearl Harbor on September 12, 1945, where it was quickly dissolved, with only the Combat Swimming Company being retained and merged into the 1st Marine Division.

Summary

In its four years of existence, the VAC Amphibious Reconnaissance Battalion had pioneered the techniques of amphibious reconnaissance as set forth in doctrine written during the interwar era and just prior to the U.S. entry into World War II. During four years of war, Major Jones' VAC Amphibious Battalion pioneered the use of submarines, seaplanes, a host of special equipment (including SCR-300 radios and camouflage uniforms), and, most important, tactics that Marine Reconnaissance teams employed as late as the 1970s. In short, Jones' Reconnaissance Marines, to paraphrase an old saying, utilized "most of the old and some of the new" equipment used by Marines during World War II.

Doctrinally, during World War II, VAC Amphibious Reconnaissance Battalion validated many of the tactics and operational concepts formulated during the interwar era, especially in the use of submarines and seaplanes as a means of being conveyed ashore to the objective area. More important was the fact that, unlike the other special Marine Corps units formed during World War II, amphibious reconnaissance not only would expand in size and missions but also enjoy a postwar resurgence as HQMC discovered that pre-assault reconnaissance was crucial to the success of an amphibious assault as well as operations beyond the beachhead.[79]

Even as VAC Amphibious Reconnaissance Battalion folded its colors in September 1945, the lessons of World War II were being absorbed. One of those lessons concluded that the Marine Corps required a force reconnaissance capability. "Reconnaissance," as carried out by the officers and men of VAC Reconnaissance Battalion, was here to stay.

3

Reconstitution and Expansion

Marine Corps Amphibious Reconnaissance (1946–1963)

Based on the lessons of World War II and Amphibious Reconnaissance Battalion's successful campaign in the drive across the Pacific, the concept of pre-assault reconnaissance remained an important element in the planning and execution of amphibious assault. At the conclusion of the war, HQMC deactivated Amphibious Reconnaissance Battalion, though its Combat Swimming Company was retained at Camp Pendleton, California, which trained pilots in survival skills such as knife fighting, combat swimming, and other self-defense measures.[1] Postwar budgetary and manpower cuts further reduced the need for a specialized unit such as amphibious reconnaissance.

Reactivation of Force Reconnaissance (1948–1950)

The postwar cuts in defense spending by the Truman administration slowly changed, however, as tensions between the United States and the Union of Soviet Socialist Republics (USSR), as well as the ongoing civil war in China between the Nationalists and Communists and a number of insurgencies from French Indochina (Vietnam), the Philippines, and the Dutch East Indies, threatened U.S. national security.[2]

In 1948, a board convened to examine the future role of amphibious warfare at HQMC concluded that "organization of the FMF [included] a requirement for raids and reconnaissance which might include: '…the destruction of hostile weather and radar stations, destruction of enemy submarine base facilities, destruction of enemy air base facilities, destruction of critical enemy industrial plants or raw materials, reconnaissance of hostile beaches and shore defenses, reconnaissance of air and submarine bases.'"[3]

The board members recommended the reactivation of a Force Amphibious Reconnaissance Battalion based on the World War II–era table of organization with a strength of 1 officer and 308 enlisted men.

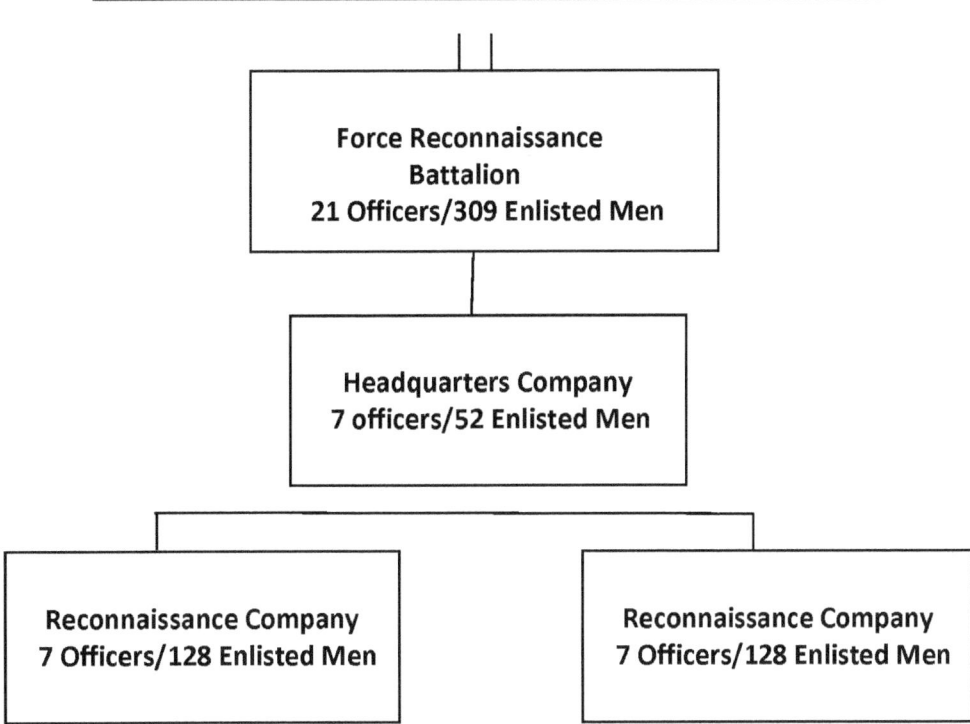

Diagram 3: U.S. Marine Corps Force Reconnaissance Battalion, 1948 (Stubbe, *Aarugha!*, 52).

Along with reactivating Amphibious Force Reconnaissance, the board likewise gave some consideration to "the improvement of transportation of amphibious reconnaissance teams to remote ... or inaccessible ... portions of the globe." Colonel William Coleman, in his review of "amphibious reconnaissance" during World War II, noted that the requirement for "improved means of transportation" was significant, as it meant that amphibious reconnaissance patrols of future "might operate on objectives at distances that today (1948) seem impossible."[4] These methods of transportation included the submarine, seaplane, and parachute.

Lessons of "Recon's 'First War'" (1945–1963)

The aforementioned principles forged from the experiences of Marine reconnaissance units in the Pacific Ocean areas during World War II, and according to which Marines would guide and initiate reconnaissance operations in Vietnam twenty years later, were reiterated and put into doctrine following the reconstitution of Marine Corps' amphibious reconnaissance units in the late 1940s.[5] These principles included the following points:

1. A patrol must be so constituted, both as to size and equipment, that it can operate in its assigned area with minimum danger of detection;

2. Personnel assigned must be well trained in amphibious patrolling and be in good physical condition;

3. Patrols must be given simple missions capable of accomplishment and of sufficient importance to warrant sending out such a patrol;

4. Patrols must be allowed sufficient time to accomplish the missions assigned;

5. Patrol leaders must be chosen for their known ability and intrepidity;

6. Before departure from base, patrols and the commander of transporting craft must be carefully briefed as to where and how they will be landed and where and how they will be recovered.[6]

As Marine planners at HQMC and FMFPac digested and integrated the lessons from Marine operations in the Southwest Pacific into amphibious reconnaissance doctrine, Marine amphibious reconnaissance units began a rigorous period of training in both land and seaborne operations.

It is important to note that besides the standard missions of beach and hydrographic surveys, which were critical to conducting an amphibious assault, the mission of ground reconnaissance patrols continuing into the hinterland was essential

A squad of Marine Raiders is shown making a practice landing during maneuvers at Camp Lejeune, North Carolina, in May 1949, using rubber rafts. Before, during and after World War II, the use of rubber rafts was essential to the reconnaissance mission (USMC photograph).

to carry out operations ashore. Ground reconnaissance had a unique ability to gain additional and more detailed information beyond what could be provided by other agencies or intelligence sources that might not be in a position to aid Marine commanders planning offensive and defensive operations. After operational experiences gained on Bougainville and Hollandia, New Guinea, in April 1944, extensive operations ashore became integral to reconnaissance training, as "information [many times] could only be obtained through ground patrolling." Indeed, in order to obtain such information, Marine reconnaissance elements would have to "search ... recent enemy camp sites, bivouac areas, and installations for abandoned documents, equipment, and indications of the size and nature of the enemy forces. Roads and trails could be inspected for recent vehicular or foot movements and an estimate made as to the number and types of vehicles, or numbers of men, which passed and the direction of the movement." Marine reconnaissance patrols could likewise report on the development of enemy outposts so as to give clues regarding the location of (enemy) bivouac areas or defensive positions. Finally, "Marine reconnaissance patrols may be able to penetrate the enemy outpost and physically observe the enemy dispositions." During the Marine involvement in I Corps in Vietnam, these same missions became standard missions for both "Force" and "Division" Reconnaissance teams.

Amphibious Reconnaissance Company, 1946–1950

Then–Captain Kenneth J. Houghton, who served with Major James Jones' Amphibious Reconnaissance Company during World War II (and later as FMFPsc CG, retiring as a major general), conducted several amphibious reconnaissance missions off Mille and Maloelap in the northern Solomon Islands. He recalled that his team trained for every possible contingency, including conducting raids, amphibious insertions, and parachuting into a target area. Perhaps the most important training came in the form of egressing from a submarine as a means of clandestine insertion. Houghton remembered that during operations in the

Major General Kenneth J. Houghton, USMC, one of the early pioneers of Marine Force Reconnaissance (USMC History Division photograph).

Southwestern Pacific theater of operations, he and his reconnaissance force were carried to the target area in a submarine to scout Japanese positions and "kind of seeing what was there," in terms of enemy defenses. Remaining in the Pacific after World War II, Major General Houghton went on to command Amphibious Reconnaissance Company, which was composed of 115 Marines, and trained in egressing from a submarine, attending jump school with the U.S. Army's 11th Airborne Division (then stationed in Japan), and patrolling.[7]

During an exercise aboard the submarine USS *Perch* (APSS-313), Houghton and his 115-man detachment prepared to evacuate the ship after it had been struck by the destroyer USS *Orlech*. The *Perch*, which sank in some 158 feet of water, eventually was able to surface, albeit with the screw of the *Orlech* embedded in its conning tower and with both periscopes sheared off.[8]

Korea (1950–1951)

During the Korean War (1950–1953), elements of the 1st Marine Division's Reconnaissance Company conducted scouting and deep reconnaissance missions of the Wonsan and Hungnam ports, as well as enemy logistical facilities. Additionally, they conducted seven raids along the North Korean coast from the USS *Horace A. Bass*. One of these raids, conducted on August 12–16, 1950, with a combined force of sixteen Marines and twenty-five Navy Underwater Demolition Team (UDT) members, raided the Posung-Myon area and destroyed three tunnels and two railway bridges without losing a man.[9]

Marine Reconnaissance's versatility in joint operations that transitioned into combined operations was on display in September 1950 when a reconnaissance force commanded by Captain Houghton conducted a training mission aboard the submarine USS *Perch*. Even as the reconnaissance team trained, the *Perch* took on a detachment of the Special Operations Group (SOG) and later some sixty-three Royal Marine Commandoes assigned to the 41st Independent Commandos, led by Lieutenant Colonel Douglas Drysdale.[10] Captain Houghton's team accompanied the *Perch* while the Royal Marines carried out their amphibious raid in conjunction with the USS *Maddox* (DD-731) along the North Korean coastline.

For the first three days after the landing at Inch'on on September 15, 1950, reconnaissance units acted as a screening force for the 1st Marine Division, operating on its right flank as they hunted down enemy stragglers and guerrillas. Prior to the division moving across the Han River, a thirteen-man reconnaissance team crossed to scout the other shoreline for enemy activity and report back to Major General O.P. Smith. Consequently, the reconnaissance team had the honor of being the first to cross and land on the opposite bank for their company. The Recon Marines later acted as a screening force, operating on the flanks of the 1st Marine Division during the battle for Seoul in late September 1950. They likewise acted as a screening force on the flanks and gaps throughout the line and hunted down partisans and enemy holdouts, in addition to releasing Korean civilians captured by the Communists during their initial offensive in June 1950.

After Seoul, Division Reconnaissance Company participated in the landings at Wonsan and then advanced with the rest of the division, leading the division to Hungnam. During this move, the company employed its first motorized patrol in jeeps in order to scout an enemy supply depot located some forty miles from Hungnam in the town of Huksu-ri. As the patrols entered the North Korean villages, civilians informed the Marines of the whereabouts of enemy stragglers who moved primarily by night in order to avoid allied aircraft.

Corporal Paul Martin, a member of one such patrol, recounted:

> As we went through each town on the route, the natives reported straggling enemy soldiers moving at night. When we reached the foot of the mountain pass, a native reported there were 4,000 Reds in the town ahead. We pushed forward anyway but did not see a single Red when we went through the town. It was dark when we arrived at the top of the pass, so we assembled our jeeps and formed a perimeter guard. Five North Koreans hit our lines during the night but none got through. The next day we moved on, finally contacting the enemy outside Huksu-ri. After making contact, we broke off and headed back to Hungnam with our information. We hadn't suffered a single casualty.

Corporal Martin stated that after Hungnam, the Recon Marines joined the 7th Marine Regiment on its advance toward the Chosin Reservoir. It was here that the unit came into contact with not only the North Korean People's Army but also, for the first time, soldiers from the People's Republic of China at Sudong-ni. Corporal Martin said that the first batch of Chinese prisoners of war reported that their main force was located at Chinhung-ni.[11] Subsequently, during the first contact with the People's Liberation Army (PLA) at Chinhung-ni, the Recon Marines encountered two Russian-made T-34 tanks and, after a brief firefight with enemy soldiers, destroyed both tanks by tossing grenades into them. Leaving Chinhung-ni, the Recon Marines conducted several flank security patrols for the 7th Marines before returning to division headquarters.

On November 27, 1950, Recon Company was ordered to Yudam-ni. Before reaching their assigned area, they were briefly detained by roadblocks at Koto-Ri, where Colonel Lewis B. "Chesty" Puller, the commanding officer of the 1st Marines, ordered the Recon Marines to "tie in with his 2d Battalion and strengthen the Koto-ri strongpoint." Leaving Koto-ri, during the fighting retrograde toward Hungnam, the Reconnaissance Marines took the rearguard position with Company B, 1st Tank Battalion, and fought through to Hungnam, where they were eventually evacuated along with the 1st Marine Division.

Reconnaissance Company later saw action from January through March 1951 during the Andong-Pohang guerrilla hunt, which also involved searching enemy weapons caches. Corporal Martin recalled, "Every day our motorized patrols ran into roadblocks and once engaged a large group of guerrillas." The Marine corporal added that "this was all good training for new men who knew little about motorized reconnaissance."[12]

During Operation "Killer" (February 20–March 6, 1950), Lieutenant General Matthew Ridgway's counteroffensive aimed at driving the Chinese PLA and North Korean People's Army (NKPA) back across the 38th Parallel, the Reconnaissance Company continued to patrol and take enemy prisoners. During the United Nations' spring counteroffensive in order to retake Seoul, the Recon Marines conducted motorized patrols into Chunchon and along the communications route to Seoul. On one such patrol, the Reconnaissance Marines remained concealed in a town for two days, tracing enemy cavalry and infantry patrols, eventually calling in air strikes on them.

In the fall of 1951, the Reconnaissance Marines once again found themselves serving alongside the 1st Marine Division in the area surrounding the "Punchbowl." Foreshadowing actions a decade later in Vietnam, they took Hill 812 and then participated in the first helicopter-borne assault on Hill 884.

During their remaining time in Korea, Reconnaissance Marines supported their infantry brethren, operating as an additional rifle company. After 1951, when the war become one of outposts and static warfare, Reconnaissance Marines were used primarily to guard command posts, protect flanks, conduct small combat patrols, and engage in company- (and battalion-)size combat operations.

The 1950s—An Era of Experimentation

During the 1950s, Reconnaissance Marines conducted numerous training exercises in egressing from submarines and conducting airborne and helicopter-borne insertions, as well as participating in numerous exercises with the three active Marine Divisions (1st, 2nd, and 3rd) at home and abroad.

Even before the end of involvement in the Korean War, Amphibious Reconnaissance Battalion (later changed to 1st Force Reconnaissance in 1957) experimented with new means of intelligence gathering, methods of delivery for the insertion of reconnaissance units, and new techniques designed to enhance the reconnaissance mission in support of the Fleet Marine Forces.

As the fighting progressed in Korea, Marine Reconnaissance units continued to hone their amphibious warfare skills. During LANTFLEX 52, 2nd Recon Battalion conducted "a series of training exercises between September 15th and November 17th, 1951," in order to "simulate ... the principal aspects of a naval campaign that might conceivably take place in the Mediterranean during the first year of war." During this exercise, FMFLant (as part of TF-22, 2nd Amphibious Recon Battalion, under direct control of Commander, Amphibious Troops) trained in unison with the USS *Sea Lion* (ASSP-315) in support of the ongoing experiments in conducting heliborne assaults from the sea. During missions on Onslow Beach, Camp

Lejeune, North Carolina (October 16–20), and later near Bogue Field (November 9–13), Recon Marines conducted successful information-gathering operations to acquire the intelligence that enabled the heliborne force to successfully capture their objectives.[13]

During the fall of 1952, 2nd Recon Battalion members conducted a series of exercises off Vieques, Puerto Rico, and later at Onslow Beach. Landing from the *Sea Lion*, team members carried out their normal intelligence information-gathering mission on the former while on the latter they acted as an aggressor force.

Due to the need for Marine replacements in Korea, Headquarters Marine Corps (HQMC) disbanded 2nd Reconnaissance Battalion, excepting Company A; this company was later redesignated the 2nd Amphibious Reconnaissance Company, Fleet Marine Force, commanded by Captain Leo Shinn. Organized in accordance with T/O K-4623, HQMC augmented the company by attaching a weapons platoon in order to provide increased firepower.

During the 1950s, Amphibious Reconnaissance Company and Division Reconnaissance conducted training exercises together based on a recommendation from the Commanding General, FMFLant, to the Commanding General, 2nd Marine Division and Force Troops, FMFLant, who proposed that 2nd Amphibious Company and the Reconnaissance Company from the 2nd Marine Division "conduct similar training and deployments." The memorandum stated that the Division Reconnaissance company should conduct landing operations from aboard the *Sea Lion* for fifteen training days during the first and third quarters. Meanwhile, 2nd Reconnaissance Company was to conduct similar training during the second and fourth quarters. Both reconnaissance elements were to be employed as one unit once a year during the annual Fleet Marine Force landing exercise in the Caribbean Sea.[14]

Similarly, and based on a recommendation from then-Colonel Victor H. Krulak, G-3, Fleet Marine Force, Pacific (FMFPac), a fifty-five-man Amphibious Reconnaissance Platoon was formed on March 12, 1951. The new formation, commanded by First Lieutenant Francis Kraince, consisted of several veteran staff noncommissioned officers (Technical Sergeants Ernest L. DeFazio and John W. Slagel, along with Staff Sergeant Neal D. King and Corporal Wiley B. Ballow). Alongside these Korean War veterans, the new platoon was "fleshed out" with recently graduated "boots" from Marine Corps Recruit Depot, San Diego, California.

Upon activation, the home for the Amphibious Reconnaissance Platoon was Camp Del Mar, on Camp Pendleton, California, due to its proximity to the ocean. For a brief time, then-Sergeant Alfred M. Gray (years later commandant of the Marine Corps) was its communications chief.

While at Camp Del Mar, the Amphibious Reconnaissance Platoon pursued a rigorous training schedule that included the use of rubber boats for insertion and extraction, combat swimming, SCUBA, parachute jumping, hydrographic beach surveys and other essential skills such as marksmanship, physical conditioning, supporting arms and land navigation. The platoon augmented its training with beach insertions from the USS *Perch* in support of landing exercises conducted at Midway and Guam on October 8, 1951. The platoon also provided instructors to train pilots in escape and evasion tactics and interrogation resistance at March Air Force Base.

One of the more notable training exercises conducted by Amphibious Reconnaissance Platoon (later Company) was carried out in Alaska. To test the effectiveness of their reconnaissance and raid training, the Marines of Amphibious Reconnaissance Platoon embarked on a submarine with the training mission to "capture" the vital communications and monitoring installation at Adak, Alaska. The facility was defended by a 1,000-man force. However, before the commencement of "hostilities," the "Marine Reconnaissance [force] had overrun the barracks, headquarters, and airfield, capturing the commanding officer."[15]

Indeed, during the mid- to late 1950s, raiding became an official part of the reconnaissance mission. In early 1956, Amphibious Reconnaissance's mission was "the execution of amphibious reconnaissance missions; to possess the capability of executing amphibious raids of limited scope; the capture of prisoners, military or civilian for interrogation purposes, contacting secret agents or informants." Other missions included:

1. Limited sabotage or harassment of enemy rear areas accessible by water
2. Minor demonstrations to cause the enemy to disclose his positions
3. Marking of beaches and landing points for the assault waves
4. Reconnoitering the road net and acting as guides for the initial assault waves of the Landing Force
5. Reconnaissance in limited force
6. Small scale amphibious raids against enemy personnel and lightly defended installations

The inclusion of the raid mission was, in fact, "built on the model used to inspire Lieutenant Colonel Evans Ford Carlson's 2nd Raider Battalion and Colonel Mike Edson's 1st Raider Battalion during World War II." It was an idea that never left the minds of the senior ranks of the Marine Corps in the 1950s and mid–1960s.

It is interesting to note that Lieutenant General Victor H. Krulak, while serving as commanding general of Fleet Marine Force, Pacific (1964–1967), attempted to "re-create" a raiding capability among Marine units in Vietnam. According to retired Marine Colonel Frederick Tolleson, who as a captain served as the commanding officer, Company E, and later S-4, 2nd Battalion, 7th Marine Regiment, during Operation "Blue Marlin" (November 7–10, 1965), and who was present at this meeting, "Lieutenant General Krulak met with Major General Lewis W. Walt and Colonel Oscar F. Peatross, commanding officer of the 7th Marines, to urge the creation of a 'raider company.' He [Walt] proposed a unit along the lines of the Marine Raiders of WWII to carry out deep missions against the VC." Colonel Tolleson added that Colonel Peatross, himself a "Raider," having served as a company commander under Lieutenant Colonel Evans F. Carlson during the raid on Makin Island, voiced his opposition to such a move. As Tolleson recalled, Peatross told Generals Krulak and Walt that such a move would diminish the strength of his rifle companies.[16] However, when pressed by both generals, Peatross "complied" with the request and designated one company per battalion as a "raider" company capable of carrying out long-range raids and reconnaissance against the Viet Cong. From then on, infantry battalions designated one of their rifle companies as a "raider" company.

In fact, as mentioned earlier, during the late 1950s, with the addition of the raid mission, the reconnaissance force was augmented with heavy weapons, including .50 caliber machine guns and mortars. The crews and weapons were added to the Table of Organization and Equipment (T/OE) of 1st Amphibious Reconnaissance Company and were employed during a follow-up exercise in Adak, Alaska, in early 1956.

Buoyant Ascents

As the 1950s progressed, further innovations were made in waterborne insertion techniques. To complement parachute and helicopter insertion techniques, attention was directed to SCUBA and buoyant ascents. Colonel Bruce F. Meyers, a pioneer in the development of the tactics and techniques of Marine Amphibious and later Force Reconnaissance during the 1950s and 1960s, recalled that the Marines of 1st Force Reconnaissance reasoned that insertion by buoyant ascents would allow scout swimmers greater flexibility en route to and on reaching an enemy beach if they were unencumbered by SCUBA gear. Meyers added, "If we could exit our submarine using underwater buoyant ascent, we would then make a surface swim—and use netting on our heads to break up the outline of our heads in the water ... moreover, such a team of surface swimmers would not be limited to one spot for both ingress or egress. We could swim into one part of a beach and have the flexibility of leaving for another."[17]

As for egressing from a submerged submarine, Marine Recon and Navy Underwater Demolition Teams used both the Momsen lung and the Steinke hood, which were both still in use when Marines from 1st Amphibious Reconnaissance Company began practicing buoyant ascents from submarines such as the *Perch* and the submarine tender USS *Nereus* (AS-17). The Momsen lung was a primitive underwater rebreather used before and during World War II by American submariners to aid in emergency escape. The device contained a canister of soda lime, which removed poisonous carbon dioxide from the exhaled air and then replenished the air with oxygen. Two tubes led from the bag to a mouthpiece: one from which to inhale air and the other for exhaling spent air. The device hung around the wearer's neck and was strapped around the waist. Besides providing oxygen for the ascent, it allowed a submariner or Recon Marine to rise slowly to the water's surface, thus avoiding an air embolism. The Momsen lung was invented by Vice Admiral Charles B. "Swede"

Momsen, USN, and remained in service up through the 1950s, later replaced by the Steinke hood. Submariners and Recon Marines trained using the Momsen lung in an eighty-foot-deep escape training tank at New London or Pearl Harbor, Hawaii, during the late 1950s.[18]

The Steinke hood (developed by Navy Lieutenant Harris I. Steinke) was intended to replace the Momsen lung; it consisted of a plastic hood with a transparent face piece for visibility, which was attached to a buoyancy compensator (life jacket). Compressed air at the bottom front was used to inflate the system prior to the ascent. The hood enclosed the entire head of the swimmer to hold breathing air, which expanded in the hood as the swimmer rose to the surface and underwater pressure decreased. Two release vents, one in the hood and the other in the buoyancy compensator, opened during ascent to vent expending air. Once the wearer was on the surface, the closed vents allowed the system to retain buoyancy and act as a life preserver.

As Colonel Meyers noted, "Both the Momsen lung and Steinke Hood were state of the art in 1958 when we [1st Force Reconnaissance] began to research the idea of using the buoyant ascent." He added that the first tests using the buoyant ascent technique took place off the Silver Strand, adjacent to Glorietta and San Diego Bay, south of Naval Amphibious Base Coronado, and later in June 1958 at Pearl Harbor. Joined during the Coronado exercise by five members of the 1st Reconnaissance Battalion out of Camp Pendleton, the Marines of 1st Force Amphibious Reconnaissance conducted the first buoyancy ascent tests from the USS *Perch*. Shortly after these tests, 1st and 2nd Force Reconnaissance "further developed methods for underwater recovery."[19]

Other Technological Developments: The "Fulton Sky Hook," McGuire and STABO Rigs, and the SPIE Rig

Other technological developments during the late 1950s and field tested by Marine Reconnaissance Test Unit 1 included the introduction of the "Fulton Sky Hook" for both ingress and egress operations, as well as the "Trooper's Ladder," the McGuire and STABO rigs, and the SPIE rig. The "Fulton Sky Hook" was invented by Robert E. Fulton, Jr., great-great-grandson of the designer of the first steamboat. It was specifically designed to rescue downed pilots on land and at sea in addition to inserting or extracting Central Intelligence Agency agents; the device evolved from World War II systems designed to recover personnel from the ground after airborne operations.[20]

The Sky Hook consisted of a droppable kit composed of three parts, similar in appearance to an aircraft wing tank divided into thirds. The tank was buoyant so that it could be dropped by parachute to a downed pilot who was too far out at sea for helicopter recovery. One compartment of the tank contained a combination body harness and padded jumpsuit. The harness portion was comparable to a standard military parachute harness. Another compartment contained several deflated balloons, about the size of large weather balloons; there were also two helium canisters to fill the balloons. The third compartment contained, according to Colonel Meyers, a five-hundred-pound pickup line. The top fifty-foot section of the line was attached to the balloon and made from hundred-pound test nylon line; it was designed to break away after pickup. The next ninety feet were six-thousand-pound test tubular nylon line; the remainder of the pickup line, down to the harness, was four-thousand-pound test tubular nylon line.

For use in an extraction, the "Fulton Aerial Retrieval System," according to Colonel Meyers, worked this way:

> A Navy P2V Neptune ... would fly over and drop the tank by parachute as close as possible to the person to be picked up. The person would then don the jumpsuit and harness and then inflate the balloon and send it aloft. The aircraft would circle back in, making a run at about one hundred twenty knots, approaching from the downwind side. Centered on the nose of the Neptune, in front of its propellers, was a twenty-two-foot yoke or "vee" made of tubular steel. The pilot would aim the plane's nose, with the two forks of the yoke immediately in front of him, at a target spot on the pickup cable that was delineated with a brightly colored piece of foil. Seizing the nylon line at that point, the yoke device would lock the line in three "triggers," creating a simultaneous lift and pull. Two of the triggers locked the line, and the third trigger spun a reel on which the line wrapped about eight turns, locking it to the airplane. The effect was to snatch the person from the surface and cause him or her immediately to rise almost two hundred feet straight up. The person would begin to trail in the air behind the aircraft and would then drop to a lower trail position, from which he or she could be winched into the aircraft using a J-Hook.[21]

Field tested by Marine Reconnaissance in 1958, the "Fulton Sky Hook" was used twice during the Vietnam War. One of those occurrences was with a pilot shot down over North Vietnam, who decided not to employ the device because the fifteen minutes it took to deploy would have put him in jeopardy of being captured. He was, as Meyers wrote, eventually picked up by an Air Force CH-53 "Jolly Green Giant" helicopter in Thailand. The other instance involved a downed pilot who deployed the balloon but moved it to avoid a nearby mountain. He was eventually captured by North Vietnamese troops.

The "Trooper's Ladder," developed in the 1960s by the U.S. Army's Special Forces to expedite helicopter insertion and extraction without having to land, consisted of specially built sixty-foot aluminum ladders of four feet in width, which were rolled up near the skids of the helicopter. The ladders enabled Special Forces and Marine Recon teams to either exit or enter a hovering helicopter from a heavily vegetated area or uneven or rugged terrain such as mountainsides. Marine Force Recon would often double the ladder length by 120 feet by placing two ladders side by side in order to enable the inserted teams to land into a heavy jungle canopy.

Colonel Meyers wrote that by March 1969, Major General Ormond R. Simpson, commanding general of the 1st Marine Division, was convinced of the ladders' efficacy and requested that the Commanding General, FMFPac, take action to have an additional eight "Trooper Ladders" added to Force Recon's table of organization. The Marines of 1st Force Reconnaissance "discovered that by utilizing the ladder and taking advantage of the more numerous small openings in terrain and vegetation, a patrol [could] be inserted or extracted in seconds versus the ten to twenty minutes required by rappelling or hoisting operations."[22]

Another method of extraction used by Force Reconnaissance teams, as well as the joint Studies and Observations Group (SOG) teams, was the McGuire rig, which consisted of one-hundred-foot nylon ropes with a six-foot loop at the lower end hooked to a padded seat (much like a child's swing seat). One drawback of the McGuire rig was that the ropes could become entangled in the dense jungle foliage, forcing the helicopter crew chief to cut the ropes and thus cause the person being picked up or inserted to slip out of the harness. After several fatalities, a slip hook was added to prevent this outcome. Unfortunately, despite the addition of the slip hook, several more fatalities occurred.

The STABO (Stabilized Body) rig was developed by Army Special Forces from the 5th Special Forces Group Recondo School after a McGuire rig fatality. The STABO rig replaced the Marine Recon team member's standard army web gear or 782 gear, as well as the Army's load-bearing equipment (LBE) harness, and it was worn throughout the entire patrol. When an emergency extraction was needed, the patrol member unfastened two straps on his belt's back, brought them through his legs, and snapped them securely in front with a climber's snap link, called a carabiner. The Huey would hover momentarily overhead, dropping a one-hundred-foot nylon line fitted with a STABO yoke, which had two "D" rings at each end. The patrol member snapped into the "D" ring and was lifted up out of the area, dangling a hundred feet below the helicopter, usually traveling around ninety knots.

Meyers stated that the STABO rig was far superior to the McGuire rig, as it allowed the "extractee" to fire his weapon while being hoisted into the air. This feature proved to be a lifesaver during the Vietnam War, as Recon Marines could fire on a pursuing enemy while being airlifted into an awaiting helicopter. Later versions of the STABO harness placed the carabiner in the front at all times, thus making it more convenient for a team in a hot extraction.[23]

One last method developed to extract teams from the jungle was the SPIE (Special Purpose Insertion and Extraction) rig. Developed in a joint effort by Marine Air Wing parachute riggers and Marines from both 1st Force Reconnaissance Company and 1st Reconnaissance Battalion, the SPIE rig was designed to enable a helicopter to simultaneously extract up to twelve heavily laden team members. According to Lieutenant Colonel Meyers, the riggers took one-hundred-foot lengths of standard two-inch-wide flat nylon parachute harness webbing and sewed them together back to back, doubling the normally high tensile strength. At the lower end of the line, they sewed a series of reinforced "D" rings.

While out on patrol, every recon team member wore what parachutists call an "integrated harness. This allowed team members to detach the harness once on the ground."²⁴ Each Recon Marine carried carabiners. During an extraction, the helicopter crew chief would drop the SPIE rig through the jungle onto the ground where the Recon team waited. After the entire team was hooked up (including wounded and those killed in action), the patrol leader would radio the pilot or crew chief that the team was ready for extraction. Using maximum thrust, the helicopter would then begin its climb straight upward. Sometimes when operating in a dense jungle canopy, the team members would be dragged through the foliage until the helicopter reached a clearing. After arriving at the home base, the helicopter would slowly set the team down without injury. The SPIE rig was a significant improvement over both the McGuire and the STABO rigs, as it enabled the team members to be either inserted or extracted all at once. The SPIE rig is still in use by members of Force and Division Reconnaissance.

The "Jungle Penetrator" was developed primarily for Search and Air Rescue (SAR) missions, but it saw limited use as an extraction device for Marine Recon teams. The penetrator was bullet shaped and weighed slightly over twenty pounds. The design allowed it to penetrate dense jungle and triple canopy. It was lowered by a small crane attached to the side of a helicopter. Typically, it would develop a significant static electricity charge that needed to be discharged on the ground before it could be mounted for extraction. The device had three narrow seats that unlatched, giving it the appearance of an anchor. Ostensibly, three people could be winched up at a time. Because it required extensive hover time, and limited ability for Marines to defend themselves from ground fire, it was not a preferred method of extraction. Interestingly, then First Lieutenant Wayne E. Rollings (later retired as a major general), while serving with 1st Force Reconnaissance Company in 1969 in Vietnam, was extracted by a jungle penetrator while on the patrol for which he was awarded the Navy Cross. During the extraction, he was dragged through heavy foliage, causing him to lose part of his finger, in addition to wounds previously suffered during the patrol's contact on the ground.²⁵

Most Marines of 3rd Force Reconnaissance Company in 1968 carried a ten- to twelve-foot length of rappelling cable and two D–Links while on patrol. The purpose of these items was to prepare a Swiss seat (rappel seat) with which they could use the D–Links to attach themselves to a rope dropped by a helicopter for an extraction where the helicopter could not land. Though theoretically feasible, there's no record of this technique having been used. However, it seemed to provide an added measure of confidence for a number of Marines.

Marine Recon Training in the 1950s

Besides combat swimming and parachute training, Marines assigned to Force or Division Reconnaissance likewise trained in weapons familiarization, including the M-1 Garand, M-1 carbine, .45 caliber pistol, M-3 machine pistol (or "grease gun"), grenades, and bayonets; map reading; use of a compass; hand-to-hand combat; cover, concealment, and camouflage; small boat handling; small-unit tactics such as patrolling; communication skills such as radio communication; use of message books; and visual recognition. Corporal Paul G. Martin, who served with Marine Reconnaissance companies in Korea, later wrote, "A Recon company should be prepared for, and equipped for, any type of work." More important was the fact that "the training program of the force reconnaissance Marine was a continuous process, in SCUBA techniques, patrolling, evasion and escape, and parachute techniques."[26]

Corporal Martin, in fact, outlined several important principles regarding the training and employment of Marine reconnaissance units, including the following: (1) size and equipment; (2) intelligence gathering and evaluation of information; and (3) close coordination with air and artillery units.

According to Martin, reconnaissance units should be "kept small," as large patrols were too easily spotted by the enemy. Martin wrote that "foot patrols should travel light and the men should carry only personal weapons." He added that due to their weight and bulky nature, heavy crew-served weapons such as machine guns

In April 1955, Marine infantrymen head for shore in rubber rafts after leaving a U.S. Navy Martin PBM. This was one of the methods utilized by Marines in making an amphibious landing or conducting amphibious raids in the 1950s (USMC Photograph A-145158, HQMC).

and mortars, which "serve only to make a reconnaissance patrol unwieldy and slow," should not be used by reconnaissance teams. Writing before the fielding of both the M-14 and the M-16 assault rifles, Martin wrote that Reconnaissance Marines should be armed with Browning automatic rifles (or BARs). Martin stated that because of the tremendous rate and volume of fire they could put out, "BARs can furnish all the firepower necessary."[27]

Concerning intelligence gathering and evaluation of information, Martin wrote, "Commanding officers and operating and intelligence officers should be fully instructed as to the functions of a Recon outfit." Looking back, it seems his words were insightful given that reconnaissance operations a decade later in Vietnam were hampered at all levels of command. Commanders and staff officers frequently demonstrated a lack of knowledge of recon capabilities; they did not understand how to employ recon teams and ignored the information gathered by their teams. Martin also wrote, "Great care should be used in evaluating information picked up" by the Marines from the locals.[28] As occurred during World War II and later in Korea, the information acquired by recon teams sometimes proved either incomplete or misleading.

As for the coordination with supporting arms, Corporal Martin wrote that greater effort should be made to contact artillery and air elements when conducting a mission. His emphasis on ensuring timely and accurate coordination and on-time fire support was to prove incredibly important as a force multiplier for small recon teams operating in Vietnam.

Corporal Martin best summed up amphibious reconnaissance's mission when he wrote that its function on the battlefield is to obtain information and get it back to those who can use it—namely, Marine infantry.

Pathfinders

One late development prior to the commitment to Vietnam was the integration of the Pathfinder teams concept into reconnaissance operations. Pathfinder operations were integral to the success of both Force Reconnaissance and Division Reconnaissance teams in the carrying out of pre-assault missions such as beach surveys in World War II and Korea. Pathfinder skills took on an added importance leading up to Vietnam with the integration of the helicopter into Marine tactical operations. Locating and designating helicopter landing zones (HLZs) was critical. A Pathfinder platoon was, in fact, a part of Amphibious Reconnaissance Force Company's table of organization, and this identity is acknowledged by the winged torch atop the parachute in the Force Reconnaissance Company's unit patch. Lieutenant Colonel Meyers wrote that the addition of a Pathfinder platoon "greatly reduced" the tactical capability of Force Recon. He explained that 1st Force Recon's Pathfinder platoon, when the unit first stood up, consisted of three teams, each having one officer and ten Marines, and was commanded by First Lieutenant David Ramsey.

Operationally, when in the field, each team would normally jump with ten pounds of gear, which averaged about ninety pounds per Marine. Meyers noted, "Our T-10 static line parachutes weighed something over forty pounds. The bulk of our equipment included (for example), a helmet, web gear, a pack, rations, an individual weapon such as a M3A1 .45 caliber submachinegun, and ammo." In addition, each Pathfinder team carried twenty three-dimensional marker panels (in the form of tetrahedrons, which could be seen as a pyramid-shaped panel from any direction), twelve SE-11 night marker lights for the landing zones, the Justine glide-path indicator (which provided a three-colored high-intensity team to guide pilots into the landing zone), air-ground wind direction marker panels, AN/PRC-6 radios (hand-held "walkie talkie"), the PRC-10 radio (VHF radio replaced in Vietnam by the AN-PRC-25 radio), the AN/GCR-9 radio (HF communications with air; also the largest piece of gear), batteries, and a supply of colored smoke grenades.[29] Pathfinder teams likewise carried the MAY radios for ground communication. In addition to their individual weapons, each Pathfinder team carried one bipod-mounted machine gun (.30 caliber M1919A1), which they used when setting up a hasty defense of a landing zone.

The mission of the Pathfinder teams was to scout out and designate landing or drop zones for incoming helicopters or airborne (parachute) operations, as well as reconnaissance teams. A Pathfinder team was flown into the combat zone by a Navy Grumman TF-1 Trader aircraft, which could carry nine team members, thus requiring Pathfinder teams to leave two members behind. The two Pathfinder Marines left behind would be used as replacements should any member of the team become wounded or killed in action. When feasible, two Navy TF-1s or a Douglas R4D-8—two of which were organic to the air repair squadron of a Marine Air Wing (MAW)—would be used to insert a full Pathfinder or reconnaissance team.

Training was rigorous for the Marines who volunteered for Pathfinder (and recon) duty. Lieutenant Colonel Berwick "Barry" Babin recalled, "After completing their basic MOS school, Marines selected for Pathfinder teams attended specialty schools offered in the Marine Corps and other services such as SERE School, Ranger school, communications schools, and Army Airborne school. Intense unit training and field exercises tied external training into a well-integrated training program that produced operationally capable pathfinder teams." Babin emphasized that during the Vietnam era, "Internal operational training took precedence over external training because it was necessary for team cohesion as well as being more time efficient and amenable to unique and specialized Marine reconnaissance needs. Selection for an external school became a motivational factor for the Marines and it was viewed as a reward. This balance between training and motivation continued on as a tradition in stateside and in-country Reconnaissance units during the Vietnam war."[30]

The prestige of a highly selective admission process continues in the Force Reconnaissance community today and was readily apparent when 5th Force Reconnaissance Company stood up in January 1967 as the Vietnam war progressed. Lieutenant Colonel Babin remembers it some 50-plus years later:

> As a Lance Corporal in January 1967, I saw an advertisement placed in the Camp Pendleton Scout newspaper stating that Marines with MOS 3516, Organizational Automotive Mechanic, were being sought to volunteer for the newly formed 5th Force Reconnaissance Company. I and about 50 or 60 other Marines were trucked out to Camp Las Pulgas where we were formed up and received a brief explanation about force reconnaissance. We were told that all Marines assigned to the new unit had to meet exacting standards. Prior to arrival, our Service Record Books had been screened to ensure we had passed the regular Marine Physical Fitness test, could swim, qualified on the rifle range, had no office hours, good proficiency and conduct marks and had a minimum 110 GCT. I don't recall the name of the sergeant giving the brief, but he explained the strenuous nature of the "max endurance physical fitness test" we were about to be administered, emphasizing that it was voluntary and we could quit anytime. He concluded by asking if anyone wanted to drop out before we began. About a third did so. We were then put at attention, and I recall the sergeant and two Marines, Lance Corporals Al Sniadecki and Bob Buda, began walking through our ranks, disparaging our character, motivations and abilities: getting in our face like drill instructors. They were immaculately groomed wearing crisply starched utilities and cover with spit shined boots and highly polished brass and jump wings. We were put on the pull-up bars, dropped for pushups and other exercises: continuous movement and stress. The entire time we were verbally harassed, belittled and advised to quit. We ate dust and sweat under a cloudless sky with no breaks. Muscles fatigued and spasmed. Sweat stung our eyes. Marines began to fall out, until only a dozen or so remained, then the run began. We took a tour of Camp Las Pulgas, running with no end in sight, and culminating at the top of the steep slope of a seemingly never-ending hill. At the top, myself and three other Marines remained. There were two positions available. We were run back to the company headquarters where we waited for what seemed a long time. Eventually, myself and Lance Corporal John Van Drasek were called into the First Sergeant's office and put at parade rest in front of his desk. First Sergeant Robert F. Snyder told us what it takes to be a Recon Marine and asked if we were ready for the commitment. When we said "yes" he told the sergeant to get us out of his sight until we had a haircut. The recon haircut involves removal of all hair on the sides and a flat top over the crown of the head with the top of the scalp slightly exposed. When we returned to the first sergeant's office, we were again centered on his desk at parade rest while he was on the phone. We heard him say "Yes, sir" a couple of times, followed by "I have two volunteers in front of me right now." After he hung up, he had us escorted at a double-time to the supply building. As we left his office, his voice trailed us, "Do not fall through your grommet on this." We were issued a complete set of 782 gear to include helmet. After donning the gear, we were double-timed to the Las Pulgas pool and ordered to climb to the top of the 30 foot tower. On command, we jumped off into the pool where we drown-proofed for about half an hour. As my head came to surface, I was able to glimpse my first sergeant and some officers wearing tropical uniform trousers with tan long sleeve shirt at pool side. One of the officers was noticeably shorter than the others and carried a swagger stick. The rank insignia on his collar shined brightly in the late afternoon sun, and I couldn't make it out. After they left, and we were told to exit the pool, the first sergeant informed us that we did okay for General Krulak's demonstration. (Lieutenant General Victor H. Krulak, Commanding General, FMF Pacific) That was day one! Upon reflection, it seems to me that the stringent entry requirement serves as a source of unit pride as well as a common bond for Marines who demonstrated, through voluntarily subjecting themselves to the initial mental and physical stress, a readiness to undergo extreme hardship to serve each other and accomplish their mission.[31]

Besides being accomplished parachutists, both Colonel Bruce Meyers and First Sergeant Donald Hamblen noted that each Reconnaissance Marine had to be in top physical shape. According to Meyers, when FMFPac organized the 1st Reconnaissance Company on June 19, 1957, physical conditioning was a major requirement of each candidate volunteering for the unit. Each Marine candidate, chosen for his infantry and communications skills, underwent a rigorous physical fitness test, administered by NCOs to weed out those deemed unable to meet the demands of the "team." As Meyers stated, each Marine was required to do as many pull-ups and sit-ups as he could until he could manage no more. Then each leatherneck had to do a three- to five-mile run, chanting all the way as a means to test their endurance. For those who made it through the exercises and run, the next test was a one-mile swim in open water. The few who survived this test were then subjected to another run, with the candidate's endurance being the key deciding factor in whether he would be admitted to the ranks of 1st Reconnaissance Company. As Meyers noted, the evaluators were looking for Marines who pushed themselves to the extremes of exhaustion, as "We knew we could develop the endurance, fitness, and style of those dedicated few."[32]

Manned with Marines in the best of physical shape, 1st Force Reconnaissance, along with their Pathfinder teams, conducted a series of exercises during the late 1950s to test their new equipment and techniques, all of which would be employed by the "teams" to great effect in Vietnam.

Organization and Mission of Force and Division Reconnaissance (1960–1963)

In 1960, 1st Force Reconnaissance Company's table of organization (T/O) called for 12 officers, 146 enlisted Marines, and 2 Navy corpsmen to man the three sections within the company: a headquarters section, consisting of five officers and seventeen enlisted men who had made up the operations and intelligence sections; the supply and service platoon, consisting of one officer and twenty-seven enlisted men who made up the communications, supply, medical, and amphibious maintenance sections; and the main body of the company—the four reconnaissance platoons, each of which had one officer and twenty-six enlisted men.

Reflecting the emphasis placed on counterinsurgency by President John F. Kennedy, changes in Force and Division Reconnaissance Battalions occurred in 1963, in both the Marine Corps and the U.S. Army, as each service began to doctrinally place more emphasis on counterinsurgency operations in its tables of organization. Improvements were made to Force and Division Recon organizations. Force Reconnaissance companies were changed to six recon platoons that had identical duties. Each platoon consisted of one officer and fourteen enlisted Marines, with each team consisting of four men. The Division Reconnaissance Battalion changed to 32 officers and 438 men with four companies. Reflecting the nature of its main mission, both the air controller and the crew-served weapons were removed from

Division Reconnaissance Battalion's tables of organization and equipment (TO/E). Its platoons were larger than those of Force Recon, consisting of one officer and twenty-three enlisted Marines organized into two recon squads of two teams of four men each. While Force Recon Marines still carried the M3A1 "grease gun," Division Recon Marines carried the standard-issue M-14 rifle. For added firepower, both Force and Division Recon teams had an M-79 grenade launcher, the M-60 machine gun, and hand grenades. The missions for both organizations likewise remained the same, and it was believed by planners at HQMC that the structure and missions of both reconnaissance levels were "sound for both conventional and unconventional warfare."

Regarding rank structure, a major served as the commanding officer of 1st Force Reconnaissance Company, while his executive officer and operations officer were both captains. Platoon commanders were lieutenants. Babin noted:

> Virtually all the Marines in the operational platoons carried a primary infantry MOS, mostly 0311 (Basic Rifleman) and 0369 (Infantry Unit Leader), while some Marines in the support sections carried an infantry MOS, most had a specialty MOS depending on their billet. As Marines continued their reconnaissance training, they picked up secondary reconnaissance specific MOS:

8652	Reconnaissance Man, Parachute Jump Qualified
8653	Reconnaissance Man, SCUBA Qualified
8654	Reconnaissance Man, Parachute and SCUBA Qualified
9952	SCUBA Marine
9952	SCUBA Marine (Officer)
9953	Parachutist/SCUBA Marine
9953	Parachutist/SCUBA Marine (Officer)
8662	Parachutist
9952	SCUBA[33]

As for the majority of Marines in the company, most if not all were basic infantrymen carrying infantry MOSs.

Commenting on the mission of both Force and Division Reconnaissance, which changed very little from its pre–World War II origins, First Sergeant Hamblen, in his autobiography *One Tough Marine*, outlined the five tasks of both reconnaissance elements:

> a. The force reconnaissance company, as part of the task organization of a landing force, is employed to acquire information on the enemy, weather terrain for that force. It accomplishes this task by introducing small scout teams oriented on specific collection missions, or by establishing observation posts at selected vantage points.
>
> b. The company had no offensive capability and is wholly concerned with the acquisition of military intelligence information.
>
> c. Introduced by aircraft and dropped by parachute into a small unprepared drop zone or landed covertly from a submarine, each reconnaissance team, utilizing movement, observes and physically reconnoiters the area or object

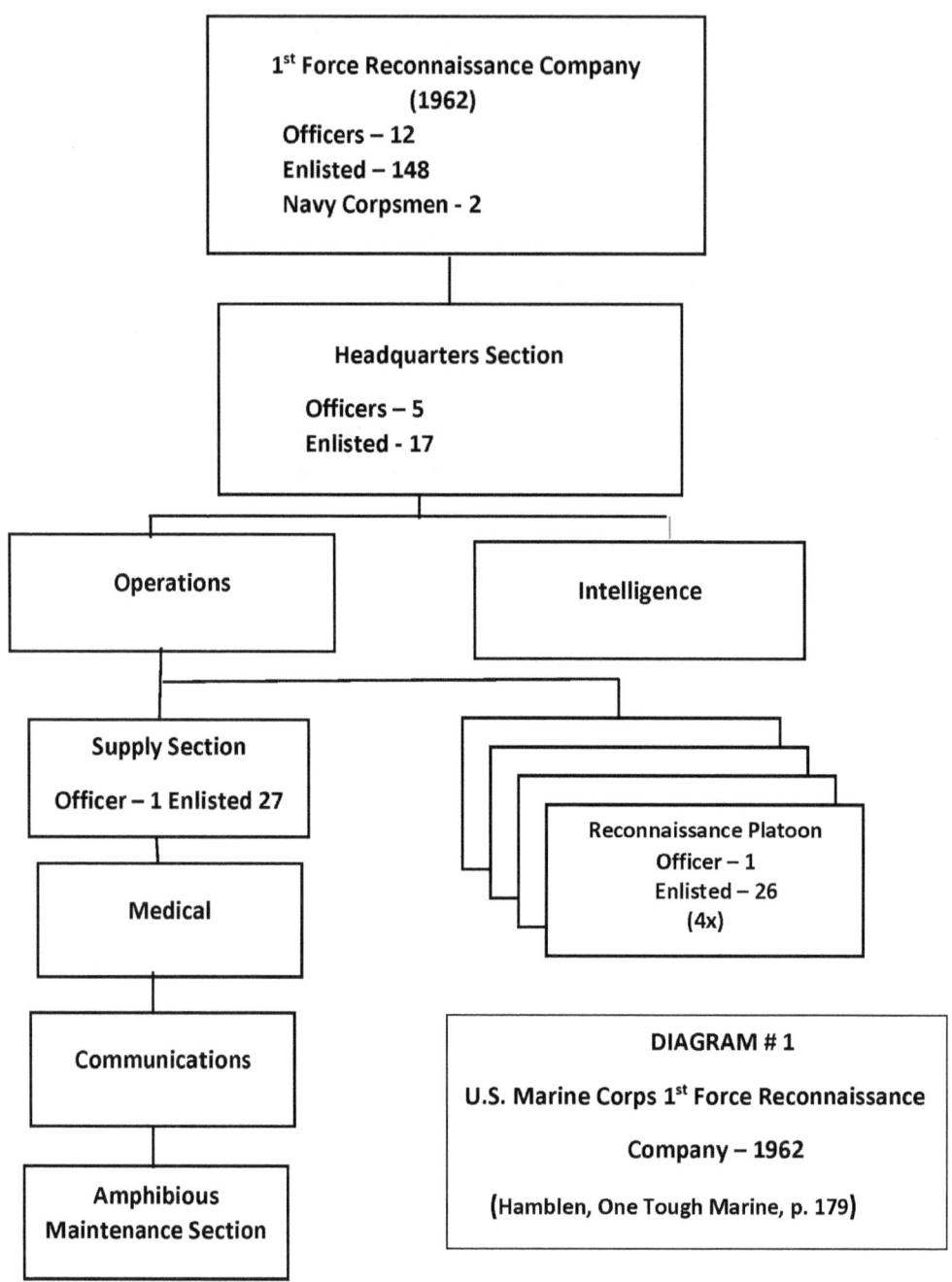

Diagram 4: 1st Force Reconnaissance Company, 1962.

of intelligence interest, and reports by radio or via a relay station or relay aircraft directly to the landing force commander. Upon recovery, the team is debriefed and a detailed supplementary report prepared and forwarded together, with any documentary, physical, or photographic data acquired.

    d. The support performed by the force reconnaissance company is

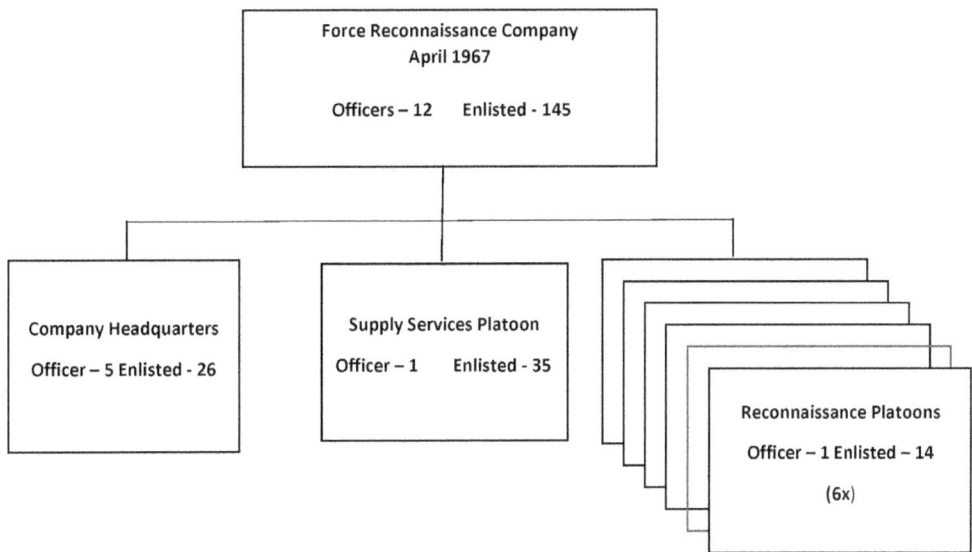

Diagram 5: 1st Force Reconnaissance Company, 1967.

not in the form of a direct service or support to a subordinate element of the landing force. Rather, it consists of the acquisition of raw information for the landing force commander. The force reconnaissance company does not produce intelligence. The unit headquarters plans, coordinates, and supervises the introduction, communications with, and the recovery of its subordinate reconnaissance teams.

e. Force reconnaissance teams have the inherent capability to provide terminal guidance to initial helicopter waves in landing zones. This capability is equally possessed by force and division reconnaissance elements, differing only in the exclusive parachute entry available in the force unit. To a lesser degree, infantry and other ground units can provide terminal guidance commensurate with the less-complex routine helicopter operations conducted within the division's zone of action. Pathfinder missions are usually executed by reconnaissance teams assigned pre-landing reconnaissance task within the general landing area. This pathfinder terminal guidance capability does not include landing-zone traffic-control functions.[34]

4

Vietnam

The Early Years (1963–1964)

There were two levels of structured reconnaissance support employed by the Marines in Vietnam. The first, Force Reconnaissance companies, tasked with conducting pre-assault and distant post-assault reconnaissance missions in support of the landing force, were first deployed to the Republic of Vietnam (RVN) in the summer and fall of 1963. Marines from the 3rd Force Reconnaissance Company were directed to conduct long-range reconnaissance missions in conjunction with the forces of the Army of the Republic of Vietnam (ARVN) along the South Vietnamese–Laotian border as part of the Strategic Reconnaissance Group.

There were four active-duty Force Reconnaissance companies in the Marine Corps during most of the Vietnam War. They conducted long-range reconnaissance missions as well as traditional "reconnaissance-type" missions, including beach surveys, artillery spotting, and target acquisition. Operating in teams that numbered anywhere from four to eight Marines, "Force Recon" supported operations for both division and Marine Amphibious Force (MAF)–level operations in I Corps. Force Recon Marines initially operated over a wider and deeper battlefield than the Reconnaissance Battalion Marines. Babin pointed out that, though structurally designed to be a Fleet Marine Force asset, the Force Reconnaissance companies were attached to their respective division's Reconnaissance Battalion for most of the war. This non-doctrinal alignment, while providing responsive and efficient support to the two infantry divisions, at times created a degree of confusion as to their employment and logistical support.[1] As such, they were not attached to either the 1st or the 3rd Marine Divisions, nor were they attached to the individual regiments and battalions.

Each Force Reconnaissance company was deployed to Vietnam with six platoons. Each platoon was structured for one officer, fourteen Marines and one Navy corpsman. These were further broken down into teams of four to five Marines. For operational purposes, the platoons were further divided into eight-man teams, and, in anticipation of possible deployment to Southeast Asia, Recon Marines were given French classes. Each Recon Marine was a marksman or above, SCUBA and/or jump qualified, and in top physical condition. Besides being qualified in parachuting and

SCUBA diving, they also trained in egressing from submarines and using rubber boat insertion and extraction techniques.

Operation "Shu Fly": Reconnaissance in Vietnam (1963–1964)

In April 1963, Marines from 3rd Force Reconnaissance Company, along with other Marine Reconnaissance elements, deployed to South Vietnam in response to the increasing U.S. commitment to the war in South Vietnam. With the arrival of Marine Medium Helicopter Squadron Unit HMM-362 during Operation "Shu Fly" in April 1962, elements of 3rd Reconnaissance Battalion, 3rd Marine Division, deployed to South Vietnam as a perimeter defense force. In April 1963, action was taken on an earlier request for the assignment of a security detachment to guard the Marine area. A reconnaissance platoon of forty-seven Marines from the 3rd Marine Division joined the task element, thus relieving the men of the helicopter squadron and the MARS-16 sub-unit of the important secondary responsibility they had held since the task unit's deployment to Soc Trang. The assignment of the ground Marines was timely in that it corresponded with a reduction by the ARVN of its forces guarding the perimeter of the Da Nang airbase. One Marine general (Major General Keith B. McCutcheon) later observed that with the arrival of the infantry unit, "the air-ground team was in being in Vietnam."[2]

Studies and Observations Group (SOG)

Starting in late 1963 and continuing into 1964, as part of Secretary of Defense Robert McNamara's Plan 34A (which was the Pentagon's undeclared, highly secret war against the North Vietnamese both in South Vietnam and along North Vietnam's coastline), members of the 1st Force Reconnaissance Company, assigned to the Naval Advisory Detachment (NAD) headquartered at Da Nang, participated in the Central Intelligence Agency's Studies and Observations Group (SOG). Here, Force Recon Marines, sometimes dressed in local Vietnamese attire (black pajamas and khaki blouses) and carrying Soviet and Chinese arms (AK-47s and SKS carbines), assisted local indigenous forces such as the "Nungs" (ethnic Chinese, who had a reputation as fierce and reliable fighters—frequently hired as camp/village guards and to fight alongside U.S. forces), as well as their South Vietnamese equivalents, on raids on North Vietnamese and National Liberation Front ("Viet Cong") forces, hitting base camps and military installations. Members of 1st Force Reconnaissance assigned to NAD likewise conducted raids with the assistance of the South Vietnamese Navy and Marine forces.

During one such "insertion" by U.S. Navy *NASTY*-class patrol boats, a team from 1st Force Reconnaissance Company, armed with 57-mm recoilless rifles, conducted one such raid along the North Vietnamese coastline. Given the strict rules of engagement, the Marines were not to actively participate or land with the South Vietnamese during the raid.³ The Marines and their ARVN counterparts were intercepted by North Vietnamese *SWATOW* (Chinese *Shantou*) boats that had been operating in the same area. On August 2, 1964, the USS *Maddox*, which had been on a DESOTO patrol, assisting South Vietnamese, was fired on by these same NVA *SWATOWs*, who mistook the *Maddox* for the boats that they had been chasing, thus initiating the so-called Gulf of Tonkin Gulf incident, precipitating the formal entry of the United States into the Vietnam War.

Lieutenant General Bernard M. "Mick" Trainor, one of the first Marines assigned to SOG in mid–1964, participated in clandestine missions from 1964 to 1966 along the Vietnamese coast north of the 20th Parallel. He later recalled:

> We were basically organized into two groups—the Navy group and the Team Group. In the Navy group we had PT Boats. We had Norwegian "Nasties," which were fantastic boats.... These were high-powered PT boats built by the Norwegians, powered by Rolls-Royce engines. They could make about 40 knots. We would use these boats to go north. The crews were all Vietnamese. Most of them were refugees from the north. Certainly, all of the officers were refugees from the north—fiercely anti–Communist, very talented guys, very brave guys, but very practical guys ... the other part was the "Teams."

According to General Trainor,

> We had ... as I recall, six teams, and these were teams to conduct commando raids ashore.... The North Vietnamese referred to our operations as "The Sea Commandos" ... They were made up of Vietnamese also, again, most of them from the north, except for one team, which was made up of Nungs, who were of Chinese extraction living in Vietnam left over from old Chinese invasions. There was always friction between the Vietnamese and the Nung [and other ethnic minorities mostly living in the mountains such as the Hmong, Muong and others, collectively referred to as the Montagnards]. But the Nung were professional. They were like the Gurkhas [Nepalese soldiers]; they were professional soldiers. As a matter of fact, each of the Americans that were involved in this thing had a Nung bodyguard, and they were totally dependable.⁴

Lieutenant General Bernard M. Trainor, USMC, was one of the first Reconnaissance Marines to serve in the Republic of Vietnam as a member of a Studies and Observation Group (1963–1964) and later as commanding officer of 1st Reconnaissance Battalion (1968–1969) (USMC History Division).

"The teams were based at a place called My Khe [Beach]," an old walled French camp, and that was where "we trained the teams," Trainor added. In addition to Marine Recon personnel, Navy SEALs helped train these Vietnamese teams. As Trainor explained, due to its strategic and tactical importance, the "site had an elaborate communications setup—intelligence setup—directly from Saigon to us, from the Philippines and various other activities. So we had first-class intelligence."

The planning process for clandestine operations was also quite elaborate, Trainor commented, primarily because "the Vietnamese leaked like sieves, and the Americans never knew who was a spy and who wasn't." He added:

> Say, we wanted to conduct a prisoner snatch somewhere north of Dong Hoi. We, the Americans, would get all the intelligence and we would plan the operation. Then, with unmarked maps, we would have the Vietnamese skippers and team chiefs in and we would go over the operation and lay out the bare bones as to the location of the operation. They would see the aerial photos; they would see the obliques; they would see the submarine shots; they would see everything that we had. But it would all be sanitized. And then the skipper, who was going to be the officer in tactical command and the team chief, would work out the details of how they were going to go about this operation still not knowing exactly where it was. Then they would be put into isolation. The teams and the crews would all be in isolation and, at the appointed time, they would board the PT boats. We usually operated three PT boats at a time in support, and the teams would go north. Now, there was a prohibition against Americans accompanying them, and that prohibition was, at least, formally adhered to. But there were certain operations that we felt the presence of an American would be useful, and we went. Saigon never knew this. Well, let me put it this way: I think Saigon knew.... But they didn't want to know. We never told them; they never asked. So we would go along on certain missions.[5]

As for reporting, Trainor said the teams reported to SOG at MACV—in other words, to General William C. Westmoreland at MACV, and to a Special Operations Group staff at CinCPac, and then back to SACSA (Special Assistant for Counterinsurgency and Special Activities), which was the old Special Operations Agency that existed in the Pentagon or directly under Secretary of Defense McNamara. Trainor stated that this was an extremely interesting "facet of the Vietnam War." So, early on, Marine Recon was playing a decisive role in the Vietnam War.

U.S. Air Force Combat Controller Teams in Thailand and Vietnam (1962–1970)

The "undeclared" war in South Vietnam involved not only Marine Reconnaissance and Army Special Forces teams but also Navy SEALs that conducted hydrographic soundings along the Vietnamese coastline and the inland waterways of the Mekong Delta. The U.S. Air Force, beginning in 1962, dispatched Combat Controller Teams (CCTs) to Thailand and South Vietnam that guided strike aircraft to ground targets against the NVA in Laos and along the Ho Chi Minh Trail in the period of the undeclared U.S. war in Southeast Asia. Indeed, as early as 1962, the U.S. Air

Force dispatched Air Commando Wings composed of SAR (Search and Rescue) helicopters as well as other ground personnel, including CCTs, to Thailand to establish bases near the Laotian border to call in air strikes by Air Force fighters flying out of Utapo and Nakhon Phantom in Thailand. The CCTs, trained in jungle warfare techniques and air commando tactics, including forward air controlling (FACs), liaised with Hmong tribesmen whom they trained and equipped to assist in the Air Force's contribution to the counterinsurgency effort against the NVA.[6]

As late as the spring of 1967, U.S. Air Force CCTs continued their efforts in directing air strikes as well as conducting civic action programs among the hill tribesmen near the Laotian border. During the siege of Khe Sanh (February–April 1968), Air Force CCTs assisted the Marines by providing on-the-spot support in guiding airstrike aircraft and C-130s resupplying the firebase with ammunition and evacuating wounded Marines.

Combat Controllers, following in the footsteps of the 1st Air Commando Group that served in Burma during World War II, were consolidated in the 606th Air Commando Squadron (606th ACS) and later the 56th Air Commando Squadron (56th ACS) and placed under the command of Colonel Harry C. Aderholt, USAF. The CCTs operated in three-man teams (one captain and two enlisted men) that either parachuted or were inserted via CH-53 "Jolly Green Giant" helicopters into a remote airstrip where they made contact with local Hmong tribesmen.[7] In addition to their combat role, the CCTs conducted civic action programs along with gathering critical weather data used in air strikes against North Vietnam. These efforts were directed by the 13th U.S. Air Force throughout various bases in Thailand.[8]

The early deployment of Marine Reconnaissance teams, Navy SEALs, Army Special Forces, and Air Force CCTs to South Vietnam and Thailand became a laboratory of sorts for the type of war these clandestine warriors encountered during the years of American involvement in South Vietnam. The deployment of these "special forces" laid the operational and tactical foundations for the Special Forces doctrine that developed during and after the war in Vietnam.

Marine Reconnaissance and the Beginnings of Recon's "Long War" (1963–1966)

Before the massive U.S. buildup that began with the landing of the 9th Marine Expeditionary Brigade in March 1965, the Marine helicopter squadron was not the only Marine unit in Vietnam. Marine Pathfinder teams and other elements of Marine Reconnaissance units likewise saw duty in Vietnam.

In October 1964, elements of 1st Force Company, operating as part of the U.S. Seventh Fleet's Special Landing Force (SLF), and in line with one of Recon's major missions, conducted an extensive survey of Cam Ranh Bay in southern II Corps. The purpose of the survey was to determine the feasibility of establishing a naval facility.

From July 6 to August 6, 1964, Sub Unit 1, 1st Force Reconnaissance Company, commanded by First Lieutenant Jack W. Philips, participated in operations connected with surveys of Cam Ranh Bay in Vietnam while assigned to Mine Flotilla ONE's USS *Epping Forest* (MSC-7) and with three mine-sweepers, including the USS *Warbler* (MSC-206). Included with Sub Unit 1 was the Navy's Underwater Demolition Team (UDT) 11. While the Navy units chartered most of Cam Ranh Bay, UDT-11 conducted hydrographic surveys on all outer beaches. Sub Unit 1 Marines conducted a variety of reconnaissance-type missions, including searching for likely Viet Cong activity in and around Cam Ranh Bay. After UDT-11 completed the hydrographic surveys in the Cam Ranh Bay area, the task group moved north to the Bay of Ben Goi while Sub Unit 1 Marines conducted similar reconnaissance missions behind each of the selected beaches. Although the teams encountered no significant enemy contact, Viet Cong snipers subjected the Recon Marines to sporadic gunfire while one frogman stepped on an enemy punji stick.[9]

In late 1964, Sub Unit 1 became increasingly involved along Vietnam's coastline. Still part of the Seventh Fleet SLF, the Recon Marines operated simultaneously with sailors from UDT-12 aboard the USS *Weiss* (APD-135). While in the Gulf of Tonkin, off the North Vietnamese coast, the ship went to general quarters when three North Vietnamese navy patrol boats attacked the *Weiss*, prompting a launch of an F-8 Crusader jet, which sunk one of the attacking boats.

In the weeks prior to the main landing by Marines from the 9th Marine Expeditionary Brigade at Da Nang in March 1965, the leathernecks from 1st Force Reconnaissance Sub Unit 1, commanded by Captain David Whittingham, landed on Red Beach, Da Nang, and, in conjunction with sailors from UDT-12, operating off the USS *Cook* (APD-130), "accomplished the reconnaissance of RED Beaches 1 and 2 at Da Nang" on February 23–27, 1965. The successful survey of both beaches, including beach exits and cross-country trafficability, resulted in the selection of Red Beach 2 as the landing site for the first major Marine combat elements in Vietnam—the 3rd Battalion, 9th Marines.[10]

As the Johnson administration stepped up its counterinsurgency efforts in South Vietnam in order to bolster the ARVN, Secretary of Defense Robert S. McNamara ordered the Marine Corps to increase its advisory role with the assignment of another group of Marines to South Vietnam in order "to employ their skills in the counterinsurgency environment." Headquarters Marine Corps assigned a small Special Operations Group of six officers and twenty-one enlisted men. This small Marine detachment conducted operations under the auspices of United States Military Assistance Command Vietnam (USMACV) in supporting the South Vietnamese Army and Marine Corps (VNMC) in counterinsurgency operations against the Viet Cong.

It should be noted that despite their different non-traditional "official" missions, HQMC assigned reconnaissance elements to the counterinsurgency effort in Vietnam in order bolster the ARVN. Marine Reconnaissance teams were to "advise"

ARVN in counterinsurgency operations, but their primary mission to carry out pre-landing beach surveys and mapping and to act as a security force for Marine aviation and communications facilities and personnel remained. SOG and other reconnaissance elements participated in the same type of missions and often in the same reconnaissance areas of responsibility.

5

"Land the Landing Force"
Recon Goes to War (1965–1967)

The Landing Force Arrives (March–April 1965)

In March 1965, elements of the 9th Marine Expeditionary Brigade arrived from Okinawa and landed at Da Nang. "Marine Recon" led the way ashore and began its six-year war in South Vietnam.

The initial commitment of Marine Reconnaissance elements included the 3rd Reconnaissance Battalion, 3rd Marine Division, and the 1st Force Reconnaissance Company, a Force Troop unit. During the first phase of the Marine landings on March 8, 1965, Marines from both units operated in and around three main tactical areas of responsibility (TAORs): Da Nang, Chu Lai, and Hue/Phu Bai.

Several days after the initial landing at Red Beach in Da Nang, elements from Sub Unit 1, 1st Force Reconnaissance Company, conducted additional beach surveys near Chu Lai, which facilitated the planning decisions that were needed to land elements of the soon-to-arrive 3rd Marine Amphibious Brigade (MAB) along a beachhead dominated by impassable lagoons and the Viet Cong. Despite the presence of a substantial enemy force, 1st Force Reconnaissance Marines successfully surveyed the coastal areas near Chu Lai and identified a suitable landing site that was eventually used by the main body of the 3rd MAB.

On April 20, 1965, two and a half weeks before the landing of 3rd MAB at Chu Lai, Force Reconnaissance Marines surveyed a beach south of the Tra Bong River, a little more than six miles south of the proposed landing beach. On April 22, while conducting a reconnaissance operation between Da Nang and Hoi An, Recon Marines from Company D, 3rd Force Reconnaissance Battalion, engaged in a brief firefight with the Viet Cong. The next day, April 23, the Recon Marines engaged a larger enemy force, and after being caught in a VC crossfire, 3rd Reconnaissance Battalion suffered its first casualties, as Corporal Lowell H. Merrell and two Navy corpsmen were mortally wounded during the firefight. Shortly thereafter, Reconnaissance Marines named their base at China Beach "Camp Merrell," in honor of their slain comrade.

"A Pioneering Night Helicopter Pathfinder Operation"—The Dominican Republic (April 1965)

Even as Recon Marines conducted combat operations in the Republic of Vietnam, elements of Force Reconnaissance supported the Marine brigade sent to the Dominican Republic by President Lyndon B. Johnson on April 28, 1965, to restore order after a Communist-inspired coup threatened to establish a Castro-like regime in that country. During this operation, a Force Reconnaissance platoon conducted a pioneering night helicopter Pathfinder operation in support of Marine operations on the ground. Later, this same type of operation was successfully employed by Marine Reconnaissance teams in South Vietnam.[1]

Reconnaissance Units—Early Non-Doctrinal Use

In May 1965, 1st Force Reconnaissance Sub Unit 1 teams reverted to their role as advisors and served as patrol leaders for the Vietnamese-manned Civilian Irregular Defense Groups (CIDGs). The CIDGs were initiated as a covert spin-off from the CIA to train ethnic minority Vietnamese into an anti–Viet Cong force and to collect intelligence information, primarily in the central highlands and Laos. The Reconnaissance Marines participated in reconnaissance-in-force patrols composed of U.S.- and Australian-led Nung (which operated out of Da Nang). A third mission required a quick-response force to provide security for downed Marine helicopters. Throughout the next few months (specifically in July and August of the same year), two platoons from Sub Unit 1 operated with the 4th Marine Regiment out of Chu Lai. Other Force Reconnaissance Marines from Sub Unit 1 assisted the naval commander of Task Force 76 with beach surveys while another force platoon served with the Special Landing Force (SLF) off the Vietnamese coastline. In October 1965, Sub Unit 1 Marines, with the addition of its fourth platoon, along with the 2nd Battalion, 3rd Marines, participated in Operation "Red Snapper."

Reconnaissance Battalions, meanwhile, supported the division in and around its TAOR, acting as a screening force. Then-Lieutenant Lawrence C. Vetter, who extended his thirteen-month tour in Vietnam as an engineer to serve seven months as a platoon commander and patrol leader with 3rd Reconnaissance Battalion, wrote, "Quite often this meant that reconnaissance units were attached to subordinate division units—that is regiments and battalions." Vetter recalled that the Recon companies or platoons attached in direct support of either a regiment or a battalion reported to the regimental or battalion commander and operated "directly" for him (as opposed to Force Reconnaissance companies, which were structured as the MAF commander's asset).[2] In short, as Lieutenant Colonel Babin explained, the Reconnaissance Battalion "is part of the Marine Division's structure and the Division commander can keep them in general support of the Division, or he can put them in direct support of, or in attachment to, other Division units. Consequently, the Reconnaissance Battalions are frequently referred to as Division Recon." Babin added, "A lack of understanding of reconnaissance capability, confused task organization and unfavorable operational intent restricted Marine reconnaissance units from conducting missions such as those carried out by the Army's Long-Range Reconnaissance patrols (LRRPs) and other Special Forces' units."[3]

Reconnaissance Units Join the War

During the Vietnam War, there were four active-duty Reconnaissance Battalions: 1st Reconnaissance Battalion (Camp Pendleton, California; deployed to Vietnam); 2nd Reconnaissance Battalion (Camp Lejeune, North Carolina); 3rd Reconnaissance Battalion (Vietnam); and 5th Reconnaissance Battalion (Camp Pendleton, California; one platoon deployed to 1st Reconnaissance Battalion in 1966). Late in the war, as Marines began to redeploy from Vietnam back to either the continental United States or Okinawa, the 5th Reconnaissance Battalion was deactivated.

The Reconnaissance Battalion was structured with an H&S company and four reconnaissance platoons. Prior to 1968, the platoon was organized with one officer and twenty-three Marines. Each platoon in the Reconnaissance Battalion was divided into two squads and one headquarters section. In 1968, as operational needs drove increased requirements for reconnaissance capability, HQMC added a third squad and, at the same time, a fourth reconnaissance company, Company E, to each battalion. Reconnaissance Battalion structure allowed for the capability to be a reconnaissance platoon in direct support of each infantry battalion in the division or a company for each regiment. Infantry battalion and regimental commanders, when supported by Recon, were provided with flexibility to augment their security and extend their "eyes and ears" to meet the needs for intelligence gathering and other requirements. Patrols varied in size from four-man teams to an entire platoon as the mission or objective dictated.

Elements of 3rd Force Reconnaissance Company and 3rd Reconnaissance Battalion, which arrived in South Vietnam during the summer and fall of 1965, along with U.S. Army Special Forces, operated in teams of four to five men in and around Saigon as well as near the Laotian border. Later, in 1964, prior to the commitment of Marines to the war in South Vietnam, both 3rd Force Reconnaissance Company and elements of 3rd Reconnaissance Battalion operated in unison off the South Vietnamese coast, conducting beach and hydrographic surveys prior to the commitment of the 9th Marine Expeditionary Brigade in March 1965. 1st Force Reconnaissance Company was attached to 1st Reconnaissance Battalion, 1st Marine Division, from October 3, 1965, until November 18, 1966, subsequently serving with the 1st Reconnaissance Battalion before returning to the United States in 1971.[4]

Two platoons of 3rd Force Reconnaissance Company deployed to Vietnam in March 1966, and a third platoon deployed in June to support the 26th Marine Regiment. The remainder of the company deployed on March 21, 1967, and, after several months, was attached to the 3rd Reconnaissance Battalion. A fourth platoon from 3rd Force Recon joined the battalion in October 1966.[5] They were attached to the 3rd Reconnaissance Battalion until October 1969, at which time they began to stand down and were eventually deactivated in early 1970. As the Force Company came together, a platoon from the recently activated 5th Reconnaissance Battalion at Camp Pendleton was deployed to join 1st Reconnaissance Battalion.

Operational Commitment: Operations "Starlite" and "Dagger Thrust" (August–September 1965)

During Operation "Starlite" (August 18–24, 1965), the first major offensive against the Viet Cong, led by 7th Marines' commanding officer, Colonel Oscar F. Peatross, 1st Force Reconnaissance Company Marines attached to Sub Unit 1 served alongside the 2nd Battalion, 4th Marines, with the 3rd Platoon, which had been part of the SLF attached to Battalion Landing Team (BLT), 3rd Battalion, 7th Marines.

Major General Oscar F. Peatross, Jr., USMC, commanded the 7th Marines during Operation "Starlite" in August 1965 (Peatross Papers, Marine Corps Recruit Depot, Parris Island, South Carolina).

During Operation "Dagger Thrust II," the 4th Platoon served with the SLF's BLT 2nd Battalion, 1st Marines, near the Hai Van Pass north of Da Nang. Unfortunately, a host of supply problems, maintenance and other command and control issues hampered Sub Unit 1's operations ashore. This in turn led Major General Lewis Walt to transfer Sub Unit 1 to operational control of the 3rd Marine Division, which in turn gave operational control of the unit to the 3rd Reconnaissance Battalion. The transfer became effective on October 30, and two days later, on November 1, 1965, Sub Unit 1, 1st Force Reconnaissance Company, became 1st Force Reconnaissance Company (-), with a strength of 9 officers and 103 enlisted men. In effect, 1st Force Reconnaissance Company became a sixth, "albeit smaller," company of the reinforced 3rd Reconnaissance Battalion.[6]

The 3rd Reconnaissance Battalion Arrives "In Country" (March–May 1965)

On March 8, 1965, a platoon from Company A, 3rd Reconnaissance Battalion, which had been attached to BLT 3/9 of the SLF, became the first Division Reconnaissance element to be permanently located in Vietnam. Other platoons from 3rd Reconnaissance Battalion arrived in attachments to BLTs: a platoon from Company B with BLT 3/4; a platoon from Company D with BLT 1/3; and a second Company D platoon with BLT 2/3. This arrangement lasted until April 13, when these "in-country" reconnaissance platoons were regrouped as Company D, 3rd Reconnaissance Battalion, with Captain Patrick G. Collin commanding. Company D commenced operations as the 9th Marine Expeditionary Brigade company. The 3rd Reconnaissance Battalion headquarters arrived in Vietnam on May 7, 1965, with Lieutenant Colonel Don H. "Doc" Blanchard, his entire staff, and the remainder of the battalion. They came ashore at Chu Lai with the 3rd Marine Amphibious Brigade (3rd MAB).

Shortly after 3rd MAB came ashore, 3rd Reconnaissance Battalion reunited with its other companies (A and C) while Company B remained at Chu Lai. Both Companies A and B were brought up to strength by integrating the Company D platoons with the 3rd Reconnaissance Battalion at Chu Lai. Company C, which had been at Da Nang, "OPCON'd" to 3rd Battalion, 4th Marines, at Hue/Phu Bai on May 26.

With 3rd Reconnaissance Battalion fragmented across the Marine order of battle, Major General Walt issued a directive on September 19 that attempted to maintain some unit integrity within reconnaissance. This directive stated that 3rd Reconnaissance Battalion was to be used in general support of the 3rd Marine Division. In fact, as one post–Vietnam history of 1st Force Reconnaissance pointed out concerning 3rd Reconnaissance Battalion's "sloppy" command relationships, toward the end of April and in May 1965, Marine Recon teams were "being used for any mission that might come up."[7] Some of the missions included Marine "Raider-type missions; they ended up on some infantry assault type missions." In fact, "The haphazard employment of reconnaissance assets denied Marine commanders the ability to fully exploit Recon's capability resulting in a loss of timely information on the enemy and terrain as both Division and the MAF [headquarters] were not receiving the information they required."[8]

Meanwhile, Company C, 1st Reconnaissance Battalion, which had arrived in Vietnam with the 7th Marines, commanded by Colonel Oscar F. Peatross, reinforced the 3rd Battalion Reconnaissance and was designated to operate as a fifth company within the newly created Reconnaissance Group ALPHA. By September 19, 1965, 3rd Reconnaissance Battalion was in position to support III Marine Amphibious Force, conducting reconnaissance patrols throughout III MAF's tactical area of responsibility (TAOR). The battalion, commanded by Lieutenant Colonel Roy R. Van Cleve, was dispersed into three enclaves. These positions included Headquarters and Companies "A," "C (-)," and "D" at Da Nang; a platoon of Company "C" at Hue/Phu Bai; and the newly designated Reconnaissance Group ALPHA, composed of Company B and the attached Company C, 1st Reconnaissance Battalion, which was detached from Da Nang to the 3rd Battalion, 4th Marines, at Hue/Phu Bai.[9] Established in their reconnaissance areas of responsibility, and reflecting the "defensive" nature of III MAF's mission, the reconnaissance companies conducted local patrols that ranged from two to six miles, scouting and engaging in limited firefights with local Viet Cong and main force units of the National Liberation Front (NLF). The mission of 3rd Reconnaissance Battalion was to "screen the regiment's left flank. Platoons from the battalion conducted screening patrols and established listening and observation posts in front of the infantry lines for two weeks."[10]

Meanwhile, while 3rd Reconnaissance Battalion operated out of the Chu Lai enclave, Delta Company, commanded by Captain Collins, continued to patrol in and around Da Nang. On May 14–15, 1965, in Elephant Valley, northwest of Da Nang, Captain Collins and First Lieutenant William Vankat led a patrol, which consisted of four ten-men teams, and engaged in a day-long firefight with a small Viet Cong unit that proved to be part of a full enemy regiment. Lieutenant Vankat later recalled, "I think we picked on a VC regiment. After sixteen hours of fighting my team suffered one killed and all the rest of us were wounded. I was hit twice. Two Army chopper pilots pulled us out of the battle and saved our butts."[11]

In support of 9th Marine Expeditionary Brigade, the 3rd Reconnaissance Battalion had by April 1965 "claimed more VC kills" than all of the "in country infantry units," despite the fact that the rules of engagement at this time in the Da Nang and Chu Lai TAORs were defense oriented. The mission would change, however, prior to the commencement of Operation "Starlite" in August 1965.

Recon Goes to War: Operation "Starlite" (August 1965)

During Operation "Starlite" (August 18–24, 1965), the first major offensive against the Viet Cong, commanded by Colonel Oscar F. Peatross, 7th Marine Regiment, Reconnaissance Marines from 1st Force Reconnaissance Company Sub Unit 1 served alongside the 2nd Battalion, 4th Marines, while 3rd Platoon, which had been attached to the SLF, continued to serve with Battalion Landing Team (BLT), 3rd Battalion, 7th Marines.

A "Busy" Month for Reconnaissance Marines (September 1965)

During September 1965, "Recon" Marines maintained an active schedule supporting the 1st Marine Division and the U.S. Navy's "Brown Water" fleet in the Mekong Delta. On September 12–15, Recon Marines participated in Operation "Piranha." A week later, during Operation "Dagger Thrust I" (September 20–21, 1965), Reconnaissance Marines and Navy Underwater Demolition Teams from the USS *Diachenko* conducted one of the first amphibious raids of the Vietnam War.

Operation "Dagger Thrust I–III" (September–October 1965)

In order to maintain pressure on the Viet Cong, III MAF launched "Dagger Thrust I, II, and III," a series of planned amphibious raids in support of Operation "Market Time" anti-infiltration operations. The concept was to conduct three successive "rapid" raids that capitalized on the element of surprise.

During Operation "Dagger Thrust I," one of the stay-behind platoons conducted a reconnaissance of a harbor near Saigon where the VC were suspected of resupplying by means of submarine and storing supplies in nearby locations. A four-man Force Recon team, augmented by two South Vietnamese UDTs, was sent to investigate. The two ARVN UDT members, in fact, made a favorable impression on the Marines, due to the fact that they had "enlisted for life, were well-trained, [and were] strong swimmers." Sailing on the USS *Diachenko* (LPR-123), a World War II–era destroyer that served as a transport for Navy UDTs and Marine Reconnaissance teams, the landing party—led by Gunnery Sergeant (later Sergeant Major) Maurice J. Jacques and including a South Vietnamese UDT—came ashore "bare foot," in order to not give away their presence, and marched inland. Sergeant Jacques' mission lasted two days, and, although they did not see an enemy submarine, they saw a considerable number of VC personnel, many carrying the new AR-15 rifles and PRC-25 radios. The Marines and ARVN UDT noted their findings and made their way back to the *Diachenko*. Shortly thereafter, Marines from the 3rd Battalion, 7th Marines, using the recon intelligence, swept the area and captured the Viet Cong.[12]

During "Dagger Thrust II," three Marine Force Reconnaissance teams, accompanied by South Vietnamese UDT personnel, went ashore in small boats on the evening of September 27. One team lost radio contact but was located by helicopters of HMM-163. None of the teams reported any enemy sightings, and the raid was subsequently cancelled.

"Dagger Thrust III" occurred on October 1, 1965, with the battalion landing team going ashore at Tam Quan. Meeting scattered resistance, the Marines were ordered to break contact and return to the ship, which soon set sail for a priority mission off the coast of Indonesia.

During the remainder of 1965, the reconnaissance detachment conducted a series of short patrols in support of friendly artillery, collectively known as "STING-RAY" operations. The following year, after Operation "Hastings" in the late summer, the name and mission became official. Similar economy of force patrols, small in number but leveraged with supporting arms, became a hallmark of reconnaissance operations and made a significant impact on combat operations throughout the remainder of the war.

The detachment was unable to conduct any long-range reconnaissance missions due largely to operational concerns and a lack of understanding of the value of long-range reconnaissance patrols such as those carried out by Special Forces units. After the redeployment of the company headquarters and two platoons back to Camp Pendleton, California, two platoons from Sub Unit 1 remained "in country" and were attached to the Special Landing Force.

1st Force Reconnaissance Company Sub Unit Recon and U.S. Army Special Forces

With the establishment of III Marine Amphibious Force on May 17, 1965, teams from 1st Force Reconnaissance Company Sub Unit 1 began to conduct long-range, clandestine reconnaissance in and around the Da Nang and Chu Lai TAORs. With the concurrence of Major General William R. Collins, who assumed command of the 3rd Marine Division on May 3, 1965, and III MAF Commanding General Major General Lewis Walt, the Force Reconnaissance detachment initiated operations with U.S. Special Forces (USSF) in I Corps with a two-fold mission: (1) gain experience in the mountain jungle approaches to the Marine TAORs, and (2) provide possibly useful information directly to III MAF. This mission was implemented in two ways: the reconnaissance teams were detailed to USSF "A" caps from Khe Sanh to Chu Lai for two-week periods, providing leaders for U.S.-advised Civilian Irregular Defense Group (CIDG) patrols from these camps; second, additional teams were used in reconnaissance-in-force patrols launched out of the Da Nang TAOR. This arrangement "proved valuable to the Special Forces since the Force Reconnaissance Company contingent included a significant number of highly-trained SNCOs and radio operators." Once Force Reconnaissance Marines completed a patrol, they submitted reports and were debriefed by Lieutenant Colonel R.E. Gruenler, III MAF G-2. Force Reconnaissance Marines operated with their U.S. Army Special Forces counterparts from the latter part of May to July 10, 1965. At this time, Sub Unit 1 was augmented with a platoon brought in country by Lieutenant David L. Grannis, which increased the detachment's strength to two officers and thirty enlisted Marines.[13]

A Month of Extensive Patrolling (July–August 1965)

From July to the end of August 1965, the teams from 1st Force Reconnaissance Company Sub Unit 1 conducted extensive patrol operations from the 4th Marine Regiment base at Chu Lai with Company B, 3rd Reconnaissance Battalion. These patrols lasted anywhere from three to four days and were limited to about twenty "clicks"[14] inland. The reconnaissance teams were either inserted individually by helicopter or dropped off from the main body of a larger deception patrol (known as a "false insertion"), or else they would "walk" into the area of operations by foot from a friendly position. Extraction of the recon teams was normally done by helicopter.

When Reconnaissance Marines from Company B were unavailable, the 3rd Battalion, 3rd Marines, and 2nd Battalion, 4th Marines, requested aid from the Force Reconnaissance Sub Unit 1 detachment. Most of these patrols were carried out by four-man reconnaissance teams, though some teams numbered five or six. Reconnaissance teams would sometimes execute a "stay-behind patrol" similar to Gunnery Sergeant Jacques' example in "Dagger Thrust." A team would travel with a larger unit and simply drop off or remain in place when the larger unit moved on. This method of insertion and patrol was considered the most clandestine (as well as the most dangerous) used by Marine Recon teams. The stay-behind patrols were often able to obtain information that otherwise could not have been obtained. Such was the case when the commander of 3rd Battalion, 3rd Marines, requested information about a village complex "vis-à-vis the infantry sweeps on the Viet Cong," in order to determine the movement of enemy fighters from village to village in reaction to the company sweeps or whether they were actually members of the village or hamlets. The recon teams sent to investigate this enemy movement "were able to maintain a covert posture for over two days and avoid compromise."[15]

During the remainder of 1965, teams from Sub Unit 1 conducted a series of patrols that were short in duration and designed to capitalize on available artillery support. Collectively, these patrols were known as STINGRAY operations. Similar economy of force patrols, small in number but leveraged with supporting arms, became a hallmark of reconnaissance operations and had a significant impact on combat operations throughout the war.

Marine Reconnaissance Team Equipment (1965–1968)

During this early phase of the Marine involvement in Vietnam, reconnaissance patrols were limited in scope and duration due to the "defensive" nature of the war. Two factors that contributed to the limited nature of reconnaissance patrols were the lack of portable communications gear and the weight of the radio equipment then in use by the reconnaissance teams. The PRC-47 (VHF/FM) was "too big and heavy for the teams to carry though it did have sufficient range." The smaller, lighter AN/PRC-10 ("Walkie Talkie"), which was hand-held with a sling, could be carried by team leaders, though it did not have the range often required by Marine or Army reconnaissance teams. This situation was alleviated by the arrival of the PRC-25 radio, which replaced the AN/PRC-10. The AN/PRC-25, a short-range, portable manpack, frequency-modulated (FM) receiver-transmitter, was used to provide two-way voice communication. Marine and Army units received the PRC-25 in November 1965, and Marine recon teams began using it almost immediately. Indeed, the PRC-25 would be the primary method of radio communications used by all Marine ground units in Vietnam War until it was replaced by the AN/PRC-77. From 1965 to 1968, some 33,000 sets would be sent to Marine and Army units in Vietnam.[16]

One of the major impediments in carrying the PRC-47 (and PRC-25) was the number of batteries that team members had to bring with them. Vietnam's harsh climate, had an adverse effect on the duration of battery life; as a result, all team members to carry extra batteries, thereby increasing each team member's combat load. This problem was only slightly alleviated (though never resolved) throughout the Vietnam War.

Recon Marines Dressed for the Occasion

Lieutenant Colonel Berwick Babin recalls, "Throughout the war there was no standard weapon(s) or equipment that reconnaissance Marines were required to take on patrol.... [I]ndividual loads were dictated by the patrol leader, but there was considerable latitude given to individual preference. Other than on special missions as mentioned earlier, the Marines wore the basic sateen green utility uniform or the lighter weight jungle utilities with the enlarged pockets. Some Marines wore the jungle utility trousers with the sateen shirt which was a heavier material that provided better protection from thorns, sharp-edged elephant grass and heavy brush."[17] Colonel Andrew Finlayson noted that 1st Force Reconnaissance Marines often wore the much-preferred U.S. Air Force "tiger stripe" uniform or Army camouflage uniforms.[18] Babin added, "To protect the hands from the brush, Marines wore dress uniform gloves from which they removed the wool lining and the index finger of the firing hand. A few Marines acquired various styles of camouflage uniforms from local merchants, the ARVN or other services. The oak leak camouflage design uniform did not begin to reach Marine reconnaissance supply lines until late 1968. Recon Marines did not wear a flak jacket or helmet while on patrol (ironically, they were mandatory in the rear at Dong Ha when I was there in 1968) in an attempt to lighten the load, reduce noise and be agile. As a result, with their camouflage face paint, it was not unusual for them to be mistaken as VC/NVA upon first glance in the field."[19]

Regarding a patrol's gear, Babin explained:

On their person you might find recon Marines with a map (encased in plastic from a radio battery), grease pencil (to plot on the plastic covering the map), lensatic compass, wrist watch, notebook, pen or pencil, 'bush' scarf, mirror, air panel(s), survival gear, pocket knife, pencil flares and a gas mask with a CS grenade inside. Hanging on the web gear, which could be either Marine 782 web gear or the Army 'H' harness, a recon Marine might have a K-Bar style combat knife (with a day-night flare taped to the sheaf), magazine pouches (usually doggy pouches with four magazines vertical and one horizontal across the top—all magazines with a tape pull-tab), fragmentation and smoke grenades, water canteens, rope and snap links, and first aid kit.

Ruck sacks (ARVN ruck sack preferred) would be loaded with food, ammunition, poncho and/or poncho liner, socks and whatever other comfort items a Marine might pack. When 3rd Force Reconnaissance

Lance Corporal Swiderski, a member of 3rd Force Reconnaissance Company, in full field gear prior to the start of a mission at their combat base near Phu Bai in 1969 (courtesy Sergeant Bill Moss, USMC Collection).

Company began running four-man teams in spring of 1968, many Marines lightened their load and switched to the Army 'ass pack.' The patrol leader carried a pair of 7 × 50 binoculars and an AN/PRC 63 UHF (survival) radio (small hand held radio to talk to fixed wing and as a backup). The patrol leader and the radioman carried shackle and authentication sheets, and because four-man teams rarely included a Corpsman, the patrol leader carried morphine syrettes. Some teams would carry the Corpsman's unit 1 medical kit, but most didn't consider it a priority.[20]

Weather and Terrain

According to Babin, "What uniform was worn and what weapons and equipment were carried was always subject to the weather and the terrain. If it couldn't

Marine Recon member James Fuhrman (KIA in February 1970) reapplies "cammie" in the morning during a patrol with 3rd Force Reconnaissance Company (courtesy Sergeant Bill Moss).

take a beating, no matter how promising a capability it had, it was of no value in the bush."[21] Colonel Finlayson, Lieutenant Larry Vetter, Babin and others wrote that Marine Recon teams operated in all types of weather and over all sorts of terrain, from the coastal lowlands to the rugged terrain of "Charlie Ridge," as well as in the hill country located south of and parallel to the DMZ and in the deep forests of the A Shau valley and along the western border with Laos. Marine Reconnaissance teams often found themselves slicing their way through seas of dense elephant grass that could reach ten feet in height or watching their balance as they climbed steep ridges. Teams could hazard movement along trails, dodge through vegetation-denuded crater-of-the-moon landscapes or crawl for hours under dense bush or over hills where vegetation was short to nonexistent. They found shelter along river banks and in thick brush. They slept on the ground as ants and insects (sometimes tigers and snakes) had their way with them. They drank from water sources enriched with Agent Orange and walked through thick mud and tripped over vines and roots as they conducted deep reconnaissance operations.

As for the weather, Vietnam's varied temperatures ranged from the cold and torrential downpours of the monsoons to the 100 percent humidity and 100-degree heat of summer, to the chill of the "crachin" (often referred to by the French as "the spit"), which brought about decreased visibility from its low-hanging mist, particularly in the mountains and their valleys, frequently preventing teams from calling in artillery, close air support or a helicopter extraction. Depending on the season, Marines might find themselves clinging to ponchos in the "freezing" or cool weather brought in by the monsoon, which started in October and lasted through March.[22]

Finlayson noted that Vietnam's weather dictated the size, length, and mission of the Recon team, as shown in his account of one mission after Operation "Knox" in November 1967:

Caught up in a typhoon for a week in the field, a member of Team Atlas, 3rd Force Reconnaissance Company, whose fingers have experienced severe water immersion, wraps up a poncho liner (courtesy Sergeant Bill Moss).

> The monsoon season had begun in central Vietnam, and with it came days of rain and colder temperatures. Due to the bad weather and the increased likelihood of poor flying conditions, our patrols planned for more than the normal four days in the bush. We took more food with us to tide us over if our patrol was extended, and we often increased the size of our patrols in case we had to walk out and move through the villages in the lowlands. Taking all of this into account I decided to take most of my platoon on this patrol, a force of 13 Marines. Our mission was to establish an OP near Phu Loc and observe enemy infiltration in that area. Marine intelligence sources continued to inform us that the enemy was planning to attack Da Nang and several other military and civilian sites sometime after the first of the year. They wanted the recon teams to find out where these enemy units were staging for the attack. For some reason unknown to us, they suspected the hills south of Hue near Phu Loc as one of the enemy staging areas.... We did not spot any enemy during our patrol, primarily because the monsoon rains kept everyone with any common sense indoors and dry. Of course, we had no sense. We spent a soggy four days in our ponchos trying to keep the lenses of our binoculars

Life in the field for Reconnaissance Marines was debilitating. Here a member of 3rd Force Reconnaissance Company displays his hands, which are pruned after a week in the field during a typhoon (courtesy Sergeant Bill Moss).

Two Recon Marines from 3rd Force Reconnaissance Company in the field (courtesy Sergeant Bill Moss).

Right: Members of Team Atlas, 3rd Force Reconnaissance Company, fill their canteens in a stream during a break in a patrol (courtesy Sergeant Bill Moss).

dry while we scanned the empty terrain below us through a veil of continuous rain. There was some traffic on Highway 1, mostly U.S. and ARVN military vehicles and civilian trucks, but that was about all we saw. The incessant rain not only made us wet and uncomfortable, it tended to sap our morale as well. By the time the patrol ended on the 11th November, we looked like prunes, and some of my men were suffering from the onset of trench foot.[23]

Members of Team Atlas, 3rd Force Reconnaissance, break for chow while on mission (courtesy Sergeant Bill Moss).

Armament of the Reconnaissance "Teams"

With regard to armament, Babin explained:

Perhaps the most important item a Recon Marine carried with him on patrol, regardless of terrain or weather was his weapon. The Force Reconnaissance T/E weapon was the M3A1 "grease" gun. It grew out of favor with most reconnaissance Marines after initial deployment to Vietnam, and logistical support for the WWII leftover could be problematic. In the field it was subject to rust and the short barrel, heavy recoil and relatively slow cyclic fire rate made it almost exclusively a close-range fighting weapon. Most reconnaissance Marines preferred the greater flexibility provided by the long rifle, and, perhaps, there was a certain comfort level with the rifle as a part of the legacy of Marine marksmanship drummed into Marine psyche from bootcamp and beyond with every Marine a *rifleman*.

What recon team members carried as primary individual weapons tracked with other infantry units. In July/August 1965, the M-14 became the primary rifle until the M-16 was fielded in 1968. The M-14 was appreciated for its larger caliber, knock down and brush cutting capability. However, it was heavy to carry, cumbersome in dense brush and prone to rust. The M-16 was lighter and easier to carry, and with the .223 caliber bullet, provided the opportunity to carry more ammunition. Early mechanical problems and its fragile design sparked a lot of derisive comments as these factors could result in jammed weapons during fire fights. Recon Marines typically taped the end of the barrel closed with electrician's tape and wrapped a cloth around the receiver area of the rifle as dirt barriers. A cleaning rod was attached to the barrel for quick access to clear failures to extract. I MAF directed Marines not to fashion a guerrilla sling by attaching a line from the front site blade to the stock because continued carry in that fashion would bend the magnesium alloy barrel. This was followed by directive not to use the three pronged flash suppressor to twist and break the wire binding c-ration boxes because it could damage the rifle. With these issues in mind many Marines looked wistfully at the AK-47. There were many captured and available to reconnaissance Marines. They were appreciated for their ruggedness and reliability with a large caliber round. From a practical point, they were not logistically supportable, ammunition and parts, so it was not carried as a personal weapon, and to the chagrin of many, was not a permitted war trophy.

The eight man or larger reconnaissance patrols and outposts were carefully balanced with personnel and weapons. They hit the bush with a Corpsman (who deemphasized his non-combatant stature and supplemented his .45 pistol with a rifle) and one or two radio operators. The M-60 machine gun with bipod only was carried and supplemented with claymore mines, an M-79 (*blooper*) and occasionally the M-72 LAAW, a night observation device and Patrol Seismic Intrusion Devices (PSIDs). Sometimes the point would carry a shotgun, but most patrol leaders preferred their point to carry an M-14 for its knock down capability or the M-16 that could empty a full magazine faster than two shot gun rounds could be pumped. In addition to their rifles, individual Marines carried a variety of equipment and weapons. Team members carried fragmentation hand grenades, smoke grenades, thermite grenades (usually the radio operator to destroy the radio before capture) and CS grenades (to break contact). Some team members carried a .45 pistol and occasionally someone would have a revolver.[24]

In terms of individual equipment, Marine Reconnaissance teams initially carried the standard M3A1 "grease gun" until the teams were issued the M-14 rifle in July–August 1965. Later, Reconnaissance Marines carried the standard M-16 assault rifle. Individual Marines were armed with the M-26 grenade, a K-Bar combat knife, M-18 smoke grenade and M-15 white phosphorous grenade. Patrol leaders, assistant patrol leaders and radio operators also carried the Colt 1911 .45 caliber pistol. As for webbing, Marine recon teams sported either the traditional 782 gear and rucksacks or the much-favored Army of Vietnam rucksack that was both light and more comfortable. Marine Recon teams likewise often sported captured Viet Cong AK-47 chest pouch webbing as they exchanged their U.S.-issued weapons for the highly efficient AK-47 assault rifle. On Colonel Finlayson's highly successful team known as Killer Kane, one of his Marines, Lance Corporal James Hager, carried the "Stoner" light machine gun or the heavier (though deadly) M-60 machine gun. Finally, some Marine Recon teams had a designated grenadier who carried the M-79 grenade launcher known as the "blooper" for increased fire support when fighting their way out of an ambush.

A Very Important Team Member—Navy Corpsmen

Colonel Finlayson emphasized that among the most important members of any Marine Reconnaissance team were the Navy corpsmen. Besides their life-saving skills, Navy "docs" assigned to either Force or Battalion Reconnaissance played a critical and vital role in Marine Reconnaissance operations.] Thus In effect, corpsmen were expected to, as Bruce "Doc" Norton and HM3 Robert Buehl noted, "carry their own weight and be part of the team."[25] Navy corpsmen, when the situation called for it, were expected to act as infantrymen, many times fighting as well as performing on-the-spot medical care for wounded Marines (and sometimes enemy soldiers). Navy corpsmen such as HM3 Buehl and Bruce "Doc" Norton, who found themselves assigned to one of the many recon companies, were, in fact, volunteers. "Once a corpsman volunteered ... and [was] accepted into recon, they underwent the same training as their Marine counterparts."[26] Navy corpsmen attended the Field Medical Service School, which functioned as "basic training" for all new corpsmen assigned to the Fleet Marine Force (FMF). Corpsmen assigned to serve with the FMF "attended infantry training, jungle warfare school, jump training and even scuba school." Navy corpsman Robert "Doc" Schoelkopf, who volunteered for recon duty, "underwent every kind of specialized training the Marines could cook up over the next 17 months. When his orders to Vietnam arrived in the fall of 1967, he was prepared as he could possibly have been" for duty with a Marine Recon team.[27]

Already in short supply due to the demands for Navy corpsmen by regular Marine line companies, "docs" were few and far in between in Force Recon.[28] Corpsmen assigned to Marine Recon teams were held to the same exacting standards that patrol leaders demanded of their Marines. In addition to their medical kit, Navy corpsmen used the same weapons, carried the same gear, ate the same food, and endured the same hardships. In fact, corpsmen were considered one more "trigger puller," and their "medical specialty served the patrol only after their tactical proficiency."[29]

"Corpsmen participated in every type of mission for which force recon was specially-suited. SCUBA-qualified corpsmen joined Marines in conducting searches for ordnance, bodies, explosives rigged to bridges and submerged tunnels for weapons caches." Corpsmen likewise earned their jump wings.

Due to their small numbers, corpsmen "ended up going out on more patrols than many of their Marine counterparts to cover teams without a corpsman assigned." Bruce "Doc" Norton recalled that he went out on more than 30 patrols with 1st and 3rd Force Reconnaissance Companies. Norton said that "it just kind of happened, that way." Put differently, due to the close bond that developed between Reconnaissance Marines and their Navy corpsmen, when asked to go on a patrol, "what are you going to say, No?"

Corpsmen assigned to Force and Battalion Reconnaissance likewise maintained a healthy respect for their comrades assigned to regular Marine line companies. Norton recalled one incident when he hitched a ride back to Da Nang aboard a medevac helicopter and met up with three corpsmen he had previously known. They were assigned to the triage unit there. "I thought they were out of their minds. You see a helicopter land with five or six casualties, or a number of dead, or guys with limbs blown off, and they were seeing this every day. My God, how do you do it?"[30] Norton added that the respect was mutual. "They thought," Norton recalled, "I was insane going out there on these long-range recon missions, where I felt very comfortable and safe with my team, never having to deal with things that they did on a daily basis. I was just in awe of them."[31]

As both "Doc" Norton and HM3 Schoelkopf recalled, Marine Recon team members could expect to see their Navy corpsmen with them, if necessary, to join in the fight against enemy units. More important, however, team members could count on their "docs" being there to either "patch them up" or perform life-saving triage when wounded prior to being evacuated to a field hospital for further treatment. Navy corpsmen thus performed a dual role while assigned to a Marine Reconnaissance team, serving as both "healers and fighters" during Recon's long war against the VC and NVA.[32] Immediately upon insertion into the RZ with a team, the Navy corpsman had to be ready to administer first aid while also potentially fighting alongside the other team members.

The Reasoner Patrol (July 12, 1965)

One of the first major engagements fought by Marine Recon occurred on July 12, 1965, when first platoon, Company A, 3rd Recon Battalion, was sent via helicopter to the town of Dai Loc, to the foot of Hill 327. The 1st Platoon—commanded by Second Lieutenant Bill Henderson and accompanied by Company A's commander, First Lieutenant Frank Reasoner, along with sixteen Marines, one Navy corpsman, and an ARVN dog handler, and airlifted by Marine UH-34s some ten air miles south of Da Nang—landed in the town of Dai Loc and quickly entered the nearby village of An My (3), where they moved cautiously as they observed the villagers, who remained in their grass shacks and appeared to be wary of the leathernecks and their ARVN counterpart.[33]

The Marines, carrying M-14 rifles, one hundred rounds of ammunition (some Marines carried two hundred rounds), one or two canteens, several grenades, and an M-79 grenade launcher, proceeded west and then north toward Dai Loc. Operating in daylight (contrary to standard recon procedures that called for movement at night), they approached the village. Operating on the left flank, some three hours into the mission, Second Lieutenant Henderson and half of the platoon entered the village of An My (3) in search of a sniper who had fired on the Marines. Meanwhile, First Lieutenant Reasoner and the remainder of the platoon continued down the road toward An My and approached the village along the main route. With their weapons at the ready, the Marines entered the village, which appeared to be empty. According to retired sergeant major Fred Murray, then a lance corporal, "the situation didn't look good," a fact he relayed to Lieutenant Reasoner.

As the Marines pushed through the village, a rainstorm opened up, drenching the leathernecks as they cautiously maintained their watch. It was at this point that Corporal B.C. Collins and then–Lance Corporal Murray saw three men wearing ponchos and helmets, brandishing AK-47 assault rifles near a clump of trees. The Marines quickly sprang into action, dropping down and firing on the enemy soldiers. Subsequently, an enemy RPK machine gun opened fire from a nearby rise. A fusillade of enemy small arms fire targeted the leathernecks as they took up positions in the village graveyard among the headstones. The Viet Cong, meanwhile, "from their tactically advantageous positions," kept the Marines pinned down and attempted to envelop the team from two flanks. Even as the VC poured their murderous fire on the Marines, Lieutenant Henderson's force continued to push through the village, where they, too, began receiving heavy enemy fire on their left flank.

"Carve His Name with Pride": First Lieutenant Frank S. Reasoner, USMC, Commanding Officer, Company A, 3rd Reconnaissance Battalion. Lieutenant Reasoner won the Medal of Honor posthumously for his bravery and leadership in the fight in the village of An My (3) in July 1965 (courtesy U.S. Marine Corps History Division).

Lance Corporal Murray and Corporal Collins, operating in front of the unit, then exposed themselves to enemy fire in order to find a better position from which to cut off another enemy unit that had joined the battle and was attempting to maneuver behind the Marines. After a furious melee, their weapons on automatic, Collins and Murray killed several enemy soldiers and blocked their attempt to outflank the Marines.

The enemy machine gunner, however, maintained a steady fire. Meanwhile, Lance Corporal Hall, who carried the M-79, had been wounded by enemy fire. With no air or artillery support, the "blooper" (as the M-79 was affectionately called by the men who used it) was desperately needed to take out the enemy machine gunner. Once again, exposing himself to enemy fire, and with Corporal Collins providing cover, Lance Corporal Murray left his protected position and ran out to retrieve Hall and his M-79.

The firefight continued on into the early evening as the dusk settled in. The two recon teams, now together, remained pinned down by what was estimated to be a force of some 75–125 Viet Cong. The Marines, "alone and outnumbered, six or seven to one, continued to fight back." Later intelligence confirmed that the Marines had fought a Viet Cong company.

The radio operator, Lance Corporal James Shockley, later remembered that he rushed to be near Lieutenant Reasoner, in order for him to "call somebody." Dodging enemy bullets, Shockley was able to reach Reasoner, though, as the radioman recalled, "we never could get comm…. Pipes' [the other radio operator] radio was shot up, and with the PRC-10, the comm was bad with them anyway." Shockley later said that the only way to make a PRC-10 work was to either stand or sit up, something he couldn't do with the enemy machine gunner "pinging away."[34]

At this time, according to Sergeant Major Murray, members of Reasoner's team received word that both Shockley and Reasoner had been hit. Unable to come to the aid of either man, the Reconnaissance Marines continued to fight off the Viet Cong, who once again tried to surround the trapped Marines by going around the village. With Marine helicopters flying above the village, bullets flying, and men shouting orders, Reasoner managed to get word to Lieutenant Henderson to make his way toward the landing zone on the south side of the village. First, the Marines would have to silence the VC machine gun that had them pinned down. This task was accomplished in short order when Private First Class Hahn, with fire direction provided by Corporal Collins, managed to knock out the enemy machine gun with his M-79. Then Hahn, Private First Class Thomas Gatlin, Private First Class Thorace L. Pannell, and Lance Corporal Murray began to low crawl some thirty yards toward both Shockley and Reasoner. By this time, however, and unknown to the Marines attempting to rescue (as they thought) two wounded men, Lieutenant Reasoner was dead, having been killed by enemy fire while trying to help Shockley.

Under the cover of darkness, the Marines managed to retrieve Shockley and Reasoner. At that time, the entire unit moved out of the ditch toward the main road and landing zone. By then, the Marines had been able to establish communication and had called for an extraction. Even as the Marines awaited the helicopters, the Viet Cong continued to pour fire down on them. At 2100 hours, the UH-34s touched down; the wounded Marines and Lieutenant Reasoner's body were loaded on the first helicopter while the rest of the platoon boarded the second. Lieutenant Henderson and a Navy corpsman, Doc Lewis, took the third one.[35]

During the firefight at An My (3), 1st Platoon, Company A, 3rd Force Recon, suffered one dead (Reasoner) and three wounded (Lance Corporals Shockley and Hall and Staff Sergeant Knee). For his bravery under fire and self-sacrifice in attempting to reach Shockley, First Lieutenant Frank Reasoner was posthumously awarded the Medal of Honor. Corporal Collins was awarded the Navy Cross. Second Lieutenant Henderson, Lance Corporal Murray, and Private First Class Gatlin received the Silver Star. In recognition of First Lieutenant Reasoner's bravery at An My, the battalion's main headquarters was named Camp Reasoner.

Tactically and operationally, the fight at An My (3) was significant. Tactically, the Marines held their own against a superior enemy force that the leathernecks not only outfought but also outmaneuvered in the nearly day-long firefight. Marine discipline and, most important, training had been vindicated in this encounter. Operationally, the 1st Platoon, Company A, 3rd Force Reconnaissance Company, effectively tied down an entire enemy company, thereby preventing it from being used in an assault on the nearby fortress of Dai Loc. Extraction of the Reconnaissance Marines from 1st Platoon, Company A, 3rd Force Reconnaissance Company, likewise demonstrated that helicopter pilots were willing to land to extract a recon team despite intense enemy fire. This action served as a precedent for future reconnaissance operations and codified the close working relationship between reconnaissance units and Marine helicopter squadrons that developed over time.

As a result of the fight at An My (3) and other engagements by Marine Reconnaissance units, the size and composition of reconnaissance patrols, especially in the Da Nang area, was reevaluated. It was recognized that patrols had to be large enough to fight their way out of any entrapment and deal with the possibility of an ambush and later North Vietnamese Army (NVA) units.

The argument of "large versus small" patrols continued for some time. Captain J.L. Compton, the leader of a Provisional Reconnaissance Group in January 1966 during Operation "Double Eagle I," opined, "It appears obvious that a platoon is too large to move clandestinely and is too small to take care of itself if hit."[36] In fact, it was not until 1967 that recon units were able to find the "right fit" for patrolling, and this only after much experimentation and many firefights.

Communications Problems Continue to Plague Operations in the Field

Part of finding the "right fit for recon patrols" was the establishment of proper communications in the field. Communication problems continued to hinder the teams' ability to transmit messages to higher headquarters and air units over long ranges as they spread throughout I Corps. This was due largely, as mentioned before, to the types of radios then used by Marine Recon units: the PRC-47 and PRC-10. The PRC-47 was both too large and too bulky for small teams, though it did have sufficient range. By contrast, the PRC-10, while light and easily transportable, did not have the range required by reconnaissance units. Also, both radio sets used batteries at a high rate, requiring Marine Reconnaissance units to carry extra batteries on all patrols. In fact, only "water had a higher precedent" when conducting patrols. One Marine commented, "Patrols were caught up in the simple equation which restricted patrol duration to the number of batteries that could be carried, which in turn was reduced still further by the amount of other equipment and supplies which had to be carried."[37]

The communicator for Team Atlas, Lance Corporal Wayne Breen, calls in a fire mission while in the field. Note the plastic cellophane around the handset (courtesy Sergeant Bill Moss).

The problem with radios was partially resolved in November 1965 with the arrival of the PRC-25 radio and its long-life BA 386 battery, which enabled Marine Reconnaissance units to carry out deeper, long-range duration patrols. Nevertheless, problems with communication continued as recon units were often faced with the "grim reality of heavier loads for longer patrols."[38]

Use and Misuse of Marine Reconnaissance Units

The size and composition of reconnaissance units was often dictated by the type and scope of the mission assigned by battalion, regimental, and division staffs. This in turn led to reconnaissance units performing many missions normally carried out by infantry units. From the time of the Marine landings in Vietnam in March through November 1965, Marine Reconnaissance units performed a variety of missions, some of which were not directly related to reconnaissance. Lieutenant Colonel Roy R. Van Cleve, commanding officer, 3rd Reconnaissance Battalion, stated that his teams were

> being used for any mission that might come up. If you didn't have somebody else to do it, why, give it to recon. They ended up on some raider-type missions; they ended up as CP security frequently on operations. As a result of this, General Walt decided that the reconnaissance effort should be controlled at the reconnaissance battalion level, and that any request for reconnaissance-type missions would come through the Division staff, the Division reconnaissance officer, G-3/2, advising, "Yes, this is a reconnaissance-type mission," or "No, this is not a reconnaissance-type mission." Division would task reconnaissance battalion to provide whatever organization was asking for the necessary forces. People were realizing there was a lot of talent in the Recon Battalion that was not being sed strictly for recon purposes, and the Divisions and MAF were losing a lot of potentially valuable information.[39]

There was also the issue of whether reconnaissance units were "fighters" or "finders."

As previously mentioned, when the first provisional M-Series table of organization was published on February 20, 1958, it stated, "The [Division] Reconnaissance Battalion may be employed as a unit to screen the advance of the Division or execute counter reconnaissance missions." These were clearly defined fighting missions. This precept was later rescinded with the publication of a revised M-1428 table of organization (Division Reconnaissance Battalion), on March 5, 1961, which stated, "The Reconnaissance Battalion ... will be employed to gain intelligence," and "It is not equipped for decisive or sustained combat.... It is not capable of screening or counter reconnaissance missions."[40] The regulation added, however, that reconnaissance units could be reinforced if the division believed that the reconnaissance unit was in danger of being overwhelmed or destroyed, as occurred on July 12, 1965, with the Reasoner patrol at An My (3).

Despite a further revision of the regulation on September 23, 1963, some confusion remained. While reiterating the fact that reconnaissance units were not "equipped for decisive or sustained combat," the regulation allowed that they could be used in the counter-reconnaissance or combat assault role. This revision reflected misunderstanding of the recon mission and utilization of Recon Marines in general. In short, there remained an attitude that Marine Reconnaissance units, because of their demanding training and aggressiveness, were "fighters" as well as "finders."

This misunderstanding led to the idea of using Marine Reconnaissance units as a "raider" force. It was not lost on anybody at the time that Major General Lewis Walt and Colonels Edwin B. Wheeler, Edward P. Dupras, Jr., and Oscar F. Peatross were World War II Raider Battalion veterans. This notion, however, was put to rest by the FMFPac commanding general, Lieutenant General Victor H. Krulak, who saw this approach as a waste of a valuable asset. He insisted that "combat assault operations, including amphibious raids, are missions to be conducted by rifle companies,

Colonel Peatross briefs General William C. Westmoreland (third from right) and General Lam (ARVN) during Operation "Texas," a combined U.S. Marine Corps and Army of the Republic of Vietnam operation that took place northwest of Quang Ngai, during March 20–25, 1966 (Peatross Papers, Marine Corps Recruit Depot, Parris Island, South Carolina).

rather than reconnaissance units." Nonetheless, during the summer and fall of 1964, Company C, 3rd Reconnaissance Battalion, had actually trained as the battalion's "raid" company. The concept of retaining a raider capability in the infantry structure was evident in the summer of 1965 prior to Operation "Starlite," when Colonel Peatross, in keeping with General Krulak's intent, designated and maintained on a rotating basis one company of the 7th Marines as a "raider" force.

Another perspective on the use and "misuse" of reconnaissance units came from Colonel Andrew Finlayson, who was one of the most successful reconnaissance leaders in Vietnam while a lieutenant in 1967–1968 with 1st Force Reconnaissance Company. Colonel Finlayson stated, "The Marine Corps was never really sure how to employ reconnaissance teams and, of course, the missions of battalion recon and force recon were somewhat different (Battalion recon was doctrinally used for close in, that is, under direct fire range, while force was doctrinally supposed to conduct deep reconnaissance). This distinction was rather blurred during the Vietnam War with both recon organizations conducting both missions, although I think force recon was more likely to be employed on the really deep missions."[41]

General Wallace M. Greene, commandant of the Marine Corps; Colonel Oscar F. Peatross (on right); and Major General Louis Walt, III MAG commanding general (foreground) at Da Nang, July 1965 (Peatross Papers, Marine Corps Recruit Depot, Parris Island, South Carolina).

Colonel Finlayson added that the concept of reconnaissance "evolved" during the Vietnam War. "In the early stages, just about all recon missions were surveillance missions (finders) and those teams were told to escape and evade (E and E) based on the doctrine developed when it was thought recon would be employed against the USSR or the People's Republic of China (PRC). The E and E idea was changed since I believe, there were some bad results early on with the teams doing this. Instead, the standard practice became to fight off the enemy or wait for extract helos take the teams out."[42] This was precisely what occurred on numerous occasions in 1965 into early 1966, and it was particularly the case with the Reasoner patrol: a platoon-size recon team fighting off a VC company.

As for the issue over whether recon teams were "finders or fighters," Finlayson said that "I don't think the Corps finally reconciled the 'finders vs. fighters' dilemma. In Vietnam, the commanding generals found that it was difficult to react in a timely manner to much of the information gained by finders since the enemy moved in small groups and commanders were reluctant to risk ground troops against small targets far from friendly lines." According to the published doctrine, from the time Marines landed at Da Nang until the summer of 1966, the tactics of Reconnaissance Marines as they arrived in Vietnam were understandable considering the backgrounds of the commanders—General Walt, a former Raider Battalion commander in World War II, had three regimental commanders who had been

Major General Louis Walt, Commanding General, III Marine Amphibious Force (center); Brigadier General Keith B. McCutcheon, Commanding General, 1st Marine Air Wing (left); and an unnamed Marine colonel in Da Nang, RVN, in summer of 1965 (courtesy U.S. Marine Corps).

platoon commanders in his raider company: Wheeler of 3rd Marines, Dupras of 4th Marines, and Peatross of 7th Marines.[43]

A Matter of Doctrine (1965–1967)

Up to 1965 there was disagreement over how the doctrinal role of Force and Battalion Reconnaissance should evolve. In fact, doctrinal publications of the time reflected the debate that would take place over Recon's battlefield role. FMFM 2-2, *Amphibious Reconnaissance*, clearly dictated a supportive (not combative) role for reconnaissance units. With regard to the Force Recon company, FMFM 2-2 specified, "The company has no offensive capability and is not employed as a tactical unit. That is … it is not assigned tactical missions, objectives, or tactical areas of responsibility."[44] The doctrine did, however, allow for some apparent offensive employment of reconnaissance units. FMFM 6-1, *Marine Division*, and 6-2, *Marine Infantry Regiment*, note a "reconnaissance in force" role as well as a mission of "control and

A map check by Corporal Bill Moss (left) and Lieutenant Corporal Donelle Kegler (right), checking grid coordinates while on patrol (courtesy Cpl. Bill Moss).

adjustment of long-range fires." However, FMFM 8-1, *Special Operations*, clearly stated that because parachute and subsurface entry were connected with raiding, and since these methods were peculiar to Force Recon companies, Force Recon teams could be utilized as raiders. FMFM 8-2, *Counterinsurgency Operations*, while noting that reconnaissance units' mobility provided a commander with a valuable asset by gathering information to conduct operations against guerrillas, also said that such reconnaissance personnel could be employed for attacking small, isolated forces. Recon teams could likewise "conduct limited tactical operations against located guerrilla bands."

In short, the doctrinal debate on how to best employ reconnaissance teams continued well into their deployment to Vietnam. As Colonel Finlayson concluded, "most Marine commanders did not know how to effectively employ recon teams and often misused them or assigned them missions that were not appropriate. They seemed to rely more on signals intelligence and would often disregard or disbelieve recon reports. Not always, but much of the time." He added that from a personal standpoint, it was his experience while leading Team Killer Kane that "recon teams should be more aggressive and attack the enemy whenever a good opportunity presented itself."[45]

STINGRAY—A New Missions Is Born

Despite the employment problems that persisted throughout the remainder of 1965, Major General Lewis W. Walt, III MAF commanding general, realized that reconnaissance units, if properly utilized, were well equipped to locate an enemy who had already established a reputation for blending into the surroundings, a phantom army that was seldom seen armed and concentrated. "Even when VC units were sighted, they were usually on the move, and presented fleeting targets at best. Regular Marine ground formations were too clumsy for this mission; the VC they found generally wanted to be found." As a result, General Walt "decided that since reconnaissance patrols could find the VC, then the patrols should be provided with a means to destroy the enemy."[46] Henceforth, Marine reconnaissance patrols were allowed to call in air and artillery strikes on enemy patrols. After several months of experimentation by reconnaissance patrols in both the Da Nang and the Chu Lai TAORs, the concept was refined and officially adopted in early 1966 as a tactic that came to be known as "STINGRAY." Over the next three years, STINGRAY missions became the standard reconnaissance mission. Indeed, Colonel Finlayson stated, "By the time I was 'in country,' in early 1967, most missions [of recon] were STINGRAY missions."[47]

Operation "Jackstay"—Riverine Operations

Operation "Jackstay" was a counterguerrilla operation involving the 1st Battalion, 5th Marines; a Force Reconnaissance platoon; a twenty-man team from Battalion Recon; two Vietnamese Marine battalions; seventy-three Navy UDT sailors; and fifteen Navy SEALS, led by Navy Commander James Robinson. The operation took place on the Long Than Peninsula in the Rung Sat ("Forest of Death") Special Zone (RSSZ) from March 26 to April 6, 1966.

The RSSZ, a marshy, mangrove swamp south of Saigon, consisted of a dense swamp that covered approximately four hundred square miles and was home to some fifteen thousand Vietnamese clustered in nine villages located on the few dry islands in the area. Travel throughout the RSSZ was primarily by sampan or small boats, as the area had no road system other than a half-completed black-top road on one island built by the French during the 1950s. Streams and rivers in the RSSZ were shallow, narrow, and winding. The area was covered by dense vegetation that "severely limit[ed] access to interior areas" and provided a natural cover for the Viet Cong that operated in the area and acted as an impediment to infantrymen attempting to move inland from the shoreline. Extensive flooding, coupled with high tides, forced the assault force to wade ashore from the rivers only to become mired down in the mud and dense foliage. The enemy-favorable terrain features made the RSSZ an important infiltration route used extensively by the VC. The RSSZ was "looked

The most essential skill Marine Force and Division Reconnaissance acquired was the ability to handle small boats and rubber rafts. Here, Recon Marines train in the use of rubber rafts: (1) Lance Corporal Scott Stout; (2) unknown; (3) Lance Corporal Sean McCarthy; (4) Lance Corporal Joe Koval; (5) Lance Corporal McKenzie (rear paddler) (courtesy Lieutenant Colonel Barry Babin).

Marines charge through the surf as their boat touches the shoreline. Shortly after landing, they established a skirmish line high on the beach to conclude an exercise held off Da Nang, demonstrating their ability to conduct raids from the sea to shore (U.S. Army Photograph A410922).

upon as an impregnable jungle where the VC had complete freedom, by planners in Saigon. Arrival of the combined Marine-Army-Navy team changed this perception as with little augmentation, they had the material, know-how, and will to fight the VC in his sanctuary and on his own terms."[48]

The "Jackstay" concept of operations was to conduct river ambush patrols every other night. Teams would depart late in the day and travel up the river in small fiberglass boats provided by U.S. Army Special Forces.[49] They would arrive at their ambush site with just enough daylight to allow them to hide their boat and then get into position under cover of darkness. The Marines subsequently extended a line passing from man to man; they would use this line to signal enemy numbers and their direction of approach. From an operational standpoint, the endeavor was a success, as the combined American task force prevented enemy boats from moving up and down the river. Gunnery Sergeant Billy M. Donaldson later said, "We were just all over the area. We took the Delta away from those people as long as we were there. Their small craft couldn't move."[50]

Operation "Trailblazer"—The Last of the Large-Scale Recon Operations (October 1965)

Prior to the "merging" of both Force and Division Reconnaissance assets, two companies from the 3rd Reconnaissance Battalion hiked into Happy Valley for Operation "Trailblazer" to conduct a reconnaissance-in-force operation. Their mission was to determine the extent of enemy concentration in the hills west of the Da Nang TAOR. During October 18–24, reconnaissance teams prowled the hills, seeking out the elusive VC. In one firefight, two enemy guerrillas were killed and five enemy base camps were uncovered by the recon teams. The Reconnaissance Marines likewise located and identified an extensive trail network that would aid future reconnaissance missions. Operation "Trailblazer" was the "last of the reconnaissance-in-force operations conducted by 3rd Reconnaissance Battalion as the emphasis began to be placed on the use of smaller patrols that concentrated on patrolling. Henceforth, company-size patrols were the exception not the rule." [51]

Force and Division Reconnaissance Merged

In November 1965, in order to maximize the efforts of both Force and Division Reconnaissance units, III MAF headquarters ordered the merger of both reconnaissance units then in the field in South Vietnam. The combination of Division and Force Recon assets enabled both units to carry out "deep patrols" during surveillance and targeting missions. However, Lieutenant Colonel Babin recalled that a degree of resentment lingered for some time over this action among Force

Reconnaissance Marines, who considered it a diminishment of the Force Reconnaissance mission and an effort on the part of higher headquarters to devalue their specialized training experience.[52]

During the last months of 1965, the 1st Force Reconnaissance Company continued to support various operations with small detachments assigned to battalion and regiment levels. At this time, the company worked as part of the 3rd Reconnaissance Battalion with mixed results and no major engagements.

Operation "Birdwatcher" (December 14–18, 1965)

The "test" for the evolving reconnaissance mission came with Operation "Birdwatcher" in December 1965. Three reconnaissance teams from 1st Force Reconnaissance Company (a total of twenty Marines and CIDG troops), as well as a one-man base defense reaction force, set out from their base camps at Ba To, twenty-six miles south-southwest of Quang Ngai and Camp A-107, which was located at Tra Bong, almost seventeen miles southwest of Chu Lai, located on the upper reaches of the Tra Bong River. The mission was to "determine [the] location, identity, strength, movement, and armament of VC/PAVN units."

On November 27, the company's 2nd Platoon was detached by III MAF to relocate to Special Forces Camp A-106 at Ba To in Quang Ngai Province. The 3rd Platoon followed on December 7, joining Special Forces Camp A-107 at Tra Bong. Both platoons were assigned to assist in Operation "Birdwatcher" with the mission "to gather intelligence about the location of enemy forces through the jungle paths and along the river routes in the interior of the countryside."

As the 2nd Platoon, commanded by Lieutenant J.C. Leaker and Gunnery Sergeant Maurice Jacques, settled into the base camp, General Walt arrived shortly thereafter to brief them. The III MAF commanding general informed the Recon Marines that "the enemy had apparently retreated to the Ba To area to regroup following several battles with the 7th Marine Regiment." General Walt added that a regiment from the North Vietnamese *325th Division* had arrived in Ba To and was set up with storage areas and a hospital unit; it was connected by high-speed trails and thought to be located in a large bowl-shaped valley.[53]

Initially, patrols based out of Ba To "resulted in contact with large enemy units armed with automatic weapons." Because of the presence of larger-than-normal enemy units, the decision was made to increase the size of the four-man recon patrols. Hence, the Marine Recon teams were augmented by three CIDG soldiers (local tribesmen) per team. In addition to their increased firepower, the CIDG soldiers brought a wealth of local knowledge of the surrounding terrain to assist the Marines.

On December 14, three four-man teams of 2nd Platoon, each with three CIDG soldiers and reinforced with a forty-two man CIDG reaction force, deployed to a kidney-shaped hill almost five miles from Ba To. Two listening posts were placed on the fingers of the hill of the grassy slope of this hill.

From their "harbor site" atop the hill, the reconnaissance force sighted some seventy enemy soldiers over the next two days. By remaining in the same location for two days in order to observe enemy activity, the team allowed the VC and NVA soldiers to pinpoint their location. By 1730 on December 16, all of the patrols had returned to the hill to prepare for their move back to Ba To, though they were delayed due to a dense fog that had settled in over their camp. This delay proved fatal, as the VC, an hour and a half later at 1900, after having pinpointed the reconnaissance team's location, launched a "walking mortar barrage" that served as preparation for an all-out assault by some 150–200 men, which came shortly after as enemy machine gun fire raked the hillside.

In the battle that ensued, the Marines, along with U.S. Army Special Forces Staff Sergeant West and CIDG and ARVN forces, split into small groups as they fought off the enemy attack. The Marines, led by Gunnery Sergeant Jacques, withdrew into a small perimeter, taking advantage of the concealment offered by the local banana leaves. Sergeant Major Jacques later recalled:

> We had moved about three thousand yards away from our hiding place before I thought it would be safe to rest. I had put the team in [a] tight 360-degree defensive position when I heard the sound of brush breaking nearby. I thought to myself, "This is it." I've done everything I can think of to get my men away from the NVA, but they don't give up. I had one magazine left, but I wasn't about to let those bastards take us alive. I pulled the last magazine of .30 caliber rounds from its pocket and struck it with my carbine and took up the slack in the trigger. One of the CIDG soldiers who was traveling in our group, placed the fingers of one hand over his mouth, gesturing for me to be quiet, and then placed his other hand over the barrel of my rifle, signaling for me not to shoot. Together we sat, waiting and watching for the approaching sound to take form.[54]

Fortunately, the approaching sounds turned out to be two CIDG soldiers who had happened on Jacques' position.

Moving out, Jacques' party then came across an enemy trail. Disregarding the standing operating procedure that warned against using an enemy trail, Jacques' force moved out along the path and came across two Marines who had been separated during the assault earlier that evening. With the wind shielding the movement of Jacques' party, the force of Marines, CIDG, and Nung headed toward Ba To. To act as a point for their movement, Jacques placed two Vietnamese stragglers out in front. Jacques thought that by doing this, the NVA "would see two Vietnamese approaching on their trail, [and] it just might give us enough time to break through any ambush." The Marines moved out and reached Ba To without incident at 1400 on December 17.

One Marine, Corporal Donald M. Woo, who had been captured by the NVA and managed to escape not once but two times, and had been given up for dead, arrived at the Special Forces camp with two enemy soldiers he had taken prisoner and forced at knife point to carry him to Ba To. Overall, the patrol suffered fourteen dead, including three Marines, the Special Forces staff sergeant, the Vietnamese lieutenant patrol leader, and nine CIDG troops, whose bodies were recovered several days later on December 21.

As a result of the firefight at Ba To and several other encounters, a long-standing Force Reconnaissance operational procedure was suspended. Previously, Recon Marines were trained to break contact on being attacked and to split up, with each member making for the extraction point on his own. After the fight at Ba To, force patrols went in together, stayed together, fought together, and were extracted together.

As nearly a year of combat operations came to an end, Force and Battalion Reconnaissance had tested, discarded, and adopted a whole range of procedures to govern patrol operations during the next several years of combat in Vietnam. Marine operations in 1965, in fact, became a "testbed" for future operations in the Republic of Vietnam. The effect they would have on Force and Battalion Reconnaissance was significant, as it set the pace of operations for the remainder of Marine involvement in Vietnam.

6

"The Year of the Offensive"

*1st Marine Reconnaissance Battalion in Action
(1966–1967)*

Even as the Marines of Company A, 3rd Force Recon, fought the Viet Cong, 1st Force Reconnaissance continued to carry out its mission in support of Marine infantry and III MAF headquarters. Throughout 1966, the Marines of 1st Force Reconnaissance Company, 1st and 3rd Reconnaissance Battalions, conducted extensive patrols in and around the Da Nang and Chu Lai TAORs, primarily in Happy Valley and Charlie Ridge, in support of operations by the 1st and 3rd Marine Divisions as well as III MAF. Indeed, as combat operations in I Corps intensified, Marine Reconnaissance units continued to conduct extensive patrols deep inside enemy territory in support of Marine combat operations against the VC and NVA.

During Operation "Double Eagle I," which lasted from January 21 to February 16, four platoons from Force Recon company combined with Company B of the 3rd Recon Battalion to form a Provisional Reconnaissance Group (PRG). The mission of the PRG was to establish observation posts and monitor any enemy activity, most notably of the *325A PAVN Division* (People's Army of Vietnam [North]), which had been operating along the borders of Quang Ngai and Binh Dinh Provinces. Recon activities by the group were in support of a joint Amy and Marine operation that covered most of I and II Corps.

During "Double Eagle I," the PRG "employed 35 team-size OP's, 5 platoon patrols, and two company patrols." Reconnaissance Marines had 153 sightings, totaling some 919 VC or NVA and 400 VC suspects. On thirty-one separate incidents, these sightings resulted in twenty-three VC KIA—fourteen by small arms and the rest by supporting arms (mortars, artillery and close air support). Recon Marines destroyed five tons of rice, five hundred pounds of salt, and sixty gallons of kerosene and captured numerous documents and equipment.

"War by Detachments": Reconnaissance Operations (January–December 1966)

Throughout 1966, reconnaissance units were frequently detached to support Marines as well as joint and combined operations with the U.S. Army, U.S. Navy and ARVN. For Marine Reconnaissance, 1966 was a "war by detachments," as both Force and Battalion Recon carried out numerous patrols in and around Da Nang and throughout I Corps (and bordering II Corps) in operations with the U.S. Army.

Beginning in January 1966, a team from 1st Force Reconnaissance Company conducted a two-day reconnaissance and surveillance operation (January 21–22, 1966) led by First Lieutenant R.F. Parker. Based at the Ba To Special Forces base camp, the team consisted of two officers and twelve enlisted men, including a Navy corpsman. As Lieutenant Parker noted in his after-action report, the firefight that ensued was typical of the engagements his team (code-named "Hateful") fought against the VC and NVA that winter. During the two-day operation, Hateful, after a brief though furious firefight with a force of some thirty to fifty VC and NVA, managed to break contact after a harrowing night at their base camp, as enemy units unsuccessfully attempted to penetrate the recon patrol's position. The Marines suffered two MIA (First Lieutenant James T. Egan and Corporal Edwin R. Grissett), though they had no KIA or WIA. Lieutenant Parker's team managed to kill seven to nine VC in the engagement. Lieutenant Parker noted in his after-action report that their corpsman alone killed five or six of the enemy after being briefly cut off from the rest of the unit. During this operation, Parker employed the newly adopted STINGRAY tactics and managed to call in 150 rounds of artillery on suspected enemy positions.[1] The aggressive nature and use of supporting arms by Hateful became typical of reconnaissance teams shifting from the traditional clandestine reconnaissance missions to the "economy-of-force" patrol concept.

As for the use of the new economy-in-force concept, Lieutenant Colonel Babin commented,

> My training in 5th Force Reconnaissance Company before getting orders for Vietnam in September 1967 emphasized the importance of clandestine insertion, patrolling operations and extraction. Ideally, the enemy should never know the team was ever there. When I started running patrols in northern I CORPS with 3rd Force Reconnaissance in February 1968, this secretive nature of reconnaissance operations was the prevalent operating concept. That's not to say that targets of opportunity were not engaged, because lucrative targets to include prisoner snatches, weren't ignored, but when discussing the difference, it was not uncommon to hear a biblical reference: "If you live by the sword, you die by the sword." Late Spring 1968, with Operation PEGASUS, the company shifted from eight-man patrols to running, almost exclusively, four-man patrols until I rotated on November 2, 1968. Smaller teams with less individual firepower were more vulnerable in a contact, but the smaller number created a smaller, less visible foot print, and we retained the ability to call in artillery and air. I recall that Warning Orders would come down as either KEYHOLE or STINGRAY missions. However, I don't recall ever getting a KEYHOLE warning order that did not have a secondary Stingray mission.[2]

In a follow-up operation, dubbed "Double Eagle II" (February 19–27, 1966), teams from 1st Force Reconnaissance Company established observation posts (OPs) and conducted patrols in support of the operation. Marines from 1st Force Reconnaissance reported 29 enemy sightings of some 130 VC/NVA as well as 50 VC suspects (VCS).

In the aftermath of Operation "Oregon" (March 19–23, 1966), a search-and-destroy mission in the Phu Bai TAOR, Phu Bai was reinforced with two reconnaissance companies (B and D) from the 3rd Reconnaissance Battalion. On March 28, they were designated Provisional Reconnaissance Group B, under the command of Captain James L. Compton. By March 31, the Marine forces at Phu Bai numbered nearly 6,400 men, including four infantry battalions, a helicopter squadron, the artillery battalion, the Provisional Reconnaissance Group, and other supporting units. A force composed of Marines from the 1st Battalion, 4th Marines, was assigned as a quick reaction force for the Marine Reconnaissance teams operating northwest of Phu Bai.

March was a slow month for 1st Force Reconnaissance, which spent most of the time absorbing and training new replacements, as well as practicing and honing traditional reconnaissance techniques such as rubber boat training and insertion, along with parachute training. However, in April, 1st Force Recon Company headquarters moved from Da Nang to Hue/Phu Bai, to Khe Sanh, and then back to Da Nang. Finally, they ended up at Chu Lai. Two platoons were put under operational control of 4th Marines at Hue/Phu Bai on April 11. The company headquarters, with the other two platoons, relocated from Da Nang to Hue/Phu Bai on April 15 and took command of Company B (Rein.), 3rd Reconnaissance Battalion. Designated as Reconnaissance Group Bravo, they provided reconnaissance operations to support 4th Marines in the Hue/Phu Bai area. During the same month, platoons from 1st Force Reconnaissance were spread throughout I Corps in support of Marine rifle battalions from the 1st and 4th Marines as well as 3rd Force Reconnaissance Battalions, where they conducted observation and surveillance missions, effectively employing STINGRAY procedures against enemy positions.

Shortly after 1st Force Reconnaissance Company consolidated at Hue/Phu Bai, the 1st Platoon (call sign "NIGHT STICKER"), on May 16–17, 1966, was inserted by helicopter a little more than a mile west of Hue City, where they set up an observation post and radio relay station on Hill 679 near Nui Bai Cay Tar. Six hours into the patrol, enemy contact was made when Corporal R.G. Cotton spotted several VC soldiers moving toward his position. The Marine corporal opened fire on the approaching enemy, killing one before he himself was killed as he attempted to return to the OP. HM2 L.W. Carper, the patrol's Navy corpsman, was likewise mortally wounded as he attempted to treat Corporal Cotton. Several days later, the 2nd Platoon (call sign "PRIMUS") was inserted into the same location and met heavy enemy fire immediately after the helicopter departed. This contact resulted in four Marine WIA and at least three VC KIA. The patrol was extracted by helicopter after only 15 minutes on the ground.[3]

Groundwork for Operation "Hastings"

By late spring of 1966, MACV became increasingly concerned about NVA infiltration across the DMZ. Subsequently, General William Westmoreland, via III

MAF, directed that reconnaissance operations be greatly expanded in northern I Corps. An NVA soldier surrendered to the ARVN on May 19 and stated that he was part of an advance reconnaissance unit for the *324B Division* infiltrating across the DMZ to operate in Quang Tri Province. The information provided by the enemy soldier was confirmed when an NVA lieutenant surrendered on July 9. In response, a 1st Force Reconnaissance Company headquarters element and its second platoon traveled from Hue/Phu Bai to Dong Ha as Task Unit Charlie, with Major Colby (Commanding Officer, 1st Force Reconnaissance Company) designated as commander of the task force (he was also commander of Task Force Bravo). The task unit included infantry and artillery as well as the reconnaissance units.

The Marines experienced an intense operational environment in which teams were frequently returned to the bush shortly after finishing the previous patrol, sometimes even on the same day. Teams made contact more often than they didn't and engaged platoon-size units of the *304th NVA Division*, some patrols lasting less than an hour before being extracted.

By this point in the war, the Marines in I Corps were engaging regular NVA units. The war along the DMZ, in fact, had become more conventional in nature as NVA units from the *324B Division* crossed the border and infiltrated into South Vietnam via the DMZ with the objective of overrunning Quang Tri Province. In order to verify this enemy movement, the 1st Force Reconnaissance Company—along with elements of the 3rd Reconnaissance Battalion, E Company, 2nd Battalion, 4th Marines, and a battery of artillery from 3rd Battalion, 12th Marines—were moved into the region just south of the DMZ. This task force, renamed "Recon Group Bravo" and commanded by Major Dwain A. Colby, was tasked with locating, pinpointing, and (if the opportunity arose) calling in artillery on the unsuspecting enemy.

Within a few weeks, the tempo of patrols increased tenfold, as Recon Group Bravo was, in fact, repeatedly coming across platoon-size enemy units, thereby necessitating the dispatch of patrols within hours of each other in order to keep the flow of intelligence to 1st and 3rd Division as well as III MAF staffs. During the period of July 1–15, 1966, Recon Group Bravo conducted eighteen patrols, which resulted in the capture of two NVA soldiers, confirming reports that the *324B Division* was in Quang Tri Province. The information gathered by the Marine Reconnaissance teams led to the initiation of a major offensive designated Operation "Hastings." More to the point was the fact that Recon had proven its true value as an intelligence-gathering force.

Operation "Hastings," which commenced on July 15 and ended on August 3, resulted in 882 enemy KIA, MIA, and WIA. It was (much like "Starlite" the previous August) one of the largest and most successful Marine operations of the Vietnam War. In one instance, which validated the STINGRAY concept, a five-man Marine Reconnaissance team located a 250-man NVA force and called in an artillery strike that resulted in the deaths of fifty NVA soldiers from that force. A follow-up close air strike called in by the same team resulted in the death of the remaining two hundred men.

The frenetic pace of patrols continued into July. Due to the increased enemy activity, Recon Group Bravo was reinforced, and the command group relocated to Cam Lo, with Task Force Delta, which was tasked with executing Operation "Hastings." From there they coordinated reconnaissance support for "Hastings." The intelligence and support provided by Marine Reconnaissance proved crucial to the operation's overall success.

More important was the fact that Operation "Hastings" was a turning point in Marine Reconnaissance's war in Vietnam, as General Walt began to realize the importance of the STINGRAY concept. As Lieutenant Colonel Babin commented:

> Earlier reconnaissance efforts that had located enemy formations and principal enemy lines of communication, influenced the development of the ground scheme of maneuver. Throughout the operation, reconnaissance patrols attrited the enemy. On one occasion, a five-man team called in artillery on about 250 NVA some 400 meters from their position. Killing about 50 with artillery, they called in fixed wing air on the remaining NVA with devastating effect from 2,000 pound bombs: an estimated 200 additional NVA KIA. HASTINGS came to an official close on August 3rd. The *324B Division* ceased to have an effective presence in South Vietnam. Significantly for the reconnaissance Marines was General Walt's official recognition of their efficacy and their deadly coordination of supporting arms by designating their patrols as "STINGRAY Patrols."[4]

The significance of "Hastings" to Marine Reconnaissance in the context of the STINGRAY concept was further emphasized by Babin, who wrote:

> it was finally realized that the need for small, mobile teams that could inflict a great deal of damage on the enemy, because they were lighter, faster, and less obvious than regular line infantry, could be met by reconnaissance units. It was a triumph over long held FMFM 2-2 doctrine that the Force Recon Company had "no offensive capability and is not employed as a tactical unit...." The point was driven home immediately after HASTINGS the end of July 1966:
>
> Team Primness, under the leadership of Sgt. Orest Bishko, was sent out to find and destroy these small elements [left after Operation "Hastings"].
>
> The team inserted by Huey in the early morning. To minimize their signature, Force Recon teams were only four to six men. This team consisted of only Sgt. Bishko, Cpl. William McWilliams, the team scout, LCpl. Thomas Moran, the radio operator, Cpl. Joe Miller, the Tail-End-Charlie, and a Marine infantry officer, Bing West, serving as the secondary radioman. West had been ordered to go along on a Force Recon patrol that intended to engage the enemy by indirect fire, in order to analyze the action and report on the concept's feasibility.
>
> Once off the bird, the Marines ran into the brush and headed uphill, onto the ridge. The next two days were a combination of moving through steep terrain and thick brush, hiding in OPs, watching and listening, and trying to find the enemy. Several times they heard the VC making noise, but were unable to find them.
>
> On the second day, they saw their first VC. McWilliams and Miller were close enough, and only hidden by tall grass, that they thought they would be seen, but the VC didn't notice them, and they crept back to join the rest of the team on the other side of the ridge. That evening, they spotted enough enemy to attempt calling fire, but the angle the 105mm howitzers had to fire, coupled with high winds, was throwing the fire off. Bishko called off any more fire missions until morning.
>
> From their hide the next morning, they heard what sounded like something close to a

company of VC in a grove below them. Bishko called for one round of white phosphorus in adjust. The first round was off, and didn't seem to alert the Vietnamese. Bishko adjusted and called for fire for effect.

As the shells started to rain down on the grove, VC began to pour out, trying to cross the stream to the west of the grove. Bishko continued adjusting fire on them, bringing down volley after volley. At one point he estimated at least 200 VC in the open. The artillery was smashing down trees and Vietcong with every salvo.

As the artillery pounded the encampment, several dozen armed VC charged out of the kill zone and up the hill to the Marines' right flank, where they began searching for the team. Their commander had evidently figured out that someone had to be directing the artillery. Team Primness stayed in place long enough to continue to direct fires until they could see no one moving below. Then, fully aware of the enemy element hunting for them, Bishko got his team up and they ran down the back side of the ridge, where they took cover in a streambed.

During the fire missions, the Company S-3, Capt. William Ostrie, had called an Air Force observation plane in over the team to provide support. As the Vietcong searched for the Recon Marines, getting closer and closer, Bishko made contact with the observation plane, establishing their position. The FO then called in an F-8 Crusader to drop bombs on the advancing North Vietnamese.

The first strike was so close that it rocked the Recon team. Bishko called up that the pilot had missed, but the FO told him that it had been a direct hit. There were no longer any enemy troops behind them. It was just their first taste of danger close with two 2000 pound bombs.

The patrol moved out to the east, looking for another good observation point. They didn't find one, but Miller and McWilliams were watching their back trail, and in the late afternoon, spotted more North Vietnamese following them. The enemy wasn't trying to be stealthy, and Moran called in more artillery, destroying the trailing force. That was the last of the enemy they saw.

The next morning, they linked up with the Huey to bring them out. They had just executed the most successful artillery strikes of the war thus far. West's report was well received, and the Stingray patrols program was born. From then on, Force Recon teams would haunt the North Vietnamese, calling down artillery and bombs wherever they could find them.[5]

During the month of August 1966, 1st Force Reconnaissance Company conducted 38 patrols with 54 enemy sightings of some 986 NVA/VC. During one of these engagements, a recon team triggered another major battle with the NVA and VC known as Operation "Prairie."

Operation "Prairie," which began immediately after the conclusion of "Hastings" on August 3, 1966, and was conducted by the 3rd Marine Division, along with the 1st Force Reconnaissance Company, had the mission of interdicting and destroying the NVA's *324B Division*, which had by now crossed the DMZ into South Vietnam. Reconnaissance's mission was to "determine the size, disposition, and location of the VC/NVA units and [determine] their infiltration routes and to engage targets of opportunity with supporting arms." In order to accomplish this task, Marine Reconnaissance units utilized the same concepts successfully employed during "Hastings," whereby five-man recon teams were inserted by UH-1 "Huey" helicopters for missions that lasted anywhere from three to six days. It is important to note that Operation "Prairie" was the first time that all six platoons from 1st Force Reconnaissance Company worked together during the same operation.

Operation "Prairie" (August 8–October 4, 1966)

On August 6, 1966, Team Groucho Marx launched the first STINGRAY reconnaissance mission during Operation "Prairie." Led by Captain Howard V. Lee, the reconnaissance team, inserted by Huey UH-1 helicopters, landed four miles south of the DMZ and thirteen miles west of Dong Ha, four clicks north-northeast of the Rockpile, and began a grueling three-day operation in an attempt to locate what was reported to be a sizeable enemy force. This was the first significant encounter that involved a STINGRAY patrol and touched off a four-month battle with the NVA.

During the next two nights, the Marine Reconnaissance team (officially known as Team 61) observed and called in artillery strikes against suspected enemy positions. On the morning of August 8, a patrol member detected enemy movement fifty meters in front of the team's position. The patrol leader called for an artillery strike at Cam Lo to fire on a suspected enemy base camp. The Marine Reconnaissance likewise observed ten to fifteen NVA troops moving into skirmish line one hundred meters away from their positions, apparently trying to locate the American patrol. The team leader, Staff Sergeant Billy M. Donaldson, radioed Major Dwain A. Colby, commanding officer of the 1st Force Reconnaissance Company, and reported the situation. Major Colby sent a pair of gunships to cover the patrol and asked Staff Sergeant Donaldson "if they thought we could get some prisoners out there if I sent in a reaction force. He answered in the affirmative and said that there was a landing zone within 150 meters of them."[6] An infantry platoon from Company E, 2nd Battalion, 4th Marines ("The Magnificent Bastards"), shortly thereafter arrived and linked up with the Reconnaissance Marines. The Marines then moved to a nearby hilltop, where they established a defensive perimeter.

A squad sent down the hill to check out the area found a series of freshly dug foxholes in and around the streambed (a typical North Vietnamese tactic), along with a few crossbow-type booby traps. After locating the enemy position, the Marines returned to report their findings. Captain Lee radioed headquarters and requested extraction. Shortly thereafter, four helicopters arrived. As the first helicopter took off at 1600, the NVA opened fire with automatic weapons from a position three to four hundred meters from the patrol. An hour later, thirty to forty enemy soldiers assaulted the hill from the north within hand grenade range. This attack lasted nearly an hour and half until contact was again broken off by the NVA at 1830.

A half hour later, 1830, the NVA initiated another assault, again with thirty to forty soldiers. As darkness swept over the hill, a helicopter was able to land and bring ten Marines along with ammunition and Captain Howard V. Lee, Company E's commander, who assumed command of the hilltop position.

Darkness, however, did not deter the enemy, who within thirty minutes of nightfall launched a furious three-sided attack on the hill, throwing grenades and peppering the Marines' position with heavy automatic fire. Once again, the Marines repulsed the assault with concentrated and accurate rifle fire. By this time, however,

"Fire Team" members of "F" Company, 2nd Battalion, 5th Regiment, wade through a waist-high stream covered by a dense jungle about four hundred meters south of the DMZ during Operation "Prairie" (USMC Photograph #A187937).

ammunition was running low. In addition, Captain Lee, who had recently arrived, had been severely wounded in this attack.

At 1930, fighting once again flared up, and Major Colby, back at base camp, realized that it would be impossible to extract the Marines until the next morning. Meanwhile, a gunship manned by an all-volunteer crew arrived with additional ammunition, but the rotor blade of the helicopter was hit by enemy fire, which disabled the vehicle. The crew of the stricken aircraft dashed out before it crashed and managed to pull off all of the machine guns and all the ammunition; they joined the rest of the defenders in the perimeter. There were no more serious assaults, although movement was heard in the area fifty to one hundred meters from the patrol's position. According to a Navy corpsman, "The rest of the night was quiet…. You could hear them [the NVA] drag off the bodies. Some would come right up to the brush line and just start talking. Every time we shot at them another grenade would come in. They were trying to feel our positions."[7]

By this time, Captain Lee, who had been seriously wounded in the face and his back and legs, turned over command to Major Vincil W. Hazelbaker, one of the helicopter pilots. Prior to Major Hazelbaker's arrival, Lieutenant Colonel Arnold

E. Bench, the battalion commander from 2/4, had radioed Captain Lee, who, due to the severity of his wounds, was unable to talk. Corporal Bacta, from 1st Force Recon Company, who was manning the radios, replied that both Major Hazelbaker (who was then unconscious) and Captain Lee (who had lost a considerable amount of blood) were "unable to do anything," while he (Bacta) had been "calling in supporting air and artillery" on the NVA. When Lieutenant Colonel Bench asked Corporal Bacta who was in charge, the Marine corporal answered, "I am."[8]

Eventually, daylight brought relief, as Company F (from 2/4) arrived along with the battalion command group, as well as the remainder of Company E, which soon fanned out and conducted an extensive sweep of the area. Much to their surprise, the Marines discovered that the NVA had melted into the surrounding jungle. In their wake, they left thirty-seven bodies strewn about the perimeter, most within fifteen meters of the Marines' position on the hill. Drag marks and blood trails revealed a higher enemy body count. Later in the day, an aerial observer spotted an enemy column hurrying from the area carrying twenty-seven more bodies. The pilot then called in an artillery strike on the NVA, which wiped out the entire formation.

The fight by Team Groucho Marx and Marines from Company E, as well as the downed Marine aviators from HMM-161, resulted in some one hundred NVA KIA. Marines suffered five KIA (four from Company E and the UH-34 gunner from HMM-161) and twenty-seven WIA (one from 1st Force Reconnaissance Company, fifteen from Company E, and the remainder from the MAG-16 helicopter crews and three pilots).

For bravery in leading the Marines in the firefight, Captain Lee was awarded the Medal of Honor. Major Hazelbaker was awarded the Navy Cross for assuming command from the wounded Captain Lee. Corporal Bacta, whose "outstanding and extraordinary work in continuing his communications while at the same time assuming partial command of troops during the time when the persons in charge were unable to function," was likewise recommended for the Navy Cross. However, Bacta's award was downgraded to a Silver Star due to a disciplinary action when he "commandeered a jeep illegally" while on leave in Da Nang.

Major Hazelbaker again came to the assistance of Reconnaissance Marines when, on October 23, 1966, he extracted, under poor weather conditions and heavy enemy fire, a recon team commanded by Staff Sergeant Larry Kester. Braving low cloud cover, limited visibility, and mountainous valleys, Major Hazelbaker managed to land his helicopter as the Marines on the ground laid down a barrage of rifle grenades and automatic weapons fire, enabling the Huey to extract the team.

Operations with the Special Landing Force: Deckhouse IV (September 15–17, 1966)

During an operation with the Special Landing Force composed of the 1st Battalion, 26th Marines (led by Lieutenant Colonel Anthony A. Monti), a platoon from the 3rd Reconnaissance Battalion encountered an NVA company five miles north of Dong Ha while reconnoitering the southwest portion of the objective area south of the DMZ in search of the infiltration points as well as the *90th NVA Regiment*, part of the enemy's *324B Division*. The well-camouflaged NVA soldiers, moving down a trail in single file, nearly "bumped" into the Reconnaissance Marines. Shortly thereafter, both the Marine Reconnaissance platoon and the NVA opened fire simultaneously. Outnumbered, the Reconnaissance Marines called for help. Within minutes, Marine helicopters hovered overhead to evacuate the platoon. Unfortunately, heavy enemy ground fire prevented them from landing. Five helicopters were hit and two crewmen wounded in the abortive attempt.

At this point, the reconnaissance team called in for supporting arms, which included a battery of 107mm "howtars" (a 107mm howitzer mounted on a pack howitzer chassis) that "pounded the area with continuous fire as Marine F4 Phantom B jets from Marine Air Group—11 (MAG-11), bombed, strafed, and rocketed the enemy positions which allowed the helicopters to land and extract the reconnaissance platoon under cover of supporting arms." [9]

During the two-hour engagement, the Marine Reconnaissance patrol suffered one KIA, six WIA, and one MIA. Prior to their extraction, the Marines attempted to locate the missing man, but enemy fire forced them to give up the search. Later on, the reconnaissance team claimed it had killed at least nine NVA and estimated that at least thirty more NVA were killed by supporting arms.

The 1st Force Reconnaissance Company's support of Operation "Prairie," one of the largest single battles engaged in by Marine Reconnaissance in Vietnam to date, was concluded on November 17, 1966, having made 170 sightings of 2,023 NVA/VC and engaged in 41 contacts, with 73 enemy confirmed KIA by small arms and 57 "probables" killed by small arms; 14 confirmed KIA by artillery, with 168 "probables"; 26 reportedly killed by air strikes; and 2 prisoners captured. During Operation "Prairie," Marine Reconnaissance teams called in 144 artillery strikes along with 27 air strikes. Friendly casualties resulted in nine WIA and no KIA.[10]

Teams from 3rd Reconnaissance Battalion during Operation "Prairie," which operated out of the Khe Sanh base camp and patrolled out to a maximum of approximately ten thousand meters, "pushed the envelope for the 'deep reconnaissance mission.'"[11] Artillery support came from the 105mm and 155mm howitzers that had respective ranges of 11,000 and 14,600 meters. At the end of this three-month-long operation, 1st Battalion, 3rd Marines, was withdrawn while one infantry company and one platoon for 3rd Force Reconnaissance Company, along with supporting artillery, remained and patrolled the area, many times out of the range of the artillery.

Major B.G. Lowrey, commanding officer of 1st Force Reconnaissance Company, noted in his after-action report for "Prairie":

> Operation Prairie was extremely beneficial to the 1st Force Reconnaissance Company. This operation in conjunction with Operation Hastings represented the first time in Force Recon

history that a Force Recon Company conducted an extensive reconnaissance operation with company headquarters and all platoons present. Unfortunately, no parachute entry was conducted therefore it was unknown how effective is the units parachute entry capability. Limited parachute training was conducted concurrently during the operation and did not interfere with the day-to-day operations … the employment of the small reconnaissance team proved successful and in keeping with the theories developed by this unit during the ten years of training. It is felt that one of the most significant advances made in patrolling techniques was the attempt to employ CS gas as a standard defensive and offensive weapon of the small patrol. Subsequent to Operation Prairie the unit has continued to explore this technique with continuing good results.[12]

By the end of 1966, with the successful conclusion of both "Hastings" and "Prairie," 1st Force Reconnaissance Company and 3rd Force Reconnaissance Battalion had "become an integral part of Marine operations in Vietnam." Indeed, Marine Reconnaissance teams had become a "lethal punch," not only conducting surveillance missions and seeking out and reporting enemy movements but, in fact, killing the enemy as well.

After Operations "Hastings" and "Prairie," reconnaissance-in-force efforts continued with the same general mission to "determine [the] size, disposition, and location of VC/NVA units and infiltration routes [and e]ngage targets of opportunity with supporting arms." The concept was to insert small patrols, usually five-man teams, by a UH-1E in order to conduct ground reconnaissance and surveillance for three to six days.

By December 1966, Marine Reconnaissance teams were conducting deeper long-range reconnaissance patrols. Occasionally, larger-than-normal formations of enemy soldiers were observed moving south. During Operation "Sierra," a patrol from 3rd Force Reconnaissance Company, on December 26, 1966, "counted over 200 VC, clad in gray and khaki uniforms with rifles and packs, and moving in groups of four- and five-man teams," entering a village, where they changed into black pajamas and departed in groups ranging from eight to ten men. A similar patrol conducted by a team from 1st Force Reconnaissance Company during "Sierra" counted 230 enemy soldiers during a 44-hour period.

7

"Anatomy of a Reconnaissance Patrol"

"Initially, Marine Reconnaissance patrols consisted of anywhere from eight to fifteen Marines." Lieutenant Colonel Babin emphasized that as Recon's missions evolved, "patrols normally consisted of anywhere from 4- to 5-man teams to joint or combined platoon sized units." Key to the patrol size was duration and mission: establishing a patrol base, setting up an observation post, reconnaissance-in-force, clandestine information gathering (KEYHOLE) and/or enemy attrition (STINGRAY). As an understanding of reconnaissance patrols' unique and efficient abilities to satisfy the information needs of I Corps commanders evolved to a level of "reliance" by the end of 1966, reconnaissance patrols in 1967 (and to the end of Marine combat involvement in Vietnam) were primarily focused on KEYHOLE and STINGRAY missions. "1st Force Reconnaissance Company and First Reconnaissance Battalion, operating in southern I CORPS, continued to occasionally be tasked with operating out of, or establishing, an observation post/patrol base, while 3rd Force Reconnaissance Company and 3rd Reconnaissance Battalion, operating in northern I CORPS, operated almost exclusively with the now *traditional* reconnaissance patrol."[1]

All reconnaissance patrols started with a warning order being issued to the patrol leader. The warning order outlined the mission, the coordinates, and other pertinent information on the terrain that he would have to know prior to the start of the mission. Some warning orders were more detailed than others and might contain instructions on the weapons to be carried, special geared to be taken along by team members, and a detailed schedule of events to take place up to and during the insertion.[2]

Once the warning order was issued, the patrol leader conducted a pre-inspection of his team to determine their fitness and health for the forthcoming mission. Team members were likewise screened in order to ensure that each man was mentally able to concentrate on the mission at hand. Those members who expressed personal problems or other issues that might distract their attention were left behind. Lieutenant Colonel Babin noted, "This was unusual, and due to the intensity of operations teams were sometimes fleshed out with Marines of dubious professional credentials, such as recently arrived Marines and Marines from company or battalion support sections." Babin went on to say, "Most patrol leaders maintained a written or mental

Sergeant Berwick "Barry" Babin after coming from a patrol with 3rd Force Reconnaissance Company in 1968 (courtesy Lieutenant Colonel Barry Babin).

patrol checklist that he would adjust depending on the mission. Time permitting and based on the experience of his team, patrol leaders would spend time assisting team members prepare weapons, equipment, uniform and supplies. Those items … remained essentially unchanged throughout the war."[3]

The patrol checklist contained all the items that individual members (and the team as a whole) were to carry on the mission. Items were added or discarded according to the nature of the mission. As mentioned previously, reconnaissance teams prior to November 1965 carried the M3A1 "grease gun." In November 1965, Reconnaissance Marines carried the M-14 and later M-16 assault rifles. Other members carried the M-60 machine gun or M-79 grenade launcher. Officers, NCOs, corpsmen, and radiomen carried the .45 caliber pistol. All Marines and Navy personnel carried the K-Bar fighting knife, fragmentation and smoke grenades, flares, and weapon-cleaning gear. On some patrols, claymore mines were carried. Radiomen carried the PRC-25 (or later PRC-77), as well as the PRC-93 or RT-10A survival radio. After Operation "Prairie," recon teams carried two CS grenades in order to facilitate a quick evasion and extraction by incapacitating the enemy with tear gas. After "Prairie," all Marine Recon team members carried a M7A2 gas mask.

Once the mission and area to be patrolled were issued, the patrol leader conducted an overflight of the area where the team was to be inserted. Two landing zones (LZs) were selected, while a third one was chosen to be a "false insertion" landing zone in order to prevent a compromise of the intended LZ. During the insertion, the helicopters carrying the team would first fly to the false LZ in order to deceive any VC attempting to ambush the team as it was inserted. An extraction LZ was likewise selected during this overflight.

"Usually, the day prior to the patrol, the patrol leader would make sure his on-calls were transmitted to artillery, issue his five-paragraph order and conduct a preliminary personnel inspection to ensure team members were getting supplies, weapons and equipment they needed for the patrol. Day of patrol, a final personnel inspection was conducted before the helicopters arrived. The pilots would get briefed by the patrol leader. Ideally company or battalion staff would assist in the brief, but this was not always possible due to number and frequency of patrols."[4]

Insertion and Extraction of a Marine Recon Team

Both the insertion and the extraction of a Marine Reconnaissance team often proved challenging. Colonel Andrew Finlayson (who led both Killer Kane and later Swift Scout) recalled that a team's insertion and extraction depended on good intelligence, sound tactical leadership and a well-trained helicopter pilot and crew. Lieutenant Colonel Babin recalled one insertion and extraction during a mission as Marines evacuated the Khe Sanh firebase in June 1968, designed to locate and observe elements of the NVA's *324th Alpha Division*:

> Success in the reconnaissance mission required insertion into the reconnaissance zone (RZ) in such a manner that the enemy was unaware of the team's location. Force Reconnaissance Marines were trained to be inserted by sea, air and land by foot, swimming (and SCUBA), rubber boat, swift boat, parachute (from helicopter or plane) and helicopter. However, in 1968, most of the Marines of 3rd Force Reconnaissance Company were untrained in parachute and waterborne insertion techniques.
>
> Marines from 3rd Force Reconnaissance Company made several administrative jumps near Da Nang and in the vicinity of Dong Ha and Quang Tri. There was some discussion about jumping from Army slicks (UH-1E with side doors that could be slid closed) at 400 feet at speed. Supposedly, this was the minimum altitude from which a chute could fully deploy, with a boost from airspeed. It was theorized that the speed and low altitude would combine to make a clandestine insertion. It was an exciting concept, but I think most were a bit relieved that we were never called upon to make a parachute insertion. There were some stories about two earlier failed parachute insertions from higher altitude attempted by 1st Force Reconnaissance Company that did not end well.
>
> Some patrols were inserted by swift boat along the Qua Viet river in 1968, but swift boats required liaison with the Navy, which seemed difficult to coordinate. I'm unaware of insertion by any other means, in the LANCASTER operation area, except by foot and helicopter.

Insertion by foot was usually preceded by a ride in a 6 × 6 (2½ ton or 5-ton truck) to a base such as Cam Lo or LZ Stud (later renamed as Vandegrift Combat Base after the General awarded the Medal of Honor for his command of Marines on Guadalcanal). Sometimes, patrols would be delivered to a base by multiple modes of transportation, such as to Oceanview, a small outpost on the DMZ at the extreme northeast corner of South Vietnam. An Oceanview mission would start with a ride on a Landing Craft Utility (LCU) to the mouth of the Qua Viet river, on the coast a few miles south of the DMZ. From there, patrols would await a ride on a Landing Vehicle Tracked (LVT) also known as an AmTrac, short for amphibious tractor, for the last leg of the trip to Oceanview.

Foot patrols would depart the perimeter at night and take the most concealed route possible to arrive at their RZ to begin operations. Insertion by foot was not desirable as there was a high likelihood the NVA were observing the perimeter from which the patrol departed.

The majority of patrols were inserted by helicopter. Helicopters were very visible and they made a lot of noise, but their main advantage was speed, firepower and quick extraction if necessary.

Ideally, a patrol leader would request a helicopter overflight of the LZ after receiving a warning order. Unfortunately, due to other priorities and the often-short time between warning order and insertion, there was no overflight. Rather than formally requesting an overflight, or after having a request denied, some patrol leaders would hang out near an HLZ, usually near Bravo Med, and ask a pilot if he could make a quick overflight for us. Many times, pilots would take us on for 30 minutes or so.

Overflights would fly to the vicinity of the RZ at several thousand feet and circle the area off-center from the actual RZ so as not to give away the likely HLZs to be used for insertion. The patrol leader would note vegetation and terrain and confirm HLZs for insertion and extraction.

An HLZ was a sufficiently large enough area of low vegetation where a helicopter could land, and have a quick and clear route of egress. Sometimes the HLZ had to be outside the RZ. Sometimes the only choice was the side of a hill which made rotor avoidance and distance to ground key considerations. A field of elephant grass could appear as a level field, good for landing, but it could also be 10 to 12 feet high growth, and unsuitable for a ground landing, a long drop for a team being inserted. There were stories about Marines injured by contact with rotor blades and long falls.

I took out a patrol where there was only one possible HLZ that I spotted on an overflight. It was ideally located. It looked to be the military crest on a finger reaching out from a long heavily vegetated ridgeline. On the day of insertion, we discovered that the HLZ was much smaller than it had appeared on the overflight, and a steep hillside made touching down impossible. The pilot skillfully swung his CH-46 into the area with the tail gate facing the hillside. He could not get us close to the ground for fear of his rotors hitting the side of the hill. This left a drop of about six feet when we deplaned. Unfortunately, as we deplaned, the helicopter swerved slightly to one side leaving about a 15-foot drop on the side from which my radioman was jumping. He hit the side of the hill landing on a small tree stump that stood out about three feet high. It poked him in the rib cage fracturing a couple ribs. I called for an immediate extract and the helicopter circled back to pick us up. We threw our gear into the helicopter as two team members pulled themselves aboard and then turned around to pull the radioman aboard as I muscled him up (without the radio already on the bird) so they could pull him aboard followed by me. It was not too pleasant a situation. When I returned to Dong Ha, I was told I would go out the following day to patrol the same RZ. I briefed a new team member, and we used the same HLZ in the same manner. With the helicopter crew's previous experience, we were inserted into the same HLZ without incident.

When the insertion helicopters arrived for a team going out on patrol, the patrol leader would brief the pilots on the mission, enemy situation, desired avenue of approach into the RZ and the primary and alternate HLZ(s). We were inserted by either CH-46 or CH-34, and escorted by two UH1E gunships, until about March of 1968. The end of March through April the Army supported us with slicks for operation Pegasus. It was about that time that the CH-34s were scratched from future insertions, with their relatively weak lift power and elevated pilot position that limited vison for take-off and landing.

Our insertion tactics called for a primary and secondary insertion helicopter of the same model to fly in tandem, one after the other, with two gunship escorts, one on either side, as wingmen. The gunships were UH-1Es (Huey) with rockets and machine guns on each side of the craft. The 46s and 38s had .50 cal's mounted on either side. The AH-1 COBRA was in-country and flew in as escort when I was extracted on some patrols in the summer of 1968, but I don't recall them escorting any of my patrol inserts.

Boarding the helicopter for insertion, the team would take seats on either side of the plane near the exit. The Team Leader would take a position between and to the rear of the pilots. He would use the plane's internal communications system, a radio hand set that hung to the rear of the cockpit. From there he could advise the pilot on the ingress and hear any instructions or changes to the situation. It was not unusual to see NVA crossing streams or moving along trails on the flight to the RZ. As the helicopters approached the HLZ the Team leader moved to the rear of the aircraft in preparation for deplaning with his team.

As the helicopters approached the RZ, they would fly a spider path (unpredictable course) and nap of the earth (NOE). NOE flight takes advantage of terrain features for cover by using valleys and folds in the earth for the flight. The low flight and engine sounds, echoing down the valleys, made it difficult for the NVA to get a fix on the flight. The reconnaissance team would be in the lead helicopter. Ideally, as the team approached the HLZ, the lead bird would drop into the zone and the team, already standing on the gate, on either side to the helicopter, would deplane in a couple of seconds, as the trail helicopter flew overhead. Once we had deplaned, the insertion helicopter flew up to trail the helicopter that had flown over it. With CH-46s, the tail gate on both helicopters was opened straight out to avoid hitting the ground and to make it difficult to distinguish between the aircraft with the team and the aircraft without the team. After the insertion, the helicopters would resume NOE and spider flight path flaring (making fake landings) into potential HLZs until they were some distance away, where they would orbit until the patrol leader advised that the team was all secure on the ground.

After deplaning, teams would move rapidly away from the HLZ to take a concealed position away from where the enemy might arrive to investigate the area. The first order of business on the ground for the team leader was to establish radio contact, get oriented with the terrain and confirm the team's position on the map. It was not unusual to get inserted in the wrong LZ, so it could take a little time to get an accurate location. This orientation was critical as any support or report must be based on the team's location.

There were two additional devices available for insertion/extraction. The jungle penetrator, a heavy bullet shaped piece of metal that could be dropped to penetrate thick canopy. It could be used as a means of insertion or extraction from a hovering helicopter. I don't recall any 3rd Force Reconnaissance Team ever having used one, and I don't recall seeing one on any aircraft. There were other test rigs such as the SPIE rig, but I never had any experience with them.

Team members always carried a length of rope and a couple of Snap Hook D-Rings for the purpose of making a "Swiss seat" that could be attached to a rope for rappelling or to hook-up for extraction. I don't recall that any team ever used a Swiss seat for patrol insertion or extraction, though there was some rappel training off the observation tower at Dong Ha.[5]

    Babin recalled another patrol and the difficulty his team had in inserting into the HLZ:

I recall that Steve Fahlstrom was my radio operator and Tim Lamontagne was the point. I don't recall the fourth team member, perhaps Gaillard Bartells. Anyway, there was no problem finding a place to land the choppers, as the area for as far as you could see was short grass and craters with a little vegetation in the draws. The area was between Khe Sanh and Lang Vei I and II. We did our best to follow the normal insertion protocol as described in the attachment. The choppers had come in late to pick us up from Dong Ha, so it was a mid-morning insert. We flew around the general vicinity of the RZ for several minutes, following nap of the earth to deceive the enemy as to our insertion point. The flying was making me more than a little queasy with the jerky turns and rapid ascents and decent until finally they inserted us exactly where we wanted. On the way in we could see the Lang Vei ruins and the remnants of the Russian tanks that were destroyed a month or so earlier. As I recall there were two of them. As we de-planed we immediately went to our knees because the grass was only about two feet high. We were on the slope of a long finger and we started crawling (literally) away from the insert point immediately. We set up in OP on the side of the hill to watch the area as we wanted to minimize movement because we were very exposed to observation from the terrain below us. We were all lying in prone position to limit our profile. After a couple hours I decided to move the team to continue covering the RZ and accomplish our stingray mission. Also, I did not want to risk staying in one place too long in case our position was compromised. We travelled just below the military crest, and parallel with the ridgeline. The grass was about waist to shoulder high in some of the down-slope areas so we could move in a crouch, while in other areas it was barely high enough to conceal us while crawling. As we moved along, with Steve about 3 or 4 meters behind me and Tim in the lead, we were passing through some higher vegetation, elephant grass, when I heard Steve right behind me open up with his M-16 and a burst of AK-47 fire. I quickly turned around and saw movement in the brush down-hill and fired a burst in that direction, without return fire. I signaled to Tim to move to higher ground. Apparently, a couple of NVA, possibly the point for a larger unit, had sighted us and was moving up the side of the hill at an angle to intercept us. We quickly moved to higher ground and found a small amount of cover in a crater. Again, the grass was about 2 feet high and the hill gradually slopped away from us. However, we couldn't see very far in front of us because even through the grass was short, it blocked our view while we were in a prone position, so I stood up which allowed me to see at least a hundred yards across our front. I could see movement in the grass and NVA crawling up the hill. So, I stood up several times to fire because it was the only way I could see them (NVA) and I figured my suppressive fire would keep them from shooting back with any accuracy. They were crawling towards us and coming to about 50 meters out. I recall Steve telling me to get down or I'd get hit, and me telling him it was the only way we could see them. Immediately after the initial contact, Steve had called for an emergency extract, using the same coordinates as the insert LZ, as we had not travelled more than a couple hundred meters. After about 15 minutes, we had helicopters coming onto our hill for the extract. That was the fastest response to an extract I ever experienced. I guessed that the helicopters were fragged from another mission in the Khe Sanh area as there was a lot of med-evac and supply activity at the time. They landed on top of the hill, and as they were coming down we started to run towards them, alternately turning back to fire automatic to keep the enemy on the ground. It took us about 20 seconds to reach the helos, and about the time we got to them the NVA had dropped a couple mortar rounds in our direction, while the choppers were on the ground. I recall the rounds landing about 50–75 meters off to one side just as we started boarding. We flew out before any more mortar rounds could land. I was told that we were the first patrol to have spent time on the ground in that area since the siege had broken and that a previous attempt to insert a team in the same area about two weeks earlier took too much fire to land, so their mission was aborted.[6]

Once established on the ground, Marine Reconnaissance teams generally proceeded along their patrol route with caution. Each team member had an assigned area of security, working in silence, taking advantage of terrain and vegetation to remain concealed and maintain a position on tactically advantageous terrain. The teams rarely spoke on patrol, instead using hand and arm signals. Unless immediate information needed to be transmitted (such as with contact), radio communications were conducted by keying the radio handset in response to questions from the radio relay.

During pre-patrol inspection, the patrol leader could check team members for smells such as from cologne; however, out on patrol, pepperoni sticks and other edibles might need to be quickly addressed. Babin recalls, "Despite having a case of c-rations (12 meals) to choose from, team members generally took one can per day of either a fruit or a 'heavy' (can of meat, egg, beans, etc.)." Team members would typically not have a bowel movement for six days of patrol to avoid the resultant smell. Conversely, they were attuned to the sounds and smells of the NVA. The NVA defecated close to their trails, and fresh smell indicated they were close. They frequently traveled with "live food" such as ducks and chickens that quacked and clucked. "They had a distinctive smell which was a blend of charcoal and fish."[7]

Lance Corporal Donald W. Vaughn, who was assigned as a door gunner on a CH-46 with Marine Medium Helicopter Squadron 161, Provisional Marine Air Group 39, 1st MAW, recalled what he described as an "ugly extraction" of a four-man reconnaissance team on June 14, 1968, in the vicinity of Hill 861, about five thousand

A team from 3rd Force Reconnaissance Company is transported into the field by a U.S. Army "Huey" helicopter. The helicopter is from the U.S. Army's 2nd Battalion, 17th Regiment (courtesy Sergeant Bill Moss).

meters northwest of the Khe Sanh Combat Base in Quang Tri Province. Lance Corporal Vaughn recalled that as the CH-46 descended into the landing zone, the co-pilot instructed him to lay down suppressive fire. Vaughn said that his first target was an enemy machine gun that was firing on the Marine helicopters as they landed. The CH-46, he recalled, "landed right almost on top of the 'freaking machine gunner,' which made my first target really easy to catch and figure out … you know … that was easy, it was about twenty yards away, I mean we almost landed on top of the damn thing.… The funny thing though, and that made it easy to hit it right away, it was very visible, all the flashes coming from it.… I don't know what they [the NVA] did … but they were exceptionally intent on killing the recon team, killing the team rather than the helicopters. Usually, we get all the rounds because it's easy to hit. It's the NVA mentality which is strange."[8]

Lance Corporal Vaughn stated that even as the skids of the helicopter touched down, the firing never ceased:

> I just started laying down suppressive fire as best I could. It was easy to see flashes because there was so many. You couldn't really pick targets. I'd have been bouncing all over, so I just started pushing down the tab of my .50 caliber machine gun. I should have fired five or six shot bursts. I think I was shooting with 30, 35 shot bursts. I'm surprised the barrel didn't melt. But it was really strange though because they were intent on killing the team, it seemed like to me. And of course, the cool thing about that, and I bet we weren't in the zone for a good 20 to 30 seconds because when the guys came in, and I mean they leaped into the helicopter, the crew chief was back on the ramp. As soon as the last man came flying through, he was still midair, I think, the crew chief said, "Go, lets go, that's it, go." And the pilot pulled up and started going away.[9]

Corporal Lou Kern, a member of 1st and later 3rd Force Reconnaissance, echoed Vaughn's account of a recon team being extracted in a "hot" landing zone and stated that it was all a matter of "technique." Kern added:

> The mission is simply to get in, gather information and then get out alive. Everything revolved around these simple tasks. Recon is a far cry from "1000 men abreast." Once in our Recon Zones our primary means of gathering intel was sight, sound and smell. The same was of course true for the enemy who was trying to either avoid us or kill us once we were on patrol.
> With a helicopter insert the enemy, if anywhere close to the insert point, darn sure knew a team had been inserted. In 67 the Annamite Mountains around The Sanh were still pretty much virgin tropical forest. There were very few places a helicopter could land. There were some mountain meadows of elephant grass but recon teams soon found these to be undesirable LZs. It was very difficult to judge just how high the elephant grass was and on several occasions the teams jumped off the hovering helicopter and discovered the jump was not 4 feet but 10 or more feet. This resulted in serious injuries and aborted the mission. A well conditioned Marine was certainly capable of jumping off a 10-foot platform but with 80 to 100 pounds on his back and no ability to see the ground it became a dangerous proposition. As the war escalated walk outs and Rough Riders became more and more dangerous. The NVA could and did put observers up in trees around the bases or along the roads. There is one story of a team walking out and into the jungle. Eight team members walked under a tree and the last man in the team just happened to look up and notice an enemy soldier sitting high up in the tree. It can be assumed this was not a single isolated incident.[10]

After a helicopter dropped the reconnaissance team into the landing zone, the Marines swiftly moved to cover ground while the radioman conducted a communications check to ensure that the patrol leader could communicate effectively with headquarters or friendly aircraft overhead. The teams then moved out along a predetermined route in which every member had been well briefed. Moving in file with the point man out front and a security man bringing up the rear of the team, the patrol would halt for a rest and conduct a communications check. The team members then formed a cigar-like position in order that both flanks and rear were adequately covered. Once on the move again, the point man, who normally went out about twenty meters from the rest of the patrol, kept a watchful eye for booby traps and signs of any enemy activity. The patrol moved stealthily, with no talking, smoking or any other activity that might tip their position off to the enemy.

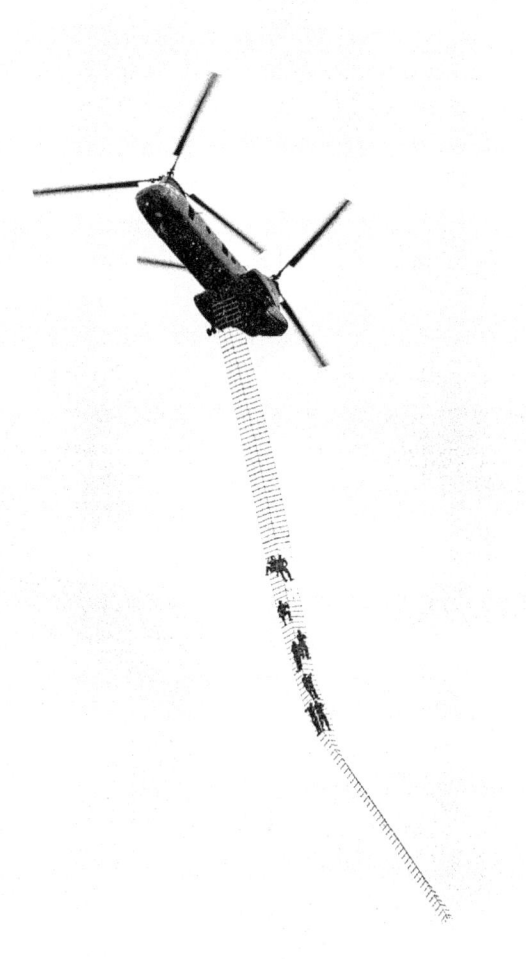

A Marine Reconnaissance team uses the "Simmons Ladder" in the Arizona Territory (reprinted with permission by photographer and retired Marine Major Barry Broman).

The insertion of a Marine Reconnaissance team could be an exacting procedure, as were extractions, particularly if friendly forces were in the area. Private First Class Randy Kington, a Marine with 3rd Battalion, 7th Marines, and part of the Special Landing Force aboard the USS *Iwo Jima*, recalled that during one insertion at Qui Nhon on June 30, 1965, his platoon sergeant warned his squad to be wary of a Marine Recon team that had been inserted into the area of operations. "The platoon sergeant," Kington noted, "emphasized that they should be careful not to shoot them."[11]

As was the case with the majority of Marine Reconnaissance teams during the

Vietnam War, most movement and surveillance was undertaken during the day; at night, the recon team clustered into a temporary encampment known as a harbor site, where one member would always be awake so as to allow the others to sleep. Reconnaissance Marines likewise had night scopes known as "Starlight" scopes that could identify enemy soldiers in the dark.

While on patrol, Marine Reconnaissance team members maintained a decent amount of space between them so as not to lose sight of each other or alert the enemy to their presence, thus preventing the team from being ambushed or surprised. Reconnaissance Marine John Edmund Delezen, who was a member of 3rd Force Reconnaissance Company (March 1967–December 1968) and served as point man on several patrols, wrote that "the interval between each man in the column [was] based on the terrain. In this ambush-prone scrub, we spread the interval until each man keeps the man ahead of him in sight. Following some thirty meters behind me is the grenadier with the M-79 grenade launcher. Behind him is the T[eam] L[eader] who is followed closely by the primary radio operator. He is followed by the Corpsman who is followed by the secondary radio operator," and then "the ATL (assistant team leader)"; at the end, as Delezen wrote, "the most important in this terrain is the rear point man."[12] Delezen noted that each team member brought "an extra complement of ammo" on many patrols. Every team member, in addition to his T/O weapon—in Delezen's case, an M-14—carried twenty magazines of twenty rounds each. Sometimes Marines carried one or two extra bandoliers stuffed into their cargo pockets. Other Marines carried additional grenades and batteries.

As night approached, Babin noted,

> The team would prepare to eat and locate a place to spend the hours of darkness. Recon teams rarely moved at night due to the limited vision, uncertainty of vegetation and terrain and relative noise of such movement. We would move to a position, usually an hour or so before darkness, to take turns eating. I would get a radio check, verify my on-calls and map location. As darkness descended, we would move maybe 50 meters,

"A Bird after an Extraction": A CH-46 used to extract Sergeant Babin's team after a reconnaissance mission (courtesy Lieutenant Colonel Barry Babin).

depending on terrain and vegetation, to our "harbor site." We'd select a location that was off any trails but close enough that we could hear movement. Ideally, we would be in heavy vegetation on the side of a hill, making it less likely that an enemy soldier would accidentally stumble upon our site or find it if specifically looking for us. Some teams, usually the eight man patrols, would incorporate claymore mines and Patrol Seismic Intrusion Devices into their harbor site security. On four-man patrols each of us would take a two-hour watch, while the other team members slept. If there was enemy movement, it was a big decision as to whether to wake the others and risk noise. Throughout the night the radio relay would contact us once an hour asking us to key our hand set twice if we were Alpha Sierra (all secure). In the morning, we'd wake up, wipe off our rifles, take a sip of cool water and move out.[13]

As for an actual firefight, Reconnaissance Marines preferred to initiate the fight with claymore mines and hand grenades and small arms fire. According to Babin:

> The chance contact could occur when the enemy detected the team and set up an ambush, or as in most cases, the enemy and the team surprised each other. These encounters rarely had an altogether good outcome. However, I think, based on my experience, the smaller four-man team had a much better chance of breaking contact and evading the enemy than larger patrols.
>
> Recon teams made three general types of contact with the enemy: undetected sightings and fire missions, deliberate contacts (ambushes) and chance contact. The undetected sightings allowed the team to continue their mission while collecting information and/or pursuing enemy attrition. Given the NVA's counter-reconnaissance efforts, teams would sometimes call for an aerial observer to fly in the general vicinity of their contact to deceive the enemy as to who was calling in a fire mission on them. Larger patrols could set up hasty ambushes to take enemy prisoners or to attrite the enemy. Such tactics compromised the team's location and usually ended the patrol. Such ambushes were also risky as in more than one case, the enemy ambushed turned out to be elements of a much larger force.[14]

After the adoption of the STINGRAY tactics, reconnaissance leaders could call in artillery and/or air strikes and even, in some cases around the coastline, offshore naval fire support from the USS *New Jersey* and its massive 16-inch guns, which could support recon teams some twenty-four miles inland. If ground support was needed, recon commanders could call in support from surrounding Marine and/or U.S. Army units. In fact, "reaction teams" code-named Bald Eagle or Sparrow Hawk were pre-staged at alternate LZs in case they were needed to support the reconnaissance team.

If enemy units proved more numerous, the team broke contact and simply "melted back" into the bush, with members heading for the extraction rendezvous or landing zone. Using TNT, claymores, C4 explosives, hand grenades and intense small arms fire (later CS gas), the team "withdrew over the most expeditious route" to the designated landing zone. On arriving there, the radioman called in for extraction. Once the team returned at the base camp, the Marines cleaned up, ate hot chow, and were debriefed by the S-2 Intelligence or S-3 Operations Officer, who then typed up a completed report that was subsequently sent to higher headquarters for further dissemination.

By mid–1966, procedures governing the insertion, use, movement, extraction, and debriefing of reconnaissance patrols were well established. More important is the fact that as the number of patrols increased, reconnaissance was able to firmly establish the standard operating procedure for all patrols and lay the groundwork for the successes enjoyed from 1967 until Marine Reconnaissance withdrew in 1970.

8

The Year of the Offensive
Recon and the Fight for the Hills (1967)

For Marines, 1967 began as 1966 ended: a year of intense combat. For Marine Reconnaissance, the new year brought with it an increased tempo of operations as their patrols penetrated deep into enemy-held territory in I Corps and more specifically along Charlie Ridge and Happy Valley, located southwest of Da Nang along the north-northwest corridor in the Arizona Territory. The new year likewise brought a more aggressive operational tempo by recon teams. More to the point was the fact that, as both Colonel Andrew Finlayson and Corporal Louis Kern recalled, 1967 was a year of transition for recon's mission. Corporal Kern added that since 1965, "recon's mission transitioned to a new phase every year." Starting with its initial reconnaissance and surveillance missions in Vietnam in the spring and summer of 1965 to what can be described as the "find 'em, fix 'em, and destroy 'em" phase by then-Lieutenant Finlayson's recon team (Killer Kane) in mid–1967, Marine Reconnaissance—both Force and Battalion—became a potent force-in-being, operating deep into enemy territory and serving as a valuable intelligence-gathering asset.

As Colonel Finlayson later wrote, Killer Kane's aggressiveness proved "to me that the only way to obtain really useful information about the enemy was to either capture a prisoner or search the bodies of enemy dead for documents of intelligence value. Before this patrol we were not unlike the other recon teams in that we considered it essential to remain covert and engage only the enemy with air strikes and artillery fire. From now on [mid–1967], we would deliberately seek out the enemy and engage them at close range with small arms if the tactical situation looked favorable. We would continue to use Stingray techniques of using supporting arms to kill the enemy, but we would not pass up any opportunity to kill them with small arms fire also. We would be far more aggressive and spend less time hiding and more time seeking the enemy. We would ambush the enemy and attempt to obtain prisoners." Finlayson noted that by mid–1967, "Killer Kane was about to embark on a one-team campaign to kill the enemy wherever we found them and to ask to go on patrols in areas that everyone knew contained significant numbers of VC and NVA troops. Killer Kane was going on the attack."[1]

The Operational Setting: I Corps (1967)

During 1967 in I Corps, the Marine Corps had in the field eighteen to twenty-one infantry battalions, numbering about one thousand Marines. These units were from the 1st and 3rd Divisions and the 26th Regiment. "Prior to the end of 1967, the U.S. Army's 23rd Division ('Americal' Division), and one brigade from the 1st Cavalry Division were re-located to I Corps, increasing the American maneuver battalion strength to those provinces by about one-third. There were, in addition, three battalions of Korean Marines and units from the Army of South Vietnam (ARVN)."[2]

As for Marine Force and Battalion Reconnaissance, their mission in the northern I Corps area of South Vietnam was three-fold: (1) locate, observe and report on NVA units; (2) engage and attrite NVA units with supporting arms; (3) develop geographical information and identify tactically useful terrain features such as artillery sites, avenues of approach, water sources and helicopter landing zones.

As for the enemy situation in I Corps, MACV intelligence estimated that by the end of 1967, not including combat support or combat service support units, there were fifty-six NVA/VC combat infantry battalions, averaging approximately six hundred men each. This estimate, in fact, led to a dispute between III MAF headquarters and reports of increased enemy infiltration across the DMZ by Marine Reconnaissance teams. As early as June 14, 1966, General William Westmoreland, in a message to III MAF headquarters, "reiterated the necessity of long-range reconnaissance" and ordered Lieutenant General Lewis Walt and his staff "to take the necessary action to improve, expand and fully utilize their long-range ground reconnaissance elements." In the spirit of that directive, 1st Force Reconnaissance Company aggressively initiated reconnaissance efforts in northern I Corps starting in June 1966. This increased effort of long-range reconnaissance, in fact, resulted in the commencement of Operation "Hastings," which in turn led to the displacement of 3rd Marine Division to the northern portion of I Corps—all the result of patrolling by the Marines of the 1st Force Reconnaissance Company.

Despite COMUSMACV's repeated insistence that the NVA were increasingly infiltrating across the DMZ (a fact substantiated by multiple reports from Marine Reconnaissance teams regarding the presence of large numbers of NVA in northern I Corps), General Walt continued to emphasize the need for civic action along the coast and persisted in his belief that there were no large-scale enemy units south of the DMZ.

Asked to brief the III MAF commander and his staff in January 1967, Captain Timothy Huff, commanding officer of Charlie Company, 3rd Reconnaissance Battalion, told the assembled officers that the NVA were "indeed" coming across the DMZ and spoke of the increasing contacts with large-scale enemy units. Huff recalled that "Walt said he was trying to show Westmoreland … that he was wrong about the NVA coming across the DMZ in big numbers, and that he wanted patrols inserted

8. The Year of the Offensive

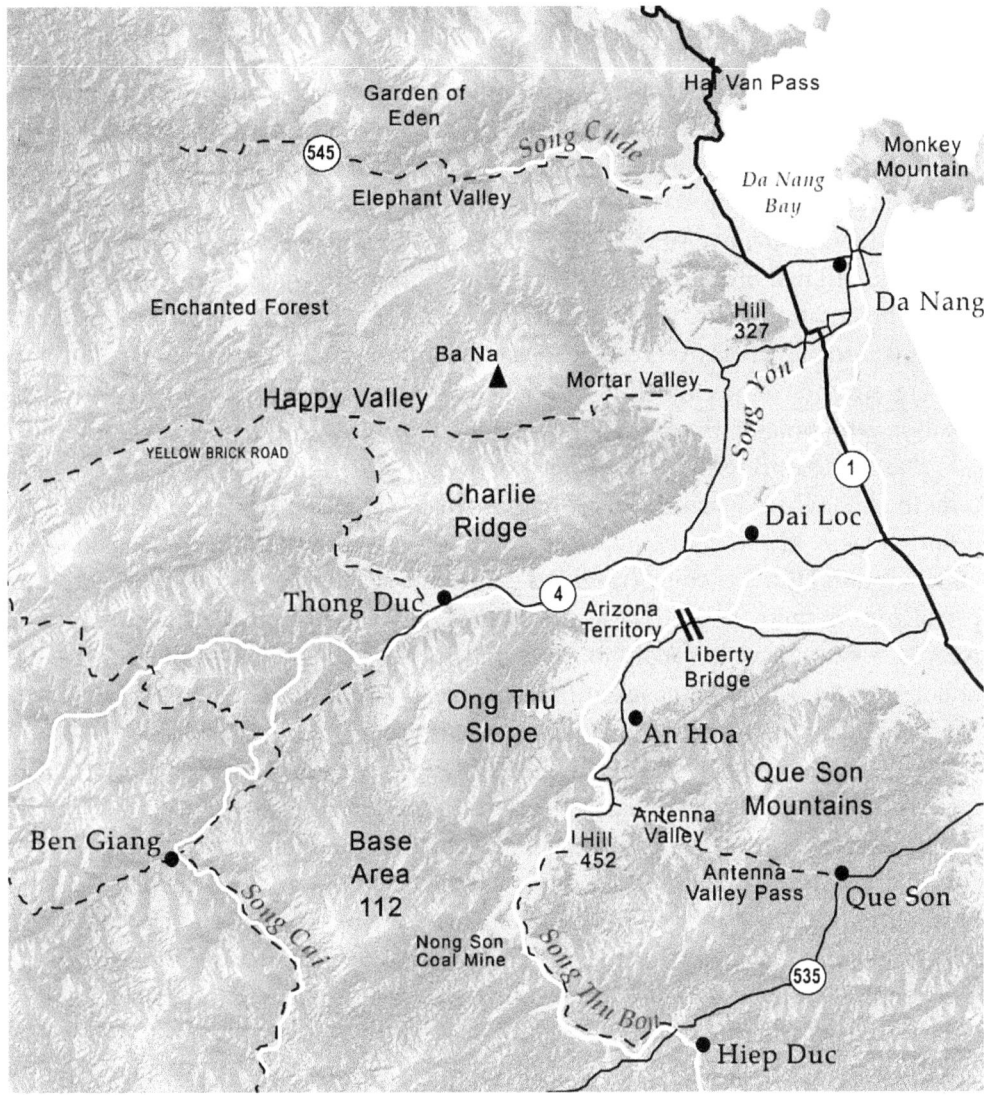

Map 4: 1st Force Reconnaissance Company's primary area of operations (AO), 1966–1969 (courtesy Colonel Andrew Finlayson; reprinted with permission).

between the Rockpile and the DMZ. He really didn't want to hear what I was trying to say."

Exasperated by Huff's repeated assertion that the enemy was coming across the border, Walt called the Marine captain into a backroom when the briefing ended; he then pointed at a map and ordered the captain to put a patrol north of the Rockpile in order to confirm the enemy's presence. When informed that there was no suitable LZ in the area, the III MAF commander ordered the insertion to take place by truck. In response to Huff's assertion that such a maneuver would be fraught with danger, Walt retorted, "That's the problem with the Marine Corps today—they're too goddamned reliant on the helicopter," and insisted that the teams be inserted the next morning by truck, a dangerous procedure in the day as well as at night.[3] The insertion nonetheless took place.

Driving at night on Route 9, and in territory "Charlie owned," according to Huff, the convoy dropped the first team off at Cam Lo before heading toward the Rockpile in order to drop off the second team (Huff all the while "hanging onto my M-16 and praying my Hail Marys"). Having dropped off both reconnaissance teams at their respective sites, Huff headed back toward the Dong Ha base. Then, at daybreak, "all hell broke loose," as the enemy, alerted to the presence of a resupply CH-46 bringing ammo to the two teams, opened fire on the helicopter with machine gun and automatic rifle fire. Huff, who was aboard to guide the helicopter to the harbor site, was hit in the calf while a Marine gunnery sergeant aboard was also hit in the foot. Dropping off the ammo, the pilot, Huff recalled, "raced back to Dong Ha."[4]

Despite the presence of the NVA north of the Rockpile, Huff stated that Walt remained convinced that the NVA's presence south of the DMZ was limited. Sergeant Gregory Menary, who had taken a reconnaissance patrol into the same area after Captain Huff's encounter, recalled, "There was no doubt among us who were patrolling out there that the NVA were in those hills in force. Sometimes at night on patrols, we would see long columns of lights that looked like Coleman lanterns. But nobody would believe you back at the base except other Marines in Recon or those from the infantry who had been on patrol out there."[5]

The skepticism expressed by higher headquarters toward reconnaissance patrol reports of enemy activity persisted well past Operations "Hastings" and "Prairie" and did not end with General Walt. Supporting Captain Huff's and Sergeant Menary's assertion that higher headquarters questioned reconnaissance reports were the recollections of the leader of Team Killer Kane, one of the most successful Marine Reconnaissance teams during the Vietnam War. Colonel Finlayson, who arrived in Vietnam in February 1967 and ran reconnaissance patrols up to the 1968 NVA TET offensive, commented:

> When I was a recon team leader, I was often surprised by the lack of credence some of division staff had for our patrol reports. They seemed to trust their agent nets and Radio Battalion more than the ground recon teams. This was not always true, but many of my colleagues in 1st Force and 1st Recon Battalion told me the division staff did not believe their reports, especially the reports dealing with patrols outside the division's TAOR. I am not sure of the reason for this, but I know it existed.[6]

The veteran reconnaissance leader added:

> When I was an infantry commander, I never, repeat never, received any worthwhile intelligence from higher headquarters and I found that when I went to 2/5 after serving as the Ops Off[icer] for 1st Force, that no one in 2/5 had ever received any intelligence generated by our teams. I passed all of our patrol reports up through the 5th Marines to division, but evidently this intelligence went up but not down. Again, I do not know why this was so. In any event, it appeared to me that a lot of good work went for naught.[7]

Sergeant Menary added "that intelligence received and processed at the higher levels of command was not routinely passed down to the battalion level. So, whether it was

Sergeant Babin snapped this photograph of the "Rockpile" during a reconnaissance patrol (courtesy Lieutenant Colonel Barry Babin).

the Recon Battalion or the infantry units, the people on the fighting level were often without a good picture of the enemy situation." Lieutenant Lee Klein, who served as both a recon team leader and an intelligence officer for the 3rd Battalion, 26th Marines, said in a taped letter home in early 1967, "The Marine Corps is not very good at intelligence.... Up in the division level they hoard information. They don't pass it down to you."[8]

As these and other Marine Reconnaissance team leaders noted, the failure to provide adequate and timely intelligence that acknowledged the presence of a significant body of enemy troops north of Khe Sanh and along Highway 9 remained a problem throughout the war. Indeed, as Colonel Andrew Finlayson and then–First Lieutenant Larry Vetter recalled, both division and MAF staffs often ignored reconnaissance reports that pointed to the presence of enemy troops, possibly to discount enemy capabilities or to challenge MACV's insistence on a change of tactics. This situation in turn resulted in a further misunderstanding of Recon's value, a problem that was only partially resolved after the 1968 TET offensive.

First Lieutenant Andrew R. Finlayson, USMC, and his team (known as Killer Kane) and Team Brisbane at Camp Reasoner. The members of 5th Platoon, 1st Marine Force Reconnaissance Company, display trophies recently captured from the Viet Cong in the summer of 1967 (courtesy Colonel Andrew Finlayson).

The ongoing debate between Generals Westmoreland and Walt over the best way to employ the Marines in I Corps further hampered Marine Reconnaissance's reporting of large enemy units after Operation "Hastings" from mid–1966 onward. For his part, General Westmoreland spent a considerable amount of time analyzing the tactical employment of American forces and how to best bring the VC (and later NVA) to battle. Any successful search-and-destroy operation had to contain several elements to achieve maximum effect; the most important element (at least according to the MACV commander) was timely, reliable intelligence. Commanders had to be able to discern the presence of enemy forces in a general area and then pinpoint the precise locations of individual units within the area before an attack could proceed. In addition, once the assault began, they had to be able to hold the enemy in place long enough to defeat him. For these reasons, Westmoreland emphasized that "commanders had to have a fairly precise appreciation of the size, location, and dispositions of an enemy force before they could launch an assault. Since only long-range ground reconnaissance could provide this information, and since few of the units in Vietnam were trained in this military specialty, Westmoreland had no choice but to make each division and brigade responsible for establishing its own reconnaissance units, an approach that put heavy reliance on the resourcefulness of individual commanders."

Westmoreland felt reasonably confident about the intelligence operations of MACV, of which III MAF was a part. By the end of 1965, the technical means for collecting information were so well-advanced that U.S. forces could often locate major Communist formations, such as battalions and regiments, within a ten- by thirty-kilometer area. In fact, General Westmoreland's vision for prosecuting the war involved dependence on intelligence assets, including long-range reconnaissance, to locate the enemy and then provide rapid mobile and lethal response to attrite his formations.[9]

By contrast, General Walt viewed control of the coastal lowlands as key to fighting the war, and, recognizing the war's insurgency nature, he emphasized civic action to gain the confidence of the Vietnamese people. The centerpiece of his strategy was the Combined Action Group (CAG). As journalist Colin Leinster noted, Walt's "CAC (Combined Action Company) units all had the same orders: help protect the villages, get to know the people, find the local Communist infrastructure and put it out of business.... If these people could be located and won over, Walt argued, the Communists would be hit where it hurts." Between 1965 and 1967, the number of secure villages went from 87 to 197. The number of Vietnamese living in "secure" areas rose from 413,000 to 1.1 million.[10]

Westmoreland's disagreement with Walt accentuated not only the differences between the U.S. Army's and the Marine Corps' operational approach to fighting the VC/NVA (i.e., search and destroy versus civic action) but also the means and interpretation of intelligence data gathered by Marine Reconnaissance teams. As observed by Captain Huff and First Lieutenant Finlayson, the staffs at 1st and 3rd Marine Divisions, as well as III MAF staffs, frequently ignored or discounted the reports sent "up the chain" of increased VC (and later NVA) activity. In his arguments with Walt, Westmoreland emphasized that this reliance on timely and accurate intelligence fell on the activities of both Force and Battalion Reconnaissance.

General Walt's disagreement with MACV's approach to fighting the war clouded his opinion of the value and use of the reports sent in by Marine Reconnaissance teams. In fact, operational differences with MACV were at the base of his skepticism of reconnaissance reports. The III MAF commander insisted that while enemy troops were, in fact, crossing the DMZ, he nonetheless believed that the best operational plan was protecting the civilian population in the coastal lowlands from the VC, not large-scale operations or "search-and destroy" operations as advocated by Westmoreland. For his part, General Westmoreland insisted that mobility and large-scale operations were key to defeating the NVA and VC—hence his desire to move the Marines from an enclave mindset to one dominated by mobile operations.

This operational debate made III MAF commanders even more reluctant to accept the reports being brought by Marine Reconnaissance teams about large numbers of enemy that were crossing the DMZ. This reluctance on the part of III MAF resulted in the major combat operations between the Marines and NVA and the enemy's buildup around the Marine firebase at Khe Sanh and the fight for the hills throughout the remainder of 1967 into 1968.

Studies and Observation Groups and Reconnaissance Along the DMZ (1966)

While not a Marine asset, the Studies and Observation Group (SOG) teams complemented the efforts of Marine Reconnaissance as General Walt "requested SOG's special recon help in the DMZ" in locating and determining the NVA's size, force composition, and infiltration routes into the south. In the immediate aftermath of Operation "Hastings," in which the Marines had "pushed two NVA divisions back toward the DMZ" and afterward occupied Con Thien and the Rockpile, Walt "needed to know if the NVA were massing for another attack." Because the "hills around Khe Sanh and the DMZ were so alive that Marine Reconnaissance teams found it impossible to" adequately monitor the positions of the enemy's artillery and troop concentrations without engaging large numbers of enemy troops, Walt reached out to SOG, as his staff identified "seventeen targets in the DMZ and adjacent areas in Laos" that were to be wire-tapped by SOG.[11]

Commencing in the fall of 1966, SOG teams, in unison with Marine Reconnaissance teams, began patrolling along the DMZ, despite the presence of a large number of regular NVA troops. The results were predictable, as the first three SOG teams were able to remain in the field for only three days, with one SOG having to "shoot their way out." The results were the same for the next three teams, which remained in the field two and a half days before being extracted after coming into contact with the enemy.[12]

Reconnaissance Operations (January to December 1967)

Despite the reporting difficulties encountered by Marine Reconnaissance teams, both the 1st Force Reconnaissance Company and the 3rd Reconnaissance Battalion continued to carry out a full schedule of reconnaissance patrols north of Khe Sah and in and around the area known as the "hill country" in northern I Corps.

Farther south in I Corps, action likewise occurred around the Chu Lai TAOR, where, in January 1967, the second platoon from 1st Force Reconnaissance Company reported thirteen sightings of 674 VC/VCS during forty-eight hours of observation and called in nine STINGRAY fire missions and five close air strikes. Another team that same month had twenty sightings, totaling 194 VC.

During Operation "DeSoto" (January 27–April 7, 1967), Marine Reconnaissance teams operating in the hills to the west of Company K, 3rd Battalion, 7th Marines, northwest of Nu Dai, carried out extensive patrols on which they reported sighting enemy units moving into the TAOR and called in supporting artillery and air strikes that yielded heavy enemy casualties.

Complementing Marine Reconnaissance operations in Southern I Corps were the rifle companies of the 1st Marine Division, which took part in both rifle battalion- and company-level actions during the first half of 1967. It is important to note that during the first three months of 1967, for example, leathernecks from the 1st Marine Division carried out no less than 36,553 company-size operations, patrols, and ambushes in the Da Nang tactical area alone. Many of these small-unit operations, which included Marines from 1st Force and 3rd Reconnaissance Battalion, were hard-fought battles with the Viet Cong.[13]

Operation "Prairie II" (February–March 1967)

For the Marines of the 3rd Reconnaissance Battalion, Operation "Prairie II" was one of the "hard-fought" battles that characterized the opening months of 1967 as enemy movement continued unabated during the Tet Nguyen Dan truce (February 8–12) both north and south of the Ben Hai River. When a Marine Reconnaissance team reported increased enemy infiltration north of the river, the Marines asked for and received permission to fire into and north of the DMZ to impede a large-scale movement of NVA troops southward.

Even as Marine artillery and air strikes pounded suspected NVA troop concentrations, the enemy was quick to retaliate against the firebases at Con Thein and Gio Linh with heavy, sustained fire. At Gio Linh, an estimated four hundred rounds fell on February 28 during a seventeen-minute period.

On the morning of February 27, Marine helicopters inserted an eight-man Marine Reconnaissance team from 3rd Recon Battalion five thousand meters northwest of Cam Lo in order to set up an ambush of opportunity. Once in position, the reconnaissance team sprung its ambush, killing four NVA. What the Marines did not know was that they had engaged an enemy counter-reconnaissance team and the lead elements of the *812th Regiment, 324B Division*. By 1045, the reconnaissance team reported that it was surrounded by at least one hundred Vietnamese. Outnumbered by about two hundred to one, the Marines quickly moved into a defensive position and called for help.

The first company sent to reinforce the recon team was "Lima" Company, 3rd Battalion, 4th Marines, minus one platoon and reinforced by a platoon of Marine M48 tanks. The Marines of Lima Company were "ordered to cover the five klicks to the reconnaissance team on the ground, but heavy brush up to twelve feet in height held them back." Meanwhile, the 2nd Battalion, 3rd Marines, commanded by Lieutenant Colonel Victor Ohanesian (which, as part of the Special Landing Force, had just completed a shore-to-ship movement), was ordered to come to the assistance of both the Marine Reconnaissance team and "Lima."

As Company L sought to protect one of its disabled tanks, the Marine Reconnaissance team continued to fight alone. Meanwhile, Company G, 2/3, commanded by Captain Carl E. Bockewitz, which had remained at Camp Carroll, began moving overland with orders to link up with the reconnaissance team. The linkup did not occur until 2342 that night, after the Marines from Company G had fought their way through heavy enemy fire and a series of well-laid ambushes. Once inside the reconnaissance perimeter, however, Captain Bockewitz's force settled in and provided added firepower in warding off further enemy attacks that night.

The next morning, Lieutenant Colonel Ohanesian, along with the command group and Company F, 2/3, linked up with the Marine Reconnaissance team and Company L and prepared to launch a counterattack. Ohanesian's plan was to sweep back against the NVA using "Lima" Company as a blocking force. "That meant that slightly more than half a battalion of Marine infantry was trying to move from different directions into at least a three-battalion enemy unit that was waiting for it."[14] The enemy, however, was not idle. On the morning of February 28, the NVA launched a series of mortar, antitank, and infantry attacks, forcing Ohanesian to change his initial plan and go to the assistance of Company L.

The NVA attacks continued into the early morning hours as Colonel John Lanigen, 3rd Marines' commanding officer, ordered both Captain Alan H. Harney's Company L and the reconnaissance team to displace to Hill 124, two thousand meters to the northwest of the battle that had threatened to overrun "Golf" Company and the reconnaissance team. This decision proved fatal, as the NVA waited in ambush on both sides of the hill. As the Marines pushed "hard right" up the hill, the NVA opened a fusillade of automatic rifle fire. As Lieutenant Vetter recounted in his postwar account of the fighting, "The fighting was so intense that the Marines who were battling uphill were not able to retrieve the bodies of those killed for hours. The heroism of the men of that unit in taking Hill 124 cannot be overstated." Killed in the attack as he led his Marines into battle was "Golf" Company's commander, Captain Bockewitz.

It was at this point that Colonel Lanigen realized he was fighting a major battle with the NVA. He therefore committed the remainder of the regiment in order to break the siege and engage the NVA. Company M, 3rd Battalion, 4th Marines, was ordered into the fight. Landing in helicopters atop Hill 162, one mile northwest of Hill 124, Company M (the first full Marine unit to be airlifted into battle) met light resistance as they took up positions.

At 0630, a "vicious mortar and infantry attack stunned Company L. More than 150 82mm mortar rounds hit the company's positions as NVA troops struck from three sides with heavy automatic weapons, small arms, and antitank (RPG) fire. RPG rounds hit two tanks," with one catching fire, though it was still able to support the Marines with its turret-mounted .50 caliber machine guns. By 0900 on February 28, the Marines had repulsed three NVA enemy attacks, due in large part to Captain Hartney and his observers calling in artillery to within thirty meters of the company position. As Major Robert F. Sheridan later remembered, "I had never seen this number of ... well-armed ... NVA troops in the open."

By early afternoon, the remaining platoon of Company L and a section of tanks reinforced Lieutenant Colonel Ohanesian's platoon. At 1450, Ohanesian's command group and Company F began to move toward Company G, leaving Company I and the serviceable tanks to guard the disabled tanks. First Lieutenant Richard D. Koehler, Jr.'s, Company F led, followed by the command group.[15]

The NVA were not finished, however, with their attacks. As the Marines withdrew from Company L's original position, the leathernecks once again came under heavy enemy automatic weapon and mortar fire as they walked right into the middle of a deliberate ambush. Company F's elements took cover from an ever-increasing volume of machine gun and automatic rifle fire from the front and both flanks, as well as enemy mortar fire that "walked down the length of the column." Due to the heavy brush, and unable to establish fire superiority, Lieutenant Colonel Ohanesian ordered a withdrawal. In a selfless act of bravery, Ohanesian picked up a wounded Marine and attempted to carry him to safety when an enemy mortar round slammed nearby and mortally wounded him. He died the next day, on March 1, from shrapnel wounds suffered the day before. Eventually, helicopters were able to evacuate the wounded and most of the dead as 2/3 withdrew back to the ship. The battle itself ended the same day, March 1, as the NVA withdrew into the surrounding hills.[16]

During this battle, Marine Reconnaissance reported four enemy KIA. By March 18, "Prairie II" ended, costing the NVA 694 KIA and 20 captured. Marine casualties were 93 KIA and 483 wounded. Of this latter figure, one-third of the casualties were due to enemy 82mm mortar fire. Despite the high enemy body count, 2/3's operations on Hill 124 and the surrounding area were the result of an enemy buildup that had been repeatedly reported by Marine Reconnaissance teams, though it was ignored by higher (III MAF and 3rd Marine Division) headquarters. As Captain Lee Klein, himself a reconnaissance team leader, later wrote, "This was one of the worst beatings the Marine Corps had taken in Vietnam to-date."[17]

5th Force Reconnaissance Company Activated (January 1967)

As the war along and in the hills south of the DMZ intensified, the need for reconnaissance teams grew tenfold. With a manpower pipeline already strained by the operational needs of the FMF in Vietnam and elsewhere, reconnaissance suffered a manpower shortage. This shortage was further compounded by the "thirteen-month tours, draft resistance, and the shrinking recruiting pool that acerbated the problem." In-country reconnaissance, like other technical specialties, suffered the additional burden of a longer pipeline needed to produce a highly skilled and well-qualified Recon Marine. In order to address these shortages, among other manpower efforts, recruiting standards were reevaluated, inductees (to include draftees) were offered the opportunity to join the Marines, and boot camp was shortened to eight weeks. In addition, HQMC formed, on January 31, 1967, a fifth Reconnaissance Company (5th Force Reconnaissance Company) in order to "train and supply" Marines in the "specialized skills required for force recon patrolling."[18]

The new Marine Reconnaissance Force, commanded by Major R.T. Henry and First Sergeant Robert F. Snyder, consisted of eight enlisted Marines and four officers. This initial cadre included veteran reconnaissance Marines who brought a wealth of operational experience and élan. By June 30, 1967, 5th Force Reconnaissance increased tenfold, with a strength of 11 officers and 130 enlisted Marines; 73 percent of its officers and 60 percent of its SNCO enlisted strength consisted of combat veterans. Also, by this time fifty-five of its members were graduates of the U.S. Army's Airborne School; twenty-four members were graduates of Amphibious Reconnaissance School, and five were from the Navy's SCUBA School. Testifying to the high standards to which Reconnaissance Marines were held, "out of the six airborne classes, four of the honor men were from Fifth Force Recon Company." Lieutenant Colonel Babin recalled:

> The company took advantage of other service schools, and we all viewed selection for a school as a measure of trust by the command, and as a reward for working hard. Many Marines started wearing what we called "hot dog" jackets when going out on liberty. These were tanker style jackets on which we sewed school and other motivational patches. Most had a parachute insignia stretching across the back. We were boisterous and animated as we blew off steam from the intense training program. This combination led to innumerable tales of interesting liberty experiences in California and Mexico. As time went on, the school assignments slowed. I remember a Sergeant Gates who returned from Army Ranger school after taking first place in his class. The First Sergeant explained that the school took too long and our company could more efficiently zero in on the specific nature of training for Marine reconnaissance operations better than some of the schools. In effect, though he didn't say it, Force Reconnaissance Marine training was beyond that which we could receive at Army Ranger or Pathfinder schools. I to this day believe that the 5th Force Reconnaissance Company of that era was the best infantry company in the Marine Corps, certainly the best I ever experienced in my 27 years of service.[19]

Babin also noted, "Despite the highly qualified 'triple threat' (recon, jump and SCUBA qualified) Marines emerging from 5th Force Reconnaissance Company, and their critical shortage in Vietnam, the Marine Corps terribly mismanaged their post company assignments." He added:

> Trained Force Reconnaissance Marines, the few that existed, were consistently mis-assigned to other units, and it was difficult to leave those units to get back into Force Recon. Force Recon replacement needs were treated pretty much like any other infantry unit, and people were assigned based on MOS, not experience or specialty skills. Ironically, it seems to me, the number of personnel trained in 5th and 2nd Force at Pendleton and Lejeune in 1967, '68 and '69 would have been sufficient to support personnel requirements for 1st and 3rd Force Reconnaissance Companies in the RVN, if it weren't for the mis-assignments. I suspect some mis-assignment was the result of personal animosities and professional jealousies. However, other than rumor, innuendo and personal experience I have nothing with which to back that up. I'm sure another factor would be ignorance and laziness in the personnel assignment sections.

I was a triple threat Recon Marine corporal when I and then Corporal John R. Van Drasek received orders to Vietnam in September 1967. After 20 days leave we were assigned to Staging Battalion for four weeks. Our platoon staff sergeant recognized the quality of our training as we frequently made "suggestions" during classes. After a few days he excused us from most of the classes which gave us the opportunity to see old friends and enjoy additional liberty time. Despite having a primary 0311 MOS (Infantry) I had retained my initial 3516 MOS (Automotive Organizational Mechanic), as did Corporal Van Drasek. I presume that is why we were transferred to Force Logistics Command in Da Nang. When we arrived, we were told that they had an over-supply of mechanics so we were assigned to Delta Company, 1st MP Battalion. Throughout that assignment we both attempted to request a transfer to a Force Reconnaissance Company. After about three months we finally got to Brigadier General Harry C. Olson's office one fine afternoon and by evening chow time I was talking to the First Sergeant at 3rd Force Reconnaissance Company in Dong Ha. I recall in February 1968 there were only five former 5th Force Marines in the Company: Corporal Lou Kern, Corporal Tim Lamontagne, Corporal Bob Nixten, Corporal John Van Drasek and myself. Lance Corporal Bierlein arrived a little later. They all had stories similar to mine. In talking with other 5th Force Marines, I learned many others found their way (or not) to the other reconnaissance units in ways other than routine assignment. By June, myself, Nixten and Van Drasek were platoon sergeants and Kern, Lamontagne and Bierlein were team leaders. To their credit, and not based on their MOS 2531 (field radio operator), but based on their patrol skills and recon training, Kern and Lamontagne were taking patrols out to the bush. I recall that Sergeant David Metz, a 2nd Force Reconnaissance Company Marine prior to arriving at the company, was a platoon sergeant as well.

After the initial waves of Reconnaissance intact units arrived in Vietnam, and their individual Marines rotated home, we patrolled with a lot of very dedicated and courageous Marines who never had the training opportunity that I and other Force Reconnaissance Marines had in the States prior to arriving in Vietnam. Though the lack of training limited versatility of the teams, the amazing lesson learned was that most of those without training picked it up "on the job" and overcame adversity on patrol with a never give up esprit de corps and full commitment to accomplish the mission. These were the Marines I depended on in a fire fight. These were the Marines that are the reason I made it back to the States. These are the Marines I was proud to serve with and admired for their élan and willingness to voluntarily and without hesitation take on a mission for which they were not fully prepared or trained, but knew its importance and necessity.[20]

Before it was deactivated on October 15, 1969, the 5th Force Reconnaissance Company continuously pursued an aggressive training program in mapping, patrolling, forward observer procedures, parachute and diving operations, long-distance swims and pre–SCUBA, and training with submarines. The unit "was later designated '5th Force Recon Company (-)' on November 14, 1967 when one platoon of two officers and 13 enlisted Marines were transferred to the 27th Marines for mount-out to WestPac on February 13–16, 1968."[21]

Reconnaissance Operations (April–September 1967)

From April through September 1967, both 1st Force and 3rd Reconnaissance Battalions maintained a heavy schedule of patrolling and STINGRAY missions. In support of Operation "Union," on April 27, 1967, Marine helicopters inserted an eight-man recon patrol on a low ridge overlooking Nui Loc Son. Once on the ground, the patrol, led by Gunnery Sergeant Bruce D. Trevathan, moved along the ridgeline under constant enemy sniper fire, which eventually pinned the entire patrol down. At 1600, the NVA launched a full-fledged assault against the Marines, with one enemy soldier able to penetrate the recon team's position. During the ensuing firefight, Gunnery Sergeant Trevathan "constantly exposed himself to enemy fire, aggressively moving from position to position to point out enemy targets at the base of the hill." Then, employing STINGRAY tactics, he called in "extremely accurate artillery fire," which caused the NVA to beat a hasty retreat down the slope of the ridge. Despite the accurate artillery support, however, the NVA maintained a staccato of heavy automatic rifle fire that prevented the team from being extracted by helicopters, which had made two attempts only to be aborted due to the intense enemy fire. Trevathan was able, however, to call in fixed-wing aircraft and Huey gunships that bombed, strafed, napalmed and rocketed the attacking NVA. The attacks continued into the evening; as darkness enveloped the besieged Marines, a third attempt was made to extract the reconnaissance team by helicopter. Still under constant enemy fire, Trevathan, with a strobe light, exposed himself and guided the rescue birds in to the patrol's position, successfully extracting the team from under constant enemy fire. [22]

New Missions for Recon: Helicopter and Aircraft Rescue Missions

On June 2, 1967, a sixteen-man reinforced platoon composed of Marines from Second Team, 4th Platoon, 3rd Force Reconnaissance Company, were sent on a rescue mission involving a downed Marine helicopter well into the hill country running parallel with the DMZ near the Ben Hai River. Upon insertion, the reconnaissance team discovered numerous "old" spider holes. As they moved out from their HL[23]Z, the Marines made contact with three enemy soldiers. As the point initiated and killed one of the other men, a large firefight erupted, with the team killing a second enemy soldier. Fighting off the enemy's attempt to encircle the team, the Marines were able to break contact and moved to the landing zone. Once aboard the rescue helicopters, though still under intense enemy automatic weapons fire, "it became apparent that they been in contact with a platoon of NVA and that the downed helicopter was being used as bait to draw a recovery party into the area."

During Operation "Great Divide II," on June 11, 1967, a CH-46 carrying a seven-man Marine Reconnaissance team from 3rd Force Recon exploded unexpectedly in midair, killing the entire team as well as the four-man helicopter crew. Aerial observation of the crash site was unable to determine whether there were any survivors. This in turn prompted the insertion of a reconnaissance team led by First Lieutenant Morris E. Riddick three days later, on June 14, 1967, near Hill 174, an area known for a heavy enemy presence that reportedly contained a fortified bunker complex. Nearing the enemy positions, the team's point man, Corporal Nicholas L. Natzke, was able to penetrate the enemy strongpoint. In the action that followed, Corporal Natzke, in complete disregard for his own safety, "exposed himself" during three points of the mission to "to lead an aggressive assault" against the NVA positions, "completely routing the enemy and inflicting numerous casualties." After a third assault, Lieutenant Riddick's patrol was ordered back to friendly lines, with Corporal Natzke, still lead man, successfully guiding them home "without casualties or further contact." Throughout the remainder of the summer of 1967, 3rd Force Reconnaissance carried out numerous similar missions in what Marines would later call "Helicopter Valley."[24]

On June 10, 1967, Gunnery Sergeant Trevathan led another team into enemy-controlled territory, where it again came under intense enemy small-arms fire. Eventually, the patrol gained fire superiority over the enemy and were able to kill three VC and capture a weapon. Despite being wounded in the firefight, GySgt Trevathan was able to break contact and lead his team around the enemy force. After moving the patrol to a safe distance from the enemy position, he directed an air strike on the enemy force that resulted in fifteen confirmed enemy KIA.

During Operation "Pecos," Team Dogma, led by Second Lieutenant Thomas W. Williamson, in support of 1st Battalion, 7th Marines, and consisting of two officers, eleven enlisted Marines, and one Navy corpsman, conducted a Pathfinder operation in order to observe NVA activity in a "little known area of Happy Valley" on July 18, 1967, near the initial helicopter landing zone (HLZ). Using gaff hooks, the reconnaissance team climbed into the surrounding trees, where they were afforded an excellent vantage point in observing enemy movement. From this position, the team was able to direct Huey gunships against the NVA in support of the Marine rifle battalion being inserted.[25]

On August 5, 1967, Gunnery Sergeant Trevathan led another long-range reconnaissance patrol; after disarming two enemy firing positions, he directed an artillery strike against a group of enemy soldiers. Three days later, during the same mission, Trevathan, once again disregarding his own safety, rescued his point man, who had become pinned down by enemy fire. Charging the enemy position with accurate automatic weapons fire, Trevathan rescued the trapped Marines.

Killer Kane

In keeping with General Walt's principle of "finding the enemy and killing him," First Lieutenant Andrew R. Finlayson's eight-man team—known as Killer Kane—became, over the course of a year, one of the most successful Marine Reconnaissance teams to operate during the Vietnam War. As Colonel Finlayson later recounted in his personal account of his team's exploits, "[By 1967] our team was

The presentation of false captured flags to Major General Donn J. Robertson, Commanding General, 1st Marine Division, FMF (center), by First Lieutenant Andrew Finlayson (left) and Captain King Dixon (right) (courtesy Colonel Andrew Finlayson).

the most productive team in the [1st Reconnaissance Battalion] with more sightings, more enemy killed, and more weapons captured." What contributed to Killer Kane's success was its tactical organization. Colonel Finlayson noted in his postwar memoir that Killer Kane went into the field with as few as five and as many as twelve Marines and Navy corpsmen. He added, "Through experience, it was decided that the 'optimum number' for a patrol was eight men," and how they were organized and positioned while in the field determined how successful they would be in achieving their mission.²⁶

Besides its tactical organization, what made Killer Kane unique among the teams assigned to 1st Force Recon was the change of its mission from being the "hunted" to the "hunters." The deaths of friends and colleagues imbued in Finlayson an aggressiveness that resulted in a high kill ratio in and around his team's area of operation in the Da Nang TAOR. Second Lieutenant Thomas Dowd, platoon commander of Company E, 2nd Battalion, 1st Marines, was killed when a Viet Cong threw a Chicom grenade during an operation southwest of Da Nang. Finlayson later wrote that he felt sick when he heard the news of Dowd's death, and then a "rage" grew inside him, so that he "wanted to strike out against the enemy that had deprived me of my friend."²⁷

The death of Captain Barnes, whom Finlayson described as a "vibrant, witty, and charismatic young man," likewise affected Finlayson and his team's approach to reconnaissance. Barnes' team (known officially as Team Countersign) operated in the area southeast of An Hoa Combat Base; sadly, the young Marine officer and his assistant patrol leader, Sergeant Godfred Blankenship, stepped on a land mine that killed both of them instantaneously. As Finlayson later wrote, what made Barnes' death even more tragic was the fact that, as a captain, Barnes had not needed to accompany the patrol. Nonetheless, Barnes' desire to be with his Marines just one more time represented the fidelity to standards of honor and duty that he, as a Marine officer, was expected to uphold. The courage exemplified by Captain Barnes and noncommissioned officers such as Sergeant Blankenship set the standard expected of Marines assigned to Reconnaissance.[28]

Killer Kane's war began in February 1967, shortly after Finlayson's arrival and assignment to 1st Force Reconnaissance Company, which was then OPCON'ed to 1st Reconnaissance Battalion. Finlayson, after conducting two "snap-in" reconnaissance missions, assumed command of an eight-man reconnaissance team and embarked on his first mission in mid–February. Prior to his assignment to his "team," Finlayson recalled that in a meeting with Colonel Donald M. McKeon, 1st Reconnaissance Battalion's commanding officer, he was reminded "that 1st Force Reconnaissance Company had been created by the Marine Corps specifically for deep reconnaissance and that the majority of these deep reconnaissance missions west of Da Nang would be carried out by my company." Finlayson added that Colonel McKeon informed him that "my company used smaller teams than sent out by the battalion, usually only six to eight Marines, because our table of organization (T/O) had platoons of only 15 men while the battalion platoons had 26 men. Most battalion teams went on patrol with 10–12 men. While the missions assigned to both the battalions and force teams were the same in most cases, the size, equipment, and the methods used were somewhat different."[29]

Colonel McKeon told Finlayson that his area of operation was to be north of the Da Nang TAOR, encompassing the A Shau Valley far to the west near the Laotian border, as well as north and west of Da Nang in areas Marines knew as "Elephant Valley," "Charlie Ridge," the "Ong Thu Slope," "Base Area 112," the "Enchanted Forest," "Happy Valley" (so named by Marines because "nothing ever 'Happy' occurred there"), and "Antenna Valley."[30] Finlayson said that at the time McKeon went over them, it was a "blur … but, in the coming months I would come to know each of these areas quite well."[31]

After settling into his unit and drawing his 782 gear and weapon, Lieutenant Finlayson met with the battalion in order to become acquainted with the area in which his team was to operate. Once introduced to his reconnaissance team, Finlayson accompanied two "recon patrols known as 'snap-ins,'" in order to become familiar with the terrain and how Recon operated in the field. After conducting a personal reconnaissance of the territory to be patrolled, Finlayson returned to Camp Reasoner for the actual mission. After these customary "snap in" missions,

First Lieutenant Andrew R. Finlayson leading Killer Kane on a reconnaissance mission (courtesy Colonel Andrew Finlayson).

Finlayson and his team began a series of deep reconnaissance patrols in enemy-held territory, employing the new STINGRAY concept with great effect.

Throughout the spring of 1967 and into the summer months, Killer Kane racked up an impressive kill ratio as they came across VC and NVA units that operated in and around their tactical area of responsibility. Operating over a period of 48–120 hours, and in teams as small as five men and as large as thirteen men, the Marines of Killer Kane soon became one of the most active (and perhaps one of the most effective) reconnaissance teams operating in I Corps.

By the midpoint of his first tour in Vietnam, Second Lieutenant Finlayson had conducted eighteen patrols and had learned the "art" of effectively employing artillery and close air strikes against suspected NVA/VC positions. During one patrol in early May 1967, which lasted 98 hours, Finlayson's team "conducted a successful ambush that resulted in two confirmed and three probable kills." More important, however, were the lessons learned in using artillery for ambushes and the "importance of never using more than one marking round before firing for effect on a moving target." Finlayson added that this patrol "reinforced the policy of never staying in one location for more than 24 hours. We were lucky on this patrol that the enemy never reacted quickly or completely to our presence, but my decision to remain in the same area of our first ambush could have led to disastrous results."[32]

Finlayson's experience on this patrol reinforced his efforts to work closely with the Fire Direction Control officer of the artillery battery (in this case, from the 12th

Marines) to better coordinate the use of supporting arms in an ambush. The FDC officer likewise gave Finlayson's team classes on how to adjust artillery fire and use it in a more "efficient and timely" manner.

Other lessons learned were how to deal with the NVA's "counter-reconnaissance teams, formed by the enemy to deny U.S. recon teams access to certain key NVA bass and infiltration routes." These "counter-reconnaissance teams" were special units organized by the NVA to "hunt down" Marine Reconnaissance teams in the A Shau Valley (more specifically, in and around Happy Valley and Charlie Ridge). Finlayson noted that in one interview with the Marine Corps Tactics Board, the members questioned him extensively on how his team dealt with such enemy units, as both Army Special Operations Group (SOG) and other Marine Reconnaissance teams were suffering heavy casualties due to these NVA "counter-reconnaissance" teams. Lieutenant Colonel Babin recalled "that 3rd Force Reconnaissance Marines used to joke about there being a price on their head, and some signs were recovered in 1968 indicating the going price as 10,000 piastres. The piastre was the currency denomination used by the French in Vietnam up to 1952, which was good for a few chuckles from recon Marines."[33]

Lieutenant Finlayson calls in an artillery strike during a mission (courtesy Colonel Andrew Finlayson).

NVA Counter-Reconnaissance Teams: Organization, Tactics and Employment

Besides the rewards posted for capturing or killing Marine Reconnaissance teams and Army Long-Range Reconnaissance Patrols (LRRPs), the North Vietnamese and Main Force (MLF or Viet Cong) elements dedicated considerable effort to hunting down these "Ghost Soldiers." At the forefront of that effort by the NVA was the People's Army of Vietnam (or PAVN). PAVN's table of organization followed the model established by Mao Zedong during the Chinese Civil War during the 1920s and 1930s.[34]

In terms of organization, Mao wrote that the regiment of the Red Army "should consist of four companies, each with seventy-five rifles, and counting the rifles of the special task company, machine-gun company, trench-mortar company, a regimental headquarters, and three battalion headquarters. Each regiment will have 1,071 rifles."[35] Over time, the Maoist model became the standard size of most Third World revolutionary (and some Western) armies, including PAVN; it was,

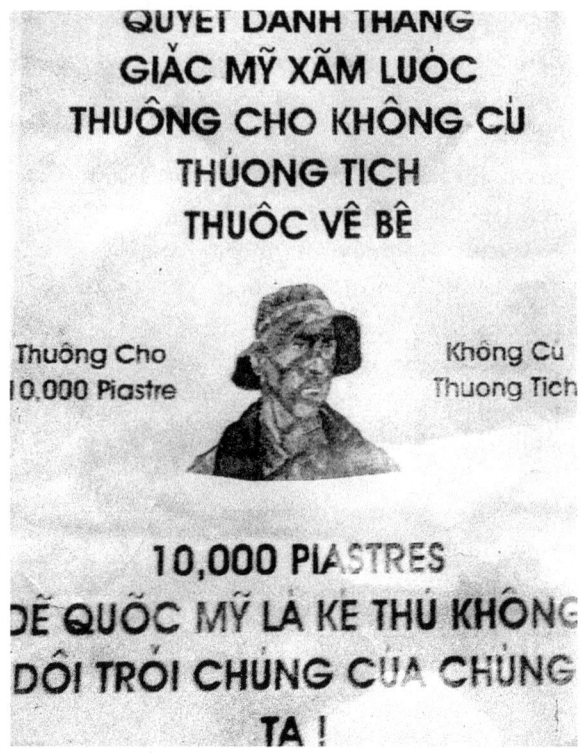

"Ghost Soldiers and Sea Commandos": A North Vietnamese Wanted poster offering 10,000 piastres for the capture or killing of a Marine Reconnaissance member (courtesy Sergeant Bill Moss).

in essence, the "3-by-3 principle," which "played a central role in the organization of the NVA and VC."[36] This principle was based on availability of cadre, fighters and equipment and proved itself to be a flexible, easy-to-maneuver force structure. This flexibility was "especially important, at higher levels (divisional and), a tank battalion, and the usual support elements of maintenance, logistics, communications and signal, motor transport, medical and engineers." One important point that is often overlooked was the fact that most Main Force units—that is, National Liberation Front or Viet Cong forces—"corresponded in organization to World War II conventional Western forces of similar size and function." In fact:

> From the division through the regiment, battalion, company, platoon, and squad there was little difference in military organization. The internal organization of main force units followed the 3-by-3 principle adopted from the Chinese PLA by General Giap for the Viet Minh and then later extended to the Vietnamese PLA.[37] According to this principle, a Maneuver unit at any level is one of three similar units subordinate to a higher maneuver unit which itself is one of three similar units.[38]

When organizing the PAVN, General Vo Nguyen Giap, who commanded North Vietnamese and Viet Cong forces in South Vietnam, adhered to the Maoist model of

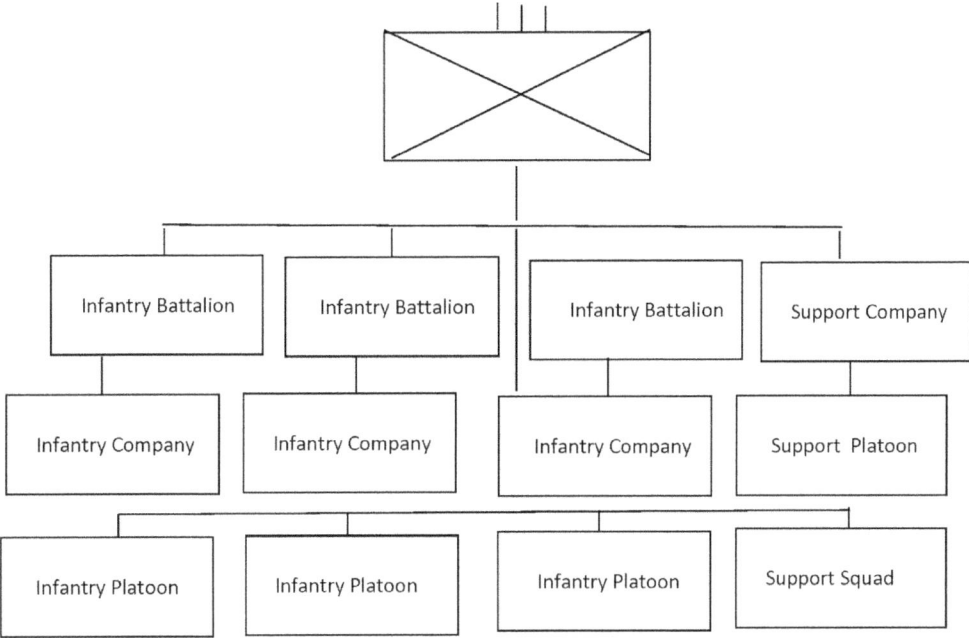

Diagram 6: A North Vietnamese Army Regiment, 1965 (Henderson, *Why the Viet Cong Fought*, 35).

the "3-by-3 principle," retaining the fourth company, platoon, and squad as support elements.[39] This approach gave PAVN both operational and tactical flexibility. As was the case in most Western armies, a company, platoon or squad would be detailed or designated as a "counter-reconnaissance" force, assigned to track (and eliminate on contact) a Marine Reconnaissance team or U.S. Army LRRP team.[40] PAVN initiated vigorous counter-reconnaissance efforts in the A Shau Valley and designated entire battalions as counter-reconnaissance teams; such was the case with the NVA's *312th Division*, which dedicated a battalion to tracking LRRP teams.[41]

Marine Reconnaissance teams normally encountered squad-, platoon-, and company-size NVA counter-reconnaissance teams. As historians Darryl Henderson and Douglas Pike noted in their studies on the Viet Cong and PAVN, both forces committed units to a particular operation based, as noted above, on "availability of cadre, fighters, and equipment," and, most of all, opportunity.[42] Based on Mao's concept of guerrilla operations, battalion-size operations offered NVA leaders both mass and concentration of firepower, important elements in countering the overwhelming U.S. superiority in the air and (in operations near the coast) naval gunfire. Contrary to the popular myth that NVA and Viet Cong units would disperse shortly after contact with U.S. forces, both groups, in keeping with Mao's tenet that "dispersion of forces has almost always led to defeat," instead concentrated their firepower, bringing in mortars and artillery.[43] Both Marine and Army reconnaissance teams presented themselves as lucrative targets, or at least that is how they appeared.

Both the NVA and the Viet Cong, based on Mao's theory regarding the necessity

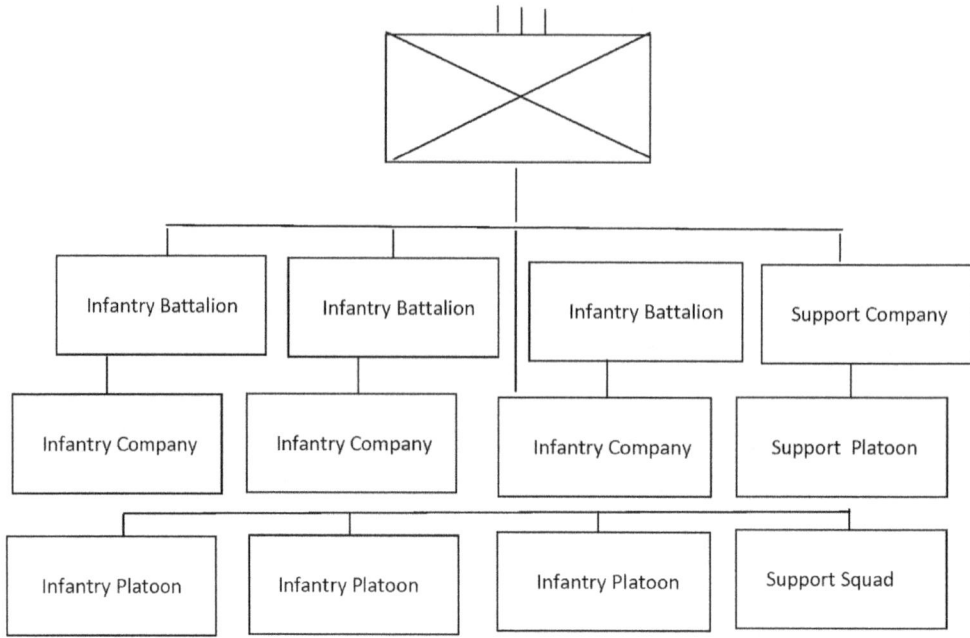

Diagram 7: North Vietnamese Infantry Battalion, 1965.

of concentrating forces, adhered to the concept that "concentration of forces to fight a numerically inferior, equal or slightly superior enemy force has often led to victory."[44] Both groups rigorously followed Mao's tenets of "mobility, firepower, and concentration," first against the French (1948–1954) and later against the United States (1965–1973).

Equipment for the six-hundred-man PAVN battalion included the Soviet/Chinese-supplied AK-47 assault rifle, Soviet/Chinese-supplied SKS 7.62mm carbines, rocket-propelled grenade launchers (RPG-2s), North Vietnamese–modified 7.62mm sub-machine guns (Type 50), Chinese Communist sub-machine guns (Type 59 "Burp Gun"), Soviet/Chinese 7.62mm light machine guns (Chinese Type 56), Soviet 82mm recoilless rifles (B-10), and Soviet 120mm, 107mm, and 82mm mortars. Some NVA troops likewise utilized captured French 7.5 semiautomatic rifles, Japanese 6.5 semiautomatic rifles, and U.S. M1 carbines and M1 Garand rifles.[45]

Operations and Tactics of PAVN and Viet Cong

Insofar as operations and tactics were concerned, the NVA combined the tenets of Mao Zedong and General Giap. General Giap, who was known as the "Red Napoleon," adhered to the principle of concentrating forces in order to defeat an equal or slightly superior enemy force.[46] It was here that the so-called Mao-Giap doctrine emerged. General Giap, however, took Mao's military principles to the next level in combating the Americans and their South Vietnamese allies.[47]

In terms of finding, fixing, and destroying Marine and Army reconnaissance teams, PAVN and the VC used the ambush as their primary tactic. This method allowed the guerrillas to "select the time, and enemy, sometimes supplying him with weapons…. It rests on mobility, offensive operations, and constant activity. It requires eternal alertness [and] it is directly related to terrain and weather, to its communication system, to its relative strength among the local population and with respect to the enemy." The ambush is offensive and not defensive in nature. In short, when conducting an ambush, "like a swarm of irate hornets surrounding an unprotected man … the guerrillas dart in, deliver a stinging attack, and retreat quickly when a powerful hand is raised against them."[48]

General Giap, in fact, wrote that ambushes became the basis for his mobile warfare strategy, one of "quick decision and fluidity."[49] The North Vietnamese general supported Mao's contention that "war is quick-decision offensive warfare on exterior lines of campaigns and battles within the framework of the strategy of interior lines, protracted war and defense, and in form, it is mobile warfare. Mobile warfare is the form in which regular armies wage quick-decision offensive campaigns and battles on exterior lines along extensive fronts and over big areas of operation."[50] Mao added that mobile warfare is simultaneously "mobile defense," which is "conducted when necessary to facilitate such offensive battles; it also includes positional attack and positional defense in a supplementary role. Its characteristics are regular armies, superiority of forces, in campaigns and battles, the offensive, and fluidity."[51]

Giap accepted Mao's contention that PAVN "must adopt offensive mobile warfare as its primary mode of operation, supplementing it by others and integrating them all into mobile warfare."[52] This approach would include PAVN's counter-reconnaissance efforts, which were a part of Giap's mobile warfare strategy. While he did not specifically include the word *counter-reconnaissance*, the intent was still present. One might say that Giap's emphasis on mobile warfare and use of counter-reconnaissance was, to use a football analogy, a form of "prevent"—preventing the enemy's ability to penetrate the NVA's "space" or territory. Although PAVN did not commit large forces to finding, fixing, and destroying Marine and Army reconnaissance teams, it used smaller formation or independent companies or squads to block their movement or ability to carry out their assigned missions. For Giap (and Mao), the ambush and guerrilla warfare were but one stage of the overall concept of mobile warfare:

> Even during the time we were using guerrilla warfare we were also using independent companies and marshaled battalions, that is to say, we sent part of our armed forces to operate as independent deep in the enemy's rear and carry out propaganda work and develop guerrilla warfare. At the same time we were using marshaled battalions to fight somewhat larger battles Thus embryo mobile warfare emerged at the time. Subsequently, we fought battles involving first one and then several regiments and in 1950 launched our first major campaign involving brigades. This campaign enabled us to wipe out important enemy military units and liberate vast areas.[53]

Operational and Tactical Effectiveness of the NVA's Counter-Reconnaissance Efforts

Giap's employment of counter-reconnaissance teams against Marine Reconnaissance and Army LRRP teams was vigorous and very effective depending on the province and location near larger NVA units. Colonel Andrew Finlayson, who led two Marine Reconnaissance teams (Killer Kane and Swift Scout), recalled that the NVA counter-reconnaissance teams his Marines encountered were "very aggressive."[54] According to Finlayson, "My experience with NVA counter-recon teams was largely a function of where I was patrolling." "If I was patrolling near the 'Yellow Brick Road' (the NVA main infiltration route from Laos into Quang Nam Province), or in Base Area 112 (West of An Hoa), then they were very aggressive."[55] He continued:

> To avoid air strikes, the NVA usually bivouacked in these areas in platoon size units spread out in a fairly large area, often many square miles. The dispersion meant that any insert was made near a platoon size NVA unit. After an insert, we often heard rifle shots which were the means of signally by the NVA to their units that a recon team had been inserted and to take appropriate action. This meant that that a squad size team of NVA, sometimes with a dog or two, would begin searching for the Marines. They would patrol along trails or start at the insert LZ and attempt to follow our trail, often pushing us to a prepared ambush. When this happened, we would take evasive action, usually moving at right angles to the direction they were pushing us, or stop and establish an ambush of our own. These anti-recon teams often made a lot of noise moving off the trails so we could hear them coming, giving us the advantage of taking them under fire before they saw us.[56]

Colonel Finlayson added, "My experience in 1967–1969 was the enemy did not use counter-recon teams outside of their base areas. I would also say the farther west we patrolled, the greater probability of encountering NVA counter-recon teams."[57]

Another view concerning the effectiveness of the NVA counter-reconnaissance teams comes from Lieutenant Colonel Berwick Babin, who recalled that as a member of 3rd Force Reconnaissance, he may "have encountered NVA

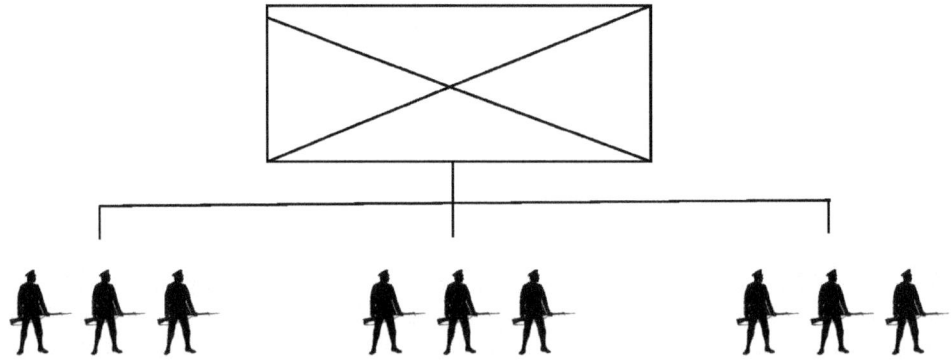

Diagram 8: A North Vietnamese Squad "Three-by-Three Principle" Organization (Henderson, *Why the Viet Cong Fought*, 35).

counter-reconnaissance units," though he questioned their battlefield effectiveness in finding, fixing, and destroying their intended targets—Marine or Army Reconnaissance units. Babin noted the lackadaisical or inattentiveness of NVA counter-reconnaissance teams that his team encountered while on patrol. He wrote, "I had three patrols during which I may have encountered NVA counter-reconnaissance units. However, on most, if not all my patrols, the NVA seemed to move about as though no one else was in the bush, that is, until we made contact. We saw them at sling arms, singing, eating, inattentive to their surroundings. This among other observations causes me to doubt they had an aggressive counter-reconnaissance operation."[58]

According to Babin, instead of a dedicated counter-reconnaissance effort, contact with enemy formations may have been accidental or coincidental encounters with well-disciplined infantry units. He noted:

> As we operated in an area of northern I Corps, where there was a large number of NVA, I would find it difficult to distinguish between a dedicated counter reconnaissance team and a group of NVA infiltrating through the jungle to simply join the fight. When we bumped into NVA formations, it seemed to me they conducted flank security tactics typical of a well-disciplined infantry unit; security patrols, listening posts and observation posts. Such security is not the same as counter-reconnaissance operations.... Aside from such security, the NVA would need to have some idea as to where our teams were operating to run an aggressive or effective counter reconnaissance operation.[59]

Babin added that the NVA possessed an aggressive counter-signals intelligence (SIGINT) or communications effort to track and locate Marine Reconnaissance teams through radio interception or triangularization:

> The NVA could easily listen to our radio transmissions and if they could understand English, they could take advantage of our terrible communications security to possibly locate the approximate position of a patrol. Then they would need to be able to communicate that info to their counter reconnaissance teams. The teams would need to have adequate land nav skills, be close enough for a timely interdiction and be somewhat fortunate to find a team that is well disciplined and moving from any previous reported location. Radio intercept is also unreliable because some of our teams were not adequately trained in land nav[igation] so their location reports were inaccurate. Another possibility might occur when an NVA unit comes under supporting arms fire. The NVA could try to identify likely O[bservation]P[osts] from which the fire is being adjusted, but once again, communication, land nav[igation] and team proximity come into play.[60]

Babin wrote that finding enemy counter-reconnaissance teams was like trying to "finding a needle in a haystack" and, in terms of manpower and effort, "was not very cost effective."[61] He cited three patrols in which his team might have encountered NVA counter-reconnaissance units. The first patrol occurred during the first week of April 1968, when his team made contact with "maybe eight NVA":

> We were operating in the mountains north of 950 and Khe Sanh and across the valley and was east from the [Hill] 881 ridgeline. The area had well traversed trails along the ridgelines and along the streams. There were signs carved into the trees and other signs of human activity such as the smell of human feces, discarded garbage and partially eaten food. It was triple canopy except where there had been artillery or bomb damage to the forest it was about 10

AM when we were walking along a ridge line on one side of the trail through an area where the underbrush had been thinned out perhaps as a rest area. Apparently by happenstance, an NVA soldier came up from the other side of the ridge line. He was dressed in a dark green uniform wearing a red neck scarf and light brown web gear. He had an AK 47 hip high with a guerrilla sling. He raised his gun hand as he yelled "Hey!" as if a friendly greeting. I was startled for maybe a second or two as he recognized I was not a friendly, and I was working out in my brain that this was a free fire zone and this was not an ARVN.[62] It was my first face to face contact. He couldn't get his hand down fast enough. I carried my M-16 hip high without a sling and a round in the chamber. A flick of my thumb cleared the safety and I went full automatic. Almost instantly I opened up so did the rest of our four man team and the NVA, not all of whom had made it up to the top of the ridg. I hit the deck reloaded and fired my second magazine full automatic into the area of Fahlstrom's front, from where it appeared someone was trying to take him and the radio out. I was about 10 feet from him. He was sitting behind a tree calling in the contact and rounds were chewing up everything around him to include blue tracers that looked like they were dancing a frenetic Watusi around his tree. It seemed like everyone was on full automatic. Bullets cracked, leaves dropped, bark flew, dirt was kicked up. I reloaded with magazine number three and shouted to break contact three times. I rose to a half crouch while firing full automatic, then turned to run downhill, breaking brush as fast as I could with Fahlstrom immediately behind me. It seemed that as soon as we broke contact all the firing stopped. I doubt we killed all of them, so I presumed they had the same idea as us—small unit, don't know enemy size, good egress available: therefore break contact.[63]

Babin's second encounter with a possible NVA counter-reconnaissance team was ever more intense, as a full-fledged firefight developed between his Recon team and the enemy troops:

The second time occurred on a patrol in June 1968 on a very hot day just south of Hill 861 about 3 or 4 clicks northwest from Khe Sanh. The area was mostly grass up to three feet high, with intermittent islands of brush, particularly in the gullies and draws along the side of the ridgeline. The terrain required us to be on our hands and knees to avoid observation, though we would be clearly visible from the opposite side of the valley, or any fingers that jutted out from the ridgeline we were on. It was early afternoon of the second day when I spotted a glint of light from a finger to our southeast. I put my 750s on it and could see a dark figure on one knee in the foliage observing us with a set of binoculars. He was no more than 150 meters as the crow flies from our position. I advised my team of the situation and we began to crawl to a position that would be out of view. As we proceeded, maybe about 20 meters away, two NVA downhill from us were observed as if they were setting into position to ambush us. Fahlstrom initiated contact and apparently both were killed. A running gun battle ensued as we moved towards the crest of the ridgeline and established a defensive position inside a bomb crater from which we had good fields of fire. We continued to engage the enemy with grenades and small arms until we were extracted under intense fire.[64]

The third encounter with an advance party of NVA resulted in a running gun battle as Babin's team attempted to board a CH-46 helicopter:

A third occasion occurred in July 1968 on a very warm morning with clear skies in the Lang Vei II area. We were inserted just off the military crest of a hill into grass no more than 3 feet high. Given the nature of the devastated landscape that reached out for several clicks all around our position I had no doubt that any NVA in the area would presume we had been inserted despite deceptive insertion measures. I moved the team on hands and knees for a couple of hours to get as much distance as I could from the insertion point. As we were moving towards a position from which to observe the area, we engaged two NVA who were crawling towards our position. We moved to a steeper side of the hill as we called for an extraction. As we waited, we had the high ground and therefore better observation than the NVA crawling towards us. We could see them by raising our eye level just above the grass. Due to the nature of the terrain, and despite the lack of cover for our team, it was difficult for the NVA to return fire without exposing themselves. The helicopter extraction crew arrived within minutes of our request. As the [CH-]46 mortars (presumably 82mm) started to hit near our location in two round volleys. As the chopper neared the ground we advised the crew we would be running toward their landing positions. As we ran towards the helicopters another volley landed closer. A third volley landed to no effect as the helicopter had gained some altitude with us on board.[65]

Both Colonels Finlayson and Babin agreed that the NVA conducted counter-reconnaissance operations, though they disagreed as to the intensity and their dedicated effort in hunting down Marine Reconnaissance teams as well as what actually constituted a counter-reconnaissance "effort." Lieutenant Colonel Babin noted that the NVA, on hearing a helicopter approaching a valley, were smart enough to realize that a recon team was being inserted and knew the "devastating effect" these teams had on their operations; thus, they made an effort to "seek and destroy" them. He added that both his team and other Marine Reconnaissance teams often encountered NVA or VC "thrashing about a recon team's harbor site seeking the leathernecks out in darkness." As Babin wrote, "Such an action could certainly be considered aggressive, but also defensive in nature." He added that "aggressive dedicated counter-reconnaissance would seem to entail specifically trained, organized, and supported units with the primary mission to destroy [Marine] recon teams.... For that reason I am skeptical that such formations existed."[66]

Finlayson and Babin agreed that "the closer you get to the enemy, particularly a well-trained and equipped enemy, the more likely you are to make contact with a numerically superior force with devastating consequences."[67] Babin stated that, in essence, "every contact between the NVA and a recon team could be considered an NVA *counter-reconnaissance operation* [Babin emphasis]." Since Babin doubted that specified counter-reconnaissance units existed, he argued that it "is better to speak simply of the NVA response to reconnaissance units, which grew in intensity the closer a team got to their formation and/or when [the] NVA observed team inserts or sloppy patrolling." He made the analogy that one should "consider the Phoenix program, in simpler terms, teams were specifically trained, equipped and deployed to destroy Viet Cong infiltration into the noncombatant population."[68]

Taking the opposite view, Colonel Finlayson stated that in his "reading of the MACV-SOG[69] patrols in Laos and Cambodia," as well as his own experience, the "NVA were highly effective against these patrols." Finlayson added that "almost all the patrols by SOG from 1968 to 1973 resulted in emergency extracts within 24 hours of insertion and in some cases the loss of the entire SOG team."[70]

Colonel Finlayson, who led a SOG team, noted the aggressiveness of the NVA counter-reconnaissance efforts "the closer I patrolled near the Laos border, especially along the 'Yellow Brick Road' that led south from the A Shau Valley to where it

"The workhorse" of the Marine Corps in Vietnam, the CH-46 "Sea Knight" helicopter, lifts off from an air base at Chu Lai (USMC photograph).

separated into two routes, one leading to Base Area 112 and the other to 'Happy Valley.' I almost always made contact with the enemy on those patrols."[71]

As the war went on, the enemy offered reward money aimed at the capture of Marine Reconnaissance and Army LRRP teams. The NVA likewise dedicated a substantial effort to "finding, fixing, and destroying" these highly effective reconnaissance teams that, as Babin noted, "were destructive toward their operations."[72]

Prisoner of War Snatches

Throughout the Vietnam War, Marine Reconnaissance patrols were encouraged to take enemy prisoners who were to be transported to Da Nang, where they would be interrogated by the battalion S-2 for useful information that included enemy unit identification, strength, and location.[73] Teams were encouraged to conduct prisoner snatches with the promise of a steak dinner and/or an in-country R&R (rest and recreation). Private John R. Rhodes, a member of 3rd Reconnaissance Battalion who walked point for Team Marketplace II, recalled one such mission. Rhodes' team was ordered to "determine the nature of the enemy activity developing along the natural infiltration routes that could be used by VC/NVA and check the area for use as a VC base camp area." Rhodes later wrote that team members were to "pay particular attention to size and direction of enemy movement ... [and] act as a forward observer for artillery on targets of opportunity. Make every effort to capture a prisoner."[74]

Inserted for the first time by Army Huey helicopters instead of Marine CH-46s, Team Marketplace II arrived over the landing zone as Marine and Navy jets prepped the area. As the helicopter banked right on its approach to the LZ, Rhodes, who sat on the floor of the helicopter with his feet dangling out of the side, was nearly catapulted out of the Huey; fortunately, one of his teammates grabbed him by the pack and pulled him back inside.

The landing zone was a large open field surrounded by a tree line. As the helicopter descended, the Marines could see the large stalks of green elephant grass waving in the wind. As the Huey came closer to the ground, the pilot turned to the Marines and told them that they would have to jump out. Rhodes wrote that this was a first, as "Marine pilots always land[ed] for us." Exiting the helicopter, Rhodes jumped down, only to become stuck in mud "that came almost up to my crotch." As the last of the team members jumped from the Huey, the Army gunship began to lift upward with the door gunner at the ready, scanning the tree line for the enemy, who were nowhere to be seen. Seeing their team member stuck, Rhodes' comrades came over and lifted him out of the mud. With that, the team moved out and, after hearing rifle shots, soon came across an enemy base camp with abandoned spider holes as well as a much-traveled trail that ran southeast-northwest. After checking the enemy camp and finding neither soldiers nor useful intelligence, the Marines moved on.

For the next several "grinding" hours, moving over terrain that included rolling hills and very dense undergrowth, the team (which had managed to travel only about one hundred meters) crossed a river. Approximately forty-five minutes into the patrol, Rhodes' team, commanded by First Lieutenant Jimmie Glenn, began to hear "clicking" noises, which continued throughout the rest of the afternoon into early evening. At 1810, after crossing a small ravine and climbing up a mountain, the Marines realized that they were surrounded by the NVA. At this point, the clicking stopped and a dead silence descended over the area.

Shortly thereafter, the quiet interlude ended, "as the quiet turned into shooting gallery, with grenades dropping into our perimeter and rounds hitting all around us on the ground and in the trees." Rhodes said, "I didn't know where the firing was coming from and the noise was deafening. The first few seconds were complete terror and we didn't know where they were or how close they were. We had no idea how many were firing at us. I fell into a prone position and faced into the jungle. I didn't see anyone directly in front of me. Rounds were hitting all around and the volume of fire was great." Rhodes recalled that during the attack, "five out of eight us were hit. Behind me I could hear someone yelling that the enemy was in the area where we had just broken a trail."[75] The attack was indeed "furious," as NVA soldiers, wearing pitch helmets and brandishing AK-47s, rushed the Marines' position, sometimes charging point-blank while letting loose a high volume of fire. Rhodes added that he and his fellow leathernecks "emptied" their magazines into the onrushing enemy. Eventually, after a firefight that lasted well into the evening, the enemy withdrew, though they continued to fire intermittently on the Marines. By nightfall, a Marine CH-34 managed to extract Team Marketplace II. Rhodes later wrote that intelligence confirmed that the field in which the team had landed was, in fact, an enemy base camp.

From Killer Kane to Swift Scout (October–December 1967)

Finlayson wrote in his memoir that each patrol brought new lessons that he and other teams incorporated into their method of operations. Throughout the summer and fall of 1967, Killer Kane continued to conduct deep reconnaissance missions. On October 20, 1967, Killer Kane's call sign was changed to "Swift Scout" in accordance with normal security protocol. Along with the change in call sign came a new mission, which was to "provide reconnaissance and screening for two U.S. Marine infantry battalions" of the 7th Marines during Operation "Knox" (October 24–November 4, 1967), south of Hue, in the vicinity of Phu Loc-Hai Van. Finlayson wrote that Swift Scout's "mission was to observe any enemy activity in the Loc Tu Sector of the Phu Loc District, Thua Thien Province, paying special emphasis on the main coastal road, Route 1, and the strategic Phu Gia Pass north of Da Nang. We were to keep 2/3 and 2/7 informed of any threat coming from the south and to call and adjust artillery on any enemy force we observed."[76] While his team failed to take an enemy prisoner (the one they did manage to capture—a NVA lieutenant—died of his wounds before he could be interrogated), Finlayson's team gathered useful intelligence on the presence of the NVA's *368B Artillery (Rocket) Regiment* (an enemy 140mm rocket team) and the latest and improved version of the Chinese AK-47 assault rifle.

For the next few days, November 9–11, 1967, Swift Scout continued to patrol along Highway 1, the so-called "Street without Joy," that ran along Vietnam's coast from the DMZ all the way to Saigon. As Finlayson noted, the NVA and VC used this route extensively and maintained a continued presence in the villages and hamlets that straddled this important highway.[77]

Three Parachute Insertions of a Recon Team

During the Vietnam War, Marine Reconnaissance carried out an extensive array of operations. In addition to ground patrols, reconnaissance teams carried out parachute drops in support of a major offensive. On June 14, 1966, Fourth Platoon, 1st Force Reconnaissance Company, executed the first combat jump in Marine Corps history, some twenty-plus "clicks" southwest of Da Nang. The paradrop, in support of Operation "Kansas," had the mission of establishing a surveillance position extending north and south of Hill 555, in order to identify any enemy units in the vicinity of the Thong Tra River. Flown over the drop zone in a U.S. Army–piloted CV-2 Caribou transport, the thirteen-man recon team, commanded by Captain Jerome T. Paull, jumped at approximately 0205 on the morning of June 14, 1966. Captain Paull recalled, "We tailgated the Caribou, in other words, we went out on the ramp in the tail of the aircraft instead of exiting the door. I was the first man to jump and we all jumped on one pass of the DZ [Drop Zone]. We used the standard T-10 parachute with static line. The jump altitude was 800 feet. The DZ was a small hill approximately 500 meters long covered by grass. It was bordered on two sides by a river, the Thong Tra, and the other side by a ridge 550 meters high. We exited the aircraft on the signal of the pilot [Captain Easterday, U.S. Army], a green light, and he put us right on target which was a difficult feat due to poor visibility. It was a moonless night and there was a lot of ground fog from the river."[78]

After landing and burying their parachutes, the Marine Recon team moved to its observation point, where, for the next eight days before its extraction on June 22, it observed large groups of enemy soldiers moving south. By the end of the mission, Paull's team had identified three enemy regiments, one Viet Cong and two others that were later identified as North Vietnamese regulars. Inserted on June 13, 1966, atop Hill 488, east of the DZ, was Staff Sergeant Jimmy Howard and seventeen Marines from 1st Reconnaissance Battalion. Howard was a veteran Recon Marine who had been awarded the Silver Star in Korea. His team had a mission similar to Captain Paull's; they also acted as a radio relay for Paull's team. On the night of June 15–16, 1967, Howard's team was surrounded by an NVA battalion of about 250 soldiers at about 2200. The reconnaissance team continued to fight through the night, hand-to-hand at times, for some twelve hours. When they were extracted, they had six KIA, with the remaining Marines WIA. They had inflicted as many as two hundred KIA on the enemy. All the patrol members were awarded medals for their part in the fight. Staff Sergeant Howard was promoted to gunnery sergeant and awarded the Medal of Honor; he retired as a first sergeant on March 31, 1977. Four of the Recon Marines were awarded the Navy Cross, and the remaining thirteen Marines received Silver Stars.

The second jump occurred on September 5, 1967. A nine-man reconnaissance team led by Gunnery Sergeant Walter A. Webb landed in Happy Valley in search of enemy 300mm Russian-made rockets that had nuclear capabilities. Gunnery Sergeant Webb's mission lasted twenty-four hours and met stiff enemy resistance, which resulted in two WIA and one MIA.[79]

Due to the experience of Sergeant Webb's team, no more combat jumps were conducted until November 17, 1969, when Team 51, led by First Lieutenant Wayne E. Rollings, made the third and final jump carried out by a Marine Reconnaissance team during the Vietnam War. It was also the first nighttime jump made by a Marine Reconnaissance team. Lieutenant Rollings' six-man team was tasked with patrolling in and around the village of Nui Tran, on the Vietnamese coastline south of Da Nang. Prior to Rollings' mission, Army and Marine infantry units had uncovered caches of enemy small arms, food, and medical supplies but no enemy. Team 51's objective was to enter the region in order to catch the enemy by surprise and flush out any VC who might be in the area. Jumping at night, from an altitude of one thousand feet, Team 51 landed on target in an area that revealed no evidence of VC activity, and they found little evidence of the VC as they swept the area looking for signs of the elusive enemy. After four days of patrolling "the entire peninsula from one end to the other," Rollings determined that there was no enemy force present. "It was apparent that the VC had not been in the area for several days at least, and no significant catches were discovered."[80]

SCUBA Reconnaissance Team Formed (October 1967)

One important mission of Force Reconnaissance remained its ability to conduct operations from the sea and along Vietnam's extensive coastline. Adding to the versatility of Force Reconnaissance Marines in Vietnam was their swimming and SCUBA capability. SCUBA provided an additional means of clandestine insertion from the sea or inland waters and enhanced their ability to conduct underwater hydrographic surveys in preparation for amphibious landings. In Vietnam, SCUBA operations took the form of collateral duty with missions that primarily involved bridge and site security. Indeed, during Force Reconnaissance's early deployment to Vietnam, Reconnaissance Marines, when not patrolling the hills and ridges in support of infantry battalions, continued to hone their skills in beach surveys and conducting operations from the sea. During Operation "Jackstay" in early 1966, Marine Force Reconnaissance teams supported infantry operations south of Saigon in the Mekong Delta in IV Corps.

In mid–1967, HQMC recognized the growing importance of underwater operations. In fact, HQMC, "in response to the destruction of over 15 bridges during a six-month period which were used to resupply both U.S. forces and ARVN along the fringes of the TAOR of Da Nang, formed a SCUBA reconnaissance team, commanded by Captain Fred J. Vogel, from First Force Recon team in October." Besides Captain Vogel, team members included Corporal E.J. Unkel, Hospitalman R.C. Schoelkopf, Sergeant R.L. Hughes, Corporal C. Thompson, Corporal C.D. Dobson, Corporal R.F. Buda, Lance Corporal R.E. Schmitt, and Lance Corporal W.J. Shaw. Lieutenant Colonel Babin added:

> In northern I CORPS, similar needs existed, but 3rd Force Reconnaissance Company in 1968 did not have any more than a handful of SCUBA qualified Marines due to the Marine Corps' poor personnel replacement program in RVN. The company did not have a designated team such as at First Force Reconnaissance Company. The Navy addressed most of the underwater needs, and on rare occasion, 3rd Force Reconnaissance Marines were called to do menial

underwater chores such as retrieving materials lost over the side of piers and bridges or clearing fouled boat screws.[81]

The mission of the 1st Force Reconnaissance Company's SCUBA team was not only to check bridges but also to be available for any mission requiring SCUBA divers, including retrieving dead bodies and searching for caves with entrances below the surface of the water. Much like the use of paradrops, the SCUBA team brought an expertise that saved Marine and ARVN lives.

Sergeant Robert Hughes, 1st Force Reconnaissance Company Dive NCOIC in 1967–1968, had many memorable dive experiences. Known as the "gentle giant" by Marines who served with him, Hughes was once tasked with locating an underwater tunnel entrance. During that particular mission,

> Sergeant Hughes searched the murky waters, he collided with an enemy swimmer exiting an underwater tunnel entrance. Hughes and the enemy engaged each other in a knife fight, with neither getting a good advantage, until Sergeant Hughes spit out his regulator mouth piece and bit into the throat of his opponent. This caused the enemy to lose his grip and provide Sergeant Hughes the opening needed to finish the fight. Sgt Hughes had at least 2 confirmed underwater kills when he rotated home. Divers tended to arm themselves with their Kabar knives, but some carried privately purchased revolvers, which were serviceable underwater whereas military issued pistols were unreliable.[82]

The value of a dedicated SCUBA team was underscored as the battle for Hue City raged in February 1968. On February 24, 1968, Captain John Vogel received word that he and his team were needed to dive on the Silver Bridge, to ensure its security as a key line of communication for the Marines fighting in the Citadel in Hue City. On arriving at the MACV, Vogel learned their orders had been modified to include inspecting eight different bridges, on both sides of the Perfume River, spread across the city. As they moved out, a squad of Marines from 1st Battalion, 5th Marines, joined to provide security. The grunts would help the SCUBA team navigate the city streets and, more important, secure the areas around dive sites as the vulnerable divers entered the water.

Captain Vogel decided to first inspect a causeway farther east of the Silver Bridge. The causeway was a solid concrete strip that crossed the waterway a few feet above the water line. When Corporals Thompson and Buda prepared to inspect the causeway, working without wetsuits and SCUBA gear, they noticed movement on the far bank. As Thompson and Buda hustled back to join the rest of the team taking cover in a nearby house, the team returned fire from across the water as recoilless shells and mortars landed near their position.

Captain Vogel, in sizing up the situation, determined that diving the causeway was untenable, as visual observation revealed it was structurally sound and crossable. Vogel's team broke contact and returned to the MACV compound, where they broke into two teams and donned their SCUBA gear. This included the standard SCUBA tanks, which are made of an anti-magnetic alloy, contain ninety cubic inches (each tank) of compressed air and weigh about seventy pounds.

First Force Recon dive team at MACV compound in Hue. Front (left to right): Lance Corporal William Shaw, Corporal Edward Unkel, Captain Frederick Vogel, Corporal David Thompson. Rear (left to right): Lance Corporal Robert Schmitt, Corporal Robert Buda, Hospitalman Robert Schoelkopf, Sergeant Robert Hughes, Corporal Clifford Dobson (courtesy Colonel John Vogel).

The causeway where the dive team first attempted a bridge inspection. The dive was aborted due to the intense enemy fire taken from the pictured buildings on the north side (courtesy Colonel John Vogel).

Corporal Bob Buda and Corporal Dave Thompson, in skivvies and dive booties, prepare to inspect the causeway (courtesy Colonel John Vogel).

Next, Vogel decided to complete the main focus of their mission and dive the Silver Bridge. Given the length of the bridge and the number of pillars to inspect, the Marine captain determined that two dive teams were needed. Vogel and Buda paired together as the first team; Thompson and Hughes were the second. As the grunts provided covering fire, the divers, despite the weight of their gear, sprinted across roughly fifty meters of open ground to reach the water, while the enemy fired from the opposite side.

Without wetsuits, and with the water temperature around 50 degrees, Vogel's team nevertheless proceeded with the mission. Once underwater, they were surprised to have about twenty feet of visibility. As they inspected the bridge pillars, which descended about fifty feet to the river bottom, two divers visually inspected the pillars close up, while the other two provided security, watching for booby traps, enemy divers, and other dangers. They found that "there were explosives and ammunition and weaponry all over, it was like an ammo dump! We saw tons of every type of projectile and thing you could dream of, but none of it was rigged to detonate on any part of the bridge," remembered Corporal Buda. After about an hour of diving, Thompson and Hughes headed back first. About halfway back, the enemy started mortaring the area. Vogel and Buda were still in the water as mortar rounds exploded on the surface. "That's one thing the NVA messed up. They should have used delayed fuses," Vogel remarked later. "Coming down straight into water like that might as well have been a brick wall. If they had used delayed fuses it might

From the south side of the river, the dropped portion of the Silver Bridge is visible. Also seen is a Navy LCU taking fire on the river (courtesy Colonel John Vogel).

have gone down far enough to knock us out. Fortunately they didn't think that far ahead." With the rest of the team and the grunts proving covering fire, Vogel and Buda reached safety.

By this time, it was about 1600, and Captain Vogel decided to inspect one more

Captain John Vogel in dive attire, shown just after returning safely to land following the dive of the Silver Bridge. The three other divers are also seen around the gear trailer returning to standard combat gear (courtesy Colonel John Vogel).

The third bridge inspected by the team, seen from the building where they took cover while under intense fire. Shown in the foreground is the destroyed tank that Captain Vogel and Corporal Buda hid behind as they attempted to inspect the structure (courtesy Colonel John Vogel).

The building where the dive team took cover and the destroyed tank near the third bridge inspected (courtesy Colonel John Vogel).

bridge before darkness. They quickly crossed the top side of the Silver Bridge and into the Citadel to have access to the remaining bridges. Their target bridge crossed a canal lining the east side of the Citadel. Marines there were engaged in a battle with the NVA across the canal. Captain Vogel and Corporal Buda moved toward the bridge to conduct a visual inspection, with the enemy about seventy meters away.

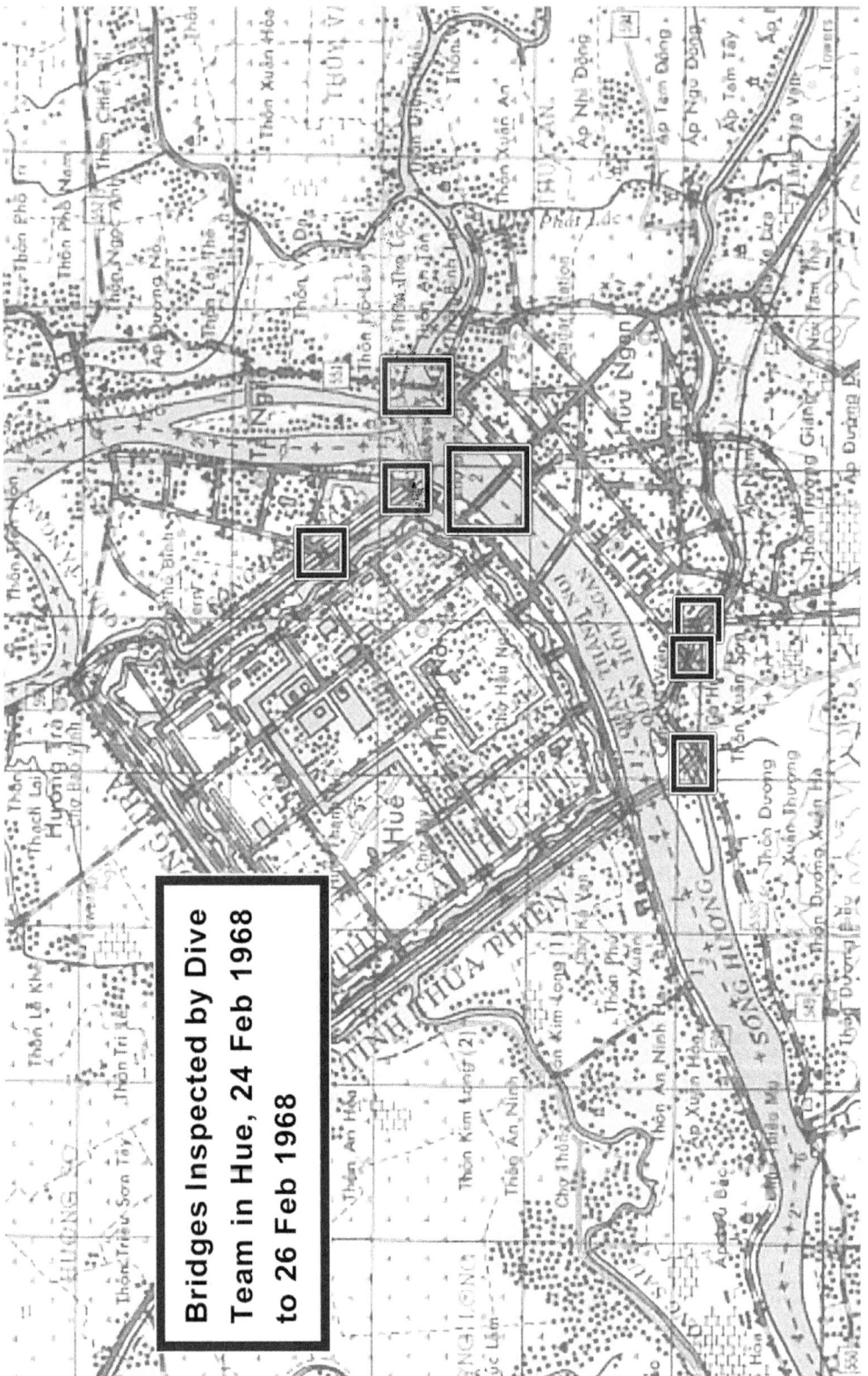

Map 5: SCUBA 1 activities during the battle for Hue (courtesy Colonel John Vogel; originally published in *Leatherneck* magazine, February 2018).

Civilians are seen crossing one of the bridges. In the center of the bridge lies one of the many bodies littering the city (courtesy Colonel John Vogel).

Vogel and Buda crawled out to entryway for the bridge amid the roar of gun fire, rockets, and exploding mortars. Bullets were pinging off the side of a burning tank, behind which they took cover. They could get no closer without getting hit. They returned to the team, broke contact and returned to the Silver Bridge.

On their second day, five more bridges were inspected, but the enemy situation at each location prevented divers from entering the water. Vogel's team visually inspected all the bridges from the ground. Some were already destroyed completely, while others appeared structurally sound.

Day two ended with their mission complete. All assigned bridges were inspected, and no evidence of rigged explosives was found. Captain Vogel's team then spent one more night in Hue and returned to Phu Bai the morning of February 26.[83]

A Year of Intense Reconnaissance Activity: A Summary

For both Force and Battalion Reconnaissance, 1967 proved to be a busy year as they conducted numerous patrols and, in the case of Killer Kane (later Swift Scout), ambushes in and around the Da Nang TAOR and in the hill country near Khe Sanh. As 1968 dawned, Marine Reconnaissance's activities continued to center in and around the Marine firebases at Con Thein and Khe Sanh, as well as in the numerous harbor sites situated in the hills and countryside outside the imperial city of Hue.

Like a thunderclap, on January 30, 1968, the enemy launched what they believed to be their war-winning country-wide offensives throughout all of Vietnam. For the next three months, Marine, U.S. Army, allied, and ARVN units battled combined NVA/VC forces in the cities, villages, and hills south of the DMZ, inflicting heavy losses and decisively defeating them in the countryside and in the cities. The enemy buildup that Lieutenant Finlayson's and other teams reported throughout 1967, largely ignored by higher headquarters, proved to be the decisive turning point of America's involvement in Vietnam.

Patrols: 1,327
Average Days per Patrol: N/A
Number of Men per Patrol: 6–8
Sightings: 1,257
NVA/VC Sighted: 14,121
Contacts: 386
Fire Missions: 884
Artillery Rounds Fired: 38,574
Air Strikes: 321

NVA/VC KIA (Confirmed): 882
NVA/VC KIA (Probable): 1,810
NVA/VC Captured: 13/2 DOW
USMC KIA: 48
USN KIA: 5
USMC WIA: 410
USN WIA: 41
Captured Weapons: 79

"The Teams in Action": Marines of 3rd Force Reconnaissance Company on patrol in northern I Corps in 1968 (courtesy Lieutenant Colonel Barry Babin).

Marine Reconnaissance's War in the "Valley of Decision"— The TET Offensive (January–April 1968)

As reconnaissance teams conducted extensive patrolling throughout northern I Corps, enemy infiltration continued into the new year, focused on the Khe Sanh Combat Base and in and around the ancient capital of Hue.[84] As patrol reports accumulated, they pointed to a clearly foreseeable conclusion: the enemy was massing for a major offensive south of the DMZ in early 1968. In fact, reconnaissance teams had reported this buildup as early as the fall of 1967. As the NVA continued to infiltrate across the tenuous border, Marine Recon teams carried on with their surveillance of the hills surrounding the Marine firebase at Khe Sanh, Con Thien, and Special Forces camps in and around Camp Carroll and the Rockpile. For the Marines assigned to both Force and Battalion Reconnaissance, the new year was to be no different from the last.

9

"Some Hard Fighting"

*Marine Reconnaissance
and the Year of Tet (1968)*

At the start of 1968, Marine Reconnaissance units consisted of the 1st and 3rd Reconnaissance Battalions and 1st and 3rd Force Reconnaissance Companies. The two reconnaissance battalions were retained by their respective parent divisions—the 1st Marine Division and the 3rd Division—with the 1st and 3rd Force Reconnaissance Companies attached to the battalions (the 1st Force Reconnaissance Company with the 1st Reconnaissance Battalion and 3rd Force Reconnaissance Company with the 3rd Reconnaissance Battalion).

Beginning in late 1967 and continuing into the winter and spring of 1968, the Marine Reconnaissance structure was increasingly OPCON'ed to large Marine and Army ad hoc task forces. These task forces were temporarily task-organized units with specific combat assets deemed appropriate to accomplish a well-defined mission or objectives and ranged in size from two to nine infantry battalions as their principal combat element. These units were often a mixture of both Army and Marine units. Such a task force could enhance the combat power of adjacent friendly units—in this case, in I Corps—and could respond to specific threats or secure critical areas or waterways. "Depending on which Marine divisions provided the major part of the task force, either First or Third Force Reconnaissance Company was OPCON'ed as its recon asset. Upon completion of the task force's specific objectives, the tasked Force Reconnaissance unit returned to division control." As Michael Lee Lanning and Ray Stubbe noted, "Force Recon support of task forces was marked by repeated successes in finding and destroying the enemy while developing new and innovative methods of patrolling, and by the spring of 1968, "Individual acts of heroism and overall team proficiency were routine."[1]

One such team was Team Laguna Point, which began patrolling the jungles only five days after its arrival at Phu Bai from Da Nang on January 4–5, 1968. During its second patrol, Laguna Point had eight sightings, totaling ninety-four NVA/VC. On its third patrol, the team became involved in a heavy firefight as it came across an NVA bunker system in the Soc Ta Trach region near Nam Hoa, which had been the reported home of an enemy base camp. As the patrol searched the abandoned bunker, it came under enemy automatic fire. In the ensuing firefight, Sergeant Nichols Hawrylak, Jr., was seriously wounded while Lance Corporal Charles E. Harris was killed. Braving enemy fire, Hospital Corpsman Second Class John L. Jackson made his way to the two stricken Marines. Despite heavy enemy fire that was now trained on him, Jackson managed to pull Hawrylak to safety and treat his wounds. A medevac helicopter hovered overhead as Hawrylak was placed on a cable that lifted him aboard. Jackson was next on the cable. As the corpsman was lifted up, the NVA turned their attention to Jackson, who by this time was suspended halfway between the ground and the helicopter. Pulling his .45 caliber pistol out and firing at the enemy below, Jackson successfully reached the helicopter. For his bravery under fire in caring for the stricken Marine, Jackson was awarded a Bronze Star.[2]

The Fight for the Imperial City of Hue (January–February 1968)

Prior to and during the enemy's TET offensive, 1st Force Reconnaissance Company conducted numerous patrols in and around Hue from their base at Phu Bai, eight miles south of the ancient imperial capital. Starting in late December 1967, 1st Force Reconnaissance Company teams amassed detailed information concerning trails, weather, landing zones, enemy strong points, and activities prior to the assault on the city at the end of January 1968. Information gathered by the recon teams revealed an increase in enemy activity. "The problem was that no one who was receiving the information was doing anything about it." In fact, Gunnery Sergeant Bruce D. Trevathan recalled that "many NVA were observed by the recon teams but that the reports were generally disregarded." One platoon commander in 1st Force Reconnaissance Company, First Lieutenant Russell L. Johnson, recalled that "he frequently talked with officers from the infantry battalions assigned to Task Force X-RAY who told him that some of the patrol's findings never made it down to their level." 1st Force Reconnaissance Company remained a part of Task Force X-Ray until September 1968, when it returned to operational control of the 1st Marine Division. For its actions in support of operations in and around Hue, 1st Force Reconnaissance Company was awarded a Meritorious Unit Citation.

Bill Hauxhurst, a member of 1st Force Reconnaissance Company from late 1967 to early 1969, stated, "Operations took on a whole new intensity in '68. We were very busy—in the bush for five days, back for a couple of days, then right back out again. We never went into an area where it wasn't expected there was enemy present." Sergeant Bob Buda, a platoon sergeant and team leader with 1st Force Reconnaissance Company, recalled that "every day, all we did was count literally hundreds of enemy troops moving into the [Hue] city."[3]

Sergeant Buda stated that as January 1968 ended, the fighting became more intense, as the Recon teams ran into larger NVA forces. The veteran Reconnaissance Marine remembered one patrol during which a large NVA force detected

The fight for the imperial city of Hue destroyed large portions of the city. A Marine observes the damage to the city in February 1968 (courtesy Colonel John Vogel).

them; a running gun fight followed as his eight-man team was chased up the side of a mountain in a game of "cat and mouse." Reaching the summit, the reconnaissance team sent out a frantic call for an extraction. The helicopters arrived just in time as the Marines were waiting on the edge of a cliff; as the CH-46 put its ramp against the side of the mountain, the team jumped one by one into the helicopter. One Marine missed and, as the team watched, fell thirty feet to what the team members felt was his certain death. Miraculously, they observed him climbing up the mountainside as they were flying away. One of the Huey gunships broke formation and turned around to retrieve the beleaguered Marine. Swooping in, the skids of the gunship touched the ground, with one of the crew members reaching out to yank the Marine inside the helicopter, which immediately took off and headed for home. Another patrol was just as harrowing, as an eight-man team had to be literally grabbed and thrown inside the Huey by the crew as its skids hit the ground.[4]

During the fight inside Hue City, one of the longest battles of the Vietnam War, 1st Force Reconnaissance Company Marines conducted thirty-five patrols throughout the month of February, during which they monitored enemy movement to and from the city and "called in more than 120 fire missions or air strikes on enemy targets." Of 180 Marines in 1st Force Reconnaissance Company, four were KIA and thirty-four WIA.[5]

A Combat Dive on the Silver Bridge

During the fight for the Citadel, Marine commanders, hoping to use the standing portion of the Silver Bridge in order to bring tanks across to reinforce Marines fighting there, called on 1st Force Reconnaissance's SCUBA team, commanded by Captain Fred Vogel, to conduct an underwater search underneath the bridge in order to determine whether enemy sappers had planted explosives underneath it. (This mission is described in the previous chapter.) While Vogel's team found a huge amount of discarded ammo and projectiles of all types, the Recon Marines "successfully confirmed nothing was rigged to drop more of the Silver Bridge." The conclusion was that "the infantry could now plan a crossing in force."[6]

"KEYHOLE Patrols": Long-Range Reconnaissance Operations

While 1st Force Reconnaissance Company was busy with the battle of Hue, Marines from 3rd Force Reconnaissance Company, as part of Task Force X-Ray, conducted STINGRAY patrols in support of the 3rd Marine Division. Beginning in March 1968, both 1st and 3rd Companies launched a number of more traditional long-range reconnaissance patrols referred to as KEYHOLE missions (four-man patrols that carried out "pure reconnaissance missions," designed to operate deep behind enemy lines that reached across the entire I Corps TAOR to the Laotian border). "The four-man [recon] teams avoided contact while keeping the enemy under surveillance and reporting his activities, lines of infiltration, supply points, and assembly areas." While Reconnaissance Marines were initially skeptical of the small size and limited firepower of the KEYHOLE patrols, "they learned to appreciate the new method in conducting Recon missions," as they proved to be very effective and there were fewer Marine casualties. During the first two months of KEYHOLE operations, 3rd Force Reconnaissance Company did not "take a single casualty." More important was the fact that these patrols were able to detect enemy arms caches, bunker complexes, and assembly areas. Lieutenant Colonel Babin noted, "The idea [behind KEYHOLE missions] was to enter the enemy's world and depart without him ever having known you were there."[7]

During the fighting in and around Khe Sanh, teams from 3rd Force Reconnaissance Company discovered roads and trails leading out of Laos to Ca Lu, the Ba Long Valley, and Khe Sanh itself; they also uncovered tracks made by enemy armor and discarded fuel drums cast aside by their crewmen.

These smaller patrols were not only more mobile but also easier to insert and extract by helicopter. During this same period, Marine Reconnaissance teams "borrowed" helicopter insertion techniques from the U.S. Army's 1st Cavalry Division prior to and during Operation "Pegasus," the relief of the Khe Sanh Combat Fire Support Base, which began on April 1, 1968:

The insertion flight team was made of three UH-1 troop carriers known as "slicks," and a pair of Huey and Cobra gunships. The slicks flew in a column, with the recon team aboard the lead bird, while the gunships remained nearby over the horizon or at a high altitude so they could come in to assist in case the slicks received ground fire. As the slicks approached the LZ, the column descended to tree-top level and the lead chopper dropped down to a few feet above the ground as the recon Marines unloaded. Meanwhile the two trail slicks flew over the lead ship. As they cleared the LZ, the chopper that had delivered the KEYHOLE patrol popped back up at the trail of the formation and all three continued on their way.[8]

This method of insertion, "combined with the team's small size and excellent camouflage procedures[,] allowed the Reconnaissance Marines to find and observe the enemy almost at will." 3rd Force Reconnaissance Company Marines benefited from the Army's relative wealth of helicopters throughout Operation "Pegasus," which ended on the morning of April 14, 1968. After "Pegasus," 3rd Force Reconnaissance Company teams used similar techniques with two CH-46s and two UH-1Es mentioned earlier.

The Summer of 1968

Teams from 3rd Force Reconnaissance Company continued KEYHOLE and STINGRAY missions in and around Khe Sanh/Phu Bai and throughout northern I Corps until the end of the war, penetrating deep into enemy-held territory, "oftentimes operating in the midst of NVA regiments and divisions."

Despite the use of KEYHOLE and STINGRAY missions during 1968, the issue of the "use and misuse of Reconnaissance teams" once again surfaced. Lieutenant Colonel William D. Kent, who succeeded Lieutenant Colonel Broman C. Stinemetz as commanding officer of 1st Reconnaissance Battalion in June 1968, expressed the opinion several years after the war that "reconnaissance" patrols were fighting the NVA rather than "watching them," thereby losing "a lot of long-range intelligence." Colonel Kent added that, once again, both division and III MAF staffs placed an "overreliance" on radio intercepts rather than on human intelligence.[9] According to Kent, "This was especially true in the NVA offensive in the Dong Ha sector at the end of April and beginning of May." In short, Marine commanders were more than willing to give recon teams a "pat on the back" for high KIA numbers but not for obtaining hard intelligence on the enemy. Lieutenant Colonel Stinemetz, in an after-action report, described the actions of one patrol in a harbor site on the nose of Charlie Ridge, west of Da Nang, that overlooked a well-known trail on January 30, 1968:

> Suddenly a major force of NVA regulars, heavily armed, came marching single file down the trail heading in an easterly direction towards the Da Nang area. At the 1st Recon Battalion's [operations center] came the whispered voice over the [tactical net] of the patrol's radio operator relaying his leaders observation. "Ask them how far they are away," the battalion's operations officer said. There was an agonizing wait as the operator relayed the request to his leader and waited for a response. Then in a barely audible whisper came: "the six [patrol commander] says they are within farting distance." The patrol leader stuck with his position for

a good thirty minutes and then called artillery strikes on points further down the trail. The darkness and the dense vegetation prohibited any damage assessment, but in debriefings patrol members reported lots of screaming from the impact area.[10]

As for the effectiveness of these patrols, from December 1967 through May 1968, Lieutenant Colonel Stinemetz reported the following reconnaissance statistics for the month of May 1968 for his battalion: 149 patrols, 476 sightings, 59 contacts, 6,606 enemy sighted, 362 fire missions and 42 air strikes; 46 enemy KIA by small arms, 681 by air and artillery. Stinemetz added, "[Recon] Marines captured five weapons and took two prisoners." As for Marine casualties, 1st Reconnaissance Battalion lost 6 Marines KIA and 45 WIA.[11]

Then-Sergeant Berwick Babin offered another perspective on STINGRAY missions versus the later KEYHOLE (four-man recon team) missions:

> Despite all the emphasis on KEYHOLE, I don't ever recall receiving a warning order that didn't include a STINGRAY mission. The difference in eight and four man patrols was the reluctance to initiate ground contact, but I don't know of any team that would pass on a lucrative target they could engage with supporting arms. In such cases, we would oftentimes request an AO to fly in the area to deflect enemy concerns that a recon team was directing fires. Staying concealed so as not to draw the enemy's attention was a practical matter regardless [of] patrol size. I recall another patrol in the Scotland II AOA which went for six days. Initial insert resulted in Sergeant Van Drasek breaking two ribs and an immediate extract, so we picked up a replacement and were reinserted the following day. We found trails and NVA shelters throughout our RZ. On the day before extract we moved closer to a river with plans to cross it at an opportune time. As we waited two unarmed Vietnamese paddled up to the bank just below us, within a couple of yards of me. They were talking and laughing. I could not see them clearly when they were up against the bank because of the brush. Lance Corporal [Steven A.] Fahlstrom called it in and then took the handset and advised Bravo to listen up. I held the handset out and kept it keyed so they could hear the Vietnamese chatter. I made a conscious decision not to attempt to capture them or ambush them to preserve our mission. The following morning, I requested permission to move out of my RZ to cross the river and was assured no friendlies would be in the area.
>
> However, as we waited for the extract a grunt company walked right over us. I was afraid they would shoot us if we stood up to let them know of our presence, so I waited until a number of them passed us by. They were very startled when I stood up, and then tried to act like they knew I was there. Then the rest of the team stood up, and they just walked on by without another word, knowing they would have been had if [we] would have been hostiles. That would have been a much riskier situation had we been an eight-man patrol.[12]

Task Force Hotel and Operation "Scotland II" (April 1968)

After April 15, 1968, III MAF assigned 3rd Force Reconnaissance Company OPCON to Task Force Hotel prior to the start of Operation "Scotland II," which took place in and around the Khe Sanh TAOR. According to Captain Phillip F. Reynolds, "Prior to participation in SCOTLAND II, the company operated with 8-9-man teams employing the STINGRAY concept." On April 15, 1968, the company began employing the KEYHOLE concept in I Corps, using four man teams that consisted of a patrol leader, point man, radio operator, and rear point. Captain Reynolds recalled, "These 4-man teams did not conduct STINGRAY reconnaissance [operations] but rather they conducted pure reconnaissance in the SCOTLAND II TAOR. We did not prep the landing zones prior to the insert. The helicopters flew directly into the reconnaissance zone. We avoided contact at all costs, and kept the enemy under constant surveillance, and reported his concept of operations, his activities, and made every effort to determine routes of infiltration, casualties, supply depots." Reynolds recounted that the KEYHOLE operations proved extremely valuable in finding helicopter landing zones for battalion-size and company-size operations in the "Scotland II" AO. The Marine Recon leader added:

> Since the start of this new concept of reconnaissance operations, this company has employed 36 reconnaissance teams under the KEYHOLE method of operations. This company since the start of KEYHOLE operations has sustained no casualties and has a credit of 15 KIAs in a period of 2½ months. The teams thus far have been credited with discovery of a large cache of arms, just east of the Laotian border. One team spotted a platoon of NVA, kept them under surveillance for 2 days, they led the reconnaissance team to a NVA assembly area, a harbor site. Located at this harbor site was an extensive bunker complex, just SW of Hill 881S. Upon extraction of the team, the next day, extensive airstrikes were called on this bunker complex, resulting in heavy destruction of the NVA and their supplies of ammunition which were located within the bunker complex.[13]

Captain Reynolds noted that during one of these missions in the "Scotland II" AO, his team discovered supply complexes and truck parks, as well as new roads under construction and tracked vehicles. He emphasized that "the results of these reconnaissance operations ... were ... invaluable in determining assembly areas and routes of infiltration."

Initially, Reynolds stated, there was some skepticism among the Marine Recon teams regarding the KEYHOLE concept. At first, team members felt "less secure because they had less people." However, as the teams employed the KEYHOLE concept more and more, they began to like it, as they discovered that "4-man teams can hide much better ... break contact much better, travel faster because they're carrying a lighter load," in addition to cutting the "duration of staying in the field" to three days. More important, from an insertion and extraction point of view, "it was easier to be extracted [and inserted] by 1 helicopter [as opposed to 2]."[14] Thus, when a team was either surrounded or needed immediate extraction, a four-man team was more manageable both logistically and operationally.

Second Lieutenant Willis M. Gregory, who commanded both 3rd and 4th Platoons of 3rd Force Reconnaissance Company, described a typical reconnaissance mission in the Khe Sanh TAOR and the close working relationship with the headquarters staff (in this case, stationed at Dong Ha):

> Since these reconnaissance operations began in the Khe Sanh area, the S3A has been stationed at Khe Sanh. He receives the missions and sends them down here to Dong Ha. As soon as the mission comes in a patrol leader is notified, and he immediately issues a warning order to his men, and they make the necessary preparations, included which is to make an

appointment with the S-2 for a briefing of the area. At the appointed time the entire team comes down and the S-2 gives a briefing on enemy troops in the area, what the terrain is like, where there are good HLZs and any other information which the team would like to know. On the morning when the mission is scheduled to take off, the chopper pilots usually come in about 6 o'clock. They are briefed along with the team members, the patrol leader, where he'd like to be put in. The entire team boards the choppers and make an overflight of the area. On this overflight the thing I try to look for is where our RZ [Reconnaissance Zone] is exactly. At times it's extremely hard to pick out where your reconnaissance zone is due to the fact that there aren't any real noticeable terrain features to guide on. If the HLZ which you have picked before hand with the chopper pilots is satisfactory you know where you are on your map then you tell the chopper pilot, "OK, just take us down." And he puts you right into the HLZ which you planned earlier. If the HLZ which you planned on the map doesn't turn out to be a good HLZ when you see it first hand, then you keep flying around the area until you find an HLZ which is acceptable to the team and to the pilots, and then you put down. As soon as the chopper comes in, the team jumps off, the chopper takes off, and the first thing the team does is make radio communication with the chopper that they are on the ground safely and are in comm with the choppers. At this point the team switches over to the primary frequency and attempts to establish communications with BRAVO relay on Hill 950. The team then moves out in a direction that the patrol leader has decided on, usually a hasty route in the reconnaissance zone, moving out in single file very slow, much slower than a regular infantry unit would move, being constantly on the alert for any sign, hearing of the enemy. Most of the time you'll hear the enemy before you see him. The enemy is usually very careless when they're out in the bush. They usually don't believe there are any friendlies in their country, and consequently they do a lot of talking, laughter, etc.

A team from 3rd Force Reconnaissance Company boards a waiting CH-46 helicopter at the Dong Ha Combat Base for an "insertion" into enemy territory (courtesy Lieutenant Colonel Barry Babin).

The movement depends on the mission of the patrol. My last patrol I had a pathfinder mission; I was to check out three possible HLZs for a grunt insertion, so I immediately headed towards the first HLZ. If the mission is just a regular surveillance of the reconnaissance zone, usually I just run a zig-zag pattern across the reconnaissance zone, trying to see if the trails are being used, but at the same time you try to keep off the trails as much as possible. Any contact I've had in the bush has taken place on or near the trail, and I've also had one booby trap, so I've learned my lessons on the trail very well.

When you're on a patrol, one of the things is to radio back any information you come across out there. You also keep a notebook and radio back any information you have on it, so that later during the debriefing, they can check it out, make sure there's nothing you've missed out there, and also it keeps the COC up to date on what's happening, whether or not you're in any danger. It's very important to keep the radio relay informed of everything you're doing.

In the evenings I usually eat chow and at this point, I usually kneel where I'm planning on making my harbor site, within 100 or 200 meters. Then I plan my on-calls and send in where I believe my harbor site will be for the night. As soon as it grows dark, I move into the harbor site for that night. With 4-man patrols there's not as much security as you had with 8-man patrols. We don't carry claymores due to the fact that there are only 4 of us. We are on 25% alert, depending on the situation. On the last patrol I was on we had movement around us the entire night, so I stayed awake the entire night until the early hours of the morning, when the movement ceased, and we went to a 50%. We usually have a 25% alert. We try to be as rested as possible for the next day because we do a lot of humping. We don't have claymores around us at night; report, and BRAVO relays keep in comm with us the entire night, so if anything happens, we can get arty on the way right away. In selecting a harbor site for the night, I usually try for the high ground. This is mainly because in the areas we've been operating, communications is so bad, that unless you're on the high ground, you don't have any communications for the night. I don't usually stay on the top of the hill, but on the slope of it. The main thing you look for in a harbor site is extremely thick brush; that way you can hear the enemy if they try to come after you, and also, they won't be able to throw in grenades on top of you.

In the patrols that we're running now we usually come out of the bush on the 3d day. In the 2d day I begin looking for a suitable HLZ for my extraction. It's really not all that difficult to find—landing zones in the Khe Sanh area—there are so many bomb craters that can be used as emergency HLZs. On the day of the extraction you're informed a little in advance by BRAVO relay that your birds are on the way, so you head for the HLZ, and guide the birds on in right on top of you. When you've extracted, you're flown right to Khe Sanh, the base itself, where we go into the COC, debriefed at Khe Sanh. As soon as our debrief is over, they tell us to hitch a ride as best we can and head back to Dong Ha. We head down to the airstrip, and how we get back to Dong Ha depends on how many birds are operating at Khe Sanh at the time and whether any of them are headed back. We've had pretty good luck on medevac birds usually heading to B Med. When we get back to Dong Ha, the team leader reports to the S-2 and gives him a general run-down of the area which might help future teams. The rest of the team usually does not take part in this."[15]

As for the effectiveness of the KEYHOLE patrols conducted in the "Scotland II" TAOR, Sergeant Robert L. Nixton, a platoon sergeant and team leader with 3rd Force Reconnaissance Company, later recounted that on one patrol north of Khe Sanh, "we were on the ground for about an hour and found this trail, 2–4 foot wide coming down from the DMZ, which we weren't too far from. We followed it to our north, approximately 3,000 meters away from the DMZ and made contact with 4–6 enemy. We broke contact, pulled back from the spot of the contact, heard movement on all 3 sides, so we pulled back a little bit further, and got extracted." Sergeant Nixton added, "There was an increase of enemy movement from the north and Laos in small groups. They were real well equipped. Their morale seems to be not too bad. They're mainly young troops and real…. The further north you get, the more the enemy is taking to the high ground."[16] Another platoon sergeant and team leader, David Metz, noted that the Marines had noticed an increase in the number of fresh enemy trails running out of Laos west of Khe Sanh and from Khe Sanh east to

A Reconnaissance Marine fords a river while on patrol in northern I Corps (courtesy Lieutenant Colonel Barry Babin).

the Ba Long Valley and to Ca Lu. Sergeant Metz likewise noted that the reconnaissance teams discovered caches of arms and equipment—gear that was in "pretty good shape."[17] This gear included AK-47s, rockets, and mortars.

Corporal Olaf L. Janis noted that in the "Scotland II" TAOR, the recon teams discovered an extensive network of bunkers as well as fresh trails running west and east of Khe Sanh. One road discovered by members of 3rd Force Reconnaissance Company was about fifteen feet wide and "had been built by structural engineers and had a big trail running alongside it"; "on that [same] road they found tank tracks, and on one point on the

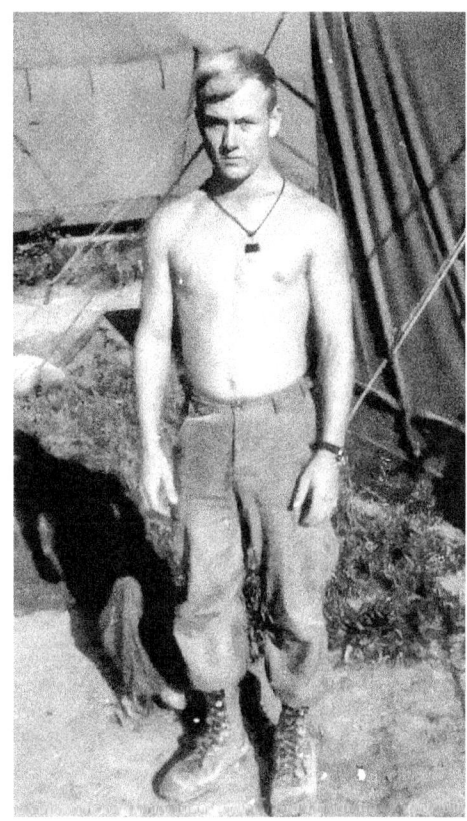

Sergeant Nixton, a platoon sergeant with 3rd Force Reconnaissance Company, poses in front of his "hooch" after a patrol (courtesy Lieutenant Colonel Barry Babin).

road they found 50-gallon fuel drums which they probably used for resupply points for those tanks." Corporal Janis noted that from April through June 1968, "We ran about 50 patrols in support of this operation ['Scotland II'] and only about 10 of these contacts was made."[18]

As Sergeant Nixton, Sergeant Metz, and Corporal Janis noted, despite the relief of Khe Sanh in April 1968, enemy infiltration across the DMZ and from Laos continued—this despite the heavy losses the NVA incurred

Lance Corporal Chuck McMullen at the Dong Ha Combat Base in a poncho in ankle-deep water (courtesy Lieutenant Colonel Barry Babin).

during the siege and subsequent withdrawal from the Khe Sanh TAOR. Sergeant Danny M. Slocum noted that many of the patrols were designed to "know the infiltration routes, HLZs throughout the area, whether the area was being used by the enemy and if so, how extensively." Sergeant Slocum later added that many of the missions were specifically designed to "find out just what the enemy was wearing, what kind of weapons they were carrying," in addition to determining the terrain, distance between the hills, and what the

Sergeant Babin snapped this photograph as an extraction helicopter took off from the Khe Sanh Combat Base in June 1968 (courtesy Lieutenant Colonel Barry Babin).

communications were like. After being wounded during one patrol, Slocum was assigned to work in the S-3, to help brief team leaders before they departed on their patrols. He had patrolled extensively across the northern I Corps. His experience included a patrol that on January 10, 1968, captured a POW. The team was extracted and subsequently given a bottle of Champagne, a steak dinner and a three-day R&R in Da Nang.[19] It was also the first patrol that Second Lieutenant Terrance (Terry) Graves made in Vietnam. Their call sign was "Box Score," and, as was the custom, because experience was considered more important than seniority in the bush, Sergeant William P. Andress, an experienced reconnaissance Marine, led the patrol.

A month later, Graves was leading Box Score in the bush when Slocum was wounded. It was a significant action and classic STINGRAY. Corporal Barry J. Butterworth provides the details:

> Team Box Score of the Third Force Reconnaissance Company reached its assigned recon zone six miles northwest of Dong Ha on 15 February 1968 by walking from the nearest firebase. Composed of eight men including patrol leader Second Lieutenant Terrence C. Graves, six enlisted Marines, and a Corpsman, Box Score had a rather typical mission, to determine enemy activity, engaging what enemy they found with supporting fires, locating landing zones and trails, and attempting to capture a prisoner. By the afternoon of the 16th, the team had reached an area overlooking a small stream pocked with bomb craters. Hearing voices in the thick brush across the waterway, the team crossed the stream to set up an ambush in a bomb crater alongside a trail. Within minutes seven NVA walked down the pathway. When the enemy was within five meters of the ambush, the recon men opened up, killing all seven. In the brief firefight, the NVA were barely able to return fire; however, two of the rounds they managed to get off struck Corporal Danny M. Slocum, tearing away shin and muscle from his thigh but not producing life threatening wounds.
>
> While the team medic, HM3 Stephen R. Thompson, was treating Slocum, Graves hastily searched the bodies and found a diary along with other documents. The patrol leader then called a med-evac for the wounded Marine and began moving the team to a better point to bring in the helicopter. Box Score made it only a few meters before the team was raked by automatic weapons fire from two different directions. Graves ordered the team into a hasty perimeter as the Marines returned fire. Several of the NVA machine guns were knocked out by accurate M-79 grenade launcher fire by Corporal Robert B. Thomson, though Thomson had been unable to spot the exact position of the automatic weapons until Private First Class Michael P. Nation exposed himself to mark their positions with tracer rounds for Thomson to zero in on.
>
> The silencing of the enemy machine guns brought only a brief lull to the fighting. Every minute, more NVA joined the battle, until at least two companies were ringing the eight-man patrol. Despite the number of NVA, Graves had to move his team to a better position from which to fight and hopefully be extracted. As the lieutenant directed in air strikes and gunships to cover their movement, the team began inching its way to the top of a small knoll. At one point a CH-46 attempted to land near the team but took several hits and had to lift off.
>
> As the CH 46 flew out of range, the NVA again concentrated their firepower on the recon team. Graves took a bullet in the thigh, but an inspection by Doc Thompson revealed that the bone was not broken. After a quick bandaging, Graves was back on the radio coordinating the supporting fires. No sooner had the Corpsman finished with the lieutenant than Corporal Thomson yelled that he too had been hit. A bullet had penetrated the Marine's left side and shattered the pelvic bone before lodging in the abdominal cavity. Doc Thompson recalls, "He said, 'I'm blacking out, Doc, I'm blacking out.' Then he passed out on me, and I think

at that moment he died. I started closed-chest cardiac massage and mouth-to-mouth resuscitation. While I was doing this, Lopez, Private First Class Adrian S. yelled, 'Doc, Emrick's (Lance Corporal Steven E.) hit, I think he's dying.' I looked over and said, 'Nation [who had been cross-trained by Thompson in medical procedures], just do what you can.'" Nation alternated between treating Emrick and doing his best to fight off the NVA. According to Nation, "Emrick kept saying, 'Get the radio off.' That was what he was talking about; he wasn't worried about himself. Lopez finally got it off by snapping off the bottom of the pack. Then Emrick said, 'Oh my God,' and that's the last thing he said. I started to give him mouth to mouth. Lopez said he could still feel a pulse."

There was no letup in the NVA fire despite the repeated runs by fixed-wing aircraft and helicopter gunships. Graves continued to fight as he directed the team to make another attempt to move to higher ground. With Doc Thompson and Private First Class James E. Honeycutt dragging Thomson and with Nation and Lopez carrying Emrick, Graves and Slocum provided covering fire despite their wounds. A few minutes later Box Score reached the low grassy ridge that was large enough for a set down extraction. Although the patrol was then in a good position for extraction, the ridge they occupied was paralleled by two higher hills, both occupied by the NVA only 100 meters away. The fight by the eight Marines against several hundred NVA had been going on for over an hour and a half.

Another CH-46 made an attempt to reach the team but took heavy fire and had to regain altitude. Captain David Underwood, orbiting the fight at 1,000 feet in his UH-34, radioed that he was coming in to make the extraction. Flying behind a Huey gunship for covering fire, Underwood came in at treetop level through a gauntlet of small-arms and machine-gun fire, touching down only a few meters from the team. Intense fire immediately centered on the UH-34, shattering the side windows and some of the pilot's instrument panel gauges. More rounds were slamming into the fuselage and fuel pods. Although practically every warning light was lit up on the still operational parts of the instrument panel, Underwood stayed at the controls, waiting for the recon team to climb aboard.

Dragging, pulling, and crawling through the elephant grass, the Marines loaded the aircraft as Graves continued to return the NVA fire. Three long minutes passed as the recon men ensured that their wounded buddies were pulled onto the aircraft that was now profusely leaking fuel and was in danger of exploding. Nation later stated, "I guess Lieutenant Graves saw how bad the plane was hit and realized if the chopper didn't leave then it wouldn't be leaving at all, because I saw him waving at the pilot and yelling 'get' or 'get out.' He did this realizing that he might get hit again and his chances of getting back were pretty slim, but he wanted to make sure that the rest of us made it back. What Lieutenant Graves did is the bravest thing I've ever seen."

As Underwood began to lift the crippled chopper, the NVA ran out of their protected positions for better shots. One burst strafed the bird, a bullet hitting Lopez in the thigh and glancing off the bone and into the Marine's stomach. As the helicopter gained a few feet of altitude, Slocum and Honeycutt realized that Graves was being left behind. With no words exchanged between the two, both Marines jumped from the helicopter to help their lieutenant. With the loss of weight of the two men, Underwood was able to gain altitude quickly and nurse the bird to the nearest medical facility. More than 20 bullet holes were later counted in the aircraft.

Meanwhile, Underwood's wingman, Captain Carl Bergman, was attempting to pick up the remaining recon men. Three passes through the NVA fire failed to find the Marines, but on the fourth try Bergman spotted the trio and set his UH-34 down near them. The chopper immediately came under intense automatic weapons fire from NVA so close that initially Bergman could not distinguish between the sounds of the outgoing from his door gunners and the incoming from the enemy. A shout from the cargo compartment revealed that the crew chief had been wounded and that the fuel cells were hit and leaking. Bergman was forced to lift off before the remaining members of Box Score were able to fight their way to the helicopter. Graves, Slocum, and Honeycutt continued to return fire as they made still another attempt to move to a more advantageous position.

The NVA dropped two mortar rounds near the trio but did no damage. Suddenly a UH-1 pilot spotted an opening and swooped in almost on top of the Marines. The Huey hovered just off the ground as the recon men threw their gear aboard and pulled themselves into the aircraft. Cross fire from the NVA zeroed in on the chopper as it attempted to lift off. Graves was hit again, as was the copilot, who slumped over the controls. The Huey nosed over and crashed on its side into the jungle. Slocum found himself on top of "a heap of bodies." As he crawled out of the helicopter, 15–20 NVA were sweeping toward him on line. The enemy spotted the Marine and opened fire as he turned and ran toward a nearby stream. Hitting the streambed at a dead run, Slocum was able to elude his pursuers. By then, darkness was closing in on the battle area.

A reaction force consisting of a platoon of B Company, 1st Battalion, 4th Marines air-landed near the crashed Huey to rescue any survivors. Before they reached the downed aircraft, they too became engaged with the NVA from three directions and suffered one killed and four wounded. Unable to proceed, the platoon formed a defensive perimeter. Slocum heard the firefight from his hiding place near the stream but decided to remain in place. He later recalled matter-of-factly, "I didn't want to go back over there. There was a firefight going on and I didn't want to get shot anymore." At daylight the next morning, the remainder of B Company was lifted in and finally reached the crashed chopper to report that Graves and Honeycutt were dead and Slocum missing.

The missing Marine's problems were not yet over. In his attempt to link up with B Company, the infantry Marines mistook him for an NVA and called in artillery on him. Slocum states, "It didn't bother me; I got down in a hole."

When the infantrymen started toward Slocum's hole, not wanting to take any more chances, he headed in the opposite direction. Finally, a chopper spotted him and coordinated his joining up with B Company. Slocum was evacuated to the Naval Hospital in Cam Ranh Bay where after two and a half months he recovered from his wounds and eventually rejoined Third Force Reconnaissance Company. Thomson, Lopez, and Emrick were not so fortunate. All three died of their wounds either aboard Underwood's helicopter or within hours of reaching the evacuation hospital.

Slocum, Doc Thompson, and Bergman later received the Silver Star. Thomson's Silver Star and Honeycutt's Navy Cross were both awarded posthumously. Underwood also had earned a Navy Cross.

Corporal James Craig, a member of 3rd Force Reconnaissance Company, sits atop a LVTP-5 amtrac with his fellow Marines (courtesy Lieutenant Colonel Barry Babin).

On 2 December 1969, in the office of the Vice President of the United States, Spiro T. Agnew presented the Medal of Honor posthumously to the family of Lieutenant Graves.[20]

As for the reaction of the enemy to the presence of the four-man KEYHOLE patrols that commenced little more than a month after the Box Score patrol, Sergeant William P. Cress noted that "we did run into a lot of the enemy out there, but they don't really believe we're out there. We're out there with 4 men usually what they're travelling at, they're just so surprised to see you they don't know if you're the enemy, one of theirs, they just stand there and look at you." Sergeant Cress added that when the recon teams discovered enemy activity in the area, "it was usually in small groups." According to him, the NVA "were just as surprised to see a 4-man team out there, dressed as they were, including camouflage which, they do wear." The Marine sergeant said that when contact was made with enemy patrols, "we broke

"Battle Ready!" Sergeant Van Drasek, a member of 3rd Force Reconnaissance, poses in front of 3rd Marine Force Reconnaissance's combat base at Dong Ha (courtesy Lieutenant Colonel Barry Babin).

contact with small arms or CS grenades, and we get pulled out as soon as we can find a HLZ."[21]

Lieutenant Colonel Babin, then a sergeant and a member of 3rd Force Reconnaissance Company, recalled one patrol in the "Scotland II" TAOR in which his team had three enemy sightings within a twenty-four-hour period. The first occurred on

> 13 June at 0900 when we spotted 1 NVA approximately 75 meters to our east on the eastern slope of a hill. He was laying on his stomach in about 2 feet of elephant grass, and he was only visible for a few seconds when he raised his head. We weren't sure we were observed, but there was a good chance of it because we were in real small open grass too.[22]

The second enemy sighting occurred the next day, on June 14, when Babin

> observed another NVA about 75 meters to our NE. He was wearing green utilities, rifle with a guerrilla sling, and he was holding something to his eyes that reflected light, which were probably binoculars. He was about 10 meters off the crest of the hill; he was Oping the SW where some airstrikes were taking place.

The third sighting occurred later that same day when Babin's team

> noted two NVA wearing green utilities and bush hats, crawling up to our rear. I think they were following us. And when we saw them, they ducked down. It was real fast. So I figured we were probably going to get ambushed. We moved up to the top of the hill and set up security on the top. During the time we were up there, we heard whispering all around us at a distance of 12–15 meters. We also heard people running around and equipment clanking. I expended 5 grenades in an effort to stop the movement which was effective at certain times, I think. When the helicopters came, just as half the team got on, my radioman was just getting on, a couple of AK-47 rounds opened up with tracers, and we silenced them, and the helicopter pulled up and there was fire from all four sides. It was estimated that there were approximately 40 Aks that opened up on the helicopter at that time.

Babin concluded by stating, "In addition to this contact there were other signs of enemy activity in that area. We located a tunnel entrance on the east slope of a hill, about 3 feet side and five feet high."[23]

As for the "other signs" of enemy activity, Corporal Harlan E. Holmes, a patrol leader with 3rd Force Reconnaissance Company and a member of Babin's platoon, whose team operated in the area just south of Khe Sanh, reported finding enemy artifacts as well as a number of

Sergeant Babin enjoys a "chew" as he takes a break after returning from a patrol (courtesy Lieutenant Colonel Barry Babin).

fighting holes dug into the ridgelines, with the majority of them being "old," though some were freshly dug. Corporal Holmes noted that the NVA used the steep ridgelines for security, as there was considerable movement down in the valleys. Another sign of the enemy's presence was the smell of campfires in the early morning hours. Holmes added that while the valleys were covered with a thick fog in the early morning hours and visibility was limited to twelve to fifteen meters, "you can smell campfire smoke in the morning, because it is 'very thick' down there."[24]

Sergeant Babin recalled Team Coral Bush's patrol of June 14, 1968, when this team, along with five other four-man teams from 3rd Force Reconnaissance Company, was inserted along possible enemy avenues of approach into the Khe Sanh Combat Base in June 1968. (Another account of this mission, as recalled by Lance Corporal David Vaughn, can be found in chapter 7.) Operating in support of Operation "Scotland II," the reconnaissance teams were tasked with locating the *324th Alpha Division* of the North Vietnamese Army, which was considered a possible threat to the security of Khe Sanh Combat Base. According to Babin, "We were briefed that the lucky team to find them, might have a serious problem. One of the briefers said that it was like [playing] Russian roulette."[25] The Coral Bush Reconnaissance Zone was located on the ridgeline running southeast from Hill 861 in the vicinity of the Khe Sanh Combat Base, in and around Hills 881 South and 861 in the "Scotland II" TAOR. Babin later recalled:

A 3rd Force Reconnaissance team led by Staff Sergeant Livingston poses for a photograph before going out on patrol in the summer of 1968 (courtesy Lieutenant Colonel Barry Babin).

Lance Corporal Steve Fahlstrom, a member of 3rd Marine Force Reconnaissance Company (courtesy Lieutenant Colonel Barry Babin).

The team was inserted on June 12, 1968. The team reported heavy movement in the valleys on either side of the ridgeline on the 12th and the 13th. Early afternoon of the 13th the team directed F-4 air strikes against enemy movement about 3,000 meters west of their position and south of Hill 881 South. Late afternoon on June 14th, the team moved north west along the southern slope, near the military crest of the ridge line, for the purpose of moving into an observation position. As they moved, the team engaged at least two enemy soldiers on their left flank. The team then moved to a higher position on the ridgeline and established a defensive position in a bomb crater. They defended their position with small arms and hand grenades against enemy forces attempting to over-run their position for about two hours. The team was extracted under intense enemy fire at about 1900 by CH-46 helicopter from Marine Medium Helicopter Squadron 161. Following the extraction, the team was flown into Khe Sanh Combat Base where they were debriefed and answered questions from Major General Raymond G. Davis, CG 3rd Marine Division concerning their actions, possible observation positions, and key terrain. Operation Charlie commenced on June 19th and successfully evacuated Khe Sanh Combat Base on July 5th, 1968.[26]

During the month of August 1968 through the end of the year, the 3rd Force Reconnaissance Company continued its assigned mission of conducting reconnaissance and surveillance of the DMZ, the Western Reconnaissance Zone and a variety of special missions, all within the 3rd Marine Division area of operations. In fact, operations conducted by 3rd Force Reconnaissance Company increased slightly beginning in August due to the mission of placing sensors in and along the known infiltration routes.

Patrols were routinely assigned and conducted as traditional reconnaissance missions. The average number of men per patrol for the month of August was seven. This total was inclusive of patrols in the DMZ, where patrol size was set at a minimum of eight men by headquarters. Lieutenant Colonel Babin stated, "In 3rd Force Reconnaissance Company, from the end of March through November (1968) when I rotted, every patrol I knew of was four Marines, except the ones of Oceanview, when we went with six in the DMZ. I never heard of the eight-man DMZ requirement."[27] Most insertions and extractions were done by helicopter, although many teams carried out a number of "walk-out" reconnaissance patrols in August 1968 from their base camps, located at LZ STUD (Vandegrift Combat Base), the Rockpile, Camp Carroll, Cam Lo, Con Thien, Cua Viet and Oceanview. The average number of hours in the field per patrol during August was "somewhere over three days or 72.2 hours from insertion to extraction. This figure included those patrols that were 'shot out' in a matter of hours on the first day."

Reconnaissance patrolling during August accounted for nineteen NVA/VC KIA (confirmed), seven enemy probable KIA, and an undetermined number of the enemy WIA. The company lost one Marine KIA (no WIA) on patrols during the period. On the night of August 31, 1968, shortly after the company relocated to Quang Tri, it came under intense enemy fire as eleven 122mm rockets crashed into the perimeter, prompting men, as Lieutenant Colonel Babin recalled, to "quip that they were safer in the bush." This attack began at 2220 and lasted some twenty minutes; it resulted in fourteen friendly WIA, of which twelve were Marines and two Navy corpsmen. Seven of the fourteen wounded were evacuated, with four of them returning to duty within seventy-two hours. The remaining three had injuries serious enough to warrant evacuation out-of-country for further treatment. Babin added, "The sand-bagged, wood framed hooches in Dong Ha stood up well during the incoming [rockets] unless they took a direct hit. The canvas hard back GP tents at Quang Tri got ripped by flying shrapnel causing them to drip water in the rain."[28]

"Firecrackers and STINGRAY": 3rd Reconnaissance Battalion (June–December 1968)

Like their counterparts in the 3rd Marine Division, reconnaissance teams from 3rd Reconnaissance Battalion remained busy with patrolling and calling in

STINGRAY strikes on enemy positions in the Arizona Territory and in and around the Hon Coc Mountain, almost four miles from Go Noi Island. These strikes took a heavy toll on enemy positions and formations in the Arizona Territory southwest of Da Nang in Quang Nam Province.

On June 10, 1968, Team Elf Skin, which had been inserted along a position on a narrow ridge overlooking the Arizona Territory and the Song Vu Gia, recorded 25 separate enemy sightings for a total of 341 Viet Cong. From its concealed position, Elf Skin also called in twenty-four artillery missions for a reported tally of over forty enemy dead. STINGRAY missions supported all major Marine operations in the I Corps TAOR throughout the remainder of 1968.

On another mission in and around Go Noi Island, Team Cayenne detected an enemy force of some one hundred men moving out of the hamlet of An Tam (1) shortly after they had been inserted. Undetected, the team leader called in a STINGRAY mission using "firecracker" fire missions, which resulted in thirty enemy KIA. According to Lieutenant Colonel Babin, Marine artillery began to employ the "new fire-cracker munitions, which came in either bombs or artillery rounds. The bomb or round exploded at a set height above ground and released a number of smaller bombs over an extended area, which in turn exploded, sending an explosive force and shrapnel over a wider area as opposed to a standard 'air burst' from traditional munitions." Babin added, "So when one said they were calling in a firecracker mission, it was usually an artillery call for fire that specified firecracker rounds to cover a wide area." Babin commented that in mid–1968 some Recon Marines started to carry the new "M-33" ball-shaped fragmentation hand grenades (known as firecracker grenades): "The [M-33] had a baseball-shape, was easier to grasp and throw, and had greater lethality than the older M-26 fragmentation hand grenade. Some Marines referred to it as a firecracker grenade, though it was a misnomer because it had a greater lethality and a sharp,

"Life in the Field": Sergeant Berwick "Barry" Babin rests between patrols at the base camp at Dong Ha (courtesy Lieutenant Colonel Barry Babin).

distinctive 'ka-rack' sound when it exploded." The veteran Recon Marine went on to say, "Some may have referred to the small material encased explosive packets dropped from the air as area denial weapons as firecracker missions. However, they were most frequently referred to as gravel, and they came in three sizes of increasing lethality. They decomposed over a period of time, possibly 90 days. When out on a patrol we could hear them explode in the night, like firecrackers, presumably as animals and NVA stepped on them." Babin said that the grenades were a "component of McNamara's Line."[29]

Later that first day, during their insertion near An Tam (1), Team Cayenne detected an eighty-man VC platoon moving west away from Go Noi Island. This was the same direction used by the enemy earlier that day. The team leader called in an air strike, which resulted in an additional thirty enemy KIA.

On the same day, another reconnaissance team from 3rd Reconnaissance Battalion, known as Parallel Bars, spotted a group of sixteen Viet Cong also moving west, some one hundred meters west of the previous sighting. Parallel Bars called in a "firecracker" mission, though, due to darkness, they were unable to confirm the effectiveness of this strike. The next day, however, as the sun rose in the early morning hours of June 26, Marine observers spotted another twenty-seven-man VC team moving along the same position almost nine hundred meters farther southwest from the first three positions. Once again Parallel Bars' team leader called in a fire mission, which resulted in five more enemy dead.

	Jul.	Aug.	Sep.	Oct.	Nov.	Dec.	Total
No. of Patrols	133	147	143	165	158	105*	851
Average Duration	2.13	2.45	2.36	3.19	8.60	3.89	3.77
Average Size	6.09	6.61	6.72	7.22	7.10	6.50	6.72
No. of Sightings	45	54	78	71	55	20	323
No. Enemy Sighted	288	778	508	289	314	114	2291
No. of Contacts	20	52	52	34	31	22	211
No. Fire Missions	16	28	39	64	64	22	233
No. Rounds Fired	416	1203	914	1742	1363	249	5887
No. Air Strikes	5	14	5	24	3	5	56
Enemy KIA (C)	22	63	102	25	23	13	248
Enemy Captured	0	0	0	1	0	0	1
Weapons Captured	2	5	8	0	7	1	23
Friendly KIA	4	1	5	1	3	1	15
Friendly WIA	26	5	20	4	6	8	69

* Includes 31 teams deployed in the field as of 12 December 1968

1st Reconnaissance Battalion Continues to Support 1st Marine Division (September–December 1968)

During the month of September 1968, 1st Reconnaissance Battalion continued to carry out KEYHOLE and STINGRAY operations against the NVA and VC in support of the 1st Marine Division (Rein.) as well as units from the U.S. Army's "Americal," 1st Air Cavalry Division, and 17th Air Cavalry Regiment. Captain John Vogel's

SCUBA team likewise continued to support operations by conducting SCUBA and salvage recovery missions.

Operation "Wheeler/Wallowa" (February 9–28, 1968)

During the "Wheeler/Wallowa" operation, teams from 1st Force Reconnaissance Company supported elements of the U.S. Army's "Americal" Division, the 1st Squadron, 1st Cavalry Squadron, 1st Air Cavalry Division, and the 7th Squadron, 17th Cavalry, in operations in the Que Son Valley that accounted for a "significant number of enemy casualties." For instance, on February 9, elements of the "Americal" Division engaged a battalion of the *29th NVA Regiment*, which resulted in two hundred enemy KIA and the capture of fifty-three individual and thirteen crew-served weapons. In a similar operation near the end of the month, elements of the 1st Cavalry Squadron, 1st Air Cavalry Division, along with 7th Squadron, 17th Cavalry, killed over 148 enemy troops and captured a further 32 individual and 9 crew-served weapons. In an operation that spanned nearly a month, the U.S. Army claimed 1,200 enemy KIA and the capture of 24 enemy POWs, 247 individual weapons and 37 crew-served weapons. It is important to note that in both instances, Marine Recon teams provided invaluable reconnaissance support to the U.S. Army units engaged in "Wheeler/Wallowa." This month-long operation to clear the VC/NVA from the Que Son Valley, in fact, involved "numerous contacts between American and NVA/VC small unit patrols." This combined Marine–Army operation, in fact, played an instrumental part in clearing the VC/NVA from the Que Son Valley.[30]

1st Reconnaissance and "Mameluke Thrust" (May 19–31, 1968)

In the aftermath of the siege and battles in and around Khe Sanh and Hue City, Recon Marines of 1st Battalion continued to conduct deep reconnaissance patrols west of the Da Nang TAOR as well as in the hills overlooking the eastern end of the So Lo Dong Valley in the area known by Marines as "Happy Valley" in support of Operations "Allen Brook," "Swift Saber," "Wheeler/Wallowa," "Mameluke Thrust," and "Houston."

Seven Months of Extensive Patrolling (July–December 1968)

Operation "Houston," which began on February 26, 1968, continued into the summer in the Phu Loc and Hai Van Pass sectors as a combined operation to reopen Route 1 between Da Nang and Hue/Phu Bai and clear the area of enemy troops. Assigned to Task Force X-Ray, a joint U.S. Marine–U.S. Army operation, was commanded by U.S. Army Brigadier General Foster LaHue and spearheaded by Colonel Robert D. Bohn's 5th Marines, supported by two battalions from Da Nang relieved by the 27th Marines, LaHue's 3rd Battalion and 2nd Battalion, as well as the 2nd Battalion, 3rd Marines. Soldiers from the U.S. Army's 1st and 3rd Battalions, 327th Infantry, as well as the 2nd Battalion, 502nd Infantry, likewise participated in the operation. Marine Recon teams from 3rd and 1st Force Reconnaissance Companies carried out an extensive number of surveillance and STINGRAY missions in support of Task Force X-Ray.

For the next seven months, teams from 1st Force Reconnaissance Company conducted numerous patrols in and around Route 545 in the vicinity of the Nam Hoa Mountain in support of Operation "Houston." Team Date Palm, an eight-man recon team led by Gunnery Sergeant G.A. Koch, had the mission of "surveillance and reconnaissance [in order to] detect possible VC/NVA troop movement or arms infiltration in the vicinity of Nam Hoa Mountain." "Gunny" Koch's team put special emphasis on "locating and fixing enemy storage areas, fortifications (trench lines, bunkers), harbor sites and the direction and trafficability of trails in the area." Prior to their departure from their base at Phu Bai, the company S-3 instructed Koch to "be prepared to call and adjust artillery and air on targets of opportunity in support of Operation HOUSTON."

Inserted by CH-46s at around 0800 on July 10, Gunnery Sergeant Koch's team landed in three-foot-high elephant grass. Throughout the patrol, they operated in an area dominated by rolling hills and scrub brush, with no canopy. About an hour after insertion, Team Date Palm came under 81/82mm mortar fire from an enemy battery. For the next twenty-eight hours, the team conducted its mission, which yielded no VC/NVA sightings, though it did uncover an older enemy trail no longer in use. Koch's team was extracted the next morning (July 11) and returned to base.[31]

On July 12, 1968, "Gunny" Koch once again led his team (code-named Team Deskwork) in the vicinity of Route 545, with the same mission of surveillance and reconnaissance of enemy infiltration routes, fortifications, and harbor sites. The patrol, which lasted seventy-one hours, uncovered a series of older enemy trails no longer in use and an overgrown landing zone, though there were no enemy sightings.

Other teams from 1st Force Reconnaissance Company conducting extensive patrols in support of Operation "Houston" included Record and Coffee Time II. In addition to their time in the field, patrol leaders spent time in direct coordination with ground combat elements of Task Force X-Ray and the 1st Field Artillery Group. Such coordination added to the professional acumen of the Recon Marines and enhanced future operations. Despite the lack of enemy sightings, these patrols brought back important information about terrain, vegetation, avenues of approach, water sources, and possible OPs and HLZs, which are helpful in planning operations. Though the teams did not inflict causalities on the enemy, they likewise did not suffer any casualties. Ironically, they also brought back information about where the enemy wasn't.

Team Record, from 1st Force Reconnaissance Company, had the mission to "conduct reconnaissance and surveillance operations with [its] assigned HAVEN to detect possible VC/NVA troop movements or arms infiltration in the vicinity of Hai Dong." In support of Operation "Houston," Team Record was instructed to place "particular emphasis on locating and fixing enemy storage areas, fortifications, (trench lines, bunkers) harbor sites and the direction and trafficability of trails in the area." Special emphasis was placed on ensuring a "thorough coordination with the S-3, 1st Field Artillery Group (1st FAG) to ensure maximum effectiveness of supporting arms, including the use of night defensive, 'on call,' and counter battery fire." Team Deskwork was likewise instructed to "ensure thorough coordination with the 5th Marine Regiment who have been assigned the mission of providing the Bald Eagle capability." Finally, Deskwork was to coordinate its movement with the 5th Marine Combat Operation Center (COC) and pass along any useful information on terrain, as well as any units "that they have operating in this area."

Team Coffee Time II, a thirteen-man reconnaissance team led by Corporal W.D. Kearney in support of Operation "Houston," was ordered, on July 19, 1968, to "establish an observation post and provide security for a radio relay site on Truoi Mountain, as well as conduct surveillance operations in order … to detect possible VC/NVA troop movement and arms infiltration in the Ben Tau area." During this particular mission, Corporal Kearney's team placed "special emphasis on surveillance in order to observe possible rocket launching sites, mortar positions, storage areas, fortifications, routes of access and egress." Kearney's team also prioritized locating "an area suitable for a helicopter landing zone (HLZ) and (a position) to adjust both artillery and air strikes on targets of opportunity in support of Operation HOUSTON." In a mission that lasted 126 hours, Team Coffee II had no visual contact or sighting of either Viet Cong or North Vietnamese regulars. The team was extracted with no casualties.[32]

From January through June 1968, both 1st Force and 3rd Reconnaissance Companies remained heavily engaged supporting both 1st and 3rd Marine Divisions as the battle for Khe Sanh consumed most Marine units in northern I Corps. During the second half of the year, Marine Reconnaissance teams executed General Raymond G. Davis' aggressive mobile tactics, which relied on reconnaissance to locate the enemy in order to rapidly engage them with infantry and supporting arms. Typical of the versatility displayed by 3rd Force Reconnaissance Company teams was Corporal Harry J. Corsetti (awarded the Navy Cross) and his team operating in the vicinity of Con Thien:

> On 15 August 1968, while conducting a long-range reconnaissance patrol southeast of the Con Thien Combat Outpost, Corporal Corsetti alertly observed a numerically superior North Vietnamese Army force approaching his team's position. Rapidly deploying his men, he assigned them fields of fire, and upon learning that a wire on a command-detonated mine was defective, he fearlessly moved to within thirty meters of the advancing enemy soldiers to repair the faulty device. During the ensuing three-hour fight, he skillfully coordinated supporting arms fires with those of his men, successfully halting the advance of the enemy until

a tank-infantry reaction force arrived. Mounting one of the armored vehicles to direct its fire, Corporal Corsetti assumed command when the tank commander was wounded, and ignoring the intense hostile fire, he directed highly effective fire against the North Vietnamese until they were forced to flee in panic and confusion. When his team came under intense fire from a numerically superior hostile force on 17 August, Corporal Corsetti immediately deployed his men and coordinated accurate artillery fire and gunship attacks against the enemy. On one occasion, he completely disregarded his own safety as he fearlessly exposed himself to draw hostile fire, enabling the supporting armed helicopter pilots to locate the North Vietnamese positions. Undaunted by the enemy rounds impacting near him, he moved across the fire-swept terrain to establish a landing zone and subsequently directed the embarkation of his men aboard an extraction aircraft.[33]

Until the end of 1968, both 3rd Force Reconnaissance and 1st Force Reconnaissance continued to support both Marine and Army operations in I Corps.

	Da Nang	*Phu Bai*	*Totals*
Patrols	96	56	150
Sightings	315	42	357
VC Sighted	2657	225	2882
Fire Missions	228	15	243
Air Strikes	15	0	15
VC KIA	175	19	196
IWC	1	1	2
VCC	0	0	0
Detainees	2	1	3
USMC Casualties	42	11	53
POW	0	0	0
KIA	10	2	12
WIA (Evac)	10	9	19
MIA	0	0	0

For Reconnaissance Marines, 1968 proved a busy year. Indeed, III MAF claimed that STINGRAY operations resulted in more than 3,800 enemy KIA. Major General Raymond G. Davis, Commanding General of the 1st Marine Division, claimed that by year's end, "he had anywhere from 58 to 60 active reconnaissance teams with about 40 to 45 out in the field at any given time," all within artillery range and conducting KEYHOLE and STINGRAY missions with the mission of "watching and reporting on enemy troop activities."[34]

10

The Eyes and Ears of the 1st and 3rd Marine Divisions

Reconnaissance from the Air

During the war in Vietnam, III Marine Amphibious Force (III MAF), which included the 1st and 3rd Marine Divisions, 1st Marine Aircraft Wing (1st MAW), and Service Support Groups, relied on ground sensors, radio intercepts and other electronic surveillance, human intelligence (HUMINT), aerial reconnaissance, and ground reconnaissance to coordinate offensive (and defensive) operations against the VC and NVA. "Marine Observation Squadrons 2 and 6 served as the airborne eyes of the 1st and 3rd Marine Divisions" and frequently operated in conjunction with Marine Reconnaissance teams in the field, to their mutual benefit.[1]

Aircraft, including the squadron's UH-1E helicopters, as well as light observation aircraft such as OV-10As ("Broncos") and Cessna 0-1Gs ("Birddogs"), "flew hundreds of observation and reconnaissance overflights of enemy territory in support of both regular Marine infantry, reconnaissance teams, and units from the U.S. Army." Marine jet fighters likewise conducted reconnaissance overflights. F-4 Phantom IIs, RF-4Bs, EA-6A "Prowlers," and F-3D "Skyknights," attached to Marine Composite Reconnaissance Squadron 1, flew "numerous conventional and infrared photographic survey missions."[2] The U.S. Air Force's Seventh Air Force and U.S. Army aviation companies likewise provided support or "filled in" when aircraft from the 1st MAW were unavailable to provide critical photo or aerial reconnaissance.

The Marine effort in Vietnam spurred many innovations in aerial reconnaissance. Helicopters equipped with the side-looking airborne radar (SLAR) and airborne personnel detector, as well as detector concealed personnel platforms, provided critical support along the DMZ.

One aircraft that proved extremely versatile was the North American OV-10 ("Bronco"). The OV-10 and OV-10A were designed to "perform a variety of military missions, including observation and reconnaissance, helicopter escort, limited ground radar, target marking, gunfire, spotting, liaison, utility and training missions," and they were armed with a 20mm gun pod, four 7.62mm machine guns, and four sponson stations equipped for rockets and AIM-9 missiles. The "Bronco" could carry a four- to six-man Marine Recon team, and it flew numerous reconnaissance

The North American Rockwell OV-10A "Bronco" (VMO-1), at Marine Corps Air Station, New River, North Carolina, June 12, 1972. The "Bronco" was used for observation, emplacing sensors along the DMZ and inserting Marine Reconnaissance teams (USMC photograph).

missions as well as helicopter support operations.[3] Team leaders frequently called for aerial reconnaissance to come on station near their location to assist in coordinating calls for fire or to deceive the enemy as to their location when adjusting fire.

The OV-10 (and Phantom II) likewise dropped airborne sensors along important road networks and the DMZ, which served to alert III MAF and U.S. Army intelligence planners of enemy movement, location and mass. Colonel David Lownds, commanding officer of 26th Marines, who defended Khe Sanh during its siege, said, "I think the casualties would have almost doubled without the sensors."[4]

During Marine Reconnaissance's war in Vietnam, one of the most important functions performed by the recon teams was gathering information that could be processed into timely and accurate intelligence. One important lesson from the use of aircraft in an observation/reconnaissance role was the expediency of photo interpretation for planners at III MAF and Marine Forces Pacific. Aircraft such as the Phantom II and OV-10 provided superb photo reconnaissance prior to major ground operations. This use of aircraft was backed up by the "Photo Imagery Interpretation Center (PIIC), which included an automatic data processing system and a direct teletype link between III MAF and XXIV Corps."[5] Supported by Marine Recon and U.S. Army LRRP teams, the PIIC provided timely, detailed intelligence information on enemy troops and positions. As a part of the ongoing intelligence-collecting efforts against the NVA and VC in I Corps, "photo interpretation teams were assigned to tactical units to assist in the planning and execution of combat operations."[6]

The Vietnam War (and, more specifically, Marine ground reconnaissance's operational experience) spurred a host of reconnaissance-oriented technological innovations in the post-Vietnam era. The need for, and value of, ground reconnaissance, so aptly demonstrated during the Vietnam War, inspired the organization of the infantry battalion's Surveillance and Target Acquisition (STA) and its successor—the Scout/Sniper platoons. In short, as Lieutenant Colonel Berwick Babin noted, during operations in Vietnam Marine Reconnaissance demonstrated that "the collection of information from a variety of sources, coupled with in-depth knowledge of the enemy and detailed analysis, provided commanders timely and relevant intelligence they were able to apply to significant advantage."[7]

Perhaps of greatest value was the integration of intelligence assets into an overall mutually supporting system now referred to generically as the Marine Air-Ground Task Force Intelligence System (MAGIS). According to Babin, "One might consider that the first generation of today's MAGIS was the Surveillance and Reconnaissance Center (SRC) stood up in Vietnam in support of III MAF in 1969." Several iterations have developed into the current form of MAGIS, which "collects, processes, analyzes, fuses, and disseminates information derived from all MAGTF intelligence disciplines (imagery intelligence, signals intelligence and human source intelligence, as well as joint theater and national systems). MAGIS connects intelligence professionals to multi-discipline data sources, analytic assessments, and collection assets. It also links them to MAGTF and joint command-and-control systems."[8]

The Grumman A-6 "Intruder," one of the finest close air support aircraft used by the U.S. Marine Corps and U.S. Navy during the Vietnam War (USMC photograph).

One last technological innovation that assisted reconnaissance teams on the ground and provided intelligence to higher headquarters was the introduction, in February 1970, of the "helicopter-mounted" forward-looking infrared radar (FLIR). The FLIR "could pick up radiation in the infrared spectrum," making it useful at night, as well as through fog, smoke haze, and the jungle canopy. Mounted on the U.S. Army's UH-1G, the FLIR's first use in combat was with the 2nd Battalion of the 17th Air Cavalry in the A Shau Valley. In a follow-up operation in the A Shau Valley, the 2nd Battalion's "Charlie Company" successfully employed the Huey-mounted FLIR along with Cobra gunships against an NVA supply column, knocking out "a four-ton truck on the valley floor." Subsequent sorties by air strikes "eliminated a second truck and a 12.7mm Russian-made anti-aircraft machine-gun."[9] Introduction of the FLIR was further confirmation that Marine Reconnaissance and U.S. Army LRRPs "owned the night" in dictating when and where to strike.

"Peeping and Snooping": Low-Level Aerial Reconnaissance in the A Shau Valley

During the fighting in the A Shau Valley, from December 1968 through mid-summer 1970, U.S. Army helicopters, from Huey gunships to "Slicks" (unarmed Huey UH-1 helicopters), as well as Cobra gunships, would go as low as the valley floor in order to conduct surveillance and reconnaissance operations and draw enemy fire, forcing the NVA to expose their anti-aircraft gun positions. This process was known as "peeping and snooping," whereby helicopters would "go down to tree top level to locate a gun emplacement or other enemy positions by an actual sighting."[10]

One such "peeping and snooping" operation occurred on April 16, 1968, prior to the insertion of the 1st Battalion of the 9th Cavalry into the A Shau Valley near A Loui during Operation "Delaware." Due to the heavy concentration of enemy anti-aircraft guns, tactical air strikes were "scheduled every half hour, with additional fighter-bombers [mostly Navy and Marine] available as needed." Forward air controllers and air officers likewise plotted targets for B-52 "Arc Light" strikes for areas with especially high concentrations of enemy installations. During the ensuing action, in which thirty enemy anti-aircraft were identified by low-level reconnaissance, tactical air and AH-1G Huey Cobra gunships assigned to the 1/9th Cavalry pummeled the NVA air defenses and, in the process, knocked out a command post and nearby vehicle park. In short, "peeping and snooping" proved effective in detecting and fixing enemy air defense and gun positions.[11]

Team Atlas prior to setting out for a mission at their base at Phu Bai in October 1969. Front (left to right): Corporal Don Premel, Lance Corporal Steve Swiderski. Rear (left to right): Corporal Wayne Breen, Lance Corporal Dave Brown, Lance Corporal Cox, Lance Corporal Gilermo Silva (courtesy Sergeant Bill Moss)

and engaged enemy forces.) In January 1969 alone, teams from 1st Force Reconnaissance Company carried out 116 patrols that sighted 1,339 enemy troops and killed 88, while sustaining 7 KIA and 37 WIA. The company likewise directed 88 artillery missions and 25 air strikes.[4] After its transfer to III MAF, 1st Force Reconnaissance Company "shifted operations" that stretched to the "far reaches of Quang Nam and Quang Tin Province." In fact, from March 9 to November 23, 1969, "Patrols from the First Recon Company sighted 7,747 enemy soldiers," as well as a massive NVA base camp "complete with a land-line communications network near Hill 434." As Marine units began to redeploy back to bases in the United States and Okinawa, 1st Force Reconnaissance Company (as well as the other reconnaissance units that remained in Vietnam) conducted fewer patrols, with the result that by December 1969 the unit carried out only five patrols.[5]

Meanwhile, teams from the 3rd Force Reconnaissance Company, as part of the 3rd Reconnaissance Battalion, and based at Quang Tri, supported 3rd Marine Division operations; in January 1969, they conducted twenty patrols and engaged sixty-two enemy troops while suffering one WIA.[6] After the redeployment of the

3rd Marine Division and 3rd Reconnaissance Battalion in October 1969, due to President Richard M. Nixon's announced troop drawdown in Vietnam, 3rd Force Reconnaissance Company continued to conduct patrols and carry out other III MAF reconnaissance missions. 3rd Force Reconnaissance Company Marines, brought up to full strength as 3rd Reconnaissance Battalion redeployed, "concentrated on patrolling the Demilitarized Zone and the newly created western reconnaissance zones of Quang Tri and Thua Thien Provinces, focusing on the A Shau Valley and surrounding terrain."[7]

Marines from 1st Reconnaissance Battalion, under the command of Lieutenant Colonel Larry P. Charon, carried out a variety of missions in support of regimental search operations. These missions included securing fire support bases and artillery observation posts, as well as training and carrying out SCUBA diving operations "within the division TAOR for demolitions and searching waterways for obstructions and weapons caches."[8] The 1st Reconnaissance Battalion's main mission, however, remained "patrol[ling] the western fringes of the TAOR." Operating in six-man teams (slightly larger than the previous year's four-man KEYHOLE patrols), the teams generally patrolled with an officer or NCO patrol leader, a radioman, three riflemen, and a Navy corpsman. The battalion spent the majority of its time in the field or at the base camp preparing for the next mission.

Lieutenant General Herman Nickerson, Jr., USMC, Commanding General, III MAF (1969–1970), was a strong proponent of the use of Marine Reconnaissance units throughout I Corps (USMC photograph).

Extensive patrolling by the 1st Reconnaissance Battalion resulted in "a steady stream of sightings and engagements." In April 1969 alone, "Reconnaissance teams from 1st Reconnaissance Battalion conducted 177 patrols, reported 2,746 enemy sightings, and directed 88 artillery and 31 air strikes." As for results, teams from 1st Reconnaissance Battalion killed some 177 NVA/VC with a loss of 7 team members KIA and 39 WIA.[9]

Reconnaissance teams from the 3rd Reconnaissance Battalion, commanded by Lieutenant Colonel Aydlette H. Perry, Jr., were likewise busy, carrying out patrols in the piedmont area along the DMZ west of Quang Tri, Quang Tri City and Dong Ha.

As Major General Raymond G. Davis noted, "every indication of enemy activity ... was 'explored by the insertion of reconnaissance teams.'"[10]

With Lieutenant General Herman Nickerson's arrival in March 1969 for a second tour in Vietnam, this time as the commander of III MAF, Major General Davis (who did not rotate until May) had an advocate for his concept of reconnaissance employment. Both officers had a keen appreciation of Marine Reconnaissance capabilities, particularly in carrying out STINGRAY and deep reconnaissance (especially KEYHOLE) patrols that collected intelligence. In contrast to Davis and Nickerson, the diminished view of reconnaissance unit capabilities that influenced recon employment by many senior officers throughout the war was exemplified by Lieutenant General Keith B. McCutcheon, an aviator, who replaced Nickerson as III MAF commander in December 1969 and gave the impression to many Reconnaissance Marines that he was "anti-recon."[11] It was widely believed that General McCutcheon did not like "an elite within an elite." Though this was a common sentiment among senior Marine leadership, Reconnaissance Marines emphatically considered themselves Marines first, and structurally they provided a technical capability, another tool in the division or force commanders' kit, just like the artillery regiment, tank battalion, AAV battalion, engineer battalion, and so forth. As Lieutenant Colonel Babin noted, "Ironically, the vast majority of Marines who served in Marine reconnaissance units in Vietnam, after the initially deployed reconnaissance Marines rotated, did not possess a recon related MOS or have previous reconnaissance training after 1967." They were Marine infantrymen, albeit dedicated, courageous and mission oriented. The idea that they considered themselves an "elite of the elite" hardly fits. They humbly let their operations and accomplishments speak for their status among warriors in Vietnam. Babin added that, "unlike other US military services, there is no special uniform style, accouterment or visible distinction separating one Marine from another. Every Marine is a basic rifleman, and all that implies. Essentially, the only visible distinction between Marines in uniform are the ribbons and devices over a Marine's left breast."[12]

Throughout the remainder of 1969 and into 1970, the STINGRAY and

Major General Raymond G. Davis, USMC, Commanding General, 3rd Marine Division, was a firm believer in the use of reconnaissance assets in supporting his more aggressive, high-mobility operations against the NVA (courtesy U.S. Marine Corps).

Lieutenant General Keith B. McCutcheon (shown here as a major general in 1966) confers with a Marine forward air controller near Da Nang in July 1966. Reconnaissance Marines felt that General McCutcheon saw them as an "elite within an elite" force (courtesy U.S. Marine Corps).

KEYHOLE patrols continued to attrite the enemy and provide critical information to commanders, vital to effective operational planning and success of operations in I Corps. The Marines of both 1st and 3rd Force Reconnaissance Companies labored on until their withdrawal from Vietnam in the summer and fall of 1970 into 1971.

In 1969 and 1970, there were two specific types of patrols carried out by Reconnaissance Marines within the 3rd Marine Division TAOR: STINGRAY operations and intelligence-gathering missions. Teams from 3rd Force Reconnaissance, for example, "using STINGRAY and deep reconnaissance techniques … in May [1969] conducted 194 patrols during which 68 contacts with enemy troops were made, resulting in 80 enemy killed and the loss of 4 Marines killed and 31 wounded. During this same period, battalion Marines directed 60 artillery missions, 35 air strikes, and conducted 14 scuba missions."[13]

Making use of Marine Reconnaissance's flexibility, teams were paired with Marine rifle squads to conduct surveillance and observation missions. One such instance occurred in the "Scotland II" TAOR on February 1–15, 1969, when teams from 3rd Reconnaissance Battalion teamed up with rifle squads from Companies F, G, and H, 2nd Battalion, 4th Marines (commanded by Lieutenant Colonel Joseph E. Hopkins), and conducted patrols along the DMZ in search of enemy forces, fortifications, and supply caches. For the next two weeks, three teams from 3rd Reconnaissance Battalion "covered less area though were involved in more fighting than the squads from 2/4 during the two-week effort." Many of the contacts led to the deployment of the division reaction force designated "Sparrow Hawk" in order to reinforce the reconnaissance teams. Lieutenant Colonel Hopkins recounted later that this technique "offered an opportunity to put a large force of Marines in, an additional platoon, and by walking them directly south, offered the opportunity to perform a good solid reconnaissance by a good size unit of a portion of the area."[14]

Operation "Neptune": In Support of Brown Water Operations on the Cua Viet River (February 1969)

Beginning in early 1968 and lasting through 1969, Marine Reconnaissance teams supported U.S. naval operations along the portion of the Cua Viet River that ran east from Dong Ha to the South China Sea. This section of the river was a major supply route for the U.S. Navy vessels supporting the Marines in I Corps with ammunition, food, and other vital equipment. Marine Joe Sloss, a 3rd Force Reconnaissance Company Marine, recalled that in 1969 he and his fellow Recon Marines were sent into the area to act as a naval security force, protecting the PBR boats as they prowled the Cua Viet River to block NVA infiltrators. The operation, dubbed "Neptune," was a joint U.S. Marine–U.S. Navy operation designed to prevent the enemy from ambushing and mining the vital waterway. According to Sloss:

> We were sent there to ambush NVA infiltrations and to disrupt [the] enemy who placed mines in the river to sabotage naval resupply [vessels]. We were told that often the NVA made mine type devices that damaged our shipping. We were assisted by the PBR boats, small naval craft, no protective armor on these vessels. They sometimes had a [M-]60 machine gun on the bow, sometimes they were positioned on the port and starboard sides of the PBR (patrol boat, river). I also saw M-79 Grenade launcher guns that were fed M-79 rounds through a belt system for increased performance. We would board these boats in the daylight to select a position for that night, able to better judge the terrain that way. We would ride past our selected position and then return back to insure/recognize the area we choose, we had to land during the cover of night. My memories are of doing this for one month straight. I will always remember passing our selected landing area then turning when we were safely away from the site, returning at a fast speed, cutting the engines to approach silently.
>
> The PBR's would glide to the river bank, we would slip over the edge of these boats, the water was usually frigid, we were soaked. Sometimes the water was too deep and we would jump quickly from the bow with our gear. We only carried our harness which held our ammo, grenades, water, usually no food since this was a night ambush and not an extended reconnaissance.
>
> We usually picked a location close to a tree line and the river, set up our claymores and used the night vision binoculars to look for the enemy, the PBR's would also be touring along the river watching for movement too.
>
> We would lay there and wait, prone position always so the Navy didn't see or suspect us. Returning routine was to get at the river's edge after calling for our PBR drop off boat, using

a strobe light to show off our position when we heard the PBR's close. The PBR would say they saw 3 strobe signals or 2 [and] they would confirm with us and come in to extract us.

After two weeks of these ambushes nightly, I was ordered to stay back, that night one team made contact. There was heavy fire between the team and the NVA. The PBR's came to extract and took fire, our team was caught between the NVA and the Navy guns. They were extracted but one dead Marine was left behind, we immediately went back to the site as a reactionary team and were able to get him back. We came into contact with intense enemy fire at the time when we were returned to get his body.

There was a Vietnamese burial mound where most of the fighting was centered, the team had used this spot as a safe vantage spot to look for the enemy soldiers and saboteurs. I remember night illumination used, support artillery, not air support. That following morning, we swept the area and found "digger tracks" where the NVA pulled their soldiers away from the area. We used these tracks to confirm enemy KIA. I don't know the count reported.[15]

As Sloss wrote, Recon's war was unlike that of fellow Marine riflemen in Vietnam. Operating under very trying conditions, in all types of weather and over all types of terrain, Force and Division Reconnaissance Marines demonstrated both tactical and operational flexibility during their service in Vietnam.

Operations in "Antenna Valley" (March–April 1969)

In southern I Corps, Team Report Card demonstrated Marine Reconnaissance's tactical flexibility. Two firefights illustrated this point. On May 23, 1969, in the southwest corner of Quang Nam Province, a team from the 1st Force Reconnaissance Company known as "Report Card," which consisted of two officers, seven enlisted Marines and a corpsman, was inserted by helicopter near the Song Thu Bon, southwest of Antenna Valley. The next morning, the team moved out along a trail in order to set up an ambush in what was an intelligence-gathering and prisoner-snatch mission.

As the team waited along the trail, a platoon of thirty-two NVA soldiers passed within two or three meters of them. It became obvious to the team leader, First Lieutenant Wayne E. Rollings, that the trail they sat alongside was a major supply route from the enemy's base camp in the An Hoa basin. Hoping to "snatch" an enemy officer, the team allowed the bulk of the enemy column to file past before they sighted an officer. The Marine Reconnaissance team managed to subdue and drag the enemy soldier into their position. Meanwhile, the team engaged "two enemy soldiers, killing both. As the Marines secured their prisoner, six more appeared to the front." In the ensuing firefight with this group of NVA, the reconnaissance team attempted to withdraw along a streambed but were "hit from all sides" by a force of some eighty to one hundred enemy soldiers.[16]

For the next thirty minutes, Lieutenant Rollings' team fended off probes by what turned out to be an NVA company. Rollings called in air support from two on-station Huey gunships, which sprayed the enemy force with rockets and machine gun fire. The Marines on the ground hurled grenades and peppered the area with fire from their M-79 grenade launcher. The battle lasted for another two and half hours before the enemy broke off contact and melted into the surrounding hills. Searching the area before being extracted by the Hueys, Rollings' team counted ten enemy soldiers killed by the gunships. As the Marine lieutenant later recounted, "I learned … that with a small unit, if you keep good security, 360 [degrees], that you can hold off a very large force that outnumbers you considerably, and suffer very few casualties. We had no casualties."[17] The same claim could not be made by the NVA, who suffered twenty-two KIA, including the prisoner the Marines originally captured.[18]

On another patrol, still led by Lieutenant Rollings, operating in the same area two and a half miles southwest of An Hoa, from June 9–13, 1969, the Marines from Team Lunch Meat faced an enemy force that intelligence estimated to be at least company strength—some 150 NVA.[19] The mission was similar to the one Team Report Card had conducted two weeks earlier: reconnaissance of a trail and ridgeline.

Shortly after insertion in the early evening of June 9, Lunch Meat maneuvered into position near the targeted ridgeline. Shortly thereafter, an enemy force estimated to be a company-size unit launched an attack. Unable to withdraw, Rollings called in fire support from a circling C-47 gunship nicknamed "Spooky," an U.S. Air Force converted C-47 transport armed with mini-guns capable of putting a round in every square yard of a football field–size target in less than ten seconds. As the enemy force moved toward the leathernecks, Rollings called in an artillery mission in order to make the enemy give up their search of the area.

The fire from the circling gunship and artillery rounds did the trick, as the enemy force was caught in a torrent of deadly crossfire. Rollings later recalled that the Marines could hear enemy soldiers screaming and groaning from the heavy fire as artillery shells crashed into the surrounding countryside: "We saw 10 NVA get within 40 yards of our position before 'arty' caught them with a barrage that finished them all off." Rollings added that between the "Spooky" gunship and artillery, "we had them [the NVA] sandwiched between us."[20] Once again, the enemy, pummeled by heavy fire and having incurred heavy losses, withdrew to the ridgeline. During the fighting, the Marines suffered only one WIA.

Another reconnaissance team from Company D, 3rd Reconnaissance Battalion, was not so fortunate. Team Flight Time, inserted into their reconnaissance zone on June 2, 1969, at 0930, was to conduct reconnaissance operations in the vicinity of Hill 471, about one "click" south, overlooking the former Khe Sanh Combat Base and Lang Vei (1) and (2), in western Quang Tri Province. Unopposed during the insertion, the six-man reconnaissance team came under small arms fire that killed one team member and wounded five others. The team leader then requested "all available 'on call' air" assets as well as a reaction force to assist the team.

At approximately 0200, a twelve-man Marine reaction team arrived in the area to assist the besieged reconnaissance team, but they arrived too late to affect the outcome of the battle. As daylight broke over the mountains, the intensity of the fighting revealed itself as the reaction force discovered the charred bodies of "three—possibly five" reconnaissance team members, which looked as though they had been hit by a flame thrower. Further investigation confirmed the presence of the bodies of five members of the team in an enemy slit trench. The sixth body, that of Corporal William A. Buck, Jr., was found some ten meters farther down the hill, with his K-Bar still in his hand. Examination of the site "indicated that that the enemy had come up the northeast side of the hill, attacking with small arms, RPGs, hand grenades, and throwing satchel charges and *bangalore torpedoes*." The leader of the reaction force "surmised" that the reconnaissance team "must have been involved in hand-to-hand fighting" before being overrun, based on the fact that equipment had been scattered around the area.[21] The members of Flight Time—First Lieutenant Michael M. O'Connor, Corporal William A. Buck, Jr., Corporal William M. Wellman, Jr., Lance Corporal Douglas W. Barnitz, Private First Class Robert L. Pearcy and Private First Class Harold A. Skaggs—were, in fact, the last full reconnaissance team to be lost in the Vietnam War.[22]

There were other threats to the recon teams, which came in the form of lightning, poisonous snakes, and wild animals. Team Centipede from the 3rd Reconnaissance Battalion faced a unique "adversary" in the form of a large tiger that stalked the Marines as they patrolled the heavy jungle area in the Ba Long Valley. "On two occasions during the four-day patrol, the tiger came to within 10 meters of the team and had to be driven off with CS grenades."[23]

Another incident involving a large tiger occurred in December 1968 when a six-man recon

The Marine Reconnaissance team members who killed the tiger. Left to right: Private First Class Maurice Howell, Corporal Jackie Blankenship (KIA June 23, 1969), Private First Class Delbert Kelly, Private First Class Thomas Shainline, Private First Class Ray Ragan (courtesy Lieutenant Colonel Barry Babin).

team from Charlie Company, 3rd Reconnaissance Battalion, had completed its mission in the vicinity of Fire Support Base Alpine, about six miles west of the Laotian border in the extreme northwest corner of South Vietnam. Due to weather, the team's helicopter extraction had been postponed. The team was secure in its harbor site when, with the approach of dawn, a tiger struck, grabbing one of the team members and dragging him away. Private First Class Thomas E. Shainline remembers hearing a scream and somebody shouting, "It's a tiger! It's a tiger." Private First Class Roy Regan, who had been sleeping beside Private First Class Richard P. Goolden, the man taken, remembers, "I jumped up and saw the tiger with his mouth around my partner. All I could think about was to get the tiger away from him. I jumped at the tiger and the cat jerked its head and jumped onto a bomb crater 10 meters away." The five remaining team members, now fully awake, took up positions around the crater and fired on the tiger. It was unclear who fired the kill shot, but the tiger released its victim, who climbed out of the crater and asked, "What happened?" He was transported away and later medically retired from the Marine Corps due to his injuries. The nine-foot-long, four-hundred-pound tiger was brought back with the team and hung on a ten-foot scaffold for display in the battalion headquarters area. Phan Van Sang, a local Vietnamese tiger hunter, later commented that some six weeks earlier a reconnaissance Marine had been killed by a tiger in the same area and that this one might have been the same tiger.[24]

Reconnaissance and Operation "Dewey Canyon" (January 22–March 19, 1969)

The first major operation in 1969 involving a heavy reconnaissance effort occurred in support of Major General Davis' three-battalion effort from the 9th Marines, designed to counter the enemy's buildup in Base Area 611 in the Da Krong Valley, located in Quang Tri Province. This area was located along Route 922 coming in from Laos and served as the enemy's infiltration route along Route 548 running through the A Shau Valley. These routes "funneled" men and supplies directed at the imperial city of Hue and the area southward toward Da Nang.[25] General Davis sought to not only forestall another "mini–Tet" offensive but also eliminate a "thorn" in the side of I Corps by reducing the enemy offensive capabilities.

Spearheading this offensive were the 9th Marines, commanded by Colonel Robert H. Barrow, USMC (later to become Commandant of the Marine Corps), who recalled, "There was some concern the North Vietnamese were going to launch another offensive, 'TET '69,' and that the area selected for the Marine offensive was, in fact, the same area used by the NVA to stage the TET 1968 offensive."[26]

Facing the 9th Marines was a well-trained, -supplied, and -equipped enemy force, armed with 122mm Soviet-supplied howitzers and backed up by a superior logistical infrastructure along the Ho Chi Minh Trail that protruded from routes

Friends from 3rd Force Recon (left to right); Lance Corporal Harry Winston (2nd Marine), Corporal Bill Moss and his friend (center). Other figures in the photograph are unidentified (courtesy Corporal Bill Moss).

coming out of Laos. Barrow's 9th Marines would be totally dependent on a heliborne support network flying supplies to Marines positioned in Fire Support Bases (FSBs) Shiloh, Razor, and Riley. Leading the effort were Marines of the 3rd Reconnaissance Battalion. Signal Intelligence, meanwhile, had detected "increased radio traffic on Route 922 that ran from Laos toward the A Shau Valley." Reconnaissance aircraft had sighted "scores of trucks, sometimes as many as 1,000 per day." The road was protected by NVA anti-aircraft guns (12.7mm, 25mm, and 37mm), which had shot down an A-6 "Intruder" with the loss of the two crewmen.[27]

General Davis realized that "something" was up and thus wanted to know "what was going on in those mountains." In order to keep pressure on the NVA and be able to counter any offensive operation on the scale of the 1968 TET offensive, Davis ordered the 9th Marines to maintain a heavy presence along Route 922 and the surrounding hills. As Davis reasoned, "if we were able to keep Marines on these trails, even from time to time, and were able to clean out his way stations, periodically, we could severely limit his [the NVA's] activity."[28]

To maintain strict surveillance of the surrounding countryside, General Davis "ordered reconnaissance teams into the mountain fastness—up to 20 teams at one time to locate enemy base camps." The 3rd Reconnaissance Battalion played an essential role in this operation. Colonel Dick Camp noted, "He [Davis] was deadly serious about this…. Every day at our staff briefing, my [Davis'] officers knew I would ask the same question: 'How many patrols do we have on the ground?' If they had less than twenty, they would have until noon to get twenty on the ground." Colonel Alexander L. Michaux, the division G-3, stated that the mission of the reconnaissance teams was "not to call in fire or anything…. Just find them and tell us where they [the NVA] are." General Davis, in fact, emphasized "that every indication of enemy activity from whatever means is explored by the insertion of reconnaissance teams … everywhere … on a continuing basis, a massive reconnaissance team effort is maintained."[29]

Team Amanda

Colonel Camp noted that, in keeping with General Davis' emphasis on "finding and fixing" the enemy units, the four-man recon teams were inserted by helicopter along Route 922. Carrying enough food, water, ammunition, and batteries to operate in the field for an extended patrol, the reconnaissance teams were tasked with identifying and locating enemy units in the A Shau Valley while being careful not to compromise their presence as they observed the enemy. This mission proved difficult, as Team Amanda ran into trouble almost immediately:

> They heard movement and almost simultaneously, began receiving a heavy volume of small arms and automatic weapons fire. The team returned fire and called for help. An aerial observer (AO) came up on station and directed air strikes. By this time, the hard-pressed Marines were trading hand grenades with the NVA who were only 50 feet away. Air strikes were brought in close—dirt clods from a bomb explosion hit one of the team members. The situation was desperate, "Amanda" was in danger of being overrun and needed immediate extraction.
>
> A last air strike was called in to clear a patch to an LZ 75 meters away. The team made a mad dash, as four helicopter gunships swooped in, guns blazing, to cover the extraction bird. The Ch-46 touched down, the team scrambled on board, and the plane leaped back into the air, taking hits as it passed out of range. Team "Amanda" was lucky; they survived the experience. Ground troops were inserted to exploit the contact…. This, in accordance with General Davis' precepts.[30]

Marine Recon teams, in fact, played a significant part in General Ray Davis' concept of high mobility operations against the NVA. Davis himself noted, "'Where we found activity we went in and smashed them' [but] the 3rd Marine Division 'never launched an operation without acquiring clear definition of the targets and objectives through intelligence confirmed by recon patrols. High Mobility operations [were] too difficult and complex to come up empty or in disaster.'"[31]

General Davis emphasized that long-range reconnaissance patrols were essential to the success of his operational concept of "high mobility" during "Dewey Canyon" and subsequent operations in I Corps along the DMZ.[32] According to Davis,

"One aspect of the mobile concept which was really proven to be a key was the use of long-range reconnaissance patrols. The 3rd Reconnaissance Battalion (Reinforced) with teams from 3rd Force Reconnaissance Company, as well as with additional platoons from the SLFs, attempt[ed] to maintain 58–60 recon teams." Davis added that this meant that at any given time, there were forty to forty-five recon teams in the field, with another "ten to fifteen teams either coming or going—being briefed, being debriefed, being inserted, being extracted."[33] As he pointed out, "This meant that every indication of enemy activity from whatever means is explored by the insertion of reconnaissance teams."[34]

One of the lessons of the 1968 TET offensive was the need for what Davis termed "a massive reconnaissance team effort." For the 3rd Reconnaissance Battalions as well as 3rd Force Reconnaissance Company, this meant that "their reconnaissance efforts were concentrated in and along the DMZ, along the Ben Hai River, west of Tiger Tooth Mountain and the far reaches above northwest of Khe Sanh, south of Khe Sanh, down the De Kron River which heads toward [the] A Shau Valley, throughout Base Area 101; the piedmont west of Quang Tri, Dong Ha, the flatlands and the village lands throughout—everywhere—on a continuing basis."[35]

General Davis directed that the reconnaissance teams be employed. This included STINGRAY and observation missions. Davis later recounted that when using the STINGRAY technique, eight- to ten-men teams "sought out the enemy … seeking opportunities to deliver fire upon them [or] the second method of well-out, smaller teams—four to five men—going on the basis of secrecy; only to observe, [and] stay out of sight." In both cases, Davis emphasized that if the enemy were encountered during these patrols, the teams were to break contact and call for extraction.[36]

General Davis emphasized that both types of teams were not to be reinforced unless artillery could be called in to support a reinforcement or an extraction: "Under an artillery fan, they [the reconnaissance teams] would normally be reinforced if the enemy presented [itself as] an adequate target. If contact occurred, the team was expected to hang in and fight it out or if it's a small contact and they start to take casualties, we might extract them. However, if it is a large contact and under the artillery fan and opportunity presents itself, they are [to be] reinforced in order to attempt to destroy the enemy force in its entirety."[37]

Davis added that once an intelligence asset detected an enemy presence, whether it was in the form of troop movement, booby traps or mines, a reconnaissance team was inserted to "prep" the area with artillery or air prior to deploying infantry units. "This system," Davis went on to say, "proved to be very effective, in the area along the DMZ, west of Khe Sanh, and up through the A Shau Valley" in support of 3rd Marine Division operations.[38]

Reconnaissance Operations (May–December 1969)

Throughout the remainder of 1969, reconnaissance teams from 1st and 3rd Force Reconnaissance Companies, as well as 1st and 3rd Reconnaissance Battalions, maintained a busy schedule of patrolling and surveillance operations in and along the DMZ into the A Shau Valley and An Hoa Basin TAORs.

For 1st Reconnaissance Marines, support of the An Hoa Combat Base and surrounding area became the focus of their reconnaissance efforts during the summer and fall of 1969. The average monthly strength of the company for the period of May 1–31, 1969, was 13 officers, 150 enlisted Marines, and 7 Navy corpsmen. This force was augmented by a platoon of one officer, thirty enlisted men, and one corpsman from 1st Platoon, Company "B," 1st Reconnaissance Battalion, as well as a platoon of one officer, twenty-nine enlisted Marines, and two corpsmen from Company "C," 1st Reconnaissance Battalion.[39]

Colonel Andrew R. Finlayson, whose team Swift Scout based its operations out of this strategically located combat base, wrote that An Hoa was one of the most important firebases occupied by the Marines. However, Finlayson wrote, "Its strategic significance was little known or understood by the Marines who fought to protect it. Most Marines lived day to day, fighting to stay alive and to keep the enemy from overrunning that particular piece of real estate in Quang Nam Province, South Vietnam. They gave little thought as to why the enemy was so intent upon trying to control the territory in its immediate vicinity."[40]

According to Finlayson, An Hoa was important to the NVA because it was situated in an area that was ideal for launching attacks on U.S. and allied forces in and around Da Nang. More important was the fact that the combat base was located along one of the major infiltration routes from the Ho Chi Minh Trail, a vital supply network that funneled men, munitions, medical supplies, and other logistical support to NVA and VC forces operating in the south. As Finlayson wrote, "The communists considered it [the Da Nang airbase] a major impediment to their war aims," so, in order to deny them control of the region, the Marines used An Hoa as a base for their operations in the area.[41]

During April and May 1969, reconnaissance teams from 1st Force Reconnaissance Company supported the 5th Marine Regiment in operations in and around Happy Valley and the surrounding terrain, dubbed "Oklahoma Hills." During these operations, battalions from the 5th, 7th, and 1st Marines, with artillery support from the An Hoa Combat Base, killed over one hundred NVA and captured a considerable number of weapons, including AK-47s, a 12.7mm anti-aircraft gun, and a short-range rocket launcher.[42] On May 19, 1969, 1st Platoon, "Charlie" Company, 1st Force Reconnaissance Battalion, departed from An Hoa and rejoined the 1st Reconnaissance Battalion in Da Nang.[43]

During the spring of 1969, 1st Marine Division Reconnaissance units continued to be tasked with conducting surveillance and intelligence-gathering missions in and around An Hoa and the A Shau Valley, reporting the number of enemy infiltrating south.

Typical of the teams executing this mission was Team Prime Cut, in support of Operation "Oklahoma Hills" in Happy Valley. Led by First Lieutenant Schanck, the team came across a sizeable enemy force and harbor site. The patrol, which lasted ninety-nine hours, had seven sightings of fifty-nine VC/NVA, twenty-four enemy bunkers and nine "hooches." The team had three contacts that resulted in one confirmed enemy KIA.[44] Linking up with a reinforced Marine platoon (thirty to forty Marines), Prime Cut encountered another enemy force that resulted in a sustained firefight and three more enemy KIA. However, their ordeal wasn't over, as an enemy machine gun pinned the force down as helicopters came in order to extract the team. With support coming from the reinforced platoon and Huey gunships, the reconnaissance team was finally extracted. During the debriefing that followed their return to the base at Da Nang, Lieutenant Schanck reported that the area was being used as a major escape route by the *NVA 31st Regiment* fleeing the pursuing Marines during the "Oklahoma Hills" operation. Lieutenant Schanck recommended that the "area should be targeted and—heavily bombed" with an "Arc Light" mission.[45]

	Danang	*An Hoa*	*Totals*
Patrols	98	26	124
Sightings	302	59	361
VC/NVA Sighted	1711	806	2517
Fire Missions	100	20	120
Air Strikes	23	25	48
NGF Missions	0	0	0
VC/NVA Killed	40	84	124
IWC	4	0	4
Detainees	2	0	2
USMC Casualties	35	3	38
KIA	6	0	6
WIA (EVAC)	16	2	18
MIA	0	0	0
NBC (EVAC)	12	1	13
KNBC	1	0	1

The fighting during the "Oklahoma Hills" operation was as intense as the previous year's fighting during the period prior to and after the TET offensive. Given the intensity in enemy activity, particularly in Elephant Valley, Marine Reconnaissance teams began carrying Claymore mines, M-60 machine guns, and the standard M-79 grenade launchers. Lieutenant Unsworth, patrol leader for Team Prime Cut, recommended in his report for a mission in Happy Valley that reconnaissance teams carry 60mm mortars and a .50 caliber machine gun.[46]

By October 1969, contrary to established doctrine in the 1950s and early 1960s that advised against carrying mortars, reconnaissance teams were taking 60mm mortars on some missions. Such was the case of Team Hireling, which added the company-size mortar to its list of special equipment.[47] However, most teams declined to trade their mobility and lighter loads for the benefit of crew-served weapons. Instead, they relied on the M-79, claymores, and M-60 machine guns on eight-man or larger patrols in order to retain their maneuverability.

Fighting and Troop Withdrawal (June–December 1969)

During the summer and fall of 1969 (May–November), teams from 1st Reconnaissance Battalion and 1st Force Reconnaissance Company maintained steady pressure on the NVA and VC in support of operations by the 1st Marine Division in the A Shau Valley and along the DMZ. With the announcement of the drawdown of twenty-five thousand troops from Vietnam on June 8, 1969, Marines maintained their combat operations in order to send a signal to the enemy that the United States remained committed to its South Vietnamese ally.[48] The announced troop withdrawals had little impact on Marine Recon's missions in and around I Corps, as reconnaissance teams continued their operations in the A Shau Valley and An Hoa Basin with both four- and seven-man patrols.

At 3rd Force Reconnaissance Company during the month of August 1969, typically, "the number of men per patrol was seven (six Marines and one Navy Corpsman)." As Captain Alex Lee noted in his report for the month of August, "this total" included those patrols operating in the DMZ, "where patrols were set at a minimum of eight men by higher authority (i.e., Division or III MAF)." As for the number of hours in the field per patrol during the reporting period, Lee noted that the average was three days (72.7 hours). The veteran recon leader added "that this total is skewed somewhat when consideration is given to the fact that the main total includes patrols that were 'shot out' in a matter of hours in the first day."[49]

As mentioned previously, one important task of Marine Reconnaissance was implanting and monitoring sensors along highly traveled roads and trails. Sensors permitted Marine planners to better determine the enemy's course of action and rate of infiltration. It also allowed Marines to use firepower, in the form of "artillery and air," to prevent the enemy from infiltrating into an area (as amply discovered during the battle for Khe Sanh) without being detected. Lieutenant Colonel Babin noted that the sensors' "effectiveness at Khe Sanh raised their importance for use at other Combat Bases."[50] General Raymond Davis commented that the use of sensors "proved to be very effective," and "[it] gave added importance to fire bases such An Hoa, for instance, if the enemy were to enter through the DMZ west from Khe Sanh, south of Khe Sanh, or up through the A Shau Valley and enters Quang Tri Province, he'll be subjected to immediate attack with artillery and mobile forces."[51]

Corporal Bill Moss's Group from 3rd Force Reconnaissance Company, Quang Tri Province, August 1969 (courtesy Corporal Bill Moss).

Semi-permanent sensor deployment by Marine Reconnaissance teams gained added importance as U.S. forces began retrograde operations in I Corps. Captain Lee reported, "Each Third Force Reconnaissance patrol that went to the field in August carried the Patrol Science Intrusion Device (PSID) consisting of four transmitters with geophones which are designed to omit radio link tones, coded #1, #2, #3, and #4, to a single receiver which is kept in the harbor site. Each of the five parts weighs less than one pound."[52]

As Captain Lee noted, during the month of August, there were a "total of 10 sightings and ten contacts or one hundred fourty three [sic] (143) NVA/VC. Patrols from the Company killed nineteen (19) NVA/VC (confirmed) and claims seven (7) more probables." Lee wrote that "1 Recon Marine was killed on patrol during the time period." The company incurred fourteen wounded, due to an NVA rocket attack in the company's firebase. This total included twelve Marines (two officers and ten enlisted men) and two Navy corpsmen. Seven of the wounded men had to be evacuated by helicopter; four returned to duty, while three (one Navy corpsman and two Marines) were evacuated to hospitals in Japan or the United States for "more extensive treatment."[53]

Teams assigned to 1st Reconnaissance Battalion and 1st Force Reconnaissance Company likewise carried out extensive deep reconnaissance operations during the same period. Patrol reports filed from August 1 through October 31, 1969, indicated increased enemy infiltration in the An Hoa and Elephant Valley TAORs. As both enemy sightings and infiltration increased, teams were instructed to "be prepared to call and adjust air/arty on all targets of opportunity." Notwithstanding the impending withdrawal of the 3rd Marine Division and "Vietnamization," of the war, Marine Recon teams were as busy as ever, supporting U.S. Marine, U.S. Army, and ARVN operations in I Corps throughout the remainder of 1969.

Training While Fighting

Despite the constant patrolling and surveillance missions, Marine Reconnaissance teams continued to hone their reconnaissance skills between missions: "When not on patrol, Reconnaissance Marines continually trained for their exacting task. In addition to the initial indoctrination for newly-arrived personnel, which included instruction in the use of the AN/PRC-25 radio, map reading, first aid, rappelling from helicopters, observer procedures, and intelligence reporting techniques, the battalions [and companies] conducted periodic refresher courses with special emphasis on weapons training, scuba diving, physical conditioning, and the use of new equipment such as extraction ladders. Selected personnel also were sent to the Army's RECONDO School at Nha Trang for more specialized training."[54]

Marine Reconnaissance team members conduct parachute training near Red Beach, Da Nang, RVN (courtesy Lieutenant Colonel Barry Babin).

Members of 3rd Force Reconnaissance Company practice an insertion technique at their combat base at Phu Bai in 1969 (courtesy Sergeant Bill Moss).

1st Force Reconnaissance's War Continues (March–November 1969)

As 3rd Force Reconnaissance Company wrapped up its operations in Vietnam, 1st Force Reconnaissance continued to conduct deep reconnaissance patrols, observing and calling in artillery on enemy formations. In fact, "During the period 9 March to 23 November 1969, patrols from First Force Reconnaissance Company had sighted 7,747 enemy, captured nine POWs as well as many enemy documents." In November 1969, as the NVA began to employ "more aggressive, well-trained counter-reconnaissance forces," "First Force Reconnaissance Company repeatedly re-entered enemy sanctuaries and provided information vital to subsequent fixing and destruction of these forces."[55]

As 1969 drew to a close, and with four years of experience in the field against a determined enemy, "reconnaissance Marines had … developed techniques and equipment in order to supply the division they supported with accurate and timely intelligence."[56] According to Lieutenant Colonel Babin, "Reconnaissance Zones, normally four to six contiguous grid squares, continued to serve a dual purpose to specify an area of interest to focus reconnaissance team efforts, and to coordinate supporting arms and maneuver."[57] With an increase in artillery-directed missions, and to ensure "prompt artillery support when needed and at the same time prevent accidental shelling, special reconnaissance zones were established for each deployed team in which only the patrol could call fire missions." To this end, both the 11th and the 12th Marines (artillery) Regiments "designated a battery or platoon of 105mm or 155mm howitzers to support each team and assigned a fire support officer to each reconnaissance battalion's command post to assist in fire planning and coordination."[58]

As for the extraction of reconnaissance teams, the 1st Marine Air Wing "designated helicopters as a part of a 'quick-reaction' package" that, augmented by a rifle platoon or company, could "ensure rapid extraction of a team under fire or in tenuous situation."[59]

As Marine forces began redeploying from Vietnam in the spring and summer of 1969, additional importance was assigned to intelligence-gathering missions, as the war was increasingly turned over to ARVN. The 1st Force Reconnaissance Company's unit citation for the period (March–November 1969) stated, in part,

> Accomplishing a total of 191 patrols, the information gathered by patrols formed the foundation and impetus for operation strikes … against enemy base camps, lines of communications and supply depots. The identity and location of the newly-infiltrated *90th NVA Regiment* into Quang Nam Province, the egress of the *21st* and *1st NVA regiments* from Quang Nam Province and subsequent return of three units was established in large measure by information gathered by the company's patrols. Intelligence derived from information provided by these patrols went on to precipitate highly successful forays including Operation Durham Peak, by the 1st Marine Division, into the Que Son Mountains, Antenna Valley area where extremely complex enemy base camps and large quantities of supplies were uncovered and destroyed.[60]

Through the efforts of the teams from 1st Force Reconnaissance Company, the NVA "were denied a vital stepping stone to Da Nang from the south and An Hoa from the east." The Marines from First Recon Company likewise disrupted the NVA's ability to launch offensive operations against these areas, in addition to being tasked with locating the enemy's *Military Region V* and *Group 44 headquarters* in

Quang Nam Province.[61] In short, through their constant patrolling and observation of the area in and around both Antenna Valley and An Hoa, the teams from 1st Force Recon Company kept the NVA "off balance" and, in doing so, prevented them from launching a "Summer 1969" offensive and thereby throwing off the timetable of the pending U.S. troop withdrawals.

	1st Recon Battalion	1st Force Recon Co.	Total
Patrols	64	18	82
Sightings	116	9	125
VC/NVA Sighted	1209	65	1274
Fire Missions	50	0	50
Air Strikes	15	0	15
VC/NVA KIA	84	1	85
Detainees	6	0	6
IWC	1	0	1
USMC Casualties	26	8	34
KIA	2	0	0
WIA (EVAC)	12	8	20
MIA	0	0	0
NBC (EVAC)	12	0	0
KNBC	0	0	0
USN Casualties	1	1	2
KIA	1	0	1
WIA	0	1	1

The pressure exerted by First Reconnaissance Company was, in fact, substantial, as patrols often took the Marines some forty miles into enemy-held territory. On these deep, long-range reconnaissance patrols, they successfully isolated pockets of enemy troops in Quang Nam Province and prevented them from being resupplied and able to launch a major offensive into early 1970.[62]

12

Redeployment and Deactivation (1969–1970)

Transfer of responsibility for I Corps to the U.S. Army's XXIV Corps signaled the end of 3rd Force Reconnaissance's war in Vietnam. Lieutenant General Melvin Zais, "the new commander, did not share [Lieutenant General Herman] Nickerson's appreciation for the Force Reconnaissance companies and pushed for their demise after the departure of the III MAF commander."[1] On March 10, 1970, 3rd Force Reconnaissance Company was stood down. Teams were extracted from the field in the A Shau Valley and joined the rest of the company, reassigned to Phu Bai, where a dozen Marines were transferred to 1st Force Reconnaissance Company. Half of the company was reassigned to Hoi An, where they trained the 2nd Republic of Korea Marines in reconnaissance techniques. "The remainder of the 3rd Force Reconnaissance Company was assigned to III MAF infantry regiments."[2]

On November 24, 1970, 1st Force Reconnaissance Company was "dropped from the operational and administrative control of 1st Reconnaissance Battalion and placed under the control of III MAF," and in December 1969 the unit was given the mission of patrolling the Thuong Duc Corridor in support of the 1st Marine Division.[3] The 1st Force Reconnaissance Company and 1st Reconnaissance Battalion centered their patrol activities on Quang Nam Province.[4]

As the 3rd Reconnaissance Battalion's activities were at first halved and then halted, patrolling and reconnaissance operations were turned over to the U.S. Army's 101st Airborne (Air Mobile) and 1st ARVN Division.

Deactivation and Redeployment (March–July 1970)

Although 3rd Force Reconnaissance Company was still officially a "unit," from March 10 to July 10, 1970, it was at "zero strength." On July 10, First Lieutenant T.S. Hodge and Staff Sergeant Frank Schemmel "were assigned to the company to 'close the books' on the unit's accounts and records."[5] On August 27, 1970, at Los Flores, in Camp Pendleton, "in accordance with the provisions of the 5th MEB's Operations Order 2-70, the Third Force Reconnaissance Company was deactivated." 3rd Force Reconnaissance Company's war was "officially" over.

Meanwhile, the 1st Force Reconnaissance Company and 1st Reconnaissance Battalion continued reconnaissance operations (albeit on a reduced scale) in the Thuong Duc Corridor after the stand-down of the 3rd Force Recon Company, with fewer patrols and enemy sightings. What remained of 1st Force Reconnaissance Company was finally withdrawn to Da Nang on August 10, 1970, where it, too, began to stand down. By the time of deactivation in August 1970, the company's strength stood at ten officers and seventy-four enlisted men.[6] However, unlike the 3rd Force Reconnaissance Company, which cased its colors, 1st Force Reconnaissance Company was relocated to Camp Pendleton, California, to remain on the active roles.

Provincial Reconnaissance Units—A Different Mission, Same War

Despite Marine Reconnaissance units being removed from the Vietnam battlefield, Marines remained very active in the reconnaissance effort. One of the least-known efforts was Marine Corps involvement in Provincial Reconnaissance Units (PRUs). As Colonel Finlayson wrote, the PRUs were part of "a secret training program at Camp Reasoner [and were] a shadowy group of South Vietnamese special operations units called the Provincial Reconnaissance Units."[7] Here, the PRU volunteers received basic reconnaissance training and classes in the English language. Wearing no rank or insignia on their tiger-striped uniforms, they were, as Finlayson described, "older and tougher than the South Vietnamese soldier."[8] The veteran Marine Reconnaissance leader was later told by his commanding officer, Major William B. Lowrey, that the PRUs "belonged to the Central Intelligence Agency, and that they were being trained for special missions as part of the Phoenix Program." This would not be the last time Finlayson had contact with the PRUs. In October 1969, as 1st Force Reconnaissance Company was standing down, he joined a PRU until his departure from Vietnam in June 1970.

Captain Andrew R. Finlayson, USMC, taken in 1972 (courtesy Colonel Andrew Finlayson).

Marine First Sergeant Donald N. Hamblen, a veteran reconnaissance man from the early pioneering days of Marine Force Reconnaissance, himself was a member of a SOG team.[9] In fact, SOG teams had many experienced Marine Reconnaissance members, who, along with their U.S. Army counterparts, provided Marine recon teams with timely, accurate intelligence.

Working with South Vietnamese provincial leaders and other U.S. team members (civilian and military), the mission of the PRUs was to "root out and neutralize" North Vietnamese cadres in the south.[10]

"A High Level of Activity" in the A Shau Valley (January–July 1970)

Beginning in January 1970, the 3rd Force Reconnaissance Company concentrated its efforts in the A Shau Valley. It continued a high level of patrolling, as well as diving missions, service as a reaction force, bomb damage assessment (BDA), target acquisition and communications relay missions. During the month of January 1970, teams from 3rd Force Reconnaissance Company conducted a total of thirty-four patrols in and around the A Shau Valley. The same month saw the company working alongside elements of the U.S. Army's 2nd Squadron of the 17th Cavalry, which provided superb gunship and recovery support to the teams in the field. The company extended its joint operations to include coordination with the U.S. Army's 10th Airborne Division, XXIV Corps, the 85th Medical Evacuation Hospital, and the Military Assistance Command Vietnam's Advisory Team/Dong Ha Training Center.[11] As a result, 3rd Force Reconnaissance Company was awarded the Army Valorous Unit citation.

During January 1970, enemy activity was "at the highest level in the six months of the Company's records."[12] Teams such as Garlic, Tinny, Pony, and Artic continued to engage the enemy in fierce but brief firefights. While in the field, teams from 3rd Force Recon Company had 159 enemy sightings, as well as eight sightings of enemy vehicles. Team members counted twenty-six confirmed enemy KIA, with ten more listed as "probables." There were no prisoners of war taken during this period. The teams lost one Marine KIA and fourteen WIA.[13]

Marine Reconnaissance teams in northern I Corps continued to engage the NVA in some of the heaviest fighting of the war. Much of the fighting, as demonstrated by Corporal Charles T. Sexton (later awarded the Navy Cross) and his team on February 5, 1970, was "vicious." Corporal Sexton was a member of a six-man reconnaissance team that was patrolling deep in the A Shau Valley when it came under a heavy volume of small arms and automatic weapons fire from approximately fifty enemy soldiers occupying well-concealed emplacements in the dense elephant grass. During the initial moments of the attack, three Marines were mortally wounded and two were seriously injured. After a rapid assessment of the precarious situation, Corporal Sexton directed the fire of his two wounded companions and moved around the fire-swept area to collect hand grenades and ammunition from his fallen comrades. Utilizing his radio, he then reported the situation to his commanding officer and requested assistance. For the next several hours, while the enemy attempted to encircle and overrun his position, Corporal Sexton repeatedly adjusted helicopter and fixed-wing air strikes on the hostile unit, hurled hand grenades, shouted encouragement to his wounded companions, and simultaneously furnished a running commentary to his company commander until a reaction force arrived to lend support. His heroic and determined actions were an inspiration to all who served with him and undoubtedly saved his fellow Marines from further serious injury or even death. As his Navy Cross citation read, in part, "By his courage, superb leadership, and valiant devotion to duty in the face of grave personal danger, Corporal Sexton upheld the highest traditions of the Marine Corps and the United States Naval Service."

In terms of supporting arms, "There was extensive use of artillery and helicopter assets during the month of January 1970." Artillery missions delivered a total of 531 rounds of 175mm on target directed by members of the patrolling units. As for fixed-wing strikes, poor visibility in the A Shau Valley restricted the number of airstrikes available to the teams. Overall, there were eighteen fixed-wing strikes during the period. As for helicopter support, helicopters from both the 1st MAW and the Army's 2nd Squadron of the 17th Cavalry provided 165 combined sorties during January.[14]

Diving teams from 3rd Force Reconnaissance Company likewise provided SCUBA assistance in searching for enemy arms caches and in salvage and recovery operations. During the month of January 1970, SCUBA teams from 3rd Force Reconnaissance Company conducted two operational dives.

Action in the Thuong Doc River Valley (June–August 1970)

As Marine Reconnaissance units approached the end of their service in Vietnam, teams from 1st Force Reconnaissance Company and 1st Reconnaissance Battalion continued their "cat-and-mouse" game in and around Quang Nam, over the same hills and trails that they had traversed in the summer of 1965.

In the Thuong Doc River Valley TAOR, teams from 1st Force Recon conducted extensive patrols in and around the Thuong Doc Special Forces Camp area, where they were involved in intense enemy contacts. During May 1970, teams from 1st Force Reconnaissance Company took heavy incoming enemy rocket fire but were eventually able to "find and fix" them to bring in artillery and air to silence them. "Further patrolling in the area of these rocket launching sites disclosed the base camp of the enemy."[15]

Meanwhile, Team Misty Cloud had twenty sightings of some 130–145 VC/NVA in the Thong Doc River Valley and uncovered an enemy base camp, in what was one of the longest patrols to date—168 hours (March 30–April 6, 1970). During this patrol, Misty Cloud called in twelve artillery fire missions that resulted in ten confirmed enemy KIA and ten "probables," as well as four air strikes that netted five more confirmed enemy KIA.[16]

During another patrol in June 1970, while operating in the vicinity of Hill 487, Team Sandhurst, led by Sergeant James R. Christopher, came under heavy enemy fire. Completely surrounded by the enemy and pinned down by heavy machine gun fire, the team was eventually extracted by the SPIE "without sustaining any friendly casualties."[17] Due to its strategic location overlooking the Thuong Doc River Valley, Hill 487 became an observation post and launching pad for "walk-out" reconnaissance teams inserted into the area.

In the early morning hours of August 4, 1970, Team Hansworth's harbor site came under enemy fire sixty meters north of the HLZ near Hill 487. At approximately 0120, the patrol leader, Lieutenant Prins, heard something crawling in the grass. Thinking that it could an enemy soldier attempting to infiltrate the team's position, Prins tossed a CS grenade into the bush, which "resulted in one trip flare being ignited" and signaled the commencement of a furious enemy assault on Hansworth's position.[18]

In the ensuing attack, the NVA fired rocket-propelled grenades (RPGs), made use of automatic weapons, and threw fragmentation grenades and satchel charges, managing to hit Lance Corporal William M. Clark with an RPG round while another enemy round wounded Lieutenant Prins. With their lieutenant out of action, Corporal James C. Holzmann seized the initiative and led the counterattack. In the action that followed, Corporal Holzmann

> personally directed the team's firepower and, in extreme personal danger from over fifteen satchel charges which exploded in and around him ... dashed among the defensive outpost [directing the fighting].... [In the same firefight] Lance Corporal M.A. Hobbs, who was located in a fighting hole well outside the team's position, used hand grenades and small arms fire around his position in an effort to break up the enemy movement.[19]

Meanwhile, Corporal Michael A. Loren, the assistant patrol leader, "completely disregarding his own safety, continually moved about to organize his men, shout encouragement, and redistribute ammunition."[20]

The fighting raged throughout the rest of the night as the NVA made several attempts to overrun the Marine Reconnaissance team, though with little success. Determined fire from Team Hansworth as well as fire from a "Spooky" gunship finally broke up the enemy attack and forced them to withdraw. As the sun rose, the full impact of the encounter could be seen, as "numerous drag marks" from enemy casualties were found all around the fighting positions. One drag mark was, in fact, only five feet from Lance Corporal Hobbs' fighting hole.[21] For his bravery and leadership during this engagement, Corporal Holzmann was awarded the Silver Star.

With the exception of a twenty-nine-man detachment that was sent to Da Nang in order to provide the 1st Reconnaissance Battalion with an airborne capability, this action was the last one for 1st Force Reconnaissance Company, as the team was withdrawn, first to Da Nang and then home to Camp Pendleton, California, where it was reunited with its parent unit—the 1st Marine Division.

"Small Wars": Recon's War Continues (August–December 1970)

Throughout the month of August 1970, and despite the drawdown of Marines, teams from the 1st Reconnaissance Battalion maintained a busy schedule in I Corps throughout the remainder of 1970 and into January 1971. Teams from 1st Reconnaissance Battalion conducted extensive patrols in Elephant Valley, Sherwood Forest, Charlie Ridge, Leach Valley, and the Que Son Mountains in direct support of the 5th Marine Regiment during Operation "Imperial Lake." A total of thirty-nine reconnaissance teams were deployed during the month, with an average of five teams deployed at any given time. The extensive patrolling by Marines of

A "Huey" helicopter belonging to the U.S. Army's 2nd Squadron, 17th Air Cavalry Regiment, shot down by enemy gunfire at HLZ X-Ray on "Zulu Relay." The pilot was killed while several Force Reconnaissance Marines were severely injured. According to Sergeant Bill Moss, leader of Team Atlas, "We used Army 'Hueys' for most of our insertions in late 1969 and early 1970" (courtesy Sergeant Bill Moss).

1st Reconnaissance Battalion resulted in ten enemy KIA and three "probable" enemy KIA, as well as the capture of six individual weapons. The "Quick Reaction Force" from 5th Marines was likewise committed on three separate occasions in response to targets identified by these reconnaissance patrols.[22]

During reconnaissance operations in the Charlie Ridge area, during Operation "Upshur Stream," a total of fifteen reconnaissance teams were deployed during the month, with an average of three teams deployed at any given time. This extensive patrolling netted twelve enemy KIA, sixteen "probable" enemy KIA, and three USMC WIA.[23] The objective of "Upshur Stream" was the exploitation of intelligence gathered by the teams regarding NVA infiltration into the area. Meanwhile, in the Sherwood Forest TAOR, eight teams from 1st Reconnaissance Battalion continued to patrol in search of signs of enemy infiltration, with negligible results. In Elephant Valley, a total of nineteen teams from 1st Reconnaissance Battalion conducted operations and had no significant sightings.[24] In addition to patrolling, SCUBA teams from 1st Reconnaissance Battalion conducted salvage and recovery operations "in general support of the 1st Marine Division (-) (Rein.), FMF."

One significant incident in December 1970 involved members of the 1st Reconnaissance Battalion's Reconnaissance Indoctrination Program (RIP) Class 14-70 during a routine training patrol on "Monkey Mountain," in which they apprehended twenty-two suspected VC, "who were in this area without authorization." The patrol members delivered the suspected VC over to the "Phoenix Committee" for processing, interrogation, and detention.[25]

Fighting and Withdrawing (November–December 1970)

Despite the pullout of U.S. forces from I Corps, there was no break in enemy activity toward the end of the year. Even as the drawdown of Marine forces from Vietnam continued, in tandem with the "Vietnamization" of the war, Marine Reconnaissance's war in Vietnam was not entirely over, as teams from 1st Reconnaissance Battalion carried out operations throughout I Corps. In fact, during the months of November and December 1970, the 1st Reconnaissance Battalion (-) (Reinforced) continued to conduct patrols in the areas of Elephant Valley, Sherwood Forest, Charlie Ridge, Leach Valley, and the Que Son Mountains, making frequent contact with the enemy as the NVA attempted to infiltrate down the Ho Chi Minh Trail toward the coast.

One patrol, carried out by Team Road Test from November 25 through December 5, 1970, lasted over 212 hours. Tasked with "conducting reconnaissance and surveillance operation" in its TAOR, Road Test was to "detect possible VC/NVA troop movement of arms infiltration and be prepared to call and adjust air and artillery on all targets of opportunity." Inserted and extracted by helicopter, the team (composed of five Marines and one Navy corpsman) reported one enemy sighting of a trail and one contact with the enemy. During the subsequent debriefing, Sergeant Kelly, the patrol leader, stated, "The team had just moved on to a trail that they had found the previous day when the Duce (second) point man sighted 1 VC/NVA moving toward the team's position. The enemy was approximately 5 meters to the west of the team. The enemy was carrying a large pack and wearing green utilities and Ho Chi Minh sandals. The Platoon Leader shouted for the enemy to '*Cheiu Hoi*' ['surrender'] causing the enemy soldiers to run down the trail. The team then initiated fire at the enemy resulting in one enemy KIA. Search of the body resulted in finding 1 large bag of rice, approximately 30 pounds in weight, 1 piece of paper, [and] miscellaneous personal gear."[26]

On a similar patrol that commenced two days later, on December 7, 1970, Team Donny Brook, led by Corporal Milleson, encountered three VC/NVA as well as a small enemy arms cache in a cave that contained a ten-pound bag of rice, documents, and a homemade backpack. Inserted by helicopter, the team requested and received close air support from a gunship hovering above the HLZ as they disembarked from the helicopter. Milleson later stated that the gunship provided "excellent coverage of the target area."[27]

During his debriefing at Da Nang, Corporal Milleson carefully recounted that the "team was following a trail when they sighted 3 VC/NVA wearing green rain gear, 3 packs, and an AK-47 assault rifle some 500 meters southeast of the Team's harbor site along a trial some 5–6 square miles in width." Alerted, the team began moving out when they spotted a cave with one enemy soldier in it and, after a brief firefight, killed him. The point man, who was carrying the M-79, then spotted another NVA soldier in cave and initiated contact and killed him with a shot from his weapon. The dead enemy soldier was wearing green utilities and a Vietnamese badge on his blouse. Both dead NVA were approximately eighteen to nineteen years of age and "appeared to be well-fed."[28]

Throughout the month of December 1970, there was no letup in enemy activity. Teams from 1st Reconnaissance Battalion continued to observe small groups of NVA moving south from their sanctuaries across the DMZ.

Another December patrol conducted by Team Road Test in the Thuong Doc River Valley was inserted and prepared to "call and adjust air/artillery on all targets of opportunity." They had the added mission of locating a previously reported enemy base camp. Much to their surprise, the Marines came upon a series of fortified bunkers and a graveyard containing the skeletal remains of what appeared to be a woman. During his post-patrol debriefing, Sergeant Kelly, the patrol leader, recounted:

> [The] Team sighted a grave site with a fence made of small trees surrounding it. The team then moved twenty-five meters to the NW where they came upon a bombed-out area. The point man then sighted two enemy 20 meters west of the team. These enemy wore green utilities,

black boots, and a state-side type of green cover. One of these uniforms had a round patch on the left shirt pocket and a red patch on the left. It was at this time that the team began receiving (Small Arms Fire or SAF) possible M-16 from their west. The team returned SAF hitting one of the enemy sighted causing him to fall (1) enemy KIA (P). The team then ceased fire and began hearing movement and enemy talking. The team utilized M-79 fire and then threw grenades with the enemy returning sporadic (small arms fire). The team utilized a WP grenade to mark the enemy position. When an (AO) ("Hostage STUD") came on station and began making gun runs. At this time the team began moving to the east with the enemy utilizing (SAF) resulting in one USMC WIA (E). While the AO was making his runs, the team received three M-79 (HE) rounds with the closest round landing 10 meters from the team. The team then continued to the east utilizing M-79 fire to cover their movement. The team was 150 meters from the original contact grid where they set up a 360 (degree) defense position in preparation for a SPIE extraction.

When the extract helo made its first attempt to extract the team it received automatic (SAF) from the west. The extract helo pulled out of the zone and the gunships made runs around team's position. Upon the second extract attempt the helo came into the zone utilizing its machine guns for cover. The enemy had ceased fire until the SPIE harness was dropped then they started firing again but not before the wounded man and another man had hooked up to the SPIE. The helo then lifted out of the zone with these two men still receiving (SAF). The team then moved to the south towards the PPB location. The teams still had [enemy] movement to their west and now east. The gunships ran gun runs around the team's positions causing the movement to cease. An (AO) ("Hostage Pogo") directed a fire mission (F/M) on the enemy position with the team's patrol leader receiving a small piece of shrapnel to the right of the foot resulting in one (1) USMC WIA (M). The team continued to the south where they were extracted without further incident.[29]

Sergeant Kelly added that Road Test's action took place in an incessant downpour with poor visibility.

Another patrol, War Cloud Training, likewise conducted a patrol in the Thuong Doc River Valley on December 16–18, 1970. Inserted by helicopter, the team managed to detain twenty-one Vietnamese civilians, though it had no contact with the enemy. After turning over the detainees to U.S. and ARVN officials, the team continued with its mission and, after being in the field for some twenty-five hours, was safely extracted by helicopter.[30]

One last December patrol occurred as Marines from Team Swift Scout, from "Alpha Company," conducted a one-hundred-hour patrol in the Thuong Doc River Valley. From the point of insertion, the team ran into heavy enemy small arms fire from fifteen NVA soldiers. As with past missions, Swift Scout was tasked with conducting a surveillance and observation mission and being "prepared to call and adjust air/artillery on all targets of opportunity."[31] Unlike the other patrols, in which contact with the enemy consisted one or two soldiers, Swift Scout landed in a virtual hornet's nest, with the NVA patiently waiting for the team as they inserted into the HLZ, unknowingly landing on top of a fortified enemy bunker complex. Following insertion, the team heard the voices of approximately five to ten Vietnamese approximately twenty to fifty meters west of their position moving toward them. In order to avoid contact, Swift Scout headed northeast.

"Happy Holidays from Vietnam!" (Left to right) Corporal Bill Moss, Lance Corporal John Hahn, and Lance Corporal George "Butch" Mennie at Phu Bai, December 25, 1969, preparing to leave for a mission (courtesy Corporal Bill Moss).

Patrols: 56	Air Strikes: 3	KIA: 0
Sightings: 124	VC/NVA KIA: 23	WIA: 3
VC/NVA Sighted: 162	Detainees: 21	MIA: 0
Fire Missions: 10	IWC: 9	NBC: 7
	USMC Casualties	DOW: 0

The team was in a security halt when they sighted approximately fifteen VC/NVA heading toward them about fifteen meters north of the point man's position. The patrol leader observed that the NVA (wearing green utilities and green soft covers while carrying AK-47s and cartridge belts but no field packs) were spread out in intervals, with one to five feet between each man. As the enemy approached the team's forward position, the leathernecks took evasive action. Taking periodic security halts in the tall elephant grass, the Marines detected a force of VC/NVA behind them heading in their direction.[32]

By this time, the team had requested an emergency extraction, and an AO was in the air for support. The AO advised the team of a possible ladder extraction point and marked the location. At this time, the team was about twenty-five meters from the site. As they moved out, they saw five enemy soldiers running toward them in an apparent effort to encircle the team. It was about 1710 when the team initiated contact, and a running gun battle ensued. Corporal Combs commented that "the smell of the enemy was strong." Continuing to the extraction point, two enemy soldiers were spotted observing the team's movements; the Marines "initiated contact with them though with negative results."[33] Huey gunships came on station with the extraction birds, laying down a heavy suppressive fire. Even as the Marines moved toward the ladder zone, the enemy sought to prevent the team's extraction. However, the team succeeded in reaching the extraction vehicles despite the heavy fire. As they were lifted away, team members reported seeing green tracers flying toward them.

While the results of Swift Scout's patrol were negative, Corporal Combs reported three "probable" enemy KIA. Combs later wrote that Swift Scout had "possibly come across an enemy base camp/bunker complex as well as numerous trails headed in that direction." He added that supporting arms were "very effective."[34]

1st Reconnaissance Battalion's Final Operations (January–March 1971)

From January through March 1971, teams from the 1st Reconnaissance Battalion (-) (Rein.) continued operations in the areas of Elephant Valley, Charlie Ridge, Leech Valley, and the Que Son Mountains during the month of January 1971. Patrols from 1st Reconnaissance Battalion, in fact, continued to saturate the Que Son Mountains in direct support of the 5th Marine Regiment during Operation "Imperial Lake." A total of forty-six teams were deployed during the month, with an average of six teams deployed at any given time. The results of this patrolling activity were ten enemy KIA (confirmed) and nine KIA (probables), with one POW taken. The teams likewise captured a number of individual weapons. There were two friendly WIA. The Marine "Quick Reaction Force" was committed on three separate occasions to targets designated by the reconnaissance teams.

Teams from the 1st Reconnaissance Battalion likewise supported elements of the 1st Marine Regiment during Operation "Upshur Stream" in the Charlie Ridge TAOR. During any given time, the battalion deployed ten teams during the same month. The results of these extensive patrols netted three confirmed enemy KIA, with another KIA listed as "probable."

In Leech Valley, ten recon teams operated, with two teams deployed at any given time. At one point, the teams made contact with a large enemy force of unknown size or composition. The results of this contact were unknown. During this operation, the 1st Marines' "Quick Reaction Force" was utilized to exploit this contact. In the eastern Elephant Valley, a total of sixteen teams were deployed at any given time, with no significant enemy contacts or sightings reported. The unit likewise conducted diving operations in support of the 1st Marine Division.[35]

In February 1971, the 1st Reconnaissance Battalion maintained its focus in the area of Elephant Valley, Sherwood Forest, Charlie Ridge, Leech Valley, and the Que Son Mountains. The unit continued to support the 5th Marine Regiment's Operation "Imperial Lake." During this operation, 1st Recon Battalion deployed fifty teams, with an average of seven teams operating in the field at any given time. As a result, there were sixteen enemy KIA (not counting two probable KIA) and seven enemy WIA (along with another probable WIA). The teams captured two enemy soldiers and one individual weapon. The recon teams experienced two WIA during this operation.[36]

While supporting the 1st Marines during Operation "Upshur Stream," in the Charlie Ridge TAOR, the 3rd Force Reconnaissance Company deployed fifteen teams, with three teams in the field at any given time. The teams reported one enemy soldier KIA (with another two probable KIA) and two enemy WIA. The unit had no casualties.[37]

During operations in the area known as Sherwood Forest, fourteen teams deployed during the month of February, with two teams out on patrol at any given time. "This patrol activity, as was the case in the Leech Valley, was in conjunction with the rocket belt security efforts of the 1st Marine Regiment."[38]

In the Elephant Valley TAOR, a total of seventeen patrols conducted operations, with three teams deployed at any given time. The results of these patrols were negligible, with no enemy contact reported.

The 1st Reconnaissance Battalion divers conducted river searches in support of the 1st Marines and discovered seven 140mm rocket warheads. Divers from 1st Reconnaissance Battalion likewise supported ARVN operations during their offensive into enemy sanctuaries in Laos during Operation "Lam Son 719." Here, the SCUBA teams "conducted daily bridge security checks along Highway 1 throughout the 1st Marine Division's TAOR searching for underwater mines and explosives."[39]

As the final patrols returned from the field and headed toward their respective combat bases, 1st Reconnaissance Battalion "stood down" at Camp Reasoner near Da Nang. On March 24, 1971—almost six years to the day when 1st Force Reconnaissance Company's Sub Unit 1 came ashore at Da Nang on March 20, 1965, in support of the 9th Marine Expeditionary Brigade's landing on Red Beach—Marines of the 1st Reconnaissance Battalion boarded the USS *Denver* (LPD-9) for their return trip home. The *Denver* departed from the Republic of Vietnam the next day, while the battalion's advance party likewise flew out of Da Nang on March 25, 1971 (Vietnam time) and arrived twenty-four hours later in the United States (March 25, 1971). With the departure of the 1st Reconnaissance Battalion, Marine Reconnaissance's war in Vietnam was over.[40]

13

"A War by Detachments"

U.S. Army Long-Range Reconnaissance Patrols in Vietnam (1966–1973)

Besides Marine Reconnaissance units, the U.S. Army fielded both Special Forces Groups and Long-Range Reconnaissance Patrols to seek out and report on enemy units. Like the Marines, the U.S. Army was not new to long-range reconnaissance operations. From the time of the Philippine Insurrection (1899–1903), the U.S. Army experimented with a variety of organizations tasked with carrying out reconnaissance, raids, intelligence gathering, and patrolling.[1]

During World War II, the U.S. Army, working with the Office of Strategic Services (the forerunner of the Central Intelligence Agency), formed a special unit, Detachment 101, that conducted a host of reconnaissance and sabotage missions behind Japanese lines in Burma.[2] In the same theater, Brigadier General Frank D. Merrill, U.S. Army, was given command of the formation known as the 5307th Composite Unit (more commonly known as "Merrill's Marauders"), which conducted hit-and-run raids behind Japanese lines in northern Burma.[3] Merrill's Marauders, a conventional organized force, was one of the Army's most successful (and highly decorated) special units, organized and ordered to "scout out," "find, fix, and destroy" Japanese units (most notably, the veteran *Japanese 18th Imperial Division*) during their successful mission to seize the vital airfield at Myitkyina.[4]

In the European theater of operations, U.S. Army Pathfinders and Rangers, working in conjunction with the 101st and 82nd Airborne Divisions, likewise conducted a series of successful operations against German positions at Ste. Mere Eglise and on the Normandy beachhead. Army Ranger units, modeled after the British Commandos, conducted a series of operations against the German Army, starting with Operation "Torch" on November 1942 through the Normandy landings on June 6, 1944.[5]

By the end of World War II, the U.S. Army had established an excellent reputation in the conduct of special operations, one that it would take into the post–World War II era with the establishment of the Army Special Forces in 1952.[6] One such organization, a direct descendant of Merrill's Marauders, was known as Long-Range Reconnaissance Patrols (LRRPs), which would work in unison with the Army's airborne forces. The LRRPs, originally a "strategic force" (that is, designed and organized to operate on a European battlefield, gathering intelligence and conducting specific missions against the Soviet Army), were soon reoriented operationally toward Latin America and Asia, particularly in Southeast Asia and Indonesia. Tensions in these areas shifted the attention of the Army's burgeoning Special Forces organizations (to be designated in 1962 as "Green Berets" by their special headgear) after 1958 toward developing a tactical force to work in conjunction with Army conventional forces. This force later operated in conjunction with the 101st Air Mobile Division during the Vietnam War, and it became one of the most effective reconnaissance assets operating after 1968 in the A Shau Valley.[7]

Origins of U.S. Army Reconnaissance Doctrine (1925–1944)

As mentioned previously, the U.S. Army has a long history in counterinsurgency. During the nineteenth century, the Army fought a long counterinsurgency campaign against the Native Americans, from the Seminole Wars in the mid-1830s through the close of the frontier in 1890.[8] At the dawn of the twentieth century, the Army (and Marines) fought a four-year long insurgency in the Philippines. Minor campaigns in Cuba (1906), and later in Mexico (1914 and 1917), involved units no larger than regiments. Involvement in World War I (1917–1918) and occupation duty in Germany from 1918 to 1920 "shifted" the paradigm of Army thinking toward that of conventional warfare.[9] Counterinsurgency and the Army's involvement in pacification campaigns were not totally forgotten (as they would be at the end of the Vietnam War).

In 1925, Brigadier General George S. Simonds, as commanding officer of the 20th Infantry Brigade, stationed in the Panama Canal Zone, oversaw the compilation of a manual that outlined the principles of conducting combat operations in a jungle environment, titled *Jungle Combat Principles*.[10] While the principles were "basic" in detail, they nonetheless laid the foundation for the Army's counterinsurgency doctrine used during World War II and afterward, and they served as the basis for the concept and objectives of the Long-Range Reconnaissance Patrol Company.[11]

Jungle Combat Principles covered subjects that ranged from "Training Regulations" and "Trails and Trail Cutting" to the general principles of offensive and defensive combat in a jungle environment, unit organization and composition, use of artillery, aviation, and tactics. While the manual acknowledged that jungle warfare was "abnormal" and unlike conventional warfare, the authors of *Jungle Combat Principles* clearly stated that fighting in a jungle was not the same as fighting "savages"; instead, it was more highly refined toward fighting "civilized and modernized forces."[12]

As for the conduct of reconnaissance, "bushwhacking" (another name for setting and springing ambushes) and intelligence gathering are covered in *Jungle*

Combat Principles. Specifically related to the need for long-range reconnaissance, this semi-official manual laid out the parameters for what it called "Jungle Intelligence," "Means of Intelligence," "Bushwhacking," and "Harassing and/or Delaying." Each of these points eventually became the foundation for both Army and Marine reconnaissance operational doctrine.

The authors of *Jungle Combat Principles* acknowledged that "distribut[ing] our forces over all of the jungle trails would amount to absolute dispersion ... [therefore] it is essential for us, and for any jungle defensive, that prompt information be obtained of the trails used or likely to be used by the enemy." The manual stressed that once the enemy's trails were discovered, troops "were to be moved in and assigned harassing missions" or the "careful location of the [enemy] forces on the flanks, away from the trails." As emphasized by both Brigadier General Dion Williams and Lieutenant Colonel Earl H. Ellis in their writings on amphibious reconnaissance, "The need for jungle intelligence is, therefore, obvious, and must be well organized and fool proof."[13]

As for the "Means of Intelligence," *Jungle Combat Principles* stated that "the primary step in intelligence is to obtain information of the general approach of large enemy forces from the sea or open terrain beyond the jungle." The authors noted that "the next step is the location of an initial screen of observation at the edge of the jungle or at the outer limit of our interest." As stressed in the manual, "Each trail would be covered at its outer limit by a double observation chain, or two posts, each of two observers, a mile apart." These posts would be connected by a field telephone and a Very[14] pistol. The communication link likewise was to have a backup in case the phone or pistol could not be used.

In a clear reference to the requirement of a ground reconnaissance force, *Jungle Combat Principles* stressed that because intelligence needed to be timely, a commander might want to send out a combat reconnaissance patrol "sufficient in size to delay the enemy advance and to get back information," holding off the enemy using harassing or delaying tactics. Ground reconnaissance would be, as the manual's authors observed, "amplified by aerial reconnaissance. Air observers could give simple warning of advance of large forces into the jungle, if the advance occurs in daylight, and in daylight could probably follow such forces, once they are located." As for aerial observation during hours of darkness or the enemy's use of jungle canopy to conceal his position, the authors conceded that aircraft would be hard pressed to locate enemy or his avenues of approach or retreat.[15]

On the subject of "Delaying Actions," the manual emphasized that "to delay [an] enemy advance through the jungle will annoy him and perhaps weaken his morale very considerably, and would generally be a primary element of the defense." According to *Jungle Combat Principles*, small units could delay and thus frustrate a larger enemy force's advance:

> Relatively small forces can hope, if properly employed to deny the use of the trails to the enemy advance elements. The ideal of delaying action is, therefore, to require the enemy, or

at least his advance elements, "to traverse the entire jungle zone away from the trails, cutting through when the jungle is thick." If this ideal is achieved, the time required by the enemy for passage of the jungle can be roughly computed as the time required to cut parallel to the trails, plus the time required to develop our various defensive positions plus the time lost through effects of ambush and other harassing actions.[16]

The manual stressed that these "small forces" or teams would be hard pressed to deny the enemy the "entire trail." Instead, the objective of the combat reconnaissance teams should be to establish a series of defenses by "leap-frogging" from position to position, thus preventing the enemy from using the trails. This approach would prevent commanders from "frittering away" troops to defend the entire trail, which could only be accomplished by larger forces. In short, "well-trained troops should be able to conduct this trail fighting in a manner to deny most of the trail to the enemy advance elements, causing his main body to delay his advance." Simply put, smaller, well-trained teams could cover longer stretches of the trail and inflict greater casualties on a larger enemy force.

While a "delaying action" can do just that—"delay" an enemy's advance—the authors of *Jungle Combat Principles* wrote that only the head of the enemy column or force would be affected. The goal of these teams was to "strike his flanks, his rear, his trains, bases, and camps. In addition to delaying him, we should plan to destroy parts of him, here and there, and to demoralize his troops in every possible way. This we do by various means of harassing."

It was here that this early "counterinsurgency manual" differentiated the concepts of "delaying" and "harassing" operations:

> The units assigned to these must be separate units. The delaying force is really a security force for our line of resistance. The harassing force must be set free, with no security mission other than to protect itself, and ultimately to withdraw for a final defensive concentration if such becomes necessary.[17]

Regarding the conduct of "harassing" missions, the combat reconnaissance patrol was to establish points of ambush along likely avenues of approach. In fact, as the manual stated, "the selection of an ambush position is very important, cannot be made from the map, and requires careful study and organization of the terrain during training periods and the readiness period. As a general rule, ambushes must be in the thick jungle, or they will be discovered. While they require certain facilities, they should not generally be in too obvious a position, or the enemy will reconnoiter and discover them."[18]

The unit or outfit assigned to such a mission would have to use stealth and fire discipline so as not to tip off their position. In direct reference to both Marine Force and Army reconnaissance teams, *Jungle Combat Principles* emphasized that the team leader was the central person who initiated and directed any action that might take place at the ambush or harassing site. The team leader would signal the rest of the team to initiate contact, hold fire, and withdraw—all on his signal lead. As for the team, they had to "lie quiet" until the order was given to withdraw, and the deeper breadth, covering more area and engaging larger enemy forces.[25] A larger, battalion/regimental-size force is also better able to provide sufficient reserve forces, mainly as a security force, in order to prevent "defeat in detail of individual ambush sites."[26] Finally, both manuals stress the need for "careful planning, efficient control, and timely intelligence" when conducting such operations.[27]

Of course, both manuals maintain that small units are still required, as they are the ones that trigger the ambush in addition to offering mutual support to the larger force in cutting off the enemy's avenues of escape. A smaller force can likewise conduct "numerous small raids against towns and outlying areas suspected of harboring guerrilla personnel and/or material."[28] Above all else, both small and large units, when conducting "harassing and delaying" operations, ambushes and raids, must be flexible and able to respond to new conditions.[29]

The concepts of counterguerrilla operations outlined in the 20th Infantry Brigade's *Jungle Combat Principles* (written primarily for soldiers in the Panama Canal Zone) represent one of the first major doctrinal publications produced by the U.S. Army in the twentieth century. These same principles of jungle warfare would later be applied during World War II by both Marine and Army units in the Southwest Pacific and in Asia. *Jungle Combat Principles*, largely forgotten in the literature of jungle warfare and counterguerrilla operations produced in the twentieth century, nevertheless laid the doctrinal foundation for Merrill's Marauders and Carlson's 2nd Marine Raider Battalion. More important, the lessons enumerated in this inter-war manual would become incorporated into the Army's counterinsurgency doctrine that emerged in the 1950s and 1960s.[30]

Marauders, Air Commandos, Scouts, and Rangers (1943–1945)

During the Second World War, the U.S. Army and Marine Corps experimented with different troop formations in the Pacific and European theaters of operations. In terms of long-range penetration units, it was in the China-Burma-India (CBI) theater of operations that the concept of a unit organized specifically for a tailored mission (in this case, the seizure of the vital Japanese airfield located at Myitkyina in northern Burma) came to the fore in the form of the 5307th Composite (Provisional) Unit. The 5307th—known by its more popular and colorful name, "Merrill's Marauders" (a name given to it by a newspaper wag in honor its first commander, Brigadier General Frank D. Merrill)—established the doctrinal criteria for the conduct of long-range penetration units used by Army LRRPs and Special Forces in Vietnam.[31]

Modeled after the 77th Indian Infantry Brigade, or "Chindits" ("Protectors of the Pagodas"), a composite force of conventional infantry and commandos[32] organized and led by its legendary commander, Brigadier (Major General) Orde C. Wingate, the 5307th (given the code-name "Galahad") began training in Deogarh, India, under Colonel Francis G. Brink. It might be noted that Brink, as a brigadier general, would lead the first U.S. Military Advisory and Assistance Group (MAAG) to Saigon, in French Indochina (Vietnam), in 1951.[33] Colonel Brink, an infantryman who had spent the bulk of his career as a trainer, had the initial task of training the three thousand volunteers for the seizure of Myitkyina. After two months of exhaustive training, the 5307th, placed under the command of Brigadier General Frank D. Merrill, began its seven-month campaign in northern Burma. On February 11, 1944, the lead battalion of the 5307th crossed into Burma from India. Followed by the remainder of Galahad, Merrill's force began its six-hundred-mile trek across the dense jungles and swamps of northern Burma. Armed with only mortars and machine guns, the Marauders came up against the veteran Japanese 18th Imperial Division. Merrill's force, dependent primarily on pack animals and aerial resupply, and marching through an almost impenetrable jungle and enduring constant fighting, at last reached Myitkyina in May 1944. Initially failing to take their objective, the Marauders finally seized the town and nearby airfield on August 3, 1944, after nearly three months of bitter fighting against the debilitated remnants of the 18th Division.

By August 1944, the 5307th was, for all intents and purposes, a decimated force. Of the 2,900 Marauders who marched into Burma, "93 had been killed in combat, 30 had died from disease, and a further 301 wounded or missing in action. An additional 1,970 Marauders had been hospitalized with sickness," with amoebic dysentery and malaria alone claiming some 503 soldiers.[34]

Even as the 5307th continued with its mission toward Myitkyina, Colonel Francis Brink authored a series of lessons learned that served as the basis for a long-range penetration force.[35] These lessons included administration and supply, training, communications, and evacuation of wounded personnel. Colonel Charles N. Hunter, Merrill's executive officer (and West Point classmate), likewise submitted a detailed after-action report of the Marauders' activities, "Overseas Observations," in February 1945, in which he elaborated on Brink's initial reports of the training activities of the 5307th Composite Unit (Provisional). Colonel Hunter, like Brink, concentrated on the organization, training and employment of the Marauders.[36]

Colonel Brink (whom this author has dubbed "the Forgotten Marauder"), in his report on the Marauders' training and organization, reached several conclusions regarding the employment of long-range penetration units, provisions of which remained relevant through the deployment of U.S. Army LRRPs to Vietnam. These conclusions included the following:

    a. A LRP force must always operate in tactical support of a specific operation to further the movement of a specific force.

    b. A defended Base of Operations from which an LRP unit operates must be established in which task forces are made up and moved out on definite missions.

    c. LRP units must be given a specific mission(s) after the performance of which it returns to a friendly base.

d. The size and composition of LRP forces should be adopted to each specific mission and set up and trained in the base area some time before moving out to attack.

e. U.S. Combat methods are best for U.S. troops and others should not be initiated.

f. There must be extremely close coordination and understanding between LRP forces and air units supplying and supporting the ground operations; otherwise the operation will fail or produce mediocre results.

g. The U.S. LRP unit is not organized or equipped for heavy attacks or for long defenses of positions.

h. The movement of LRP forces on long distant strategic missions which affect the advance of main forces is only justified if their objectives cannot be struck by the air arm, or by quick raids of air-borne glider troops which return preferably by glider after the operation.[37]

The "Forgotten Marauder": Colonel Francis G. Brink, U.S. Army (shown here as a brigadier general), was largely responsible for the training of the 5307th Composite Unit (Provisional) prior to its campaign in northern Burma (U.S. Army photograph).

The U.S. Army, in its postwar analysis of special operations during World War II, incorporated Colonel Brink's observations on the employment of long-range penetration units in its doctrinal publication dedicated to this topic. In fact, while FM 31-16 was written with operations in a European theater of operations against the Soviet Army in mind, much of what Brink wrote ended up being practiced by Army LRRP units in the A Shau Valley in Vietnam in 1968–1970.[38]

"Raiders, Reconnaissance, Aerial Spotters": Detachment 101 (1942–1945)

Organized by the Office of Strategic Services, Detachment 101 (led by first by Major Carl F. Eifler and later Lieutenant Colonel William R. Peers) conducted guerrilla operations behind Japanese lines, many times in conjunction with Orde Wingate's Chindits and Merrill's Marauders or independently with the native Kachin guerrillas. The members of Detachment 101, supplied primarily by the air, carried out long-range penetration operations against the Japanese in northern Burma. They likewise conducted sabotage and long-range reconnaissance and penetration operations deep into Japanese territory. As one U.S. Army study concluded, Detachment 101, with its Kachin Rangers, was "an invaluable source of intelligence information" during the reconquest of northern Burma. This was especially true during the 5307th's campaign against Myitkyina in the spring of 1944, at which time Detachment 101 played a significant role scouting out trails and reporting on Japanese troop movements.[39] In fact, at the start of the Marauders' campaign into northern Burma, the Kachin Rangers had formed one of the "most efficient intelligence gathering organizations" in the CBI theater.[40]

"Reconnaissance Support from the Air": The 1st Air Commando Group

One rather unique unit formed in the CBI theater to support both the American and the British long-range penetration missions was the 1st Air Commando Group, otherwise known as the 5318th Provisional Unit (Air) or by its classified name at the time—Project 9.[41] The 1st Air Commando Group, commanded by Colonel Phillip G. Cochran, was a hodgepodge collection of C-47 "Dakota" transports, UC-64 Norsemen light transport aircraft, "Vultee" L-1 Vigilant aircraft, Stinson L-5A Sentinel observation aircraft, and Sikorsky YR-4 helicopters, as well as P-51A fighter aircraft, which provided aerial resupply, medical evacuation, and close air support to both the Chindits and Merrill's Marauders as well as Lieutenant General William Slim's 14th Army and Lieutenant General Joseph W. ("Vinegar Joe") Stilwell's Chinese divisions in their drive to evict Japanese forces from northern Burma. The 1st Air Commando Group was organized to be self-sustaining units, "equipped to establish island-airfields in the heart of enemy-held territory."[42]

Alamo Scouts

The CBI theater was not the only area where special forces were organized to conduct intelligence and reconnaissance operations. General Walter Krueger, commanding general of the 6th Army, organized ten teams of thirty men each, dubbed "Alamo Scouts," to collect intelligence and conduct reconnaissance against the Japanese occupying the islands of New Britain, Noemfoor, and Sansapor, as well as during operations in the Philippines. The scouts were used to reconnoiter landing beaches and enemy positions prior to the landings by Krueger's 6th Army.[43]

"Rangers Lead the Way": U.S. Army Rangers (1942–1944)

Formation of the U.S. Army's Ranger battalions came as a result of a directive by Colonel Lucian K. Truscott at the behest of General George C. Marshall, chairman of the Joint Chiefs of Staff, who had hoped to "provide American soldiers with at least some combat experience" in a possible cross-channel invasion in 1942.[44] Influenced by the British Commando organization, the first group of American soldiers were trained and recruited by Colonel William O. Darby, a graduate of West Point. Volunteers for this new American army formation came primarily from the 34th Infantry Division, 1st Armored Division, and other American units then stationed in Northern Ireland. Formed into a headquarters company and six line companies of sixty-seven men each, the new organization (dubbed "Rangers") "sacrificed firepower and administrative self-sufficiency for foot and amphibious mobility."

Brigadier General William O'Darby observes soldiers from the 1st Ranger Battalion (courtesy U.S. Army).

After extensive training in the use of small arms, explosives, hand-to-hand combat, street fighting, night operations, patrolling, and handling of small boats from British trainers, the Rangers conducted a series of exercises, some of them carried out with live ammunition. Moved to Argyle, Scotland, in amphibious operations with the Royal Navy, Darby's force concluded its training "practicing attacks on pillboxes and coastal defenses" in Dundee, Scotland.

The Rangers' first combat experience came in the failed Dieppe Raid of August 12, 1942. The Rangers had been assigned to clear the way for the assault by the 2nd Canadian Division and two British Commandos (along with another Ranger battalion) and seize two coastal batteries flanking the port. While one battalion of Rangers succeeded in destroying the battery west of Dieppe, the German defenders managed to scatter the second battalion and British troops. Overall, the Allies suffered 3,400 casualties of the 5,000 troops used in the Dieppe Raid, with many of the British Commandos and American Rangers captured.[45]

After the disaster at Dieppe, the Army reconstituted the 1st Ranger Battalion in time for the invasion of Northwest Africa. During Operation "Torch," the 1st Ranger Battalion led the assault landing at Arzew, Algeria, on November 8, 1942.[46] A Ranger battalion participated in the assault on Sicily (Operation "Husky") in July 1943 and later at Anzio on the Italian mainland. Two Ranger battalions "were in the forefront of the D-Day landings on the Normandy beachheads on June 6, 1944 at Point d Hoe, France." The 6th Ranger Battalion, assigned to the U.S. 6th Army, participated

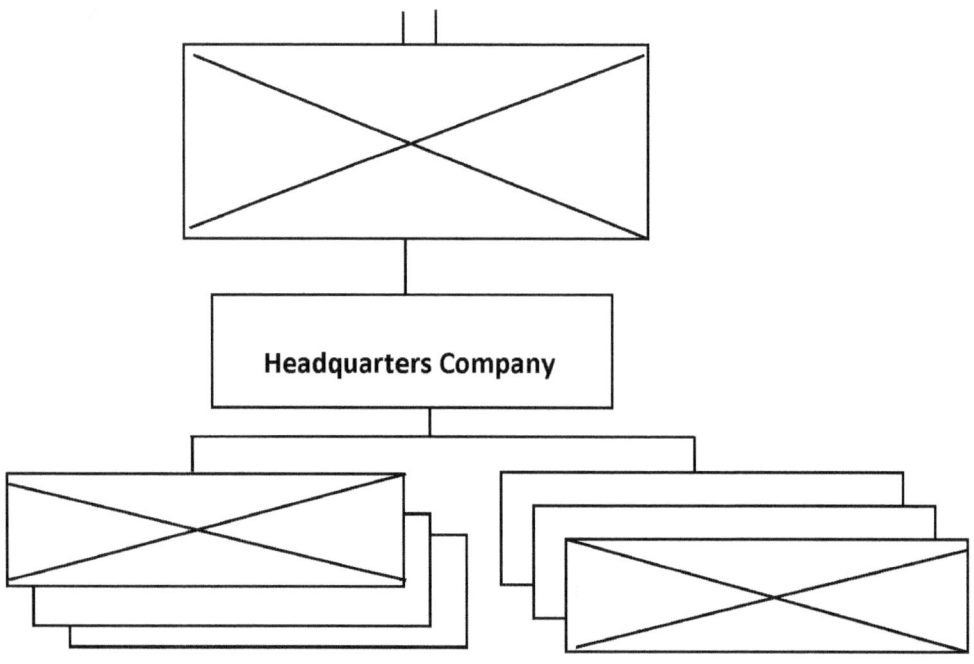

Diagram 9: U.S. Army Ranger Battalion, 1942 (Hogan, *U.S. Army Special Operations in World War II*, 12).

in combat operations in the islands off Leyte Gulf and conducted reconnaissance and intelligence-gathering operations for General Douglas MacArthur's forces in the Philippines in September–October 1944.[47]

During World War II, the U.S. Army, based on the work of the British Commandos and Orde Wingate's Chindits, experimented with a number of light infantry formations, with great success.[48] Organized primarily as a raiding force, these same formations (particularly Detachment 101) were soon gathering intelligence and conducting reconnaissance operations in addition to supporting conventional units. Based on the success of these same units in World War II, and later during the war in Korea, the U.S. Army changed the name LRRP over to "U.S. Army Rangers" during the Vietnam War.[49] It is a fact that the Army's experiments with these light infantry formations set the stage for the organization and use of similar forces in the jungles and central highlands of South Vietnam.

"The White Tigers": The Korean War (1950–1953)

During the Korean War, U.S. soldiers were assigned to various formations organized by the United Nations Partisan Infantry Korea (UNPIK). The U.S. Army's contribution to this formation was the 8240th U.S. Army Unit of the 8th U.S. Army. Known as the "White Tigers," these soldiers conducted hit-and-run raids and intelligence-gathering missions, in addition to leading South Korean Commandos on enemy positions located in the offshore islands of North Korea.[50]

Based on its experiences in World War II and Korea, the U.S. Army, during the 1950s, continued to experiment with Special Forces, including the formation of the first Long-Range Penetration Patrol forces.[51] By the time the U.S. Army became heavily involved in the Vietnam War, LRRPs were prepared to take to the field in support of both Army and Marine operations in the A Shau Valley in the spring of 1968.

Army LRRP Forces (1965–1968)

By the time the U.S. Army arrived in the Republic of Vietnam in the summer of 1965, the doctrinal precepts of how it would reverse the gains made by the National Liberation Front (or "Viet Cong") and North Vietnamese Army (NVA) or People's Army of Vietnam (PAVN) had been well established. The idea that the Army was doctrinally not prepared to fight a counterinsurgency in Asia or elsewhere is a myth, one that has been perpetuated over the decades.[52] In fact, the opposite is the case. The John F. Kennedy Center for Special Warfare, located at Fort Bragg, North Carolina (named in honor of the U.S. Army's strongest advocate for counterinsurgency), had, by 1965, produced a large body of literature and classroom instruction geared toward unconventional warfare, from which Army officers benefited prior to their deployment to Vietnam in 1965.[53] Moreover, by 1967, the Army had geared its training of company-grade officers (second lieutenant through captain) toward an emphasis on small-unit operations.[54] At this time, General Harold K. Johnson (Chief of Staff of the Army) and General William Westmoreland, as well as such individuals as the head of the U.S. Army's Infantry School at Fort Benning, Georgia, took counterinsurgency seriously and trained the men who would lead platoons and companies in small-unit warfare accordingly.[55]

In order to assess the demands Vietnam would place on the training of officers (and enlisted men), General Johnson initiated a comprehensive review of the Army's education and training base to better prepare that service for what was now a major commitment of U.S. combat forces. Johnson appointed Lieutenant General Ralph E. Haines, Jr., to take charge of the review process. Known collectively as the Haines Board and consisting of eleven officers (four general officers and seven colonels and lieutenant colonels), Johnson charged the board with determining the adequacy of the Army's school and training system over a ten-year period (1965–1975). Special emphasis was given to the "training requirements for newly commissioned officers, taking into consideration sources of new officers and the requirements for attendance at the basic officer's course."[56] While the results of the study were still being disseminated throughout the senior command echelons of the Army as U.S. troops deployed to Vietnam, the Army's Infantry School at Fort Benning conducted a full review of its own and, as a result, implemented those provisions that directly affected the preparation of newly commissioned officers as platoon leaders.

The Haines Board conducted a thorough examination of the Army's school and training system, which included on-site visits to the Army's major education installations, the most important of which were Fort Monroe, Virginia (headquarters to the Continental Army Command), and Fort Gordon and Fort Benning in Georgia. The most important school visited by the board was the U.S. Army Infantry School (USAIS) located at Fort Benning. Prior to the visit of General Haines' study group, the commandant of the Infantry School asked each department to write a critique of "its contribution to the army's school system" and its "attitude of Infantry toward training."

It is important to note that even before the arrival of the Haines Board, the Infantry School had initiated a fifteen-week course, known as the Combat Platoon Leader Course (CPLC), in order to prepare company-grade officers with the basics of infantry and leadership.[57] In its findings, the Haines Board concluded that the primary aim of the officers' basic course was to develop leaders. Skills such as infantry tactics and weapons were acquired over time, which the young officer would learn from experienced noncommissioned officers once assigned to a unit.

The USAIS faculty disagreed with the findings of the Haines Board insofar as the training of newly commissioned officers was concerned. With the increased demand for small-unit leaders for service in Vietnam, the faculty at the

Infantry School concurred with the head of the Ranger School, who wrote that "the newly-commissioned officer does not receive enough practical experience in small-unit leadership before he is required to perform as a leader," a view the Haines Board partially adopted in its recommendation that "the Ranger Course offered the best training in small unit leadership and tactics."[58] This latter point is important, given the Army's need for officers trained in small-unit operations (to include long-range reconnaissance and special operations) once assigned to Vietnam.

Regarding the preparation of newly commissioned officers for the demands of the Vietnam War, the Haines Board concluded that "all newly-commissioned officers (except Officer Candidate School graduates) attend an officer basic course covering company/battery fundamentals relevant to their first duty of assignment and emphasizing practical work and field instruction."[59] The board further recommended "that entry training for Regular Army officers include a shortened basic course six weeks in length (five for infantry officers) and a Ranger Course of eight weeks' duration; that the entry training or other than Regular Army officers include a basic course not more than nine weeks in length without Ranger Training; that airborne training be limited to those officers being assigned to airborne units."[60]

While the Haines Board emphasized the importance of Ranger training as a means of developing small-unit leaders, it maintained (as mentioned previously) that airborne training be limited to those officers assigned to airborne units. It was here that the commandant of the Infantry School disagreed, emphasizing instead that while airborne training should be primarily for those officers assigned specifically to airborne units, "it should nonetheless be made available for those officers who volunteer when space is available." He added, "The Airborne Course instills in the junior officer those most important characteristics of leadership necessary for him to function effectively as a combat leader.... The most aggressive and motivated officers are those who volunteer. Every attempt must be made to take advantage of this source for the Army hard cops of officers and future leaders."[61]

As for the battlefield value of airborne training for junior officers, the commandant wrote, "With the requirements for officers to fill vacancies in Airborne and Airmobile Divisions and Special Forces Groups, a pool of qualified Airborne officers must be maintained to provide for combat losses, normal rotation of assignments, and mobilization in time."[62] Put another way, airborne training provided a ready pool of qualified officers for specialized units such as Rangers, Special Forces, or Long-Range Reconnaissance Platoons.

The emphasis the U.S. Army's Infantry School placed on small-unit training and Ranger training filtered down to the training of Reserve Officer Training Corps (ROTC) cadets. Beginning in 1967, when ROTC basic training moved from Fort Knox, Kentucky, to Fort Benning, Georgia, new, two-year enrollees in the Army Reserve officer program received an introduction to basic infantry tactics and small-unit operations, including Ranger training. While the review committee at the Infantry School agreed that the graduates of the U.S. Military Academy received an adequate introduction to leading platoons, shortcomings existed in the General Military Science Courses in ROTC. This shortcoming, the committee hoped, would be corrected with the newly implemented five-week Combat Platoon Leader's Course, added to the curriculum at Fort Benning in order to introduce the new lieutenant to platoon tactics and leadership.[63] Moreover, the relocation of ROTC training to Fort Benning provided the Army with the opportunity to introduce cadets to basic infantry tactics regardless of their assigned branch. While the infantry training cadets received at basic training was not comprehensive, it nonetheless underscored the Army's emphasis on and commitment to developing small-unit leaders.[64]

The Small-Unit Warfare vs. Large-Unit Warfare Debate

General Westmoreland has been wrongfully criticized for the adaptation of large-unit operations often referred as "search-and-destroy" or "clearing operations." Much of this criticism centered on Westmoreland's belief that the Army's main task was to defeat the main enemy forces in the field while the Army of South Vietnam (ARVN) concentrated on pacification and local security.[65] As the U.S. Army gradually shifted its operations from an advisory role to that of an active combatant, Westmoreland believed that until the enemy's main forces had been brought to battle and destroyed in the field, pacification could not occur with any guarantee of success. In fact, he adopted the Army's doctrine that "insurgencies were multifaceted … requiring a multifaceted approach." In crafting a strategy to defeat the Viet Cong and NVA, Westmoreland embraced "three broad categories of military operations, each designed to meet a particular aspect of the overall mission" of defeating the enemy and gradually turning the fighting over to ARVN. The three categories included: (1) "search-and-destroy" operations; (2) clearing (or "clear and hold") operations, and (3) "securing operations." Each category is important insofar as to the requirement of a long-range reconnaissance force is concerned.

Regarding search-and-destroy operations, the main emphasis was the execution of "offensive thrusts," which were designed to destroy the enemy's main forces and base of operations. This type of operation involved units that ranged in size from corps to companies, and it encompassed a wide area of operations. "Tactically, they usually involved the execution of some manner of sweep or encirclement."[66]

The second type of operation Westmoreland employed was "clearing" or "clear and hold." The U.S. Army utilized clearing operations "to break up the enemy's guerrilla forces in an area slated for pacification."[67] According to Army doctrine,

> an Army brigade would move to the targeted area, establish base camps, and create a liaison with indigenous civil, military, and intelligence agencies. The brigade commander would then divide the area among his subordinate battalions. Depending upon the terrain and strength of the enemy, MACV estimates that a battalion could clear an area up to 373 kilometers[68] in size. Once established, the battalions would subdivide their assigned territory among their component companies being careful to keep a reserve for rapid reaction operations.[69]

At this point of a "clear and hold" operation, small units (companies, platoons, and squads) conducted extensive patrols, both day and night, harassing the enemy and keeping him off balance. Army doctrine stated that once the enemy had been engaged, reinforcements would be rushed to "destroy them" in operations that Army officials nicknamed "net and spear," a concept U.S. Army advisors introduced to ARVN in the early 1960s. Overall, the idea was that once the enemy had been defeated en masse, pacification could proceed unhindered as smaller patrols continued to track and destroy the remaining enemy units, laying the foundation for the final type of operation, known as "securing."

Securing operations differed little from "clear and hold." During this phase, while U.S. units continued to destroy what remained of the enemy's main or guerrilla forces, ARVN would assert control of the area and, at least according to doctrine, introduce civil authority as well as medical, education, and agrarian reforms. Paramilitary and government forces would also conduct extensive patrolling to essentially "finish off" what remained of the enemy forces.[70]

It was at this point that Army doctrine diverged, as advocates of the "small-unit war" pointed out that large-unit operations, while effective in destroying the enemy's main infrastructure, could not penetrate those areas inaccessible to either U.S. or ARVN forces. Those who favored the use of smaller units (battalions, companies, platoons, or squads) believed that the best way to defeat the VC or NVA was "by saturating an area with innumerable small patrols that would relentlessly hound the enemy until he was destroyed." With regard to securing and pacification operations, the advocates of the small-unit war likewise believed that smaller units offered the "best method of protecting the people from the guerrillas."[71]

There was a "second school of thought, insofar as the type of operation, small unit versus large unit operations that embraced the Maoist concept of the importance of the guerrilla base." Mao wrote that one of the six principles of defeating a larger enemy force was the necessity of establishing a "base area" from which the guerrillas could "expand and preserve ourselves ... and destroy the enemy."[72] Those who subscribed to this line of thought believed that destruction of the enemy's base of operations was essential to defeating the guerrilla force and thus "securing" the area for pacification efforts. Therefore, these individuals believed, "we must not be diverted by fighting every small, scattered band that may be encountered. These actions are only incidental to the primary objective of destroying the guerrilla's base of operations."[73]

General Westmoreland, for his part, "embraced both points of view." While he maintained the primacy of large-scale operations and destruction of the enemy's base camps (which were, according to Major General Frederick C. Weyand, "the number one mission of U.S. units" in Vietnam), Westmoreland nonetheless saw the use of small units as an important component of putting "unrelenting pressure on the enemy's major combat forces."[74] In fact, "at no time did Westmoreland or any of his senior lieutenants ever advocate the exclusive use of either large-scale or small unit operations." Instead, Westmoreland embraced what can be labeled a "three-tiered" operational approach in the war against the VC and NVA. This strategy included "combined" large-scale operations (or "sweeps") into enemy territory, followed by clear-and-hold operations conducted by smaller brigade or battalion-size operations, while small units, from companies to squads, conducted "securing" or smaller-scale operations that harassed and interdicted enemy forces while pacification took place.[75] In turn, each "tier" depended on the other in order to be successful.

There were critics of Westmoreland's large-scale search-and-destroy missions, most notable among them Brigadier General Ellis W. Williamson, commander of the 173rd Airborne Brigade, who, in September 1965, wrote, "I am thoroughly convinced that running into the jungle with a lot of people without a fixed target is a lot of effort, a lot of physical energy expended. A major portion of our effort evaporates into the air."[76] Williamson and other Army officers who shared similar views regarding the use of large-scale sweeps into enemy territory sought to find alternate methods to approaching the fighting in Vietnam, ones that reached into the Amy's experience in the nineteenth century against the Plains Indians and later counterinsurgencies. Two such officers were Brigadier General Willard Pearson, commander of the 101st Airborne Division's 1st Brigade, and Colonel David H. Hackworth, Pearson's one-time subordinate. Both men believed that to defeat the enemy, the Army had to adopt similar methods of operation—in other words, semi-guerrilla tactics. While Pearson and Hackworth believed that large-unit sweeps and search-and-destroy operations had a legitimate place in fighting a counterinsurgency, they advocated a more radical departure from MACV's approach to the war that emphasized the "use of small reconnaissance and ambush patrols, night operations, and the use of clandestine methods such the establishment of a network of informers and deception."[77] It is important to note that the use of semi-guerrilla tactics, as advocated by both Pearson and Hackworth, was designed not to replace large-scale operations but instead to augment them, with the ultimate objective being to keep the VC and NVA continually off-balance.

"Reconnaissance, Commando, and Doughboy": RECONDO School (1965–1966)

General Westmoreland, as mentioned earlier, was an advocate of such small-unit tactics as proposed by Brigadier General Pearson and Colonel Hackworth. In order to train soldiers and Marines in carrying out semi-guerrilla tactics, on September 15, 1966, Westmoreland officially opened a RECONDO School, headed by Colonel Francis J. Kelly, commanding officer of the 5th Special Forces Group. Westmoreland had, in fact, been a strong advocate of RECONDO, having established a similar school when he commanded the 101st Airborne Division at Fort Campbell, Kentucky, between 1958 and 1960. RECONDO—based on the Army's DELTA project, used in Vietnam during the last phase of the advisory period (1964) with the creation of the Civilian Irregular Defense Groups (or CIDGs), led by Colonel Charles A. Beckwith—was one of the most innovative concepts employed by Army Special Forces up until the advent of the use of Long-Range Reconnaissance Patrols by units of the 101st Airborne Division.[78]

The RECONDO School opened by MACV in September 1966 had a staff of five officers and forty-one sergeants, with another eight positions added as the war went on. The instructors came with vast experience in special operations, airborne operations, and reconnaissance training. All were members of the 5th Special Forces Group. The school lasted three weeks, with a student body that included Army Rangers, Marine Reconnaissance personnel, Navy SEALS, Australian Special Air Services, South Koreans, and ARVN soldiers. The course of instruction was three weeks and was broken into three distinct phases:

> 1st Week: Academics that included combat intelligence, terrain analysis, reading, basic photography, handling of POWs, and basic first aid. Students were also expected to learn the ins and outs, and sounds of every weapon used by the Communists. Students were taught to anticipate and think like the enemy.
> 2nd Week: Instruction and conduct of heliborne operations and field training conducted on Hon Tre Island, located five miles off the coast of Nha Trang. Students put into practice the techniques learned during the first week of classroom and their battlefield applicability.
> 3rd Week: The third week students were broken up into teams of six and deployed 4–5 days reconnaissance patrol in hostile territory west of Nha Trang. Students were expected to be able to put into practice in a real battlefield situation in which contact with the NVA was expected to be made. Along with the team was a Special Forces observer who would grade each member of the team as they operated in every team position, from team leader to point man. In short, it was a typical Long Range Reconnaissance Patrol.[79]

The Army's RECONDO School was both physically and mentally challenging. While it was not a "substitute for Ranger training," it nonetheless "served an essential role in improving recon and ranger operations in Vietnam," with many of its students, both Marine and Army, taking with them improved skills in jungle warfare and long-range reconnaissance techniques.[80]

Long-Range Reconnaissance Patrols and Long-Range Reconnaissance Ranger Companies (1965–1970)

In October 1965, the 173rd Airborne Brigade became the first Army unit to organize a long-range reconnaissance patrol force from organic units in the brigade. In August 1966 (coinciding with the start of RECONDO), MACV likewise began to organize "mobile guerrilla forces" designed to supplement the conventional Army units in Vietnam.[81] Other unit commanders developed a "variety of patrol procedures, each tailored to a particular need or environment." While conventional infantry units carried out patrols on a daily basis, every Army division in Vietnam by the fall of 1967 contained a "provisional" company dedicated to long-range reconnaissance patrols capable of carrying out short- and long-range operations deep into enemy territory.[82] The Army's leadership, always averse to the creation of "elite" units, which they saw as a drain on conventional military units (in terms of both manpower and resources), at first established such units (like Merrill's Marauders during World War II) as "provisional units," to be resourced and manned entirely by the battalion or brigade.[83] It was not until March 1969 that the Army officially recognized the provisional LRRPs as "Ranger" companies. At this time, the Army officially designated LRRP companies as "Long-Range Reconnaissance Ranger Companies" (LRRRs). The directive defined the mission of the LRRRs: "to provide ground reconnaissance, combat surveillance, and target acquisition capabilities to he supported units under the operational control of the G-2/S2." It was only in 1969 that the LRRR became a strategic asset, operating in such places as the A Shau Valley. By the time the Army left Vietnam in 1973, it had raised over thirteen Ranger companies spread through I, III, and IV Corps.[84]

Officially, the Army defined the Long-Range Reconnaissance Patrol as "a military unit specially organized, equipped, and trained to function as an information-gathering agency responsive to the intelligence requirements of the tactical commander."[85] "Like Marine Force and Division Reconnaissance battalions, the LRRP Company consists of members qualified to perform reconnaissance, surveillance, and target acquisition within the dispatching unit's area of interest." Most LRRP platoons had between ten and thirty men and were equipped with their organic infantry weapons (i.e., M-16s, M-60 machine guns) and wore[86] standard web gear, helmets or "boony" hat. The Long-Range Reconnaissance Patrol was "employed to maintain surveillance over enemy routes, areas, or specific locations beyond the capability of organic reconnaissance units for extended periods, reporting all sightings of enemy activity within the area of observation."[87]

One major difference between Army LRRP units and Marine Force and Division Reconnaissance detachments was the flexibility local Army field commanders had in organizing ad hoc or "provisional" LRRPs to "meet particular mission requirements which cannot be accomplished by existing LRRP units or other information-gathering agencies." Provisional LRRP units were organized and equipped from the commander's (division and/or separate brigade's) existing resources and trained to perform LRRP missions.[88]

The success of the Army's LRRP concept lay in the fact that LRRPs were organized not to duplicate other organic reconnaissance assets but to "reinforce" or work in unison with them. In the A Shau Valley, from January 1969 through 1971, Army LRRPs and Marine Force Reconnaissance units combined their reconnaissance efforts to forge a highly effective partnership in seeking out and destroying NVA units filtering into the coastal areas of Quang Nam Province.[89]

As for its organization, an LRRP company consisted of a company headquarters and three patrol platoons and was made up 8 officers and 206 enlisted men. Each of the three patrol platoons comprised a platoon headquarters and eight patrols. The platoon operated under company control and, at times, was augmented with indigenous personnel who acted as guides and interpreters. A patrol consisted of five men: a patrol leader, one assistant patrol leader, two radio operators, and one scout observer.

As outlined in FM 31-18, both division and brigade commanders employed LRRP companies to do the following:

1. Determine and report the strength, equipment, disposition, organization, and movement of enemy forces; determine location of [enemy] reserves, command posts, and key installations.

2. Perform reconnaissance and surveillance of specific sites, routes, or areas, and determine enemy movement patterns.

3. Conduct tactical damage assessment such as BDA (Bomb Damage Assessment).

4. Provide information on possible drop zones and landing zones for airborne and airmobile operations.

5. Operate in enemy-held territory to locate targets for airstrikes and ground attack and act as a ground component of long-range survey systems.

6. Deploy on periphery of area of operation (AO) to detect an enemy's attempt to break contact and evade friendly forces.

7. Maintain surveillance over suspected infiltration routes and avenues of approach.

8. Perform other appropriate ground information collection functions as required.[90]

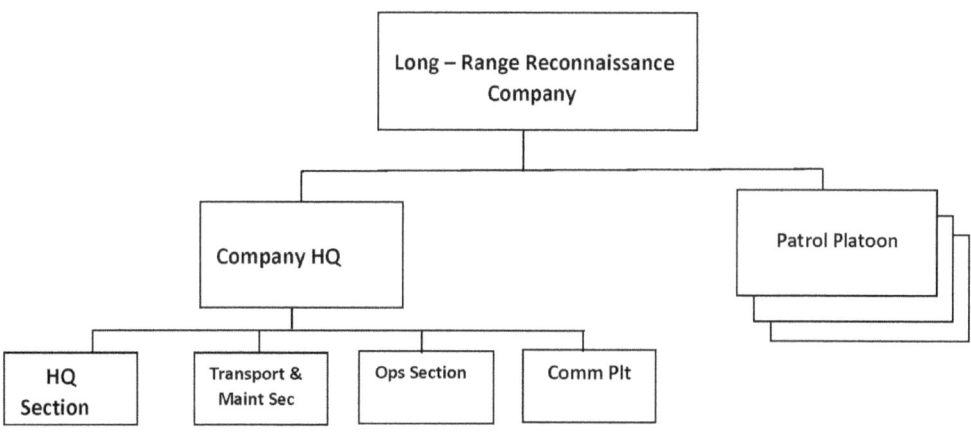

Diagram 10: A Long-Range Reconnaissance Patrol Company (FM 31-18, *Long-Range Reconnaissance Patrol Company*, 6).

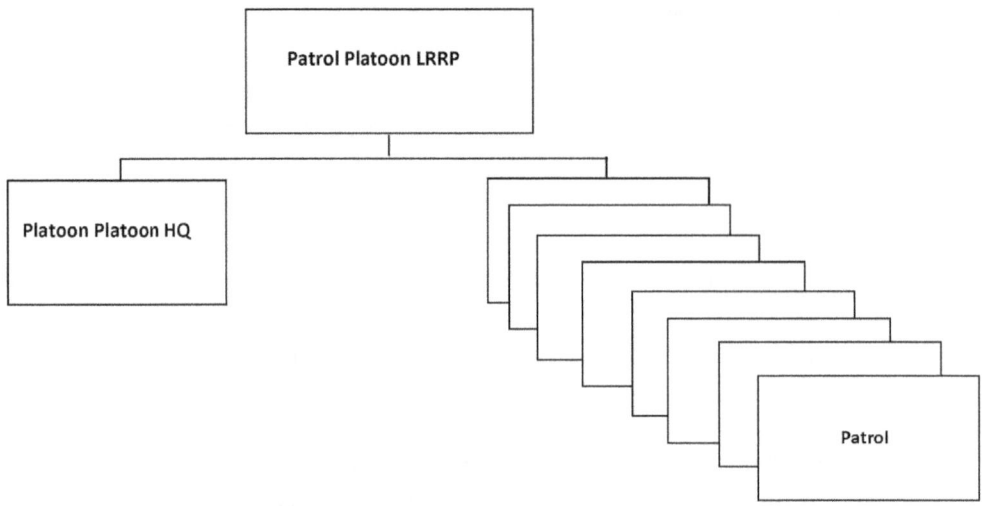

Diagram 11: Long-Range Reconnaissance Patrol Platoon (FM 31-18, *Long-Range Reconnaissance Portal Company*, 6).

LRRPS—An Operational Assessment

According to historian Andrew Krepinevich, Army LRRPs and other Special Forces units maintained a higher enemy contact rate than conventional units "engaged in search-and-destroy operations."[91] In addition, Army LRRP units and other strike teams enjoyed a higher kill ratio than conventional units and incurred "proportionally lower casualty" rates. Krepinevich ignores the fact that both Marine Recon units and Army LRRPs often avoided enemy contact in order to carry out their missions. Contact with NVA units (at least according to Marine Reconnaissance reports cited in this study) was never deliberate, nor were they intended to be. From the time both MACV and III MAF employed reconnaissance assets, the mission was to seek out and target enemy units for artillery and close air support to eliminate. That was the intended mission and purpose of Marine STINGRAY missions discussed in earlier chapters. Krepinevich likewise fails to mention that such units did not have the manpower or firepower to take on larger enemy units. A good example of this discrepancy occurred when a platoon from 3rd Marine Reconnaissance Battalion under First Lieutenant Frank Reasoner on July 12, 1965, at Dai Loc, came up against a reinforced VC company and suffered disproportionate casualties.[92] A five- or six-man reconnaissance team purposely taking on a larger NVA company or battalion simply would not have happened unless they "bumped" into the latter, at which point they would have called in artillery or air strikes to deal with the larger enemy unit.

By the time the Army departed the A Shau Valley in 1971, LRRPs/LRRRs were at the peak of efficiency, having benefited from nearly six years of trial and error in the use of small units.[93] Furthermore, Army LRRP units had perfected a close working relationship with larger, conventional units such as the 101st Airborne Division that today serves as a model for the continued value of special operating forces.

14

"Ghost Soldiers" and "Sea Commandos"

Marine Recon's War in Vietnam (1963–1971)

Throughout the U.S. involvement in Vietnam from the early 1960s until the end of the ground commitment to South Vietnam, Marine Reconnaissance played an integral part in every major and minor combat operation through conception, planning and execution. Reconnaissance patrols were not only the "eyes and ears" of I Corps commanders but also instrumental in maintaining the security of military bases throughout the TAORs. Marine Recon teams provided a wide range of skills for commanders with their ability to conduct short- and long-range patrols, as well as airborne and waterborne operations. The "can-do" spirit, courage under fire, and "never quit" attitude displayed by Marine Reconnaissance teams made them "combat multipliers" and ensured battlefield success. From the early days of "Shu Fly" in April 1963 to their participation in the Provincial Reconnaissance Units and SOG teams in the closing stages of the war, Marine Force Reconnaissance companies and battalions left an inspiring legacy as one of the most successful chapters of Marine involvement in Vietnam. Overcoming initial skepticism about their reliability, capability and value to the warfighting efforts, Reconnaissance Marines proved themselves on the battlefield time and time again with their dedication and endurance against unconventional and regular enemy forces that were both resourceful and "tough."

The highlight of Marine ground reconnaissance operations occurred before, during and immediately following the enemy's 1968 TET offensive through the spring of 1969. Their economy-of-force multiplier was exploited to the fullest by the 3rd Marine Division's commanding general, Major General Raymond G. Davis, and his concept of mobile operations in the A Shau Valley and along the Laotian border during the winter and spring of 1969. As Lieutenant General Robert Cushman (Commanding General, III MAF) pointed out, Marine Reconnaissance proved its value many times over, due in large part to Vietnam's climate, which often limited aerial observation, thereby requiring a reconnaissance team to be sent in prior to a major operation. General Cushman added that "ground reconnaissance" provided by the teams from Marine Reconnaissance proved "more important than ever" in "finding, fixing, and destroying" NVA and VC formations.¹

Marine Reconnaissance's contributions to the war in Vietnam extended beyond their legendary patrols. As Colonels Bruce Meyers and Andrew Finlayson, as well as Ray Stubbe, have written, Marine Reconnaissance's war was one of experimentation and development of new tactics, techniques, and procedures. During Marine Reconnaissance's time in Vietnam, night vision and communications equipment, the SPIE rig, "The Ladder," and STABO extraction methods were field tested through almost eight years of a grueling land war. More important is the fact that many of these same techniques used in the insertion and extraction of Marine Reconnaissance and U.S. Army Special Forces teams are still in use today.² As Lieutenant Colonel Berwick Babin noted, many of these procedures and equipment were validated by Marine Reconnaissance teams "in an unforgiving environment of weather, terrain and enemy." Babin added, "The need for accurate position reporting, effective communications, rapid response supporting arms, night vison, sensors and other personal and unit gear and equipment has inspired the development of a wide range of operational technology. Recon Marines in Vietnam laid the foundation for the techniques and practices Marine special operating forces carry forward today."³

General Robert E. Cushman, USMC, twenty-fifth commandant of the Marine Corps, said as commanding general of III MAF, "Marine Reconnaissance proved its value time and time again" in Vietnam's harsh climate (courtesy U.S. Marine Corps).

Referred to as "Ghost Soldiers" and "Sea Commandos" by a respectful enemy, due to their stealth and swift movement, the Reconnaissance Marines who endured endless patrols under trying conditions left a legacy of field performance unrivaled in Marine Corps history. The service that Force Reconnaissance and Reconnaissance Battalions provided to the Marine Corps and other branches of the U.S. military and ARVN was acknowledged in 1970 at a joint service symposium in El Paso, Texas, by Lieutenant General Raymond G. Davis, and the former deputy commander of XXIV Corps. Former commanding general of 3rd Marine Division in Vietnam, and eventual assistant commandant of the Marine Corps, Davis, himself a proven warrior who wore the Medal of Honor, Navy Cross, Silver Star and other medals for valor on the battlefield, said of Force Recon, "Our most

Appendix A
Marine Reconnaissance Equipment

a. **Uniform:** Olive drab utilities; Marine jungle utility uniform made of poplin (Recon teams also wore the U.S. Air Force "Tiger Stripe" uniform; jungle or "boonie" hat; and green T-shirt)

b. **Boots:** Marine Corps–issued jungle boots

c. **Cartridge Belt:** Known as 782 gear; M-14 ammo pouches that could carry four twenty-round magazines of 7.62 and later 5.56mm ammo; suspenders

    K-Bar combat knife
    Two canteens with water purification tablets
    Two snap links (for SPIE rigging)
    Lensatic compass
    Four mini-pencil flares

d. **Explosives: Grenades**

    C-4 plastic explosive compound
    Claymore land mines
    2 M-26 fragmentation hand grenades
    M7A2 gas mask (fall 1966)
    CS tear gas grenades (fall 1966)
    TNT (optional)

e. **Communications Equipment:**

    PRC-25 radio with spare batteries
    PRC-77 radio with spare batteries
    RT-10A survival radio
    PRC-93 radio

f. **Weapons:**

    M3A1 sub-machine gun or "grease gun"
    M-14 rifle (7.62mm ammo)
    M-16 assault rifle (5.56 mm)
    M-79 grenade launcher

M-60 machine gun
.45 caliber pistol

g. **Miscellaneous Equipment:**
7 × 50 binoculars
Starlight night infrared scope
Rucksack
Camouflage sticks
Colt 1911 hip holster
M-1946 .45 ammunition pouch
First aid kit

Appendix B
The Medal of Honor Citation for 1st Lieutenant Frank Reasoner, USMC

The President of the United States in the name of the Congress takes pride in presenting the MEDAL OF HONOR posthumously to

FIRST LIEUTENANT FRANK S. REASONER

UNITED STATES MARINE CORPS

In service set forth in the following

CITATION

For conspicuous gallantry and intrepidity at the risk of his life above and beyond the call of duty while serving as Commanding Officer, Company A, 3d Reconnaissance Battalion, 3d Marine Division in action against hostile Viet Cong forces near Da Nang, Vietnam, on 12 July 1965. The reconnaissance patrol led by Lieutenant Reasoner had deeply penetrated heavily controlled enemy territory when it came under extremely heavy fire from an estimated 50 to 100 Viet Cong insurgents. Accompanying the advance party and the point that consisted of five men, he immediately deployed his men for the assault after the Viet Cong had opened fire from numerous concealed positions. The slashing fury of the Viet Cong machine gun and automatic weapons fire made it impossible for the main body to move forward. Repeatedly exposing himself to the devastating attack he skillfully provided covering fire, killing at least two Viet Cong and effectively silencing an automatic weapons position in a valiant effort to effect evacuation of a wounded man. As casualties began to mount his radio operator was wounded and Lieutenant Reasoner immediately moved to his side and tended his wounds. When the radio operator was hit a second time while attempting to reach a covered position, Lieutenant Reasoner, courageously running to his aid through the grazing machine gun fire, fell mortally wounded. His indomitable fighting spirit, valiant leadership and unflinching devotion to duty provided the inspiration that was to enable the patrol to complete its mission without further casualties. In the face of almost certain death he gallantly gave his life in the service of his country. His actions upheld the highest traditions of the Marine Corps and the United States Naval Service.

Appendix C
Summary of Event Concerning VC Contact 21–22, 1966

1st Force Reconnaissance Company Patrol Report for January 21–22, 1966

TEAM HATEFUL[1]

At about 211430H Hateful stopped at BS 521369, to await better visibility, since poor visibility (50 feet) made accurate movement of the hilltop impossible. About 211700H four VC, wearing black, approached the patrol base from the southeast, moving cross-country. They detected the rear position of the patrol base, without being detected themselves, and opened fire. They fired only two .30 caliber rounds before they were scattered by M3A1 return fire. They ran screaming and yelling, with at least one probable WIA. Due to heavy vegetation and terrain, the main body of the patrol was unable to see the action, and hearing all the firing and yelling, took off in the other direction. The patrol had been often briefed that VC initiated contact would be broken immediately. About 40 yards from the patrol base, Lt. Parker assembled those near him, and immediately returned, on line, to the scene of the action. There they found OBERHAUS, who had remained after firing his M3A1. [1st] Lieutenant [James T.] Egan was missing.[2] Teams were sent out to search for him, and his name yelled from the position. He was not found, nor were any tracks or signs of movement in another direction found. Conflicting reports by witnesses make it impossible to determine whether or not Lt. Egan was wounded, or in which direction he might have moved. He did have his rifle with him, and no subsequent firing was heard. The rally point was the USSF [United States Special Forces] camp. Having searched the immediate area and waited until near darkness, the patrol departed at 1830H, and located themselves for the night, several hundred yards from the incident. A patrol base was established about 1530H at BS523372.

About 220745H, the patrol moved out to the northeast to continue the mission. Visibility remained the same and the patrol had to move by dead-reckoning, since it was too hazardous to remain. About 0900H, further movement to the north or east became impossible due to the severity of the grade. The patrol was forced back-track, losing an hour and move to the southeast along the contour line, trying to locate a place to descend. Such a place was found, and the patrol was moving straight downhill, when attacked from the rear at BS 524369 about 1015H.

Upon contact, the patrol was in a dispersed column, moving straight down a steep incline. The attack was made by an estimated 30 to 40 VC/PAVN, who were observed to have been following Hateful's tracks. When, in tracking, the VC made contact with the patrol's rear point, they began the attack. Due to the vegetation and terrain, only those two men in the rear point, upon initial contact, saw or engaged the enemy. The remainder of the patrol immediately attempted to break contact by rapid downhill movement, through 6 to 8 foot elephant grass and brush. The two men on the rear fired about 70 rounds into the VC, killing at 2 to 4, and wounding several. They then joined the rapid descent. The VC attacked initially with large numbers of grenades and automatic weapons (heavier than carbines, lighter than M3A1's). They pursued both physically and by fire, now using primarily semi-automatic .30 cal weapons at longer ranges. The entire descent was made under conditions of heavy attack, and was not a controlled movement. During this time, the corpsman stopped, thinking that the rest had stopped, and found himself in the midst of the VC. He killed five, and probably six, and continued moving.

Seeking cover, concealment, and terrain without great disadvantages, Lt. Parker led six men to a position in heavy vegetation, high up in a draw, where they set up an ambush for anyone tracking them (about 1100H at BS528368). The VC at this time were searching the entire area. About 1130 other men from the patrol came into the ambush, and linked up. Lt. Parker then called in over 150 rounds of artillery on suspected and possible VC positions.

At 1223H, helicopters picked up three men who had linked up at BS536368, at 1325H, helicopters picked up the nine men at BS 529367. GRISSETT was the only man missing in this incident, and is still listed as MIA. He was the point for the patrol and was seen several times during the descent, in good condition and further down the hill than the rest. It is reasonable to assume that he escaped unharmed from this incident, and began his movement back to the USSF camp.

The VC were observed by five men to be wearing khaki uniforms, one man observing khaki rain-type hats and wrap-around leggings, another observing grey or darker uniforms. From the attack, it is apparent that they were armed with sub-machineguns, semi-automatic .30 cal weapons, and a great number of hand grenades. They were aggressive and fairly well-trained, and their morale appeared to be high.

It is reasonable to assume that the four VC involved in the incident on 21 January moved to inform a VC/PAVN unit they knew to be in the area. Due to vegetation, terrain, and weather, night movement by units in the area is virtually impossible. Thus the VC/PAVN unit appears to be located no more than one hour's march from BS521369, since this would allow day-break movement there, and subsequent tracking, to the sight of the attack.

R. F. Parker, Jr.
1st Lt USMC

Appendix D
The Strategic Importance of An Hoa Combat Base

BY COLONEL ANDREW R. FINLAYSON, USMC (RET.)

For most US Marines who lived in, or fought near it, the An Hoa Combat Base (CB) was just a place they found themselves in while they fought their war against the North Vietnamese Army's (NVA) 2nd Division and local VC units. Its strategic significance was little known or understood by the Marines who fought to protect it. Most Marines lived day to day, fighting to stay alive and to keep the enemy from overrunning that particular piece of real estate in Quang Nam Province, South Vietnam. They gave little thought as to why the enemy was so intent upon trying to control the territory in its immediate vicinity. I hope this short paper will help to explain how the base was viewed by the North Vietnamese Army in the context of their overall strategy for the war and to give the Marines who were based at An Hoa CB a better understanding of why they were there.

To understand the base's importance, it is essential to understand the enemy's overall strategy and its influence on Quang Nam Province. The communist leadership in Hanoi decided in May 1959 to overthrow the South Vietnamese government (GVN) by force and began to plan for the eventual invasion of South Vietnam using conventional, mobile NVA units. To prepare the way for this eventual conventional attack, they began sending political cadres south to assist local communist cadres in a massive effort to organize the rural population of South Vietnam under the leadership of the communist party (the Lao Dong Party). Once they had organized large areas of South Vietnam, they initiated a guerrilla campaign that that was designed to demoralize the GVN and the Army of the Republic of Vietnam (ARVN), and so weaken these institutions that the NVA forces could easily overrun all South Vietnamese once the Lao Dong Party deemed the strategic situation suitable for a conventional attack. They hoped that their political organization and guerrilla units in South Vietnam would lay the foundation for what they termed "a general uprising" of the people of South Vietnam so they could seize power quickly with a minimum of casualties. They realized that southern communist forces alone were incapable of defeating the ARVN, so they planned from the very beginning to use NVA conventional military units to carry out the final attacks.

When the United States entered the war with ground troops in 1965, the Lao Dong Party assessed the situation and determined that this complicated their plans considerably, but they did not change their overall strategy. Instead, they simply decided to use the same strategy but lengthen the timeline it would take to achieve their goals. In essence, their strategy called for an integrated assault against the ARVN and American forces, using the same strategy they employed against the French from 1946 to 1954. VC local and territorial units, working in close cooperation with NVA conventional units, and supported by the communist infrastructure in the villages would fight a war of attrition against the GVN and America. It was a sophisticated strategy based upon their experience during the 1st Indo-China War and the experience of the Chinese communists in their wars against the Japanese and the Chinese nationalists. In almost every respect, the Vietnamese communists used the same strategic template that they had developed against the French, applying it to their war against South Vietnam. And just as they had done during the 1st Indo-China War, they began to develop a series of supply lines from their protected bases in North Vietnam to South Vietnam using a complex system of roads, trails and waterways in the western side of the Annamite Mountains in southern Laos and eastern Cambodia. This supply system was so important to them they formed a special unit, Unit 559, to build, maintain, and protect it, using over 100,000 North Vietnamese and 15,000 Chinese in Laos and northeastern Cambodia.

For the Marines fighting in Quang Nam Province, this meant they faced both local VC units, as well as the conventional 2nd NVA Division. It also meant that in some areas of the province they faced a highly organized VC political organization. For instance, the Arizona Territory, west of An Hoa CB, was in an area of the province that was never under GVN control and was solidly organized by the communists. It was also a place where the 2nd NVA Division obtained most of their rice and other locally produced foodstuffs. For these reasons, US Marine units seldom entered this area without encountering either VC guerrilla units or main force NVA units. The VC units were locally recruited and the NVA units came down the Ho Chi Minh Trail, but both were supplied with their ammunition, medical supplies, weapons, and communications equipment using the Ho Chi Minh Trail supply system. Although the numbers varied somewhat during the war, the Ho Chi Minh Trail system provided 8,000 NVA replacement troops and approximately 5,000 tons per month to the communist forces fighting in South Vietnam. I will go into more detail about the enemy supply system later in this paper.

During the war, the airbase at Danang was vitally important to the US. It was the most important airbase in all of I Corps and was used by the US to bomb North Vietnam when the US conducted its air campaigns over that country and it was also used to launch air attacks against NVA units and supplies moving down the Ho Chi Minh Trail in Laos. For that reason, the communists considered it a major impediment to their war aims. Early in the war, the communists in North Vietnam decided they needed to attack the airbase at Danang, and they sent the 2nd NVA Division south with this mission. It was this decision that led to the strategic importance of An Hoa CB.

The enemy knew that powerful US, ARVN and Republic of Korea (ROK) Marine forces were protecting the Danang Airbase, forces that could not be easily overcome. Instead, they resorted to sapper and indirect fire attacks on the airbase. They soon found that they could disrupt operations at the airbase and gain valuable propaganda victories by simply making low-cost sapper attacks or, more often, mortar and rocket attacks. These attacks caused the US to concentrate their forces around the airbase, leaving many areas south and west of the airbase open to NVA infiltration and VC political organizing. One area that was particularly vulnerable to NVA infiltration and VC political activity was the An Hoa Basin and the surrounding areas west and south east of it. In order to counter this enemy activity and deny this area to the enemy, the US Marines decided to occupy the An Hoa CB in 1966 and use it as a base for operations in southern Quang Nam Province.

Here, I will take a moment to explain the enemy's supply system, which was so important to their strategy and determined the level of violence they could sustain in Quang Nam Province. It all began at a spur off the Ho Chi Minh Trail in Laos that crossed the Laos–South Vietnam border at the northern edge of the A Shau Valley in Thua Thien Province (the province immediately north of Quang Nam). From the A Shau Valley, a series of trails ran south along the eastern edge of the Annamite Mountains until there was a split at the western edge of Happy Valley in Quang Nam Province, near Tat Lay Mountain (ZC0266). One trail went east and ended in Happy Valley north of Charlie Ridge. This trail supported one regiment of the *2nd NVA Division* which was based in and around Happy Valley most of the time. The second trail ran south, crossed the Song Huong River, and then ran in parallel to the old French road, Route 14, to An Giang, a deserted village on the Song Cai River vic. YC9636. It then split into several trails that ran east and ended in Base Area 112, a vast 25 square-mile area of steep, jungle-clad hills and mountains, where another regiment of the *2nd NVA Division* was based, along with the division headquarters and, at times, the political group known as Front 4. The third regiment of the *2nd NVA Division*, the *1st VC Regiment*, was, at times, based in the central Que Son Mountains in what the enemy called Base Area 116, although it was more often found operating in Quang Tin and Quang Ngai provinces.

As I stated earlier, most of the enemy's manpower, ammunition, weapons and heavy equipment came down the Ho Chi Minh Trail from North Vietnam. However, the vast majority of foodstuffs were obtained from South Vietnamese villages, either through voluntary donations, taxation or outright confiscation. To obtain these locally produced foodstuffs, the main force VC and NVA units depended on local VC political cadres known as Finance-Economy cadres. The Finance-Economy cadres collected rice taxes and party membership dues, and they also organized local labor parties to build and maintain bunkers that could be used by main force units to hide in during the day, safe from aerial or ground observation. Without these Finance-Economy cadres from the villages, the enemy main force units would not be able to be fed or to move from one location to another. Very few Marines ever heard of these Finance-Economy cadres, but they were central to the success of the enemy's mobile warfare. By occupying many of the villages in the An Hoa Basin, the Marines were able to effectively deny the enemy the ability to employ these Finance-Economy cadres, thus limiting the ability of enemy main force units to conduct sustained operations in Quang Nam Province.

If one looks at a map of Quang Nam Province, you will see that An Hoa CB is strategically located south of Happy Valley, east of Base Area 112, and northwest of Base Area 116. US Marines stationed at An Hoa CB posed a significant threat to all three of these enemy base areas, and, therefore, caused the enemy a great deal of concern. It also meant that Marine units were very close to the infiltration routes enemy units would use to launch attacks against Danang Airbase and the provincial capital at Hoi An. Furthermore, Marines in the An Hoa Basin could hamper VC political organizing efforts, prevent rice harvests falling into the hands of the enemy, and respond rapidly to enemy attempts to infiltrate into the coastal lowland areas, such as Go Noi Island or the Que Son Valley. In sum, the Marines in An Hoa CB were a serious threat to the enemy's plans and for this reason the enemy launched a series of attacks against the base and the key supply route to An Hoa that ran from Liberty Road Bridge south to the base. The *2nd NVA Division* was never able to take An Hoa CB as long as it was manned by US Marines and they suffered huge losses whenever they attempted to take it.

As long as US Marine units occupied the An Hoa Combat base, a major impediment to the communist strategy of controlling Quang Nam Province was thwarted.

Appendix E
"A Reconnaissance Patrol in 'Happy Valley' by 'Killer Kane' 1st Force Reconnaissance Company by 2nd Lieutenant Andrew R. Finlayson, USMC, Commander, 5th Platoon, 1st Force Reconnaissance Company, III MAF"

Three days ago received a frag order that I was to conduct a clandestine reconnaissance operation on suspected enemy routes of access through Happy Valley. To pay particular emphasis on trail networks that traversed my NFZ/FFZ between Hills 537 and 372. Told to call and direct air strikes on targets of opportunity. Immediately upon receiving my frag order, I called together my assistant patrol leader, my point, and my corpsman—issued to them a warning order telling them in general terms our mission, also any information of enemy, friendly situation in the area in which we were to be operating and also what equipment, what weapons, what chow to bring on this patrol. I set forth a time schedule for a patrol order, rehearsal, and test firing of the weapons. After this had been accomplished, after all weapons and ammunition had been drawn, I gave my patrol order.

Previous to this patrol order I went on an overflight over the area I was to be inserted in and also received an intelligence report from our S-2 as to the general enemy situation in that area. I was informed that this area was a transit route for troops moving into the Da Nang TAOR and was also a staging area for the *402nd Sapper Battalion*. All the intelligence information that had been received from the S-2 was incorporated into my warning order, I ensured that all the steps that I had outlined in my warning order were accomplished. After the patrol order was given, I had my patrol test fire all their weapons. These included the M-16, M14 with M76 grenade launcher, M79 grenade launcher, and the Stoner light machine gun. I then made an inspection of the special equipment that we'd be taking on the patrol. This included two PRC-25 radios, and one 750 binoculars. I also inspected the corpsman's A-1 unit to ensure that all necessary medical equipment was contained therein. After the test firing of weapons and inspection of equipment, I held a slight rehearsal. Emphasis was placed on hand and arm signals that were to be used on the patrol and also hasty ambush and formation and order of movement.

On the 3d, at 1800, I departed Camp Reasoner for Happy Valley. When we arrived over the insert area, I was informed that the Huey gunships had received fire from our primary HLZ at which time the helo pilot informed me that we'd go to our alternate HLZ. On the approach run into our alternate HLZ, we again received fire. As I looked down I could see that there were cultivated areas in an area that was supposed to be uninhabited. I could see a farm with several rows of Yuca and Wheat. The helo pilot aborted the insertion into this alternate zone and asked me if we should return home. I informed the helicopter pilot that even though we were taking fire, I still would like to get in and asked him to find another alternate HLZ in the area. This we found on top of Hill 582. As we came in, we landed in a small 30' × 40' HLZ consisting of high elephant grass. We also took a few roads upon entering the HLZ, but we managed to get in and hide without taking any casualties.

I moved into the thickest brush possible, set my team up in a 360-degree defense, and I awaited darkness. All our men kept on all their web gear and packs in order to ensure that if we were hit we could move out quickly. However the night passed without any incident.

The next morning, at 0600, we collected ourselves, took the leeches off that had gotten on us the night before, and began to move out. After moving 150 meters through the thick elephant grass, we came upon an extremely well-used trail, a trail that had been used fairly recently.

We moved in a southeasterly direction along this trail for about 400 meters. Just as I was about to turn off this trail, my point opened fire on three VC coming down the trail. He killed the lead VC and the other two ran off into the brush. In order to break contact and ensure we didn't receive any fire when we were breaking contact, I had two of men throw out CS gas grenades.

After breaking contact, I moved back up the trail about 300 meters. I realized the trail was perhaps not the best place for use to be in an area where there were a lot of VC, so I decided to move north off into very thick elephant grass.

I moved 50 meters off the trail in order to hear any movement on the trail indicating that the VC were following us. We waited silently for four hours until finally we heard movement approaching us from the southwest, the opposite direction of our contact. The movement passed our position and then it stopped. Two minutes later we saw an Asiatic face peering through the elephant grass right into our position. LCpl. Russell fired his Stoner machinegun at point blank range. The VC seemed to double up and fall backward as if someone had tied a rope about his waist and pulled him back. At least 30 rounds hit the VC. A fire fight ensued at very close range. The VC employed carbine fire. However, we gained fire superiority through the use of our Stoner machinegun and M14 rifles. Huey gunships were called into our area, but the VC broke contact before they arrived.

After waiting three more hours to see if the VC were going to close in on our positions, I began to move out. I moved 150 meters north, back towards our initial HLZ. I did this because I felt there was a great number of VC in the area and that if we got hit again before the night, I wanted to be sure we were near a HLZ so I could get my people out as quickly as possible.

After moving into an area near our initial HLZ, I set up a 360 defense in very thick elephant grass and I waited to see if the VC would hit us before dark fell.

We heard voices, signal drums, and rifle fire throughout the night. However, the VC did not come close to our position. The night passed without incident.

The next morning, we felt quite safe. We felt that the VC did not know where we were and they were and that they were probably looking in a different area. However, at 0800 we began to hear movement in the brush to our north. This movement came closer. We could hear brush breaking and then we heard what sounded like a canteen hitting against metal. The movement came closer and closer, until finally we were able to see one VC [within] ten feet of our position. Due to our camouflaged utilities and face paint and our complete silence and lack of movement, the VC did not see us. The other two VC moved to our left, no more than fifteen feet from our position. While approximately ten VC moved to our right. They appeared to be on line and sweeping the entire HLZ area. They were extremely well-trained, well-disciplined troops. They moved through extremely high elephant grass and made very little noise. They stopped about ten feet from our position. They were almost 360 degrees around us. Finally, we heard movement to our rear and two VC began to move into the harbor area. My corpsman, Doc Willis, allowed them to come within six feet of our position before he opened fire. His initial burst killed two VC and they fell backwards. The Stoner machinegun and everyone else in the patrol opened up and we threw grenades. In the first twenty seconds of the fire fight we killed five VC, all which lay dead within fifteen meters of our position. We received two incoming grenades. One wounded LCpl Russell in the face; another LCpl Williams in the back. We informed our S-3 who immediately called for an extraction. After about twenty minutes of shooting and throwing grenades, the VC moved away. We called in Huey gunships and fixed wing [aircraft] on their positions with unknown results. The Hueys left station and returned fire after refueling. However, after this interim, no contact was made.

We heard some movement in the brush to our north and east, however, it seemed to be moving away from us. After a half hour wait, the Hueys returned with fixed wing and CH-46 helicopters. After two more air strikes, the helicopters came in and extracted us. We took fire on this extraction; two rounds hit the helicopter in the fuselage.

On the 5th at 1100 we returned to Camp Reasoner.

Results of this patrol: 42 hours, 3 sightings, all of which were contacts, totaling 30 VC/NVA KIA (confirmed) and two (probable). Two USMC WIA (minor) and 1 USN WIA (minor). Four air strikes with unknown results.

Uniforms of VC were gray with black web gear and camouflaged utilities. Also, they had charcoal on their faces, used as camouflaged paint. Armed with AK47s and American (M1) carbines.

Terrain was extremely thick with bamboo up to fifteen foot high. Very little water, had to maintain water discipline. Extremely hot—estimate 115 degrees–120 degrees. This made noise discipline extremely difficult.

Recommend this area be burned by napalm and that B52 strikes be conducted followed by a thorough infantry sweep. It is believed that the VC/NVA had at least a squad in each grid square and they are actively patrolling and defending it. Troops encountered were superior in quality to any VC encountered and their training and discipline were outstanding.

Second Lieutenant Andrew R. Finlayson, USMC

Appendix F
Lessons from Marine Recon's War in Vietnam: Colonel Andrew R. Finlayson, USMC (Ret.)

Editor's note: Colonel Andrew R. Finlayson, USMC (Ret.), led two of the most successful Marine Reconnaissance teams during the Vietnam War as part of the 1st Force Reconnaissance Company (1967–1969), known as Killer Kane and Swift Scout. Colonel Finlayson offered some comments on the lessons learned during his time in Vietnam.[1]

Patrols Size and Reconnaissance Doctrine (1965–1966)

During the early years in Vietnam, 1965–1966, doctrine for Force Recon called for 4-man teams, but this had changed when I arrived in February 1967 in 1st Force. We never sent out a 4-man patrol to my knowledge. According to the CO and S-3 of 1st Recon Battalion (we were attached to them at Camp Reasoner) the 4-man patrol was eliminated because of several serous losses due, in their opinion, to the inability of a 4-man patrol to survive once one of their members was wounded or killed. I cannot speak with any authority about the experience of 3rd Recon Battalion or 3rd Force Recon Company since all of my experience was with 1st Division AO [area of operations]. I did have a 3rd Recon Battalion platoon attached to us at An Hoa in 1969 and they sent out 12-man patrols.

The optimal size of the patrol is best determined by the operational objectives and the situation. The four-man patrol is more agile and concealable, operating beyond the reach of indirect fire support. The eight-man team operating inside the arc of field artillery, in direct support of a battalion closing with the enemy, requires additional fire power to sustain itself as a maneuver units close with the enemy. This was the T/O [table of organization] before, during, and after the Vietnam War. In 1968, with more contacts than any other year, the four-man team worked very well for the 3rd Force Reconnaissance Company in spite of much initial skepticism.

Perhaps one of the greatest innovations from Vietnam reconnaissance operations was the enhanced efficacy of the four-man team, which became dual-hatted with KEYHOLE missions and the addition of STINGRAY missions. Doctrinally these teams were to be inserted and extracted without the enemy knowing of their presence during or after their mission, even when lucrative targets were presented. STINGRAY[2] [missions] changed that.

Size of Marine Reconnaissance Teams (1967–1969)

Recon battalions had much larger platoons (26) than Force Recon Companies (15) which often resulted in different patrol sizes for those units. When I was in South Vietnam (1967–1969) with 1st Force Recon Company, Force [Recon] usually sent out patrols made up of 6–8 men, while battalion often sent out patrols made up of 12–14 men.

Insertion and Extraction Techniques

Insertion time and technique (vehicle, leave behind, walk-in, river/ocean boat, parachute, helicopter) is determined by the needs of the operation and predominantly those elements of the first paragraph of the order; enemy and friendly situation, weather, and terrain. We determined the optimum time for helicopter insertion was early morning. The NVA were mostly nocturnal, primarily moving at night, so they rested during the day and were less responsive to the insertion. Certainly there were exceptions in the heavily forested areas, or where they operated with impunity, but those areas did not generally have many viable LZs and teams needed to be inserted outside their RZ and walk in. It is much easier to coordinate support and orient yourself on the ground in the daylight. That could take some time as the pilots did not always drop teams off at the designated LZ for a number of reasons such as enemy activity on the way in, urgent calls for reassignment, poor navigational skills … more than once, we had to climb a tree to look for terrain features we could triangulate or from which we could shoot a back azimuth. More than once, within hours of insertion, I had to call for an extract that would not have happened in darkness. I don't know of any extracts that took place in darkness.

As a result of operational experience in Vietnam, several new means of extraction and insertion techniques were developed. Two of those are the Fast Rope (insertion) and the SPIE rig (extraction).

A new insertion technique was developed with helicopters. It involved two identically configured CH-46s flying knap of the earth in tandem, with the team in the lead bird. Upon insertion the trail bird leap frogs the insertion bird and they resume flight in tandem and make several more flares to confuse the enemy of the actual insertion point.

Team Leadership and Training

As for who should be a team leader, that changed dramatically over time in 1st Force Recon Company. When I arrived in country, teams were most often led by lieutenants and SNCOs, but on occasion sergeants and corporals were team leaders. This was the case throughout 1967. When I returned to 1st Force Recon Company in December 1968, almost all patrols were led by NCO's and even L/Cpl's until an infusion of recon-trained officers were assigned in February 1969. From then until I left the company in May 1969, patrols were taken out by lieutenants, SNCO's, and NCO's. Personally, I saw little difference in how well these patrols operated whether they were led by officers, SNCO's or NCO's. Again, I think reasons we have staff sergeants as the platoon sergeant in the infantry. It is why the T/O of a reconnaissance unit calls for enlisted team leaders. Once again, not a lesson learned but a lesson reinforced. I have vivid memories of unfortunate results led by officers who made operational errors when more competent enlisted Marines were available. They made many of the mistakes poorly trained enlisted Marines made. However, the average number of patrols led by enlisted Marines is exponentially higher than that run by officers. An unwritten lesson reflected in the T/O reiterates that rank by itself does not give one more experience, skill, or intellect.

When I was assigned as XO of the newly-formed Company E, 1st Recon Battalion, in December 1967, after ten months in the bush as a team leader, we received a large draft of Marines who had attended the recon school in California prior to leaving for Vietnam. When they arrived, we had to spend nearly a month training them in how to conduct patrols in Vietnam. In my opinion, and the opinion of everyone in this newly-formed unit (all experienced team leaders), these stateside Marines were not adequately trained for long-range patrols. They were good Marines and responded to training quickly, but we did not feel they were ready for combat patrols. Why this was so, I do not know. At other times and at other places state-side trained Marines might have arrived ready to go on patrol. I would add that my experience in the infantry was similar with Marines trained in the states in [a] staging battalion or elsewhere. It took a month of two in-country experience for a Marine to have the skills needed to survive in combat with the NVA.[3]

Organizational Lessons and Innovations

There are several new *organizational lessons* [commentator's emphasis] learned that come to mind. In addition, there are many more individual and personal lessons learned that are found on a learning curve that grows with each successive patrol. They have something to do with such things as bug spray, leeches, sleeping, noise, eating, water, gear configuration, rifle maintenance, camouflage, observation, security, movement, patrol prep, and so on as varied as the idiosyncrasies of each Marine. These are discretionary but not universally accepted. One Marine may wear his knife on his belt while another on his chest. Few organizational lessons arrive on the shoulder of previous lessons learned, but come from the advent of new technology, innovative use of established thinking or items, or a new threat. Several areas come to mind.

The observable success and utility of the battalion reconnaissance mission had a direct impact on the development of the Surveillance and Target and Acquisition (STA). Battalions needed reconnaissance and other combat skills without depleting rifle platoons when battalion reconnaissance was not available. I recall standing up the first STA platoon in the 1st Marine Division when I was [Alex] Lee's "deuce." [S-2] Though different from recon structure and T/E [tables of equipment], we certainly looked at it as a means to partially fill reconnaissance gaps.

Prior to Vietnam, SCUBA played a doctrinal role as a means of insertion or of conducting beach reconnaissance. With minimal support available from Navy divers, greater utility opened up for SCUBA qualified Marines to support recovery, bridge security, and riverine operations. I recall clearing a fouled LHA screw for the SCUBA scarce Navy in the Dong Ha River. Upon arrival in Vietnam, I was given the option of assignment to Charlie Company, 1st MP Battalion to do regular bridge inspections in the Da Nang area. I later learned that 1st Force Reconnaissance provided additional support … during the Battle of Hue City.

Non-Traditional Reconnaissance Assignments

Given their readiness and availability, reconnaissance units were tasked with a variety of non-traditional reconnaissance missions to include reaction force, crash recovery, radio relay and Observation Posts.

Appendix G
Weapons of the Viet Cong and North Vietnamese Army

ASSAULT RIFLES/SUB-MACHINE GUNS

    AK-47—Soviet/Chinese 7.62mm assault rifle
    Type 50—North Vietnamese modified 7.62mm Type 50 sub-machine gun
    Type 59—Chinese Communist sub-machine (Soviet PPSh M1941)
    Type 43—Soviet PPSh1943 (Chinese Type 43 7.62mm)
    M1949—French 9mm sub-machine gun

RIFLES/ BOLT ACTION/SEMI-AUTOMATIC

    M1944 (SKS)—Soviet 7.662 carbine/Chinese Type 53
    M1916—French 8mm carbine
    M1—U.S. carbine .30 caliber
    M1949—French 7.5 semi-automatic rifle
    Type 99—Japanese 7.7mm rifle

MACHINE GUNS (HEAVY AND LIGHT)

    M1910—Soviet Maxim heavy machine gun
    Type 53—Soviet/Chinese 7.62mm heavy machine gun SG-43 (Type 57)
    Type 24—Chinese 7.92mm maxim heavy machine gun
    Type 99—Japanese 7.7 mm light machine gun (1939)
    M1931A—French 7.5mm machine gun
    M1924/M29—French 7.5mm automatic rifle
    Type 56—Chinese/Soviet 7.62mm light machine gun RPD
    Type 54—12.7mm heavy Machine gun DsHk38/46

MORTARS

    Type 53—Chinese 82mm mortar (1942–1943 version)
    M1938—Soviet heavy mortar 107mm
    Type 53—Soviet/Chinese 120mm heavy mortar (regimental level)

Recoilless Rifles

   Type 52—Chinese 75mm recoilless rifle

Source: Department of the Army, Pamphlet 381-10, *Weapons and Equipment Recognition Guide, Southeast Asia* (Washington, DC: HQDA, January 1966).

Appendix H
Reflections of a Reconnaissance Marine—Lieutenant Colonel Berwick Babin, USMC (Ret.), 3rd Force Reconnaissance Company (1967–1969)

Editor's note: Lieutenant Colonel Berwick Babin, USMC (Ret.), served as a member of 3rd Force Reconnaissance Company from 1967 to 1969. Here he and offers some thoughts on Force Reconnaissance during the Vietnam War.[1]

Training as a Reconnaissance Marine

Successful long-range recon patrols begin long before insertion, and is a key to success throughout Marine Corps training before, during, and after Vietnam. This is not a lesson learned but is a lesson reinforced by operations in Vietnam. We put untrained Marines, officer and enlisted, into reconnaissance combat operations while ignoring the assignment of highly skilled Marines. For example, I was an 8651 [Reconnaissance Marine] when I arrived in Vietnam. I was assigned to Fleet Logistics Command (FLC) as an automotive mechanic.

Learning on the job was not a satisfactory replacement for formal training. The success that recon teams had through the determination and courageous acts of poorly trained reconnaissance Marines leaves a bloody legacy of about 40 percent casualties, an incalculable opportunity cost and mission hampering skepticism by senior officers. All classic reconnaissance training in the states addressed most if not all of the very points other Recon Marines [such as Colonel Andrew Finlayson] present such as patrol orders, individual weapons, and equipment, battle drills, patrol organization, movement, land navigation, supporting arms, etc. Again, not lessons learned but an example of what happens when you fail to follow combat tested and established doctrine, tactics, and procedures.

Patrols and Patrol Leaders

In 3rd Force Reconnaissance Company 1967 and 1968, it was rare and unusual for an officer to take out a patrol. There are two principal reasons for this. First, most of the officers had little or no prior experience in reconnaissance and those that did spent less time in operational reconnaissance training than in attending to the administrative duties of an officer. Secondly, it was critical to have an officer to address reconnaissance operations in terms of support and employment at the Division level and other headquarters down to the company level, where logistics, horsepower and other support plays a role.

Reconnaissance Patrols are better led by well-trained and experienced enlisted Marines for both the reasons mentioned in the preceding paragraph. Though not a perfect analogy, it is for similar reasons we have staff sergeants as the platoon sergeant in the infantry. It is why the T/O of a reconnaissance unit calls for enlisted team leaders. Once again, not a lesson learned but a lesson reinforced. I have vivid memories of unfortunate results from patrols who made operational errors when more competent enlisted Marines were available. They made many of the same mistakes poorly trained enlisted Marines made. However, the average number of these patrols led by enlisted Marines is exponentially higher than that run by officers. An unwritten lesson reflected in the T/O reiterates that rank by itself does not give one more experience, skill, or intellect.

Final Reflections of a Reconnaissance Marine

The weather, the bush, are unforgiving. It was neither for you or against you. You dealt with it. If you didn't properly prepare, it was on you—bugs, scratches, rain, heat, water, gear, exhaustion, etc.

The enemy was focused on killing you. There was not a place for you to be his friend. This was an understanding—if you have an engagement, he will attempt to kill you and you him. Like a law of nature.

As for coming back from a patrol, despite the best training, rehearsals, thorough patrol orders, teamwork and skill the best you could ever hope for is to minimize the likelihood of being wounded or killed.

The outcome of the fight is very personal. You live, you are wounded, or you are dead. Your friends return, die or are hurt. That's personal. However, the fight itself cannot be personal, if you want a consistent and satisfactory outcome. I call recognition of this the zone. I entered it every time I was in a firefight. In doing so the enemy's capabilities are appreciated and weather and terrain are considered. You coldly calculate and methodically employ the appropriate tactics to accomplish the mission.

[Combat] it's like motorcycle riding. It's inherently dangerous. All you can do is minimize the danger with riding skill, muscle-mind memory and protective equipment. Maybe this similarity is what makes one like the ride. Getting home safe. Accomplishing the mission. If while making a fast turn you get scared, lose the zone, and apply the brakes or put the bike upright, you shed skin and break bones.

Appendix I
"My Story": One Reconnaissance Marine's War in Vietnam—Sergeant William Moss and Team Atlas

Editor's note: Corporal William Moss, USMC, has provided a vivid account of his service in Vietnam as a member of 3rd Force Reconnaissance Company as a member of Team Atlas. His account of his first patrol reflects the experiences of many Reconnaissance Marines in Vietnam.[1]

I enlisted in the Marine Corps in August 1968 and completed Boot Camp, ITR [Infantry Training Regiment] and B.I.T.S. [Basic Infantry Training School] in Marine Corps [Recruit Depot] San Diego and Camp Joseph H. Pendleton in California. I then went to Recon School and graduated in 1969. I was sent to Vietnam in early April and was assigned to 3rd Force Reconnaissance Company, based in Quang Tri. The first several weeks consisted of in-house training on combat and relevant classes.

My first patrol was to recover an enemy body and then six of us were transported to a deserted ARVN [Army of the Republic of Vietnam] artillery base by a USMC CH-46 helicopter.

I tripped a wire to a booby trapped bomb, but it did not detonate, so that was my first lucky break. My patrol leader scolded me for not being alert, then 5 minutes later he tripped crude smoke booby trap, and suddenly the NVA [North Vietnamese Army] within 10 miles see where we were.

That night we saw distant flashlights coming towards us, but because of s heavy rain they stopped their advance. We had been … warned prior to that tigers were sometimes found in that area that we were in and smelled a tiger close by, but we had no interaction with it. (In the prior year, a recon team member had been grabbed by a tiger, but was saved [by] the team shooting it. In 1970, a Force Recon Marine was killed and partially eaten by a tiger while on patrol.)

We were on full alert all night and at first light we could hear the enemy coming up the hill toward us.

Many of our patrols were far away from friendly forces, as was this one, so we requested close air support.

A flight of 4 tan and green Air Force F-4 Phantoms arrived and began dropping napalm on the advancing enemy. I looked up to see a napalm canister drop from the F-4 and tumble over my head to splash downhill. The area erupted in flames and smoke and it seemed to suck the air from my lungs. I could feel … the flash of heat and smell and the noise of the jets combined to create an inferno that shocked the senses of anyone that had never been exposed to this before.

The enemy had stopped firing at us, which was fortunate because two of the jets were hit by small arms fire and had to leave the scene. The two remaining jets dropped 250 lb "snake eye" bombs on the remaining troops surrounding us.

I watched as the bombs were dropped off the F-4s and the tail fins snapped out to slow its descent. The concussions and explosions were deafening.

The jets departed as the clouds began to close in around us. We had requested an extraction, but because of the weather closing in, it was in doubt that the helicopters could get in.

Luckily for us two USMC CH-46's were able to drop down through the decreasing visibility, and one quickly landed and we … jumped on board as the door gunners fired to cover us.

We ran to the open windows and continued shooting as we took off.

We returned safely to base (Quang Tri) and were later told that the enemy troops were possibly Chinese or Korean because they were much larger in stature than the Vietnamese.

It was the first of 19 patrols. Welcome to Vietnam!

Chapter Notes

Preface

1. For an evolutionary history of the development of amphibious warfare doctrine and the Marine Corps, see Jeter A. Isley and Phillip A. Crowl, *The U.S. Marines and Amphibious War: Its Theory, and Its Practice in the Pacific* (Princeton, NJ: Princeton University Press, 1951), and Leo J. Daugherty, III, *Pioneers of Amphibious Warfare, 1898-1945: Profiles of Fourteen American Strategists* (Jefferson, NC: McFarland, 2009).

2. Ray W. Stubbe, *Aarugha! Report to the Director, Historical Division, Headquarters, Marine Corps, on the History of Specialized and Force-Level Reconnaissance Activities and Units of the United States Marine Corps, 1900-1974*, reprinted as FMFRP (Fleet Marine Force Reference Publication) 12-21 (Quantico, VA: HQMC, Marine Corps Combat Development Center, May 1989).

Chapter 1

1. See Leo J. Daugherty, III, "The U.S. Marine Corps and the Advanced Base Force, 1898-1903" (MA Thesis, John Carroll University, Cleveland, Ohio, 1985), 1-20; Daugherty, *Pioneers of Amphibious Warfare*, 1-133.

2. Bernard C. Nalty, *The United States Marines in the War with Spain* (Washington, DC: Historical Branch, G-3 Division, HQMC, 1967), 8.

3. Daugherty, "The U.S. Marine Corps and the Advanced Base Force, 1898-1903," 21-22; Nalty, *The United States Marines Corps and the War with Spain*, 8; John J. Reber, "Huntington's Battalion Was the Forerunner of Today's FMF," *Marine Corps Gazette* 63, no. 11 (November 1979), 73-74; Alan R. Millett, *Semper Fidelis: The History of the U.S. Marine Corps* (New York: Macmillan, 1980), 132.

4. Commander McCalla's task force consisted of the USS *Panther*, USS *Marblehead* and two auxiliary cruisers, the USS *Dolphin* and USS *Yankee*. See Reber, "Huntington's Battalion Was the Forerunner of Today's FMF," 74-75; Daugherty, "The U.S. Marines and the Advanced Base Force, 1898-1903," 25; Jerry A. Roberts, *U.S. Marines in Battle: Guantanamo Bay, 10 June-9 August 1898* (Quantico, VA: Marine Corps History Division, Marine Corps University Press, 2020), 23-25.

5. Daugherty, "The U.S. Marines and the Advanced Base Force, 1898-1903," 25-26; Roberts, *Guantanamo Bay*, 23.

6. Stubbe, *Aarugha!*, 5. For a biographic sketch of Brigadier General Dion Williams, USMC, see Daugherty, *Pioneers of Amphibious Warfare*, 123-33.

7. Major General Commandant Charles Heywood, *Annual Report of the Secretary of the Navy for 1903* (Washington, DC: U.S. Government Printing Office, 1903), 1231; Millett, *Semper Fidelis*, 273.

8. Daugherty, "The U.S. Marines and the Advanced Base Force, 1898-1903," 98-109.

9. Stubbe, *Aarugha!*, 5.

10. *Ibid.*

11. *Ibid.*

12. Major Dion Williams, USMC, *Naval Reconnaissance: Instructions for the Reconnaissance of Bays, Harbors, and Adjacent Country* (Washington, DC: Government Printing Office, 1906), 8.

13. Lieutenant Colonel Earl H. Ellis, USMC, "Advanced Base Operations in Micronesia," approved by Major General Commandant, Headquarters, Marine Corps, 1921 (copy in possession of the author), 18.

14. *Ibid.*, 22-23.

15. Williams, *Naval Reconnaissance*, 11, as quoted in Stubbe, *Aarugha!*, 5.

16. Williams, *Naval Reconnaissance*, 11, as quoted in Stubbe, *Aarugha!*, 5; Ellis, "Advanced Base Operations in Micronesia," 5, 6, 26, 29, 61 (on aviation) and 40-41 (submarines).

17. See Major Dion Williams, *Naval Reconnaissance: Instructions for the Reconnaissance of Bays, Harbors, and Adjacent Country*, second edition (Washington, DC: Government Printing Office, 1917), 3, as quoted in Stubbe, *Aarugha!*, 6.

18. Major Dion Williams, USMC, "The Advanced Base Force," lecture delivered at the United States Naval War College, July 26, 1917 (Washington, DC: Government Printing Office, 1912), 22. Found in Historical Amphibious File 211, Marine Corps History Division, Reference Section, Marine Corps University, Marine Corps Combat Development Center, Quantico, Virginia.

19. Stubbe, *Aarugha!*, 6.

20. *Ibid.*

21. Division of Fleet Training, Office of Naval Operations, *United States Navy, Landing Operations Doctrine, Fleet Training Publication 167* (Washington, DC: Government Printing Office, 1938), 7.
22. Ibid., 5.
23. Ibid.
24. Stubbe, *Aarugha!*, 7.
25. Ibid., 7-8.
26. Stubbe, *Aarugha!*, 6; Millett, *Semper Fidelis*, 327-29.
27. Daugherty, *Pioneers of Amphibious Warfare*, 158-268.
28. Stubbe, *Aarugha!*, 7.
29. Ibid., 8.
30. Ibid., 9.
31. Ibid.
32. Ibid.
33. Ibid., 10.
34. Ibid., 15-17.
35. Lieutenant Colonel David L. Brewster, USMC, Executive Officer, 5th Marine Regiment, Fleet Marine Force, Training Directive, Number 8-39, "Debarkation from Boats," October 17, 1939, in Historical Amphibious File 60, Marine Corps History Division, Reference Section, Marine Corps University, Marine Corps Combat Development Center, Quantico, Virginia.
36. Ibid., 3.
37. First Lieutenant C. Van Ness, USMC, "The Development and Procurement of Special Landing Boats for the Marine Corps," in Historical Amphibious File 124, Marine Corps History Division, Reference Section, Marine Corps University, Marine Corps Combat Development Center, Quantico, Virginia, 1.
38. Ibid.
39. Ibid.
40. Ibid., 6.
41. Ibid., 6-7.
42. Bruce F. Meyers, *Fortune Favors the Brave: The Story of First Force Recon* (New York: St. Martin's, 2000), 243-45.
43. Stubbe, *Aarugha!*, 10.
44. Stubbe, *Aarugha!*, 11; Meyers, *Fortune Favors the Brave*.
45. Stubbe, *Aarugha!*, 11.
46. Colonel William R. Arnold, USAF, "Colonel James L. Jones Sr., Father of Amphibious Reconnaissance and World War II Hero," *American Intelligence Journal* 35, no. 1 (2018): 29-35.
47. Ibid., 29.
48. For a description of these special Marine Corps units formed prior to the U.S. entrance into World War II, see Charles L. Updegraph, Jr., *U.S. Marine Corps Special Units of World War II* (Washington, DC: History & Museums Division, HQMC, 1972 [reprinted 1977]); Lieutenant Colonel Jon T. Hoffman, USMCR, *Silk Chutes and Hard Fighting: U.S. Marine Corps Parachute Units in World War II* (Washington, DC: History & Museums Division, HQMC, 1999); Major Robert E. Mattingly, USMC, *Herringbone Cloak—GI Dagger Marines of the OSS* (Occasional Paper) (Washington, DC: History & Museums Division, HQMC, 1989), 1-21.
49. This is extracted from the author's book, *Counterinsurgency and the United States Marine Corps: Volume I, The First Counterinsurgency Era, 1899-1945* (Jefferson, NC: McFarland, 2015), 288.
50. Arnold, "Colonel James L. Jones, Sr., Father of Amphibious Reconnaissance," 30; Stubbe, *Aarugha!*, 12.
51. Stubbe, *Aarugha!*, 10; First Lieutenant Leo B. Shinn, USMC, "Amphibious Reconnaissance," *Marine Corps Gazette* 29, no. 4 (April 1945), 51.
52. Stubbe, *Aarugha!*, 20; Arnold, "Colonel James L. Jones, Sr., Father of Amphibious Reconnaissance," 30.
53. Ibid., 288-91; Lieutenant Colonel William S. Riddle, U.S. Army, Assistant Military Attaché, "Planning and Execution of a Seaborne Raid," attached in a letter from G. I. Russell, by direction for Commander-in-Chief, United States Fleet, to the Commandant of the Marine Corps, March 16, 1942, Subject: "Planning and Execution of a Seaborne Raid," London, Report 46174, College Park, Maryland, National Archives and Records Administration, FF-1/A82, Serial No. 0392, U.S. Marine Corps War Planning Section, File No. 13048.
54. Daugherty, *Counterinsurgency and the United States Marine Corps: Volume I*, 289.
55. Ibid.
56. Ibid.
57. Ibid.
58. Ibid.
59. Daugherty, *Counterinsurgency and the United States Marine Corps: Volume I*, 290; Riddle, "Execution of a Sea-Borne Raid," 4.
60. Riddle, "Execution of a Sea-Borne Raid," 4.
61. Ibid.
62. Riddle, "Execution of a Sea-Borne Raid," 4; Updegraph, *U.S. Marine Corps Special Units of World War II*, 39-40.
63. Daugherty, *Counterinsurgency and the United States Marine Corps: Volume I*, 290-91; Riddle, "Execution of a Sea-Borne Raid," 7.
64. Riddle, "Execution of a Sea-Borne Raid," 8-9.
65. Riddle, "Execution of a Sea-Borne Raid," 7; Stubbe, *Aarugha!*, 13-16.
66. Daugherty, *Counterinsurgency and the United States Marine Corps: Volume I*, 291.
67. Stubbe, *Aarugha!*, 12-17.
68. This section is extracted from the author's paper "Commandos, Royal Marines, Paratroops, and Leathernecks, 1940-1944," delivered at the University of Portsmouth, United Kingdom, 75th Anniversary of the Normandy Landings, July 21-24, 2019; David W. Hogan, Jr., *U.S. Army Special Operations in World War II* (Washington, DC: Center of Military History, 1992), 11-22, 37-38, respectively; George F. Howe, *United States Army in World War II: The European Theater of Operations—Northwest Africa: Seizing the initiative in the West* (Washington, DC: Center of Military History, 2002), 60-63; Brigadier John Durnford-Slater,

Commando: Memoirs of a Fighting Commando in World War II (Annapolis, MD: Naval Institute Press, 1991), 90–118, 119–122, respectively; David Lee, *Beachhead Assault: The Combat History of the Royal Navy Commandos in World War II* (New York: Skyhorse Publishing, 2017), 130–219.

69. Combined Operations Command (COC), Ministry of Information, *Combined Operations* (London: Her Majesty's Stationary Office, 1942), 11.

70. Durnford-Slater, *Commando*, 14.

71. COC, *Combined Operations*, 11. After the armies of Lord Roberts and Kitchener had scattered the Boers, the guerrilla tactics of its individual units (which were styled "Commando") had, for many months, prevented decisive victory by forces vastly superior in numbers and arms.

72. *Ibid.*, 11–12.

73. COC, *Combined Operations*, 10; Durnford-Slater, *Commando*, 15–16.

74. Durnford-Slater, *Commando*, 14.

75. COC, *Combined Operations*, 12.

76. M. R. D. Foot, *SOE in France: An Account of the Work of the British Special Operations Executive in France, 1940–1944* (London: Her Majesty's Stationery Office, 1966), 180–95.

77. COC, *Combined Operations*, 12.

78. See Hogan, *U.S. Army Special Operations in World War II*, 12–14.

79. Hogan, *U.S. Army Special Operations in World War II*, 12–14; George F. Howe, *U.S. Army in World War II: Seizing the Initiative—Northwest Africa* (Washington, DC: Office of the Chief of Military History, 1957), 50.

80. Howe, *Seizing the Initiative—Northwest Africa*, 50.

81. Howe, *Seizing the Initiative—Northwest Africa*, 50; Hogan, *U.S. Army Special Operations in World War II*, 11–13.

82. Foot, *SOE*, 56.

83. *Ibid.*, 56–57.

84. F. O. Cooke, "They Took Thirty Marines," *The Leatherneck* 28, no. 7 (July 1943), 26.

85. Sergeant Jeremiah A. O'Leary, USMC, "Marine Describes Casablanca: Detachment Manned Ship's Guns," *The Quantico Sentry*, U.S. Marine Historical Division, Reference Section, "Marines in Europe Folder," Marine Corps University, Marine Corps Combat Development Center, Quantico, Virginia.

86. Lieutenant Colonel L. E. Vaughan, Commandant, Commando Depot, Inverness-shire, Scotland, Report on United States Marine Corps, June 29, 1942, in Mattingly, *Herringbone Cloak—GI Dagger*, 279.

87. Foot, *SOE*, 182.

88. Foot, *SOE*, 183.

89. Foot, *SOE*, 182–84; Stubbe, *Aarugha!*

90. Foot, *SOE*, 102.

91. Troy J. Sacquety, *The OSS in Burma: Jungle War Against the Japanese* (Lawrence: University of Kansas Press, 2013), 28.

92. Foot, *SOE*, 102.

93. Sacquety, *The OSS in Burma*, 28–29.

94. *Ibid.*, 29.

95. Foot, *SOE*, 102–3.

96. *Ibid.*, 105.

97. Stubbe, *Aarugha!*, 15; Bruce F. Meyers, *Swift, Silent, and Deadly: Marine Amphibious Reconnaissance in the Pacific, 1942–1945* (Annapolis, MD: Naval Institute Press, 2004), 11–12.

98. Foot, *SOE*, 62.

99. Williams, "The Advanced Base Force," 22.

100. Meyers, *Swift, Silent, and Deadly*, 12; Foot, *SOE*, 62–64.

101. The *Argonaut* was lost in January 1943 when it was sunk while on patrol duty. A second *Argonaut* (*Guppy* class) was launched in 1944 and served in the more traditional role as an attack submarine. Meyers, *Swift, Silent, and Deadly*, 12.

102. Meyers, *Swift, Silent, and Deadly*, 12.

103. Foot, *SOE*, 62.

104. Meyers, *Swift, Silent, and Deadly*, 11.

105. APDs were converted destroyers used as transports by the U.S. Navy and Marine Corps during World War II.

106. Meyers, *Swift, Silent, and Deadly*, 11.

107. *Ibid.*, 11–12.

108. *Ibid.*, 12.

109. *Ibid.*

110. Foot, *SOE*, 185.

111. *Ibid.*, 182.

112. *Ibid.*

113. Foot, *SOE*, 183; COC, *Combined Operations*, 10–15.

114. William J. Donovan, Memorandum to the President, December 22, 1941, No. 94, W-21, and the Major General Commandant to Major General H.M. Smith, U.S. Marine Corps, Marine Barracks, Quantico, Virginia, January 14, 1942, both located in Mattingly, *Herringbone Cloak—GI Dagger*, 236 and 245, respectively; Updegraph, *U.S. Marine Corps Special Units of World War II*, 1–3.

115. Updegraph, *U.S. Marine Corps Special Units of World War II*, 2.

116. Updegraph, *U.S. Marine Corps Special Units of World War II*, 2–10; Jon T. Hoffman, *Once a Legend: "Red Mike" Edson of the Raiders* (Novato, CA: Presidio Press, 1994), 47–94.

117. Updegraph, *U.S. Marine Corps Special Units of World War II*, 2–4; Daugherty, *Counterinsurgency and the United States Marine Corps: Volume I*, 288–89 and 305–9; Captain James Roosevelt, USMC, to the Major General Commandant, the Commanding General, Second Joint Training Force, January 13, 1942, Subject: "Development Within the Marine Corps of a Unit for Purposes Similar to the British Commandos and the Chinese Guerrillas," in Mattingly, *Herringbone Cloak—GI Dagger*, 238–39.

118. Stubbe, *Aarugha!*, 13.

119. *Ibid.*

120. *Ibid.*

121. "More Than Just Good Stories: Special Operations Units as a Lens on Wars and Institutions," panel at the 2022 Annual Meeting of the

Society of Military History, Fort Worth, Texas, April 28–May 1, 2022.
    122. General Holland M. Smith, USMC, "Comments: Outline of Volume V, History of U.S. Marine Corps Operations in World War II," #27, in the General Holland M. Smith, USMC Papers, Marine Corps History Division, Reference Section, Marine Corps University, Marine Corps Combat Development Center, Quantico, Virginia, Box 9 of 12, PC 382, "Special Units, VI, 2:77–2:82."
    123. Stubbe, *Aarugha!*, 14.
    124. Stetson Conn, Rose C. Engelman, and Byron Fairchild, *United States Army in World War II: The Western Hemisphere, Guarding the United States and Its Outposts* (Washington, DC: Center of Military History, U.S. Army, 1989), 253–300.

Chapter 2

    1. Meyers, *Fortune Favors the Brave*, 1.
    2. Stubbe, *Aarugha!*, 18; Meyers, *Swift, Silent, and Deadly*, 12.
    3. Stubbe, *Aarugha!*, 18; Conn et al., *Guarding the United States and Its Outposts*, 277–28.
    4. Conn et al., *Guarding the United States and Its Outposts*, 281.
    5. *Ibid*.
    6. *Ibid.*, 283. For the Navy's role in the assault on Attu and Kiska in the Aleutians, see Gerald E. Wheeler, *Kinkaid of the Seventh Fleet: A Biography of Admiral Thomas C. Kinkaid, U.S. Navy* (Washington, DC: Naval Historical Center, Department of the Navy, 1995), 295–342; for the Marine Corps' take on the operations in the Aleutians, see General Holland M. Smith, USMC (Ret.), and Percy Finch, *Coral and Brass* (New York/Washington, DC: Charles Scribner's Sons/Zenger Publishing Company, 1949/1979), 102–7.
    7. Stubbe, *Aarugha!*, 12–13.
    8. Conn et al., *Guarding the United States and Its Outposts*, 285.
    9. Conn et al., *Guarding the United States and Its Outposts*, 285–87; Wheeler, *Kinkaid*, 322.
    10. Wheeler, *Kinkaid*, 337–41.
    11. Stubbe, *Aarugha!*, 13.
    12. Meyers, *Swift, Silent, and Deadly*, 25.
    13. *Ibid*.
    14. *Ibid.*, 28.
    15. Major John L. Zimmerman, USMCR, *The Guadalcanal Campaign* (Washington, DC: Historical Division, HQMC, 1949), 58.
    16. Meyers, *Swift, Silent, and Deadly*, 28–29.
    17. Meyers, *Swift, Silent, and Deadly*, 31–32; Henry I. Shaw and Major Douglas T. Kane, USMC, *Isolation of Rabaul: History of U.S. Marine Corps Operations in World War II* (Washington, DC: Historical Branch, G-3, HQMC, 1963), 152–53.
    18. Shaw and Kane, *Isolation of Rabaul*, 153.
    19. *Ibid.*, 195.
    20. *Ibid*.
    21. *Ibid.*, 41; Meyers, *Fortune Favors the Brave*, 2–4; Shaw and Kane, *Isolation of Rabaul*, 173–75.
    22. Meyers, *Swift, Silent, and Deadly*, 42.
    23. *Ibid*.
    24. Stubbe, *Aarugha!*, 20.
    25. *Ibid*.
    26. Dirk A. Ballendorf and Merrill L. Bartlett, *Pete Ellis: Amphibious Warfare Prophet, 1880–1923* (Annapolis, MD: Naval Institute Press, 1997), 123–41; Jeffrey M. Dorwart, *Conflict of Duty: The U.S. Navy's Intelligence Dilemma, 1919–1945* (Annapolis, MD: Naval Institute Press, 1983), 30–61.
    27. Henry I. Shaw, Bernard C. Nalty, and Edwin T. Turnbladh, *Central Pacific Drive: History of U.S. Marine Corps Operations in World War II* (Washington, DC: Historical Branch, G-3, HQMC, 1966), 3–19; Ballendorf and Bartlett, *Pete Ellis*, 120–23; Dorwart, *Conflict of Duty*, 30–35; Millett, *Semper Fidelis*, 325–27.
    28. Stubbe, *Aarugha!*, 2–3; Shaw et al., *Central Pacific Drive*, 5.
    29. Stubbe, *Aarugha!*, 3; Ballendorf and Bartlett, *Pete Ellis*, 121; Frank O. Hough, *The Island War* (Philadelphia, PA: J. Lippincott, 1947), 7.
    30. Dorwart, *Conflict of Duty*, 36–37.
    31. *Ibid.*, 37. For a biography on Colonel Richard M. Cutts, USMC, see Daugherty, *Pioneers of Amphibious Warfare*.
    32. *Ibid.*, 63.
    33. *Ibid.*, 212.
    34. General Robert H. Barrow, USMC (Deceased), "Oral History of General Robert H. Barrow," interviewed by Edgar F. Puryear, Tape 121, Side B-13-14, Washington, DC, 2004.
    35. "Oral History of General Robert H. Barrow"; Leo J. Daugherty, III, and Rhonda L. Smith-Daugherty, *Counterinsurgency and the U.S. Marine Corps, 1945–2016: Volume 2, An Era of Persistent* Warfare (Jefferson, NC: McFarland, 2018), 122–25.
    36. Dorwart, *Conflict of Duty*, 91–92, 135 and 212, respectively.
    37. *Ibid.*, 63–64, 74–75. See also Del Valle's biography in Daugherty, *Pioneers of Amphibious Warfare*, 271–97; and Lieutenant General Pedro A. Del Valle, USMC (Ret.), *Semper Fidelis: An Autobiography* (Hawthorne, CA: Christian Book Club of America, 1976), 75–105.
    38. Del Valle, *Semper Fidelis*, 75–105.
    39. Daugherty, *Counterinsurgency and the United States Marine Corps, Volume I*, 305–7; Dorwart, *Conflict of Duty*, 87–88.
    40. Meyers, *Swift, Silent, and Deadly*, 43; Stubbe, *Aarugha!*, 19–20.
    41. Meyers, *Swift, Silent, and Deadly*, 43.
    42. *Ibid.*, 44.
    43. Shaw et al., *Central Pacific Drive*, 100.
    44. *Ibid*.
    45. Stubbe, *Aarugha!*, 27.
    46. Stubbe, *Aarugha!*, 28–29; Shaw et al., *Central Pacific Drive*, 100–102.
    47. Herbert Best, *The Webfoot Warriors: The Story of the UDT, the Navy's Underwater Demolition Teams* (New York: John Day Publishers, 1962), 28.

48. Shaw et al., *Central Pacific Drive*, 142; Stubbe, *Aarugha!*, 329–30.
49. Shaw et al., *Central Pacific Drive*, 143.
50. *Ibid*.
51. *Ibid.*, 197.
52. *Ibid*.
53. Meyers, *Swift, Silent, and Deadly*, 66.
54. Stubbe, *Aarugha!*, 36.
55. *Ibid.*, 39.
56. Meyers, *Swift, Silent, and Deadly*, 72–73; Stubbe, *Aarugha!*, 36–37.
57. Meyers, *Swift, Silent, and Deadly*, 73.
58. For a description of both Force and Division Reconnaissance, see FMFM 2-2, *Amphibious Reconnaissance* (Washington, DC: HQMC, 1976), 31–37.
59. Shaw et al., *Central Pacific Drive*, 231–37.
60. Meyers, *Swift, Silent, and Deadly*, 74.
61. *Ibid.*, 74–76.
62. Shaw et al., *Central Pacific Drive*, 355.
63. *Ibid.*, 355–56, 361, respectively.
64. *Ibid.*, 368.
65. Shaw et al., *Central Pacific Drive*, 368; Meyers, *Swift, Silent, and Deadly*, 79–82; Stubbe, *Aarugha!*, 38–39.
66. Shaw et al., *Central Pacific Drive*, 368.
67. Shaw et al., *Central Pacific Drive*, 368; Meyers, *Swift, Silent, and Deadly*, 80–81; Stubbe, *Aarugha!*, 39.
68. DUKWs were amphibious trucks designed to be launched from the well decks of amphibious transports and could carry supplies and men directly ashore.
69. Shaw et al., *Central Pacific Drive*, 369; Meyers, *Swift, Silent, and Deadly*, 81.
70. Shaw et al., *Central Pacific Drive*, 369–70.
71. Meyers, *Swift, Silent, and Deadly*, 87–88.
72. George W. Garand and Truman R. Strobridge, *Western Pacific Operations: History of U.S. Marine Corps Operations in World War II* (Washington, DC: Historical Division, HQMC, 1971), 698.
73. *Ibid*.
74. Stubbe, *Aarugha!*, 40.
75. *Ibid*.
76. *Ibid*.
77. *Ibid.*, 40, as reprinted from Commendation, HQ, Tenth Army, to Fleet Marine Force Reconnaissance, Battalion, signed by General Joseph W. Stilwell. The letter of commendation can be found in the Colonel James L. Jones Papers, located at Marine Corps History Division, Reference Section, Marine Corps University, Marine Corps Combat Development Center, Quantico, Virginia.
78. Stubbe, *Aarugha!*, 41.
79. Stubbe, *Aarugha!*, 59–60; Meyers, *Swift, Silent, and Deadly*, 132–38; Meyers, *Fortune Favors the Brave*, 15–18.

Chapter 3

1. Stubbe, *Aarugha!*, 42.
2. For an excellent overview of post–World War II Asia, see Steven L. Rearden, *History of the Office of the Secretary of Defense: Volume 1, The Formative Years, 1947-1950* (Washington, DC: Historical Office, Office of the Secretary of Defense, 1984), 209–73; Gary R. Hess, *The United States' Emergence as a Southeast Asian Power, 1940-1950* (New York: Columbia University Press, 1987), 83–371.
3. *Ibid.*, 51–52.
4. *Ibid*. See also Colonel William F. Coleman, USMC, "Amphibious Recon Patrols" (Part 1), *Marine Corps Gazette* 29, no. 12 (December 1945): 22–25.
5. Coleman, "Amphibious Recon Patrols" (Part 1).
6. Colonel William F. Coleman, USMC, "Amphibious Recon Patrols" (Part 2), *Marine Corps Gazette* 30, no. 1 (January 1946): 13–15.
7. Major General Kenneth J. Houghton, USMC (Ret.), "The Oral History Interview of Major General Kenneth J. Houghton, USMC," interviewed by Benis Frank (Washington, DC: History & Museums Division, HQMC, 1978), 10–22 (hereafter cited as "Houghton Oral History Interview"). For a synopsis of the evolution of reconnaissance in the Marine Corps, see "Brigadier General Dion Williams, USMC" (chapter 5) in Daugherty, *Pioneers of Amphibious Warfare*, 123–33; Charles D. Melson (Chief Historian), Headquarters, Marine Corps, "Marine Recon: From World War to Cold War" (unpublished paper delivered at the Society of Military History); First Lieutenant R. B. Finn, USMCR, Assistant S-2, 5th Marines, "Amphibious Reconnaissance Training"; Information Sheet: "Recon Marines," all in Reference Folder 1, Marine Corps Reconnaissance, at History Division, Marine Corps University, Marine Corps Combat Development Center, MCB, Quantico, Virginia.
8. Stubbe, *Aarugha!*, 59–66.
9. "The Oral History Field Interview of Colonel Kenneth J. Houghton, USMC," Field Interview No. 1189, conducted by Master Sergeant Robert H. Olivia, USMC, Command Post, 5th Marine Regiment, 1st Marine Division, Quang Nam Province, Da Nang TAOR, RVN, June 29, 1967 (interview in Oral History Section, History Division, HQMC, Marine Corps University, Marine Corps Combat Development Center, Quantico, Virginia), 49–50.
10. "The Oral History Field Interview of Colonel Kenneth J. Houghton," 50; Stubbe, *Aarugha!*, 57. Lieutenant Colonel Douglas Drysdale, commanding officer of 41st Independent Commando, would later command Task Force Drysdale during the Chosin Reservoir campaign in November–December 1950. See Leo J. Daugherty, III, *Train Wreckers and Ghost Killers: Allied Marines in the Korean War* (Washington, DC: History & Museums Division, HQMC, 2003), 1–22.
11. Corporal Paul B. Martin, USMC, "We Stalk the Enemy," *The Leatherneck* 37 (May 1953): 28–32; "Houghton Oral History Interview," 27.
12. Martin, "We Stalk the Enemy."
13. Stubbe, *Aarugha!*, 60.
14. Stubbe, *Aarugha!*, 60; Commanding Officer,

Naval Amphibious Test and Evaluating Unit to Commander, Amphibious Force, U.S. Atlantic Fleet, via Commander, Amphibious Training Command, U.S. Atlantic Fleet, Subject: "Final Report on ASSP Project: Evaluate the U.S. SEA LION (ASSP-315) as a Troop Carrier Submarine," June 16, 1952, in Historical Amphibious File 792, Marine Corps History Division, Reference Section, Alfred M. Gray Library, Marine Corps University, Marine Corps Combat Development Center, Quantico, Virginia.
15. Ibid., 62.
16. Phone conversation between Leo J. Daugherty, III, and Colonel Frederick Tolleson, August 2, 2018.
17. Meyers, *Fortune Favors the Brave*, 163–64.
18. Ibid., 162.
19. Ibid., 165–79.
20. Ibid., 218–23.
21. Ibid., 219.
22. Ibid., 224.
23. Ibid., 225–26.
24. Meyer, *Fortune Favors the Brave*, 226.
25. Rollins Oral History Collectiin, *loc.cit*; Stubbe, *AArugha!*, 269–72; Lanning and Stubbe, *Inside Force Recon*, 219–21.
26. Martin, "We Stalk the Enemy," 31.
27. Ibid.
28. Martin "We Stalk the Enemy," 31-2.
29. Meyers, *Fortune Favors the Brave*, 76–79.
30. Lieutenant Colonel Berwick "Barry" Babin, USMC (Ret.), to Leo J. Daugherty, III, PhD, in comments on reconnaissance in Vietnam manuscript, December 6, 2019 (hereafter cited as "Babin comments").
31. Ibid.
32. Meyers, *Fortune Favors the Brave*, 121.
33. Babin comments.
34. First Sergeant Donald H. Hamblen, USMC (Ret.), and Major Bruce H. Norton, USMC (Ret.), *One Tough Marine: The Autobiography of First Sergeant Donald H. Hamblen, USMC* (New York: Ballantine Books, 1993), 179–80.

Chapter 4

1. Babin comments.
2. See Lieutenant General Keith B. McCutcheon, USMC, "Marine Aviation in Vietnam, 1962–1970," in Brigadier General Edwin H. Simmons, USMC (Ret.), et al., *The Marines in Vietnam, 1954–1973: An Anthology and Annotated Bibliography*, second edition (Washington, DC: History & Museums Division, HQMC, 1985), 264; for background to Operation "Shu Fly," see Captain Robert H. Whitlow, USMCR, *U.S. Marines in Vietnam: The Advisory & Combat Assistance Era, 1954–1964* (Washington, DC: History & Museums Division, HQMC, 1977), 111–23.
3. Stubbe, *Aarugha!*, 139–40.
4. "Oral History Transcript: Lieutenant General Bernard M. Trainor, USMC (Ret.)," interviewed by Benis M. Frank, U.S. Marine Corps History Division, Quantico, Virginia, 2015, p. 112.
5. Ibid., 113.
6. Forrest L. Marion, *Brothers in Berets: The Evolution of Air Force Special Tactics, 1953–2003* (Montgomery, AL: General Curtis E. LeMay Center for Doctrine Development and Education, Maxwell Air Force Base, 2018), 61–121.
7. Ibid., 61–65.
8. Ibid., 61.
9. Stubbe, *Aarugha!*, 142; Michael Lee Lanning and Ray William Stubbe, *Inside Force Recon: Recon Marines in Vietnam* (New York: Ivy Books, 1989), 58–60.
10. Stubbe, *Aarugha!*, 142.

Chapter 5

1. Meyers, *Fortune Favors the Brave*, 82.
2. Lawrence J. Vetter, Jr., *Never Without Heroes: Marine Third Reconnaissance Battalion in Vietnam, 1965–1970* (New York: Ballantine Books, 1996), 5.
3. Babin comments.
4. Stubbe, *Aarugha!*, 185.
5. Ibid.
6. Shulimson and Johnson, U.S. Marines in Vietnam 1965, p. 164.
7. Ibid., 155–56.
8. Babin comments.
9. Jack Shulimson and Major Charles M. Johnson, *U.S. Marines in Vietnam: The Landing and the Buildup, 1965* (Washington, DC: History & Museums Division, 1978), 174.
10. Vetter, *Never Without Heroes*, 11.
11. Vetter, *Never Without Heroes*, 11-2.
12. Stubbe, *Aarugha!*, 148.
13. Ibid., 146.
14. A "click" is one thousand meters, or one grid square on a 1:50,000 scale maps used by Reconnaissance Marines.
15. Stubbe, *Aarugha!*, 146.
16. See Communications Section in U.S. Marine Corps, United States Marine Corps Reference Data, Volume II (Washington, D.C., HQMC, 1968).
17. Babin comments.
18.
19. Ibid.
20. Ibid.
21. Ibid.
22. Colonel Andrew Finlayson, USMC (Ret.), *Killer Kane: A Marine Long-Range Recon Team Leader in Vietnam, 1967–1968* (Jefferson, NC: McFarland, 2013), 203–9.
23. Ibid., 211.
24. Babin comments.
25. For the role of Navy Corpsmen with Force and Battalion Recon see Kyle Watts, "Recon Doc," Leatherneck, April 2018, Volume No. 102, No. 4, 54-9.
26. Kyle Watts, "Recon Doc," *Leatherneck* 102, no. 4 (April 2019): 54–59.

27. *Ibid.*, 55.
28. *Ibid.*
29. *Ibid.*, 55–56.
30. *Ibid.*, 56. For a more detailed account of "Doc" Norton's tour in Vietnam, see Bruce H. Norton, *Force Recon Diary, 1969* (New York: Ivy Books, 1991), 57–116.
31. Watt, "Recon Doc," 56.
32. *Ibid.*, 56–58.
33. Vetter, *Never Without Heroes*, 20–21.
34. *Ibid.*, 22.
35. *Ibid.*, 23.
36. Lanning and Stubbe, Inside Force Recon, p. 99.
37. Shulimson and Johnson, *U.S. Marines in Vietnam*, 175.
38. *Ibid.*
39. *Ibid.*, 177.
40. *Ibid.*
41. Colonel Andrew R. Finlayson to Leo J. Daugherty, April 19, 2019, Subject: "Comments on Marine Recon in Vietnam" (hereafter cited as Finlayson comments, April 19, 2019); Shulimson and Johnson, *U.S. Marines in Vietnam*, 177.
42. Shulimson and Johnson, *U.S. Marines in Vietnam*, 177.
43. *Ibid.*
44. See Lanning and Stubbe, *Inside Force Recon*, 109–10; U.S. Marine Corps, FMFM 2-2, *Amphibious Reconnaissance* (Washington, DC: HQMC, 1965), 1.
45. Finlayson comments, April 19, 2019.
46. Shulimson and Johnson, *U.S. Marines in Vietnam*, 179.
47. Finlayson comments, April 19, 2019.
48. Stubbe, *Aarugha!*, 199.
49. See Lieutenant Commander Robert E. Munford, Jr., USN, "'Jackstay': New Dimensions in Amphibious Warfare," in Frank Uhlig, Jr., *Vietnam: The Naval Story* (Annapolis, MD: Naval Institute Press, 1986), 344–64.
50. Stubbe, *Aarugha!*, 149–50.
51. Shulimson and Johnson, *U.S. Marines in Vietnam 1965*, 179.
52. Babin comments.
53. Lanning and Stubbe, *Inside Force Recon*, 68.
54. Major Bruce H. Norton and Sergeant Major Maurice J. Jacques, USMC (Ret.), *Sergeant Major, U.S. Marine Corps: The Biography of Sergeant Major Maurice J. Jacques, USMC* (New York: Ivy/Ballantine Books, 1995), 260.

Chapter 6

1. Lanning and Stubbe, *Inside Force Recon*, 99–101.
2. Babin comments.
3. *Ibid.*
4. *Ibid.*
5. As quoted in Babin comments. See also Pete Nealen, "The Beginning of the Stingray Patrols," February 20, 2013 (https://sofrep.com/news/stingray-patrols/#ixzz2LSb3jPv1).
6. Stubbe, *Aarugha!*, 182–83; Lanning and Stubbe, *Inside Force Recon*, 105–6.
7. Shulimson, *U.S. Marines in Vietnam: An Expanding War, 1966*, 161.
8. Lanning and Stubbe, *Inside Force Recon*, 107.
9. Shulimson, *U.S. Marines in Vietnam*, 179; Lanning and Stubbe, *Inside Force Recon*, 182–4.
10. See 3rd Reconnaissance Command Chronology for 17 November 1966, Commanding Officer, 3rd Reconnaissance Battalion, to Commanding General, 3rd Marine Division, FMF, Subject: Command Chronology for November 1–30, 1966 (Texas Tech University, Sam Johnson Vietnam Center).
11. Babin comments.
12. See 3rd Reconnaissance Command Chronology for 17 November 1966, Commanding Officer, 3rd Reconnaissance Battalion, to Commanding General, 3rd Marine Division, FMF, Subject: Command Chronology for November 1–30, 1966 (Texas Tech University, Sam Johnson Vietnam Center).

Chapter 7

1. Babin comments.
2. Lanning and Stubbe, *Inside Force Recon*, 89 and 92, respectively.
3. Babin comments.
4. *Ibid.*
5. *Ibid.*
6. Lieutenant Colonel Berwick "Barry" Babin, USMC (Ret.), to Leo. J. Daugherty, III, PhD, April 9, 2019.
7. Babin comments.
8. For the full version of Lance Corporal Vaughn's account, see Appendix A; Lance Corporal Donald W. Vaughn, USMC, "Eyewitness Statement: Donald W. Vaughn," email, Corporal Barry Babin to Leo J. Daugherty, April 9, 2019; Lance Corporal Donald W. Vaughn, USMC, "Eyewitness Statement" (copy in possession of the author), 1 (hereafter cited as Vaughn Eyewitness Testimony).
9. *Ibid.*, 1.
10. Corporal Lou Kern USMC, to Leo J. Daugherty, III, PhD, email (copy in possession of the author).
11. See Randy Kington, *What a Life: How the Vietnam War Affected One Marine*, third printing (Marco Island, FL: Keller Publishing, 2010), 58.
12. John Edmund Delezen, *The Eye of the Tiger: Memoir of a United States Marine, Third Force Recon Company, Vietnam* (Jefferson, NC: McFarland, 2003), 19.
13. Babin comments.
14. *Ibid.*

Chapter 8

1. Finlayson, *Killer Kane*, 76–77.
2. Vetter, *Never Without Heroes*, p. 127.

3. Vetter, *Never Without Heroes*, 128–29.
4. *Ibid.*, 129–30.
5. *Ibid.*, 130.
6. Colonel Andrew R. Finlayson to Leo J. Daugherty, III, PhD, email, March 11, 2019.
7. *Ibid.*
8. Vetter, *Never Without Heroes*, 131.
9. Vetter, *Never Without Heroes*, 80-81; Shulimson, *U.S. Marines in Vietnam*, 157–61.
10. Colin Leinster, "The Two Wars of General Walt," *LIFE*, May 26, 1967, 83–84.
11. John L. Plaster, *SOG: The Secret Wars of America's Commandos in Vietnam* (New York: NAL Caliber, 1997), 37–38.
12. *Ibid.*, 38.
13. See Major Gary L. Tefler USMC, Lieutenant Colonel Lane Rogers USMC, and V. Keith Fleming, *U.S. Marines in Vietnam: Fighting the North Vietnamese* (Washington, D.C., HQMC, History and Museums Division, 1984), 51.
14. Vetter, *Never Without Heroes*, 132–34.
15. For a detailed account of this battle, see Major Gary L. Telfer, USMC, Lieutenant Colonel Lane Rogers, USMC, and V. Keith Fleming, Jr., *U.S. Marines in Vietnam: Fighting the North Vietnamese, 1967* (Washington, DC: History & Museums Division, HQMC, 1984), 9–15.
16. Vetter, *Never Without Heroes*, 133–34.
17. Vetter, *Never Without Heroes*, 133–34.
18. Stubbe, *Aarugha!*, 210.
19. Babin comments.
20. *Ibid.*
21. Stubbe, *Aarugha!*, 210.
22. Stubbe, *Aarugha!*, 186–7.
23. *Ibid.*
24. Stubbe, *Aarugha!*, 236–37.
25. "Happy Valley" (so named by the Marines) was located between Da Nang and the VC-controlled valley to the west; this locale consisted of a range of heights that formed a natural wall. See Phillip Caputo, *A Rumor of War* (New York: Holt, Rinehart, and Winston, 1977), 67.
26. Finlayson, *Killer Kane*, 110.
27. *Ibid.*, 59.
28. *Ibid.*, 59–60.
29. *Ibid.*, 22.
30. Caputo, *A Rumor of War*, 67.
31. Finlayson, *Killer Kane*, 84–89.
32. *Ibid.*, 94.
33. Babin comments.
34. Mao Tse-Tung, *Selected Military Writings of Mao Tse-Tung* (Peking: Foreign Language Press, 1963), 30–32; Douglas Pike, *PAVN: People's Army of Vietnam* (Novato, CA: Presidio Press, 1986), 14–104; Douglas Pike, *Viet Cong: The Organization and Techniques of the National Liberation Front of South Vietnam* (Cambridge, MA: MIT Press, 1966), 241–52; William Darryl Henderson, *Why the Viet Cong Fought: A Study of Motivation and Control in a Modern Army in Combat* (Westport, CT: Greenwood Press, 1979), 25–47.
35. Mao, *Selected Military Writings*, 31.
36. Henderson, *Why the Viet Cong Fought*, 34 and 46.
37. *Ibid.*, 34. The author is referring to what became known as the People's Army of Vietnam, not to be confused with the Viet Cong or the National Liberation Front. Pike, *PAVN*, 102–5; Pike, *Viet Cong*, 31–56.
38. Henderson, *Why the Viet Cong Fought*, 34.
39. M. Anderson, M. Arnsten, and H. Averch, *Insurgent Organization and Operations: A Case Study of the Viet Cong in the Delta, 1964-1966*, Memorandum RM-5239-I-ISA/ARPA (Santa Monica, CA: Rand Corporation, August 1967), prepared for the Office of the Assistant Secretary of Defense/International Security Affairs and the Advanced Research Projects Agency, 5–15.
40. Henderson, *Why the Viet Cong Fought*, 34–36; Jay Phillips, *A Shau: Crucible of the Vietnam War* (Salt Lake City, UT: Izzard Ink Publishing, 2021).
41. Phillips, *A Shau: Crucible of the Vietnam War*, 122.
42. Henderson, *Why the Viet Cong Fought*, 34–47; Pike, *PAVN*, 101–4; Pike, *Viet Cong*, 37–38.
43. Mao, *Selected Military Writings*, 31.
44. *Ibid.*
45. Department of the Army Pamphlet, 381-10, *Weapons and Equipment Recognition Guide, Southeast Asia* (Washington, DC: Headquarters, Department of the Army, January 1966).
46. Mao, *Selected Military Writings*, 31; Pike, *PAVN*, 36–56; Pike, *Viet Cong*, 33–39.
47. Pike, *Viet Cong*, 32–38, 50–51, 323, 378–79, respectively.
48. *Ibid.*, 37.
49. *Ibid.*, 38.
50. Pike, *Viet Cong*, 39–40; Mao, *Selected Military Writings*, 244–45.
51. Mao, *Selected Military Writings*, 245.
52. Mao, *Selected Military Writings*, 245; Pike, *Viet Cong*, 39.
53. Pike, *Viet Cong*, 39.
54. Comments of Colonel Andrew R. Finlayson to Leo J. Daugherty, III, PhD, email, June 23, 2022.
55. *Ibid.*
56. *Ibid.*
57. *Ibid.*
58. Lieutenant Colonel Berwick Babin to Leo J. Daugherty, III, PhD, Colonel Andrew R. Finlayson, Corporal William D. Moss, June 24, 2022, Subject: "NVA Counter-Reconnaissance Teams."
59. *Ibid.*
60. *Ibid.*
61. *Ibid.*
62. Army of the Republic of (South) Vietnam.
63. Lieutenant Colonel Berwick Babin to Leo J. Daugherty, III, PhD, Colonel Andrew R. Finlayson, Corporal William D. Moss, June 24, 2022.
64. *Ibid.*, 2.
65. *Ibid.*
66. Lieutenant Colonel Berwick Babin to Leo J. Daugherty, III, PhD, June 24, 2022.
67. *Ibid.*

68. *Ibid.*
69. Military Assistance Command–Studies Observation Group teams.
70. Andrew Finlayson to Lieutenant Colonel Berwick Babin, Leo J. Daugherty, III, Corporal William D. Moss, June 24, 2022.
71. *Ibid.* See also Finlayson, *Killer Kane*, 110–98.
72. Lieutenant Colonel Berwick Babin to Leo J. Daugherty, III, PhD, June 24, 2022.
73. John B. Rhodes, *Rejoice or Cry: Diary of a Recon Marine Vietnam, 1967–1968* (Danbury, CT: Economy, 1996), 118–19.
74. *Ibid.*
75. *Ibid.*, 121–22.
76. Finlayson, *Killer Kane*, 199.
77. See Central Intelligence Agency Intelligence Memorandum, "The Status of the North Vietnamese Divisions in Coastal II Corps" (Directorate of Intelligence, November 25, 1967; declassified June 28, 2018), 5–15.
78. Lanning and Stubbe, *Inside Force Recon*, 116–17.
79. Lanning and Stubbe, *Inside Force Recon*, 120–22; Stubbe, *Aarugha!*, 193–200. See also First Lieutenant Wayne E. Rollings Oral History Collection, USMC, Marine Corps History Division, HQMC, Marine Corps History Division, Marine Corps Combat Development Center, Quantico, Virginia, No. 4688, "Paradrop Insertion in RVN."
80. Rollins Oral History Collection, loc.cit; Stubbe, *Aarugha!*, 269–72; Lanning and Stubbe, *Inside force Recon*, 219–21.
81. Babin comments.
82. Watts, "'First to Fight,'" 28.
83. Kyle Watts, "'First to Fight': 1st Force Reconnaissance in Hue City," *Leatherneck* 101, no. 2 (February 2018): 24–35.
84. See entries February 18–March 4, 1968, in *Diary of Sergeant Major W. Jack, 1st Force Reconnaissance for 1968* (Quantico, VA: Marine Corps Archives, Collection #2544, PC 3286, 1968–1969, Marine Corps University, Marine Corps Combat Development Center).

Chapter 9

1. Lanning and Stubbe, *Inside Force Recon*, 145–46.
2. See Kyle Watts, *Recon Doc*," Leatherneck, April 2019, Vol. 101, No. 4, 54-5; Lanning and Stubbe, *Inside Force Recon*, 144-45.
3. Watts, "'First to Fight,'" 24.
4. *Ibid.*, 25.
5. Kyle Watts, "First to Fight" 1st Force Reconnaissance in Hue City," Leatherneck, February 2018, No. 2, Volume 100, 26.
6. *Ibid.*
7. Babin comments.
8. Lanning and Stubbe, *Inside Force Recon*, 149.
9. Shulmison, et al., *U.S. Marines in Vietnam*.
10. *Ibid.*, 552.
11. *Ibid.*
12. Lieutenant Colonel Berwick (Barry) Babin to Leo J. Daugherty, III, email, August 30, 2019, Subject: "Babin Statement, Fahlstrom Statement, Lamontagne Statement" (copy in possession of the author).
13. "Reconnaissance Operations in the 'Scotland II' Area of Operations" (interview with Captain Phillip F. Reynolds, USMC), Dong Ha Combat Base, June 18, 1968, Tape 2918, Marine Corps History Division, Oral History Section, Marine Corps University, Marine Corps Combat Development Center, MCB, Quantico, Virginia.
14. *Ibid.*
15. "Reconnaissance Operations in the 'Scotland II' Area of Operations" (interview with Second Lieutenant Willis M. Gregory), 255–61.
16. "Reconnaissance Operations in the 'Scotland II' Area of Operations" (interview with Sergeant Robert L. Nixton).
17. "Reconnaissance Operations in the 'Scotland II' Area of Operations" (interview with Sergeant David E. Metz).
18. See "Reconnaissance Operations in the 'Scotland II' Area of Operations" (interview with Corporal O. L. Janis), 263–65.
19. Babin comments.
20. Lanning and Stubbe, *Inside Force Recon*.
21. "Reconnaissance Operations in the 'Scotland II' Area of Operations" (interview with Sergeant William Cress), 269–70.
22. Babin comments, 272.
23. *Ibid.*
24. "Reconnaissance Operations in the 'Scotland II' Area of Operations" (interview with Corporal Harlan E. Holmes), 273.
25. Babin comments.
26. *Ibid.*
27. *Ibid.*
28. *Ibid.*
29. *Ibid.*
30. Jack Shulimson, Lieutenant Colonel Leonard A. Blaisol, USMC, Charles R. Smith, and David A. Dawson, *U.S. Marines in Vietnam: The Defining Year, 1968* (Washington, DC: History & Museums Division, HQMC, 1997), 238.
31. See Shulimson, *U.S. Marines in Vietnam*, 385–87; Stubbe, *Aarugha!*, 272–76.
32. Ibid.
33. Babin comments.
34. Shulimson, *U.S. Marines in Vietnam*, 556.

Chapter 10

1. Charles R. Smith, *U.S. Marines in Vietnam: High Mobility and Standdown, 1969* (Washington, DC: History & Museums Division, HQMC, 1988), 251.
2. *Ibid.*
3. U.S. Marine Corps, *United States Marine Corps Reference Data, Volume II* (Washington, DC: HQMC, 1968), XVII-32–XVII-34.
4. Colonel David Lownds, USMC, *Comments by*

Colonel David Lownds, USMC, United States Congress, Senate Armed Services Committee, Permanent Investigations Subcommittee, Hearings on the Electronic Battlefield Program, 91st Congress, 2nd Session (Washington, DC: Government Printing Office, 1971), 95.
    5. Smith, *U.S. Marines in Vietnam*, 251–52.
    6. *Ibid.*, 252.
    7. Babin comments.
    8. *Ibid.*
    9. Phillips, *A Shau: Crucible of the Vietnam War*, 405.
    10. *Ibid.*
    11. *Ibid.*, 130.
    12. The idea behind both MAGIS and SCAMP was to have an aerial platform (jet, helicopter or propeller-drive aircraft) take photographs or "implant aerial-delivered sensors" along likely avenues of approach (much like Marine Recon teams would do along the DMZ in 1968 and 1969). Aircraft would then "drop" the collected data at designated points, where they were retrieved and taken to a trailer equipped with photo interpretation equipment and processed into intelligence. MAGIS and SCAMP were later disbanded as new technologies, such as unmanned aerial vehicles and drones, came into use.
    13. Phillips, *A Shau: Crucible of the Vietnam War*, 231.

Chapter 11

    1. Smith, *U.S. Marines in Vietnam*, 252.
    2. *Ibid.*
    3. *Ibid.*
    4. *Ibid.*
    5. Lanning and Stubbe, *Inside Force Recon*, 175.
    6. Smith, *U.S. Marines in Vietnam*, 252. See also 3rd Force Reconnaissance Command Chronology for January 1969.
    7. Smith, *U.S. Marines in Vietnam*, 252.
    8. *Ibid.*, 253.
    9. *Ibid.*
    10. *Ibid.*
    11. Lanning and Stubbe, *Inside Force Recon*, 225.
    12. Babin comments.
    13. Smith, *U.S. Marines in Vietnam*, 254.
    14. *Ibid.*, 22.
    15. Joe Sloss to Leo J. Daugherty, III, email, June 1, 2019.
    16. Smith, *U.S. Marines in Vietnam*, 254.
    17. *Ibid.*
    18. *Ibid.*, 254–55.
    19. *Ibid.*, 255.
    20. *Ibid.*
    21. *Ibid.*
    22. Babin comments.
    23. See footnote 930 in Stubbe, *Aarugha!*, 228.
    24. Babin comments. See also Dan Doyle, "For These Marines in Vietnam, Unexpected Dangers Were Ferocious," https://blog.theveteranssite.greatergood.com/vietnam-tiger/, and Sergeant Bob Morris, "Growl No More…" *Northern Marine Magazine* (1968), http://www.3rdrecon.org/tiger.htm.
    25. Brigadier General Edwin H. Simmons, USMC (Ret.), "Marine Corps Operations in Vietnam, 1969–1972," in Simmons et al.'s *The Marines in Vietnam, 1954–1973*, 133.
    26. General Barrow became the twenty-seventh commandant of the Marine Corps in January 1979; Colonel Richard D. Camp, USMC (Ret.), manuscript on General Robert H. Barrow, USMC, in the General Robert H. Barrow Papers, Box 16, Folder 1 (Marine Corps Museum, Reference Section, Marine Corps Recruit Depot, Parris Island, South Carolina), "Maneuver Section," Box 161, Folder 1 (hereafter cited as Camp manuscript).
    27. *Ibid.*
    28. *Ibid.*
    29. *Ibid.*
    30. *Ibid.*
    31. See General Davis' comments in Camp manuscript.
    32. General Raymond G. Davis (Ret.), "Oral History Transcript of General Raymond G. Davis, USMC (Ret.)," interviewed by Benis M. Frank (Washington, DC: History & Museums Division, HQMC, 1978), 284 (hereafter cited as "Davis Oral History Interview").
    33. *Ibid.*, 284–85.
    34. *Ibid.*, 285.
    35. *Ibid.*
    36. *Ibid.*
    37. *Ibid.*, 285–86.
    38. *Ibid.*, 284.
    39. *Ibid.*, 7.
    40. See Colonel Andrew R. Finlayson, Jr., USMC, "The Strategic Importance of the An Hoa Combat Base" (copy in possession of the author), 1 (see Appendix D).
    41. *Ibid.*, 3.
    42. Smith, *U.S. Marines in Vietnam*, 118.
    43. See Command Chronology, 1st Force Reconnaissance Company (Rein.), 1st Marine Division (Rein.), FMF, An Hoa Command Chronology, 010001H May 1969 to 202400H May 1969, Narrative Summary and Sequential Listings of Significant Events, June 10, 1969 (Texas Tech University, Sam Johnson Vietnam Center).
    44. *Ibid.*, 17.
    45. An "Arc Light" mission was a targeted air strike by three B-52 bombers on station from bases in Guam and Thailand. See Lieutenant Schanck's comments in his patrol report, enclosed with Command Chronology, 1st Force Reconnaissance Company (Rein.), 1st Marine Division (Rein.), FMF, An Hoa Command Chronology, 010001H May 1969 to 202400H May 1969, Narrative Summary and Sequential Listings of Significant Events, June 10, 1969; Babin comments.
    46. See Lieutenant Unsworth, Patrol Report, Operations Order, 365-69, 041330H May 69, in Command Chronology, 1st Reconnaissance Battalion, May 1969, A-4.

47. See Lieutenant Merry, Patrol Report, 862-69, Patrol Hireling, Company B, 1st Force Reconnaissance Battalion, 10 October 1305H October 1969, in 1st Reconnaissance Battalion Command Chronologies, August–December 1969, 1.

48. There would be two more announced withdrawals by the Nixon administration—September 16 and November 4, 1969—which brought the Marine strength in I Corps by December 15, 1969, to 55,300. See Smith, *U.S. Marines in Vietnam*, 355–57.

49. See Captain Alex Lee, Commanding Officer, 3rd Force Reconnaissance, Via: 3rd Force Reconnaissance Battalion, (-) (Rein.), Commanding General, 3rd Marine Division (-) (Rein.), FMF; Commanding General, Fleet Marine Division, Pacific, to Commandant of the Marine Corps, September 15, 1969, Subject: Command Chronology for period 01000H Aug69 to 312400H Aug69, Enclosure 1 (Texas Tech University, Sam Johnson Vietnam Center), 9 (hereafter cited as Lee, Command Chronology, August 1–31, 1969).

50. Babin comments.

51. "Davis Oral History Interview," 284.

52. See Lee, Command Chronology, August 1–31, 1969, Enclosure 1, 9.

53. *Ibid.*, 11.

54. Smith, *U.S. Marines in Vietnam*, 257.

55. Stubbe, *Aarugha!*, 308.

56. Smith, *U.S. Marines in Vietnam*, 256.

57. Babin comments.

58. Smith, *U.S. Marines in Vietnam*, 256.

59. *Ibid.*, 256–57.

60. Stubbe, *Aarugha!*, 308–9.

61. *Ibid.*, 309.

62. *Ibid.*

Chapter 12

1. Lanning and Stubbe, *Inside Force Recon*, 225.

2. *Ibid.*, 225–26.

3. *Ibid.*

4. Stubbe, *Aarugha!*, 309.

5. Lanning and Stubbe, *Inside Force Recon*, 226.

6. Lanning and Stubbe, *Inside Force Recon*, 226–27; Vetter, *Never Without Heroes*, 290–306.

7. Finlayson, *Killer Kane*, 95.

8. *Ibid.*

9. Hamblen and Norton, *One Tough Marine*, 254–72.

10. *Ibid.*, 261–64.

11. Commanding General, Fleet Marine Force to Commandant of the Marine Corps (Code HD), March 3, 1970, Subject: Command Chronology for period January 1–31, 1970, Third Force Reconnaissance Company (Texas Tech University, Sam Johnson Vietnam Center), 5.

12. *Ibid.*

13. *Ibid.*, 6.

14. *Ibid.*

15. Stubbe, *Aarugha!*, 310.

16. *Ibid.*

17. *Ibid.*

18. *Ibid.*, 311.

19. *Ibid.*

20. *Ibid.*, 311–12.

21. *Ibid.*, 312.

22. 1st Reconnaissance Battalion Command Chronology, December 1970, Part II, Narrative Summary, January 2, 1971 (Texas Tech University, Sam Johnson Vietnam Center), 9.

23. *Ibid.*

24. *Ibid.*

25. *Ibid.*

26. See Patrol Report, Operation Order: 1206-70, Patrol: Road Test, debriefed by Gunnery Sergeant Roberts, 1st Reconnaissance Battalion, Da Nang, RVN, in Command Chronology, 1st Recon Battalion, December 1970 (Texas Tech University, Sam Johnson Vietnam Center).

27. Comments by Corporal Milleson, Operation Order: 1230-70, Patrol: Donny Brook, Co. "B," 1st Recon Battalion, Da Nang, RVN, December 10, 1970, debriefed by Corporal John L. Hilbo, in Command Chronology, 1st Recon Battalion, December 1970 (Texas Tech University, Sam Johnson Vietnam Center).

28. *Ibid.*

29. See Sergeant Kelly, USMC, Operation Order: 1233-70, Patrol: Road Test, Company "B," debriefed by Sergeant White, 1st Reconnaissance Battalion, Da Nang, RVN, December 17, 1970, in Command Chronology, 1st Recon Battalion, December 1970 (Texas Tech University, Sam Johnson Vietnam Center).

30. See Lieutenant Wellman, Operation Order: 1237-70, Patrol War Cloud Training, H&S CO., debriefed by Sergeant White, 1st Reconnaissance Battalion, Da Nang, RVN, December 27, 1970, in Command Chronology, 1st Recon Battalion, December 1970 (Texas Tech University, Sam Johnson Vietnam Center).

31. See Corporal Combs, Operation Order: 1244-70, Patrol Swift Scout, Co. "A: (PPB-DATE-PALM)," debriefed by Corporal J. L. Bilbo, 1st Reconnaissance Battalion, Da Nang, RVN, December 17, 1970, in Command Chronology, 1st Recon Battalion, December 1970 (Texas Tech University, Sam Johnson Vietnam Center).

32. *Ibid.*

33. *Ibid.*

34. *Ibid.*

35. Commanding Officer, 1st Reconnaissance Battalion, to Commanding General, 1st Marine Division (-), FMF, Attn: (G-3), Subject: Command Chronology for period of 010001H to 312400H January 1971, "Narrative" (Texas Tech University, Sam Johnson Vietnam Center).

36. Commanding Officer, 1st Reconnaissance Battalion, to Commanding General, 1st Marine Division (-) (Rein.), March 10, 1971, Subject: Command Chronology for period of 01001H to 282400H February 1971, "Narrative" (Texas Tech University, Sam Johnson Vietnam Center), 3.

37. *Ibid.*

38. *Ibid.*

39. *Ibid.*

40. Commanding Officer, 1st Reconnaissance Battalion, to Commandant of the Marine Corps (Code HD), via the Commanding General, 1st Marine Division (-) (Rein.), FMF; Commanding General, Fleet Marine Force, Pacific, April 23, 1971, Subject: Command Chronology for period March 25–April 13, 1971 (Texas Tech University, Sam Johnson Vietnam Center), 3.

Chapter 13

1. See Andrew J. Birtle, *U.S. Army and Counterinsurgency and Contingency Operations Doctrine, 1860–1941* (Washington, DC: Center of Military History, Headquarters, Department of the Army, 1997), 99–139; Andrew J. Birtle, *U.S. Army and Counterinsurgency and Contingency Operations Doctrine, 1942–1976* (Washington, DC: Center of Military History, Headquarters, Department of the Army, 2007), 171; Brian Linn, *The U.S. Army and Counterinsurgency in the Philippine War, 1899–1902* (Chapel Hill: University of North Carolina Press, 1989).

2. Richard J. Dunlop, *Behind Japanese Lines: With the OSS in Burma* (Chicago: Rand McNally, 1979); Sacquety, *The OSS in Burma*.

3. James E. T. Hopkins, in collaboration with John M. Jones, *Spearhead: A Complete History of Merrill's Marauder Rangers* (Baltimore, MD: Galahad Press, 1999); Colonel Charles N. Hunter, *Galahad* (San Antonio, TX: Naylor Company, 1963); Charles Ogburn, Jr., *The Marauders* (New York: Harper & Brothers, 1959); Gavin Mortimer, *Merrill's Marauders: The Untold Story of Unit Galahad and the Toughest Special Forces Mission of World War II* (Minneapolis, MN: Zenith Press, 2013).

4. The author is presently writing a full-length biography on the life and career of Major General Frank D. Merrill, titled *Marauder! The Life and Career of Major Frank D. Merrill, Jr., U.S. Army* (forthcoming from McFarland Press). See also Colonel Charles N. Hunter, "North Burma Campaign," from October 23, 1943, through the capture of Myitkyina, August 3, 1944, and subsequent reorganization of the NCAC, approved C/S/NCAC, November 27, 1944, in the General Joseph W. Stilwell, U.S. Army Papers, Hoover Institution, Stanford University, Stanford, CA, China-Burma-India File, File No. 15.5, Folder 1, Section 2, Part 1.

5. For an excellent overview of Army Special Operations Forces in World War II, see David W. Hogan, Jr., *U.S. Army Special Operations in World War II* (Washington, DC: Center of Military History, 1992).

6. Birtle, *U.S. Army Counterinsurgency and Contingency Operations Doctrine, 1942–1976*, 131–278. The single best monograph on the formation of the Army's Special Forces in Vietnam is Colonel Francis J. Kelly, *U.S. Army Special Forces, 1961–1971*, Vietnam Studies (Washington, DC: Department of the Army, 1973), 3–32.

7. Phillips, *A Shau: Crucible of the Vietnam War*, 203–456.

8. Birtle, *U.S. Army and Counterinsurgency and Contingency Operations Doctrine, 1860–1941*, 1–75; Linn, *The U.S. Army and Counterinsurgency in the Philippine War*. In the mid-1960s, the U.S. Army Infantry School at Fort Benning, Georgia, compiled a set of readings on counter-guerrilla operations: U.S. Army Infantry School, *Selected Readings in Guerrilla and Counterguerrilla Operations* (Fort Benning, GA: U.S. Army Infantry School, Brigade and Battalion Operations Department, August 1966).

9. Birtle, *U.S. Army and Counterinsurgency and Contingency Operations Doctrine, 1860–1942*, 55–208; Donald W. Smythe, *Guerrilla Warrior: The Early Life of John J. Pershing* (New York: Charles Scribner's Sons, 1973), 144–204 and 217–82; Julie Irene Prieto, *The Mexican Expedition, 1916–1917* (Washington, DC: Center of Military History, 2016).

10. Brigadier General George S. Simonds, *Jungle Combat Principles*, by the 20th Infantry Brigade, U.S. Army, Panama Canal Zone, 1925 (copy in possession of the author; hereafter cited as U.S. Army, *Jungle Combat Principles*).

11. U.S. Marine Lieutenant Colonel (later Brigadier General) Samuel Griffith, II, authored a similar study on jungle warfare, based on his experience as executive officer for the 1st Raider Battalion and operations on Guadalcanal in 1944. See Lieutenant Colonel Samuel B. Griffith, II, USMC, "Jungle Warfare," unpublished manuscript written at Marine Corps Schools, Marine Barracks, Quantico, Virginia; Historical Amphibious File 537, Marine Corps History Division, Reference Section, Marine Corps University, Marine Corps Combat Development Center, Quantico, Virginia.

12. U.S. Army, *Jungle Combat Principles*, 1.

13. *Ibid.*, 15. See also Lieutenant Colonel Earl H. Ellis, USMC, "Bush Brigades," *Marine Corps Gazette* 6, no. 1 (March 1921): 1–15.

14. "Very" pistol is a flare pistol.

15. U.S. Army, *Jungle Combat Principles*, 16.

16. *Ibid.*

17. *Ibid.*, 17.

18. *Ibid.*

19. *Ibid.*, 18.

20. *Ibid.*

21. *Ibid.*

22. *Ibid.*

23. *Ibid.*

24. Department of the Army, FM 31-16, *Counterguerrilla Operations* (Washington, DC: Headquarters, Department of the Army, March 1967), 50 (hereafter cited as FM 31-16, *Counterguerrilla Operations*).

25. FM 31-16, *Counterguerrilla Operations*, 50; U.S. Army, *Jungle Combat Principles*, 18.

26. FM 31-16, *Counterguerrilla Operations*, 50.

27. U.S. Army, *Jungle Combat Principles*, 18; FM 31-16, *Counterguerrilla Operations*, 50.

28. FM 31-16, *Counterguerrilla Operations*, 50.

29. U.S. Army, *Jungle Combat Principles*, 19.
30. Birtle, *U.S. Army Counterinsurgency and Contingency Operations Doctrine, 1942–1976*, 131–219.
31. See Hunter, *Galahad*, 1–26; U.S. Army, *Merrill's Marauders*, 8–30.
32. The 77th Indian Brigade consisted of the 13th King's (Liverpool Regiment), 3rd Bn/2nd Gurkha Rifles, 142 Commando, a force of Burma Rifles, signalers from the Royal Signal Corp, RAF detachments, and headquarters personnel. See Michael Calvert, *Chindits: Long Range Penetration* (London: Ballantine Books, 1973), 10.
33. Hunter, *Galahad*, 3–4; Ronald H. Spector, *Advice and Support: The Early Years—The U.S. Army in Vietnam* (Washington, DC: Center of Military History, 1983), 105–57.
34. Mortimer, *Merrill's Marauders*, 195. See also Colonel Charles N. Hunter, "North Burma Campaign," from October 23, 1943, through the capture of Myitkyina, August 3, 1944, and subsequent reorganization of the NCAC, approved C/S/NCAC, November 27, 1944, in the General Joseph W. Stilwell, U.S. Army Papers, Hoover Institution, Stanford University, Stanford, CA, China-Burma-India File, File No. 15.5, Folder 1, Section 2, Part 1.
35. See Colonel Francis G. Brink, U.S. Army, "Summary of Organization & Training of the 5307th Composite Unit (U.S. Long Range Penetration Unit) for Burma Operations," CBI, April 4, 1944, U.S. Army Maneuver Center of Excellence HQ Donovan Research Library, Armor Research Library, Fort Benning, Georgia, Call #D787.2.B77, 1–6.
36. Colonel Charles N. Hunter, "Report on Overseas Observations: Report Summary of the 5307th Composite Unit (Provisional), Merrill's Marauders, and Other Units in the China Burma Theater," February 17, 1945, U.S. Army Maneuver Center of Excellence HQ Donovan Research Library, Armor Research Library, Fort Benning, Georgia, Call #D787.2.H91, 1–13.
37. Colonel Francis G. Brink, "TAB G, Conclusions Reached with Regard to Employment of LRP Units," in Brink, "Summary of Organization & Training," 3.
38. Birtle, *U.S. Army Counterinsurgency and Contingency Operations Doctrine, 1942–1976*, 374–76.
39. U.S. Army Infantry School, *Selected Readings in Guerrilla and Counterguerrilla Operations*, 106; Sacquety, *The OSS in Burma*, 112–33.
40. Alan Barker, *Merrill's Marauders* (New York: Ballantine Books, 1972), 37–39; Sacquety, *The OSS in Burma*, 125–33.
41. See Dennis R. Okerstrom, *Project 9: The Birth of Air Commandos in World War II* (Columbia: University of Missouri Press, 2014), 35–95; R. D. Van Wagner, *Any Place, Any Time, Any Where: The 1st Air Commandos in World War II* (Atglen, PA: Schiffer Military/Aviation History, 1998).
42. Wagner, *Any Place, Any Time, Any Where*, 21–82.
43. U.S. Army Infantry School, *Selected Readings in Guerrilla and Counterguerrilla Operations*, 106.
44. Hogan, *U.S. Army Special Operations in World War II*, 11–12.
45. Ibid., 13–15.
46. Ibid., 15–23.
47. U.S. Army Infantry School, *Selected Readings in Guerrilla and Counterguerrilla Operations*, 106.
48. Hogan, *U.S. Army Special Operations in World War II*.
49. Birtle, *U.S. Army Counterinsurgency and Contingency Operations, 1942–1976*.
50. Colonel Ben S. Malcom, U.S. Army (Ret.), *White Tigers: My Secret War in North Korea* (London: Brassey's, 1996), 30–120.
51. Kelly, *U.S. Army Special Forces, 1961–1971*, 1–18; Birtle, *U.S. Army Counterinsurgency and Contingency Operations, 1942–1976*, 85–250.
52. Historians Andrew F. Krepinevich and George Herring are but two examples of individuals who have perpetuated this "myth" that the Army was unprepared to fight a counterinsurgency in South Vietnam. Andrew F. Krepinevich, Jr., *The Army and Vietnam* (Baltimore, MD: Johns Hopkins University Press, 1986), 100–127, 194–233, respectively; George Herring, *America's Longest War: The United States and Vietnam, 1950–1975* (New York: John Wiley and Sons, 1979).
53. There is an abundance of literature insofar as Army doctrine for counterinsurgency operations is concerned produced prior to and during the U.S. Army's deployment to South Vietnam in the summer of 1965. See FM 31-15, *Operations Against Irregular Warfare* (1961); FM 33-5, *Psychological Operations—Techniques and Procedures* (1961); FM 41-45, *Joint Manual for Civil Affairs* (1966); FM 100-20, *Field Service Regulations: Internal Defense and Development* (1967); FM 31-23, *Stability Operations: U.S. Army Doctrine*; FM 31-16, *Counterguerrilla Operations* (1967); and FM 31-18, *Long-Range Reconnaissance Patrol Company* (1968).
54. Ron Milam, *Not a Gentleman's War: An Inside View of Junior Officers in the Vietnam War* (Chapel Hill: University of North Carolina Press, 2009), 50–95.
55. Milam, *Not a Gentleman's War*; Leo J. Daugherty, III, PhD, "A New Page in the ROTC Concept: ROTC Entry-Level Training and Fort Knox, 1965–2014," *Register of the Kentucky Historical Society* 119, no. 4 (Autumn 2021): 387–420.
56. Milam, *Not a Gentleman's War*, 51.
57. Brigadier General J. S. Timothy, U.S. Army, Assistant Commandant, U.S. Army infantry School, Fort Benning, Georgia, to Major General Kelsie L. Reaves, Deputy Chief of Staff for Individual Training, United States Continental Army Command, Fort Monroe, Virginia, March 6, 1967, Subject: "Haines Board Recommendations," U.S. Army Maneuver Center of Excellence HQ Donovan Research Library, Armor Research Library,

Reference Section, Fort Benning, Georgia; Lieutenant Colonel H.R. Smothers, U.S. Army, Chairman, Curriculum Review Committee, February 24, 1967, Subject: "Curriculum Review Committee, Combat Platoon Leader's Five-Week Course, for the Purposes of Reviewing and Recommending Improvements in the Content of the Program of Instruction (POI) and the Five and Nine Week Basic Course," at U.S. Army Maneuver Center of Excellence HQ Donovan Research Library, Reference Section, Fort Benning, Georgia.
  58. Milam, *Not a Gentleman's War*, 51–52.
  59. Haines Board Recommendations and U.S. Army Infantry School Comments on the Haines Board Report, March 21, 1966, Reference U408.3, U.S. Infantry School Library, U.S. Army Maneuver Center of Excellence HQ Donovan Research Library, Armor Research Library, Reference Section, Fort Benning, Georgia, 75.
  60. *Ibid.*, 76.
  61. *Ibid.*, "Recommendation 5, para.5 (cont)," 4.
  62. *Ibid.*
  63. Smothers, "Curriculum Review Committee, Combat Platoon Leader's Five-Week Course, for the Purpose of Reviewing and Recommending improvements in the Content of the Program of Instruction (POI) and the Five and Nine Week Basic Course," 3.
  64. Daugherty, "A New Page in the ROTC Concept."
  65. Krepinevich, *The Army and Vietnam*, 164.
  66. Birtle, *U.S. Army Counterinsurgency and Contingency Operations Doctrine, 1942–1976*, 368.
  67. *Ibid.*
  68. 321 kilometers equals approximately 278 square miles.
  69. Birtle, *U.S. Army Counterinsurgency and Contingency Operations Doctrine, 1942–1976*, 368–69.
  70. *Ibid.*, 369.
  71. *Ibid.*, 370.
  72. Mao, *Selected Military Writings*, 154.
  73. Birtle, *U.S. Army Counterinsurgency and Contingency Operations Doctrine, 1942–1976*, 370.
  74. *Ibid.*, 371.
  75. *Ibid.*, 371–73.
  76. *Ibid.*, 374.
  77. Birtle, *U.S. Army Counterinsurgency and Contingency Operations Doctrine, 1942–1976*, 375; Larry Chambers, *RECONDO: LRRPs in the 101st Airborne* (New York: Ballantine Books, 2003), xi–xix. See also Gary Linderer, *Black Berets and Painted Faces: The Story of a LRP in Vietnam* (New York: Doubleday Book & Music Clubs, 1991), 5–27.
  78. Chambers, *RECONDO*, xii–xiii.
  79. *Ibid.*, xvii–xviii.
  80. *Ibid.*, xix.
  81. Birtle, *U.S. Army Counterinsurgency Doctrine and Contingency Operations Doctrine, 1942–1976*, 376; Krepinevich, *The Army and Vietnam*, 231.
  82. Birtle, *U.S. Army Counterinsurgency Doctrine and Contingency Operations Doctrine, 1942–1976*, 376.
  83. Frank Camper, *L.R.R.P.: The Professional* (New York: Dell, 1988), 8.
  84. See Change No. 1, "Long-Range Reconnaissance Ranger Companies," Headquarters, Department of the Army, March 7, 1969, in FM 31-18, *Long-Range Reconnaissance Patrol Company* (Washington, DC: Headquarters, Department of the Army, August 1968), C-1 (hereafter cited as FM 31-18, *Long-Range Reconnaissance Patrol*).
  85. *Ibid.*, 3.
  86. Camper, *L.R.R.P.*, 9.
  87. FM 31-18, *Long-Range Reconnaissance Patrol*, 3.
  88. *Ibid.*, 4.
  89. Phillips, *A Shau: Crucible of the Vietnam War*, 370–402.
  90. FM 31-18, *Long-Range Reconnaissance Patrol*, 5.
  91. Krepinevich, *The Army and Vietnam*, 232.
  92. *Ibid.*
  93. Phillips, *A Shau: Crucible of the Vietnam War*, 402–41.

Chapter 14

  1. Vetter, *Never Without Heroes*, 307.
  2. Meyers, *Fortune Favors the Brave*, 42–190; Stubbe, *Aarugha!*, 65–125; Kyle Watts, "'The Flying Ladder': Emergency Extractions and the Lifesaver from the Sky," *Leatherneck* 101, no. 4 (April 2018): 22–31.
  3. Babin comments.
  4. Dwight Jon Zimmerman, "Marine Force Recon in Vietnam and the Killer Kane Operations," Defense Media Network, July 8, 2010, https://www.defensemedianetwork.com/stories/marine-force-recon-in-vietnam-and-the-killer-kane-operations/.
  5. Babin comments.

Appendix C

  1. Team Hateful, a platoon from 1st Force Reconnaissance Company, consisted of two officers, twelve enlisted Marines, and one Navy corpsman. Commanded by First Lieutenant Richard F. Parker, Jr., the platoon-size force was part of a "Provisional Reconnaissance Group," combining elements of 1st Force Reconnaissance and 3rd Reconnaissance Battalion. The action occurred near Quang Ngai and Binh Dinh Provinces bordering I and II Corps during Operation "Double Eagle I" (January 21–February 16, 1966).
  2. First Lieutenant James T. Egan, Jr., USMC, from Mountainside, New Jersey, was officially listed as missing in action; his body was never found.

Appendix F

  1. Colonel Andrew R. Finlayson, USMC (Ret.), to Lieutenant Colonel Berwick Babin, Leo J. Daugherty, III, December 3, 2021.

2. See chapters 5 and 6 in this book for more information about STINGRAY missions.

3. Colonel Andrew R. Finlayson, USMC (Ret.), to Lieutenant Colonel Berwick Babin, USMC (Ret.), Leo J. Daugherty, III, PhD, December 3, 2021, Subject: "Marine Corps Reconnaissance during the Vietnam War 1963–March 1971."

Appendix H

1. Lieutenant Colonel Berwick Babin, USMC (Ret.), to Colonel Andrew R. Finlayson, USMC (Ret.), Leo J. Daugherty, III, PhD, December 2, 2021.

Appendix I

1. Sergeant William Moss, "My Story," original unpublished manuscript in possession of the author. Reprinted with permission from Corporal Moss.

Bibliography

Primary Sources

Personal Interviews

Babin, Lieutenant Colonel Berwick, USMC (Ret.), 3rd Force Reconnaissance Company and 3rd Reconnaissance Battalion.
Broman, Major Barry, USMC (Ret.).
Fahlstrom, Lance Corporal Steven A., USMC (Ret.), 3rd Force Reconnaissance Company; 3rd Reconnaissance Battalion, 3rd Marine Division.
Finlayson, Colonel Andrew R., USMC (Ret.), 1st Force Reconnaissance Company; Provincial Reconnaissance Unit.
Kern, Corporal Lou, USMC, 3rd Force Reconnaissance Company.
Menning, Sergeant Butch, USMC, 3rd Force Reconnaissance Company.
Moss, Corporal William, USMC, 3rd Force Reconnaissance Company.
Norton, Major Bruce H. "Doc," USMC (Ret.).
Sloss, Joseph, 3rd Force Reconnaissance Company.
Tolleson, Colonel Frederick, USMC (Ret.) (Deceased).
Vogel, Colonel John, USMC (Ret.), 1st Force Reconnaissance Company.

Oral Histories

Barrow, General Robert H., USMC (Deceased). "Oral History of General Robert H. Barrow," interviewed by Edgar F. Puryear. Tape 121, Side B-13–14. Washington, DC, 2004.
Davis, General Raymond G. (Ret.). "Oral History Interview of General Raymond G. Davis, USMC (Ret.)," interviewed by Benis M. Frank. Washington, DC: History & Museums Division, HQMC, 1978.
First Lieutenant Wayne E. Rollings Oral History Collection, USMC, Historical Division, HQMC, Marine Corps History Division, Marine Corps Combat Development Center, Quantico, Virginia. No. 4688: "Paradrop Insertion in RVN."
Houghton, Major General Kenneth J., USMC (Ret.). "The Oral History Field Interview of Colonel Kenneth J. Houghton, USMC," Field Interview No. 1189, conducted by Master Sergeant Robert H. Olivia, USMC, Command Post, 5th Marine Regiment, 1st Marine Division, at Quang Nam Province, Da Nang TAOR, RVN, June 29, 1967. Interview in Oral History Section, History Division, HQMC, Marine Corps University, Marine Corps Combat Development Center, Quantico, Virginia.
———. "The Oral History Interview of Major General Kenneth J. Houghton, USMC," interviewed by Benis Frank. Washington, DC: History & Museums Division, HQMC, 1978.
Peatross, Major General Oscar F., USMC (Ret.). "The Oral History Interview of Major General Oscar F. Peatross, USMC," interviewed by Benis M. Frank. Washington, DC: History & Museums Division, HQMC, 1973.
"Reconnaissance Operations in the 'Scotland II' Area of Operations." Interviews done at Dong Ha Combat Base, June 18, 1968 (Captain Phillip F. Reynolds, USMC; First Lieutenant Donald W. Blair, USMC; Second Lieutenant Willis M. Gregory, USMC; Corporal Arthur W. Wheat, USMC; Corporal O. L. Janis, USMC; Sergeant Danny M. Sloan, USMC; Sergeant David E. Metz, USMC; Sergeant William P. Cress, USMC; Corporal Billy (Berwick) P. Babin, USMC; Corporal Harlan E. Holmes, USMC; Sergeant Robert L. Nixton, USMC; HM3 David T. Tolleson, USN; Corporal Alston E. Lancaster, USMC). Tape 2918, Marine Corps History Division, Oral History Section, Marine Corps University, Marine Corps Combat Development Center, MCB, Quantico, Virginia.
Trainor, Lieutenant General Bernard M., USMC (Ret.). "Oral History Transcript: Lieutenant General Bernard M. Trainor, USMC (Ret.)," interviewed by Benis M. Frank. U.S. Marine Corps History Division, Quantico, Virginia, 2015.
Wycoff, Don P. Interviewed by Second Lieutenant J.F. Zachian, USMC, Henderson Hall, Washington, DC. Washington, DC: Oral History Section, History Section, HQMC.

Personal Papers

The Papers and Correspondence of General Joseph W. Stilwell, U.S. Army (Deceased), Hoover Institution, Stanford University, Stanford, California.

The Papers of Major General Frank Dow Merrill, U.S. Army (Deceased), University of New Hampshire, Special Collections, Library, Durham, New Hampshire.

The Papers of Major General Oscar F. Peatross, USMC (Deceased), Marine Corps Recruit Depot, Parris Island, South Carolina, Command Museum, Reference Section.

Command Chronologies

United States Marine Corps, Command Chronologies for 1st Force Reconnaissance Company, FMF, 1966–1970. Texas Tech University, Sam Johnson Vietnam Center.

United States Marine Corps, Command Chronologies for 1st Marine Reconnaissance Battalion, FMF, 1966–1971. Texas Tech University, Sam Johnson Vietnam Center.

United States Marine Corps, Command Chronologies for 3rd Force Reconnaissance Battalion, FMF, 1966–1970. Texas Tech University, Sam Johnson Vietnam Center.

United States Marine Corps, Command Chronologies for 3rd Force Reconnaissance Company, FMF, 1966–1970. Texas Tech University, Sam Johnson Vietnam Center.

Official Documents and Reports

Anderson, M., M. Arnsten, and H. Averch. *Insurgent Organization and Operations: A Case Study of the Viet Cong in the Delta, 1964–1966*. Memorandum RM-5239-I-ISA/ARPA. Santa Monica, CA: Rand Corporation, August 1967. Prepared for the Office of the Assistant Secretary of Defense/International Security Affairs and the Advanced Research Projects Agency.

Brewster, Lieutenant Colonel David L., USMC, Executive Officer, 5th Marine Regiment, Fleet Marine Force. Training Directive, Number 8-39, "Debarkation from Boats," October 17, 1939. In Historical Amphibious File 60, Marine Corps History Division, Reference Section, Marine Corps University, Marine Corps Combat Development Center, Quantico, Virginia.

Brink, Colonel Francis G., U.S. Army. "Summary of Organization & Training of the 5307th Composite Unit (U.S. Long Range Penetration Unit) for Burma Operations," CBI, April 6, 1944. U.S. Army Maneuver Center of Excellence HQ Donovan Research Library, Armor Research Library, Fort Benning, Georgia, Call #D787.2B77.

Central Intelligence Agency Intelligence Memorandum. "The Status of the North Vietnamese Divisions in Coastal II Corps." Directorate of Intelligence, November 25, 1967. Declassified June 26, 2018, #C02902656.

Commanding Officer, Naval Amphibious Test and Evaluating Unit to Commander Amphibious Force, U.S. Atlantic Fleet, via Commander, Amphibious Training Command, U.S. Atlantic Fleet. Subject: "Final Report on ASSP Project: Evaluate the U.S. S. SEA LION (ASSP-15) as a Troop Carrier Submarine," June 16, 1952. In Historical Amphibious File 79, Marine Corps History Division, Reference Section, Alfred M. Gray Library, Marine Corps University, Marine Corps Combat Development Center, Quantico, Virginia.

Ellis, Lieutenant Colonel Earl H., USMC. "Advanced Base Operations in Micronesia." Approved by Major General Commandant, Headquarters Marine Corps, 1921.

Finn, First Lieutenant R.B., USMCR, Assistant S-2, 5th Marines. "Amphibious Reconnaissance Training"; Information Sheet: "Recon Marines," all in Reference Folder 1, Marine Corps Reconnaissance, at History Division, Marine Corps University, Marine Corps Combat Development Center, MCB, Quantico, Virginia.

Haines Board Recommendations and U.S. Army Infantry School Comments on the Haines Board Report, March 21, 1966. Reference U408.3. U.S. Army Infantry School Library, U.S. Army Maneuver Center of Excellence HQ Donovan Research Library, Armor Research Library, Reference Section, Fort Benning, Georgia.

Heywood, Major General Commandant Charles. *Annual Report of the Secretary of the Navy for 1903*. Washington, DC: Government Printing Office, 1903.

Hunter, Colonel Charles N., U.S. Army. "Report on Overseas Observations: Report Summary of the 5307th Composite Unit (Provisional), Merrill's Marauders, and Other Units in the China Burma Theater," February 17, 1945. U.S. Army Maneuver Center of Excellence HQ Donovan Research Library, Armor Research Library, Fort Benning, Georgia, Call #D787.2.H91.

Riddle, Lieutenant Colonel William S., U.S. Army, Assistant Military Attaché. "Planning and Execution of a Seaborne Raid," attached in a letter from G.I. Russell, by direction for Commander-in-Chief, United States Fleet, to the Commandant of the Marine Corps, March 16, 1942, Subject: "Planning and Execution of a Seaborne Raid," London. Report 46174, College Park, Maryland, National Archives and Records Administration, FF-1/A82, Serial No. 0392, U.S. Marine Corps War Planning Section, File No. 13048.

Smith, General Holland M., USMC. "Comments: Outline of Volume V, History of U.S. Marine Corps Operations in World War II," #27, in the General Holland M. Smith, USMC Papers, Marine Corps History Division, Reference Section, Marine Corps University, Marine Corps Combat Development Center, Quantico, Virginia. Box 9 of 12, PC 382, "Special Units, VI, 2:77–2:82."

Smothers, Lieutenant Colonel H.R., U.S. Army, Chairman, Curriculum Review Committee, February 24, 1967, Subject: "Curriculum Review Committee, Combat Platoon Leader's Five-Week Course, for the Purposes of

Reviewing and Recommending Improvements in the Content of the Program of Instruction (POI) and the Five and Nine Week Basic Course." U.S. Army Maneuver Center of Excellence HQ Donovan Research Library, Reference Section, Fort Benning, Georgia.

Timothy, Brigadier General J.S., U.S. Army, Assistant Commandant, U.S. Army Infantry School, Fort Benning, Georgia, to Major General Kelsie L. Reaves, Deputy Chief of Staff for Individual Training, United States Continental Army Command, Fort Monroe, Virginia, March 6, 1967, Subject: "Haines Board Recommendations." U.S. Army Maneuver Center of Excellence HQ Donovan Research Library, Armor Research Library, Reference Section, Fort Benning, Georgia.

Van Ness, First Lieutenant C. P., USMC. "The Development and Procurement of Special Landing Boats for the Marine Corps." In Historical Amphibious File 124, Marine Corps History Division, Reference Section, Marine Corps University, Marine Corps Combat Development Center, Quantico, Virginia.

Williams, Major Dion, USMC. "The Advanced Base Force." Lecture delivered at the United States Naval War College, July 26, 1917. Washington, DC: Government Printing Office, 1912. Found in Historical Amphibious File 211, Marine Corps History Division, Reference Section, Marine Corps University, Marine Corps Combat Development Center, Quantico, Virginia.

_____. *Naval Reconnaissance: Instructions for the Reconnaissance of Bays, Harbors and Adjacent Country*. Washington, DC: Government Printing Office, 1906.

_____. *Naval Reconnaissance: Instructions for the Reconnaissance of Bays, Harbors and Adjacent Country*. Second edition. Washington, DC: Government Printing Office, 1917.

U.S. Army Doctrinal Publications

Department of the Army. Field Manual (FM) 31-16, *Counterguerrilla Operations*. Washington, DC: Headquarters, Department of the Army, March 1967.

_____. FM 31-18, *Long-Range Reconnaissance Patrol Company*. Washington, DC: Headquarters, Department of the Army, August 1968.

_____. FM 31-21, *Guerilla Warfare and Special Forces Operations*. Washington, DC: Headquarters, Department of the Army, May 1958.

_____. FM 31-22, *U.S. Army Counterinsurgency Forces*. Washington, DC: Headquarters, Department of the Army, November 1963.

_____. FM 31-23, *Stability Operations: U.S. Army Doctrine*. Washington, DC: Headquarters, Department of the Army, 1967.

_____. FM 33-5, *Psychological Operations—Techniques and Procedures*. Washington, DC: Headquarters, Department of the Army, 1961.

_____. FM 100-20, *Field Service Regulations: Internal Defense and Development*. Washington, DC: Headquarters, Department of the Army, 1967.

_____. Pamphlet 381-10, *Weapons and Equipment Recognition Guide, Southeast Asia*. Washington, DC: Headquarters, Department of the Army, January 1966.

United States Army Infantry School. *Selected Readings in Guerrilla and Counterguerrilla Operations*. Fort Benning, GA: United States Army Infantry School, Brigade and Battalion Operations Department, August 1966.

U.S. Marine Corps Doctrinal Publications

U.S. Marine Corps. *Amphibious Reconnaissance: Landing Force Manual*. Washington, DC: HQMC, 1958.

U.S. Marine Corps. FMFM 2-2, *Amphibious Reconnaissance (1963), Coordinator, Marine Corps Landing Force Development Activities*. Washington, DC: HQMC, 1963.

U.S. Marine Corps. FMFM 2-2, *Amphibious Reconnaissance (1965), Coordinator, Marine Corps Landing Forces Development Activities*. Washington, DC: HQMC, 1965.

U.S. Marine Corps. FMFM 2-2, *Amphibious Reconnaissance (1976)*. Washington, DC: HQMC, 1976.

U.S. Marine Corps. *United States Marine Corps Reference Data, Volume II*. Washington, DC: HQMC, 1968.

U.S. Navy Doctrinal Publications

Division of Fleet Training, Office of Naval Operations. *United States Navy, Landing Operations Doctrine, Fleet Training Publication 167*. Washington, DC: Government Printing Office, 1938.

Unpublished Manuscripts and Theses

Camp, Colonel Richard D., USMC (Ret.). Manuscript on General Robert H. Barrow, USMC (Deceased) in the General Robert H. Barrow Papers, Box 16, Folder 1. Marine Corps Museum, Reference Section, Marine Corps Recruit Depot, Parris Island, South Carolina.

Daugherty, Leo J., III. "The U.S. Marine Corps and the Advanced Base Force, 1898–1903." Master of Arts Thesis, John Carroll University, Cleveland, Ohio, 1985.

Griffith, Lieutenant Colonel Samuel B., II. "Jungle Warfare." Unpublished manuscript written at Marine Corps Schools, Marine Barracks, Quantico, Virginia; Historical Amphibious File 537, Marine Corps History Division, Reference Section, Marine Corps University, Marine Corps Combat Development Center, Quantico, Virginia.

Melson, Charles D. (Chief Historian), Headquarters, U.S. Marine Corps. "Marine Recon: From

World War to Cold War." Unpublished paper delivered at the Society of Military History, 1993.

Simonds, Brigadier General George S. *Jungle Combat Principles*. 20th Infantry Brigade, U.S. Army, Panama Canal Zone (Xeroxed copy, 1925, in possession of author).

U.S. Congress, House of Representatives, Congressional Testimony (1971)

Lownds, Colonel David, USMC. *Comments by Colonel David Lownds, USMC, United States Congress, Senate Armed Services Committee, Permanent Investigations Subcommittee, Hearings on the Electronic Battlefield Program, 91st Congress, 2nd Session*. Washington, DC: Government Printing Office, 1971.

Official Histories (United States)

Birtle, Andrew J. *U.S. Army Counterinsurgency and Contingency Operations Doctrine, 1860–1941*. Washington, DC: Center of Military History, Headquarters, Department of the Army, 2011.

———. *U.S. Army Counterinsurgency and Contingency Operations Doctrine, 1942–1976*. Washington, DC: Center of Military History, Department of the Army, 2007.

Conn, Stetson, Rose C. Engelman, and Byron Fairchild. *United States Army in World War II: The Western Hemisphere, Guarding the United States and Its Outposts*. Washington, DC: Center of Military History, U.S. Army, 1989.

Daugherty, Leo J., III. *Train Wreckers and Ghost Killers: Allied Marines in the Korean War*. Washington, DC: History & Museums Division, HQMC, 2003.

Frank, Benis M., and Henry I. Shaw, Jr. *Victory and Occupation: Volume V, History of U.S. Marine Corps Operations in World War II*. Washington, DC: Historical Branch, G-3 Division, HQMC, 1968.

Garand, George W., and Truman R. Strobridge. *Western Pacific Operations: History of U.S. Marine Corps Operations in World War II, Volume IV*. Washington, DC: Historical Division, HQMC, 1971.

Hoffman, Lieutenant Colonel Jon T., USMCR. *Silk Chutes and Hard Fighting: U.S. Marine Corps Parachute Units in World War II*. Washington, DC: History & Museums Division, HQMC, 1999.

Hogan, David W., Jr. *U.S. Army Special Operations in World War II*. Washington, DC: Center of Military History, 1992.

Howe, George F. *United States Army in World War II: The European Theater of Operations—Northwest Africa: Seizing the Initiative in the West*. Washington, DC: Center of Military History, 2002.

Kelly, Colonel Francis J., U.S. Army (Ret.). *U.S. Army Special Forces, 1961–1971*. Washington, DC: Department of the Army, 1973.

Marion, Forrest L. *Brothers in Berets: The Evolution of Air Force Special Tactics, 1953–2003*. Montgomery, AL: General Curtis E. LeMay Center for Doctrine Development and Education, Maxwell Air Force Base, 2018.

Mattingly, Major Robert E., USMC. *Herringbone Cloak—G.I. Dagger: Marines of the OSS* (Occasional Paper). Washington, DC: History & Museums Division, HQMC, 1989.

Nalty, Bernard C. *The United States Marines and the War with Spain*. Washington, DC: Historical Branch, G-3 Division, HQMC, 1967.

Prieto, Julie Irene. *The Mexican Expedition, 1916–1917*. Washington, DC: Center of Military History, 2016.

Rearden, Steven L. *History of the Office of the Secretary of Defense: Volume I, The Formative Years, 1947–1950*. Washington, DC: Historical Office, Office of the Secretary of Defense, 1984.

Roberts, Jerry A. *U.S. Marines in Battle: Guantanamo Bay, 10 June–9 August 1898*. Quantico, VA: Marine Corps History Division, Marine Corps University Press, 2020.

Shaw, Henry I., and Major Douglas T. Kane, USMC. *Isolation of Rabaul: History of U.S. Marine Corps Operations in World War II*. Washington, DC: Historical Branch, G-3, HQMC, 1963.

Shaw, Henry I., Bernard C. Nalty, and Edwin T. Turnbladh. *Central Pacific Drive: History of U.S. Marine Corps Operations in World War II*. Washington, DC: Historical Branch, G-3, HQMC, 1966.

Shulimson, Jack. *U.S. Marines in Vietnam: An Expanding War, 1966*. Washington, DC: History & Museums Division, HQMC, 1982.

Shulimson, Jack, Lieutenant Colonel Leonard A. Blaisol, USMC, Charles R. Smith, and David A. Dawson. *U.S. Marines in Vietnam: The Defining Year, 1968*. Washington, DC: History & Museums Division, HQMC, 1997.

Shulimson, Jack, and Major Charles M. Johnson. *U.S. Marines in Vietnam: The Landing and the Buildup, 1965*. Washington, DC: History & Museums Division, HQMC, 1978.

Simmons, Brigadier General Edwin H., USMC (Ret.), et al. *The Marines in Vietnam, 1954–1973: An Anthology and Annotated Bibliography*. Second edition. Washington, DC: History & Museums Division, HQMC, 1985.

Smith, Charles R. *U.S. Marines in Vietnam: High Mobility and Standdown, 1969*. Washington, DC: History & Museums Division, HQMC, 1988.

Spector, Ronald H. *Advise and Support: The Early Years—The U.S. Army in Vietnam*. Washington, DC: Center of Military History, 1983.

Stubbe, Ray W. *Aarugha! Report to the Director, Historical Division, Headquarters, Marine Corps, on the History of Specialized and Force-Level Reconnaissance Activities and Units* of the United States Marine Corps, 1900–1974. Reprinted as FMFRP (Fleet Marine Force Reference Publication) 12-21. Quantico, VA: HQMC, Marine Corps Combat Development Center, May 1989.

Tefler, Major Gary L., USMC, Lieutenant Colonel Lane Rogers, USMC, and V. Keith Fleming. *U.S. Marines in Vietnam: Fighting the North Vietnamese, 1967.* Washington, DC: History & Museums Division, 1984.

Updegraph, Charles L. *U.S. Marine Corps Special Units of World War II.* Washington, DC: History & Museums Division, HQMC, 1972 (reprinted 1977).

West, Captain Francis J., Jr., USMCR. *Small Unit Action in Vietnam, 1966.* Washington, DC: History & Museums Division, 1967 (reprinted 1977).

Whitlow, Captain Robert H., USMCR. *U.S. Marines in Vietnam: The Advisory & Combat Assistance Era, 1954–1964.* Washington, DC: History & Museums Division, HQMC, 1977.

Zimmerman, Major John L., USMCR. *The Guadalcanal Campaign.* Washington, DC: Historical Division, HQMC, 1949 (reprinted: Chicago: Lancaster Publications).

Official Histories (United Kingdom)

Combined Operations Command (COC), Ministry of Information. *Combined Operations.* London: Her Majesty's Stationary Office, 1942.

Foot, M.R.D. *SOE in France: An Account of the Work of the British Special Operations Executive in France, 1940–1944.* London: Her Majesty's Stationary Office, 1966.

Memoirs

Camper, Frank. *L.R.R.P.: The Professional.* New York: Dell, 1988.

Caputo, Phillip A. *A Rumor of War.* New York: Holt, Rhinehart, and Winston, 1977.

Chambers, Larry. *RECONDO: LRRPs in the 101st Airborne.* New York: Ballantine Books, 2003.

Delezen, John Edmund. *Eye of the Tiger: Memoir of a United States Marine, Third Force Recon Company, Vietnam.* Jefferson, NC: McFarland, 2003.

Del Valle, Lieutenant General Pedro A., USMC (Ret.). *Roman Eagles Over Ethiopia.* Harrisburg, PA: Military Service Publishing Company, 1940.

_____. *Semper Fidelis: An Autobiography.* Hawthorne, CA: Christian Book Club of America, 1976.

Finlayson, Andrew R. *Killer Kane: A Marine Long-Range Recon Team Leader in Vietnam, 1967–1968.* Jefferson, NC: McFarland, 2013.

_____. *Rice Paddy Recon: A Marine Officer's Second Tour in Vietnam.* Jefferson, NC: McFarland, 2014.

Fleming, Richard. *Chasing Charlie: A Force Recon Marine in Vietnam.* Jefferson, NC: McFarland, 2018.

Hamblen, First Sergeant Donald H., USMC (Ret.), and Major Bruce H. Norton, USMC (Ret.). *One Tough Marine: The Autobiography of First Sergeant Donald H. Hamblen, USMC.* New York: Ballantine Books, 1993.

Hemingway, Al. *Our War Was Different: Marine Combined Action Platoons in Vietnam.* Annapolis, MD: Naval Institute Press, 1994.

Hodgins, Michael C. *Reluctant Warrior: A Marine's True Story of Duty and Heroism in Vietnam.* New York: Ballantine Books, 1996.

Hunter, Colonel Charles N. *Galahad.* San Antonio, TX: Naylor Publishing Company, 1963.

Jack, Sergeant Major W., USMC. *Diary of Sergeant Major W. Jack, 1st Force Reconnaissance for 1968.* Quantico, VA: Marine Corps Archives, Collection #2544, PC 3286, 1968–1969, Marine Corps University, Marine Corps Combat Development Center (unpublished).

Kington, Randy. *What a Life! How the Vietnam War Affected One Marine.* Third printing. Marco Island, FL: Keller Publishing, 2010.

Lee, Lieutenant Colonel Alex, USMC (Ret.). *Force Recon Command: 3rd Force Recon Company in Vietnam, 1969–1970.* New York: Ballantine Books, 1995.

Linderer, Gary. *Black Berets and Painted Faces: The Story of a LRP in Vietnam.* New York: Doubleday Book & Music Clubs, 1991.

Malcom, Colonel Benjamin S., U.S. Army (Ret.). *White Tigers: My Secret War in North Korea.* London: Brassey's, 1996.

Mao Tse-Tung. *Selected Military Writings of Mao Tse-Tung.* Peking: Foreign Language Press, 1963.

Norton, Bruce H. *Force Recon Diary, 1969.* New York: Ivy Books, 1991.

Ogburn, Charlton, Jr. *The Marauders.* New York: Harper & Brothers, 1959.

Peters, Bill. *First Force Recon Company: Sunrise at Midnight.* New York: Ballantine Books, 1999.

Rhodes, John R. *Rejoice or Cry: Diary of a Recon Marine Vietnam, 1967–1968.* Danbury, CT: Economy, 1996.

Smith, General Holland M., USMC, and Percy Finch. *Coral and Brass.* New York/Washington, DC: Charles Scribner's Sons/Zenger Publishing Company, 1949/1979.

Smith, James. *Diary of James Smith, 3rd Reconnaissance Battalion, 3rd Marine Division, Dong Ha, Republic of Vietnam, 1967, "3-Charlie-1"* (copy in possession of the author).

Biographies

Ballendorf, Dirk A., and Merrill L. Bartlett. *Pete Ellis: An Amphibious Warfare Prophet, 1880–1923.* Annapolis, MD: Naval Institute Press, 1997.

Camp, Colonel Richard D., USMC (Ret.). *Three War Marine Hero: General Raymond G. Davis, USMC.* Philadelphia, PA: Casemate, 2020.

Norton, Major Bruce H., and Sergeant Major Maurice J. Jacques, USMC (Ret.). *Sergeant Major: The*

Biography of Sergeant Major Maurice J. Jacques, USMC. New York: Ivy/Ballantine Books, 1995.
Smythe, Donald W. *Guerrilla Warrior: The Early Life of John J. Pershing*. New York: Charles Scribner's Sons, 1973.
Wheeler, Gerald E. *Kinkaid of the Seventh Fleet: A Biography of Admiral Thomas C. Kinkaid, U.S. Navy*. Washington, DC: Naval Historical Center, Department of the Navy, 1995.

Conferences

Daugherty, Leo J., III, PhD. "Commandos, Royal Marines, Paratroops, and Leathernecks, 1940–1944." Delivered at University of Portsmouth, United Kingdom, 75th Anniversary Conference of the Normandy Landings, July 21–24, 2019.
"More Than Just Good Stories: Special Operations Units as a Lens on Wars and Institutions" (panel), Annual Meeting of the Society of Military History, Fort Worth, Texas, April 28–May 1, 2022.

Secondary Sources

Barker, Alan. *Merrill's Marauders*. New York: Ballantine Books, 1972.
Best, Herbert. *The Webfoot Warriors: The Story of the UDT, the Navy's Underwater Demolition Teams*. New York: John Day Publishers, 1962.
Calvert, Michael. *Chindits: Long Range Penetration*. London: Ballantine Books, 1973.
Daugherty, Leo J., III. *Counterinsurgency and the United States Marine Corps: Volume I, The First Counterinsurgency Era, 1899–1945*. Jefferson, NC: McFarland, 2015.
_____. *Pioneers of Amphibious Warfare, 1898–1945: Profiles of Fourteen American Strategists*. Jefferson, NC: McFarland, 2009.
Daugherty, Leo J., III, and Rhonda L. Smith-Daugherty. *Counterinsurgency and the United States Marine Corps: Volume II, An Era of Persistent Warfare*. Jefferson, NC: McFarland, 2018.
Demiquels, Mark. *U.S. Elite Forces: Uniforms, Equipment, and Personal Items, 1965*. Madrid, Spain: Andrea Press, 2015.
Dorwart, Jeffrey M. *Conflict of Duty: The U.S. Navy's Intelligence Dilemma, 1919–1945*. Annapolis, MD: Naval Institute Press, 1983.
Dunlop, Richard J. *Behind Japanese Lines: With the OSS in Burma*. Chicago: Rand McNally, 1979.
Durnford-Slater, Brigadier John. *Commando: Memoirs of a Fighting Commando in World War II*. Annapolis, MD: Naval Institute Press, 1991.
Henderson, William Darryl. *Why the Viet Cong Fought: A Study of Motivation and Control in a Modern Army in Combat*. Westport, CT: Greenwood Press, 1979.
Herring, George. *America's Longest War: The United States and Vietnam, 1950–1975*. New York: John Wiley and Sons, 1979.
Hess, Gary L. *The United States' Emergence as a Southeast Asian Power, 1940–1950*. New York: Columbia University Press, 1987.
Hoffman, Jon T., USMCR. *Once a Legend: "Red" Mike Edson of the Raiders*. Novato, CA: Presidio Press, 1994.
Hopkins, James E. T., in collaboration with John M. Jones. *Spearhead: A Complete History of Merrill's Marauder Rangers*. Baltimore, MD: Galahad Press, 1999.
Hough, Frank O. *The Island War*. Philadelphia, PA: J. Lippincott, 1947.
Isley, Jeter A., and Phillip A. Crowl. *The U.S. Marines and Amphibious War: Its Theory, and Its Practice in the Pacific*. Princeton, NJ: Princeton University Press, 1951.
Krepinevich, Andrew F. *The Army and Vietnam*. Baltimore, MD: Johns Hopkins University Press, 1986.
Lanning, Michael Lee, and Ray William Stubbe. *Inside Force Recon: Recon Marines in Vietnam*. New York: Ivy Books, 1989.
Lee, David. *Beachhead Assault: The Combat History of the Royal Navy Commandos in World War II*. New York: Skyhorse Publishing, 2017.
Linn, Brian. *The U.S. Army and Counterinsurgency in the Philippine War, 1899–1902*. Chapel Hill: University of North Carolina Press, 1989.
Meyer, Bruce F. *Fortune Favors the Brave: The Story of First Force Recon*. New York: St. Martin's, 2000.
_____. *Swift, Silent, and Deadly: Marine Amphibious Reconnaissance in the Pacific, 1942–1945*. Annapolis, MD: Naval Institute Press, 2004.
Milam, Ron. *Not a Gentleman's War: An Inside View of Junior Officers in the Vietnam War*. Chapel Hill: University of North Carolina Press, 2009.
Millett, Alan R. *Semper Fidelis: The History of the United States Marine Corps*. New York: Macmillan, 1980.
Mortimer, Gavin. *Merrill's Marauders: The Untold Story of Unit Galahad and the Toughest Special Forces Mission of World War II*. Minneapolis, MN: Zenith Press, 2013.
Okerstrom, Dennis R. *Project 9: The Birth of the Air Commandos in World War II*. Columbia: University of Missouri Press, 2014.
Parner, Joe, and Robert Dumont. *SOG Medic: Stories from Vietnam and Over the Fence*. Philadelphia, PA: Casemate Publishing, 2018.
Peters, Bill. *First Force Recon Company: Sunrise at Midnight*. New York: Presidio Press/Random House, 1999.
Phillips, Jay. *A Shau: Crucible of the Vietnam War*. Salt Lake City: Izzard Ink Publishing, 2021.
Pike, Douglas. *PAVN: People's Army of Vietnam*. Novato, CA: Presidio Press, 1986.
_____. *Viet Cong: The Organization and Techniques of the National Liberation Front of South Vietnam*. Cambridge, MA: MIT Press, 1966.
Plaster, John L. *SOG: The Secret Wars of America's Commandos in Vietnam*. New York: NAL Caliber, 1997.
Sacquety, Troy J. *The OSS in Burma: Jungle War*

Against the Japanese. Lawrence: University of Kansas Press, 2013.
Telfer, Major Gary L., USMC, Lieutenant Colonel Lane Rogers, USMC, and V. Keith Fleming, Jr. *U.S. Marines in Vietnam: Fighting the North Vietnamese, 1967*. Washington, DC: History & Museums Division, HQMC, 1984.
Uhlig, Frank, Jr. *Vietnam: The Naval Story*. Annapolis, MD: Naval Institute Press, 1986.
Vetter, Lawrence C., Jr. *Never Without Heroes: Marine Third Reconnaissance Battalion in Vietnam, 1965-1970*. New York: Ballantine Books, 1996.
Wagner, R.D. Van. *Any Place, Any Time, Any Where: The 1st Air Commandos in World War II*. Atglen, PA: Schiffer Military/Aviation History, 1998.

Articles

Arnold, Colonel William A., USAF. "Colonel James L. Jones, Sr., Father of Amphibious Reconnaissance and World War II Hero." *American Intelligence Journal* 35, no. 1 (2018): 29-35.
Coleman, Colonel William F., USMC. "Amphibious Recon Patrols" (Part 1). *Marine Corps Gazette* 29, no. 12 (December 1945): 22-25.
_____. "Amphibious Recon Patrols" (Part 2). *Marine Corps Gazette* 30, no. 1 (January 1946): 13-15.
Cooke, F.O. "They Took Thirty Marines." *The Leatherneck* 28, no. 7 (July 1943).
Daugherty, Leo J. "A New Page in the ROTC Concept: ROTC Entry-Level Training and Fort Knox, 1965-2014." *Register of the Kentucky Historical Society* 119, no. 4 (Autumn 2021): 387-420.
Ellis, Lieutenant Colonel Earl H., USMC. "Bush Brigades." *Marine Corps Gazette* 6, no. 1 (March 1921): 1-15.
Leinster, Colin. "The Two Wars of General Walt." *LIFE*, May 26, 1967.
Martin, Corporal Paul M., USMC. "We Stalk the Enemy." *Marine Corps Gazette* 37, no. 5 (May 1953).
O'Leary, Sergeant Jeremiah A., USMC. "Marine Describes Casablanca: Detachment Manned Ship's Guns." *The Quantico Sentry*, U.S. Marine Historical Division, Reference Section, "Marines in Europe Folder," Marine Corps University, Marine Corps Combat Development Center, Quantico, Virginia.
Reber, John J. "Huntington's Battalion Was the Forerunner of Today's FMF." *Marine Corps Gazette* 63, no. 11 (November 1979): 73-79.
Shinn, First Lieutenant Leo B., USMC. "Amphibious Reconnaissance." *Marine Corps Gazette* 29, no. 4 (April 1945): 50-51.
Watts, Kyle. "'First to Fight': 1st Force Reconnaissance in Hue City." *Leatherneck* 101, no. 2 (February 2018): 24-35.
_____. "'The Flying Ladder': Emergency Extractions and the Lifesaver from the Sky." *Leatherneck* 101, no. 4 (April 2018): 22-31.
_____. "Recon Doc." *Leatherneck* 102, no. 4 (April 2019): 54-59.
Zimmerman, Dwight Jon. "Marine Force Recon in Vietnam and the Killer Kane Operations." Defense Media Network, July 8, 2010. https://www.defensemedianetwork.com/stories/marine-force-recon-in-vietnam-and-the-killer-kane-operations/.

Index

Numbers in ***bold italics*** indicate pages with illustrations

Admiralty, Royal Navy (UK) 25, 29
Advanced Base Operations in Micronesia (1921; Ellis) 10–11, 49–55
Advanced Bases 1, 16; "Advanced Base Auxiliaries" 11; Advanced Base Doctrine 1, Advanced Base Exercises (Culebra, Puerto Rico) 8; Advanced Base Force 8
"Agent Orange" 104
Air Officer (AO): "Hostage Pogo" 249; "Hostage Stud" 249
Aircraft, B-29 59; B-52 Bomber 220, 291; C-47 "Dakota" transport 262; C-130 Transport 90; Cessna O-1G "Birddog" 215; Douglas R4D-8 80; EA-6A Prowler 215, 219; F-3D "Skynights" 215; F4 Phantom B 135, 215, 219, 301; F-8 Crusaders 91, 131; Grumman A-6 Intruder ***217***, 230; Grumman TF-1 Trader aircraft 80; OV-10A "Bronco" 215, ***216***, 219; "peeping and snooping" 218; P2V Neptune (U.S. Navy) 75; Phantom II 215, 216; Sikorsky (Helicopter), YR-4 Helicopter 262; "Spooky" C-47 gunship 227, 245; 250-lb "snake eye bombs" 301
Alaska, Adak 40, 72, 73
Aleutians Islands 40–44
Amphibious Corps, Atlantic Fleet 21–22
Amphibious Transport 33
Apamama Islands, Gilbert Islands 43, 44, 51–58
"arc-light" strike 218, 220, 234
ARVN (Army of the Republic of Vietnam) 86, 87, 251, 252, 268–269; 1st ARVN Division 241; Government of Vietnam 284; in Lam Son 719, 252, 271; Navy Underwater Demolition Teams 99, 103, 127, 237, 239; South Vietnamese Navy 87, 88, 91, 92, 181, 188, 284, 286, 300
Attu 42
Australia, Special Air Services 271

Babin, Lt. Col. Berwick "Barry," USMC 80–81, 83, 86, 94–95, 102–104, 107, 122, 127, 130–131, 137, ***138***, 140; insertion of a Recon patrol 141–143, 146–147, 153, 160–161, 167; on the NVA's counter-reconnaissance tactics 173–176, 180–181, 193, 195, ***205***–209, 217, 223, 235, 239, 276–277, 298–299
Bacta, Corporal, USMC, Team GROUCHO MARX 134
Bailey, 1st Lt. Kenneth D., USMC 14–15, 16
Ballow, Corp. Wiley B., USMC, Amphibious Reconnaissance Platoon 71
Barnes, Captain, USMC 164–165
Barrow, 1st Lt. Robert H., USMC, SACO Mission 50; Commanding Officer, 9th Marine Regiment, Operation DEWEY CANYON 229–231
Base Two, Roseneath, Scotland 28
Beckwith, Col. Charles A. 271
Bench, Lt. Col. Arnold E., Commanding Officer, 2nd Bn, 4th Marine Regiment 133–134
Bennett, Admiral (USN) 28, 29
Bergman, Capt. Carl, USMC 202–203
Bierlein, Lance Corporal, USMC 161

Bishko, Sergeant, USMC, Team PRIMNESS, operation Hastings 130–131
Blanchard, Col. Donald H. "Doc," USMC 97
Blankenship, Sgt. Godfred, USMC, 165, ***228***
boats: Bay Head 17; folding canvas 21, 32; Freeport 17; Greenport 17; Higgins 45; kayaks 21, 32; LCM (landing craft, men) 60; LCR [L] inflatable 33; LCR [M], raft 33; MKIV rubber raft 33; NASTY-Class Patrol "Nasties" 87–88; Navy life raft 32; PBRs 225–226; PT (patrol boats) 88–89; Red Bank 17; "rum runners" 30; Sea Sled 17; SWATOWs (Chinese *Shantou* boats) 88
Bockewitz, Carl F., Commanding Officer, Company G, 2nd Bn, 3rd Marine Regiment 158–159
Bohn, Col. Robert D., USMC, Commanding Officer, 5th Marine Regiment 211–212; Task Force X-Ray 212
Bomb Damage Assessment (BDA) 13, 220, 243, 273
Boyd, Capt. Clay A., USMC 46
Bradbeer, 1st Lt. John D., USMC 47
Breen, Lance Corp. Wayne, Team "Atlas," USMC 114, ***221***
Brewster, Lt. Col. David L., USMC 16
Brink, Brig. Gen. Francis G. Brink, U.S. Army: "The Forgotten Marauder" 260–***261***; lectures 260–261
Brown, Maj. Gen. Albert E., Commanding General, U.S. Army, 7th Division 42, 43

327

Index

Brown, Capt. Charles C., USMC 49–50
Brown, Lance Corp. David, USMC **221**
Brown, Maj. Lee H., USMC, 1st Marine Brigade intelligence officer 15
Buck, Corp. William A., Jr., USMC, Team FLIGHT TEAM 228
Buckner, Maj. Gen. Simon Bolivar, U.S. Army 43
Buda, Lance Corp. Robert "Bob," USMC 81, **182**, **183**; SCUBA Team 1, 1st Force Reconnaissance Company 180–187, 191–192
Buehl, Corpsman Robert, HM3, U.S. Navy 109
Burma 253; China-Burma-India Theater 259–262; Myitkyina 253, 259–261
Butterworth, Corp. Barry J., USMC, Team BOX SCORE, 3rd Force Reconnaissance Company 201
Bougainville (Northern Solomons Islands) 41
Bouyant Ascents 73–74
Buck, Corp. William A., USMC, Team FLIGHT TIME, killed in action 228

Cambodia, and the /Ho Chi Minh Trail 285–287
Camp, Col. Richard, USMC, Operation "Dewey Canyon" 231
Canada, 2nd Canadian Division, Dieppe Raid August 12, 1942 264
Cape May, New Jersey 17
Carabiners 77
Caribbean Sea 71
Carlson, Lt. Col. Evans Fordyce, USMC, 2nd Raider Battalion 32, 36, 37, 40; Eighth Route Army (Chinese Communists) 37, 49, 50–51, 72, 259
Central Intelligence Agency (CIA) 74, 87, 253; Office of Strategic Services (OSS) 253
Charon, Lt. Col. Larry P., USMC, Commanding Officer, 1st Reconnaissance Battalion 222
Chiang Kai-shek 50
Chindits, ("Protectors of the Pagodas") 26; Maj. Gen. Orde C. Wingate 259–260, 262; 77th Indian Infantry Brigade 259–260
Choiseul Islands 41, 46

Christopher, Sgt. James R., USMC, leader, Team SANDHURST 245
Churchill, Prime Minister Sir Winston S. 25, 26, 29
Civilian Irregular Defense Groups (CIDG) 94, 100, 123, 124, 271; Col. Charles A. Beckwith, U.S. Army, advisor to 271
Clark, Lance Corp. William M., USMC 245
Clarke, Lt. Col. D.W., Royal Artillery 25, 26
Cochran, Col. Philip G. 262
Colby, Maj. Dwain A., USMC: Commanding Officer, 1st Force Reconnaissance Company 129; Commanding Officer, "Task Force Bravo" 129; Recon Group Bravo" 129, 132, 133
Coleman, Col. William, USMC 65
Collins, Corp. B.C., Reasoner Patrol, An My (3) 112–113; Navy Cross 113
Collins, Capt. Patrick G., USMC, Commanding Officer, Company D, 3rd Reconnaissance Bn. 97–98
Collins, Maj. William R., USMC, Commanding General, 3rd Marine Division 100
Colombia, Republic of, U.S. Marine landing 8
Combined Operations (UK) 26, 29, 34, 38
Combs, Corporal, USMC 251
ComGenUSMACV, Commanding General, U.S. Military Assistance Command, Vietnam 150, 155
Commando Depot 29; Lt. Colonel L.E. 29
Compton, Capt. J.L., USMC: Commanding Officer, Provisional Reconnaissance Group 113; Commanding Officer, Provisional Reconnaissance Group B 129
Corey, Lt. Ralph, USMC 45
Corcy, 1st Lt. Russell, USMC 57
Corsetti, Corp. Harry J., USMC 213–214
Cotton, Corp. R.G., USMC, 128
Courson, Corporal, USMC, 14
Cox, Lance Corporal, USMC, Team ATLAS, photo of), 221
Craig, Corp. James, USMC, 3rd Force Reconnaissance Company, (picture of), 203

Cress, William P., Sergeant, USMC, comments on KEYHOLE patrols, pp 204–205
Crosby, Lt. B.F. "Bing," USN, 52
Cuba, Guantanamo Bay, Marine landing at, 5–7; (Map of), 6; Fisherman's Point (Guantanamo Bay) 5–7, 49
Cullen, Frank L., Colonel, U.S. Army, Commander, 32nd Infantry Regiment, 43
Currie, Private, USMC, 14
Cushman, Robert E, General, USMC, Commanding General, 3rd Marine Division, III MAF, 275276; photo of, 276
Cutts, Richard M., Colonel, USMC, 49, 50

"D" Rings 77
Darby's Rangers 27, 28
Davis, Maj. Gen. Raymond G., USMC, Commanding General, 3rd Marine Division, FMF 207, 213, 214, 223, **223**, 229–232, 235, 276; Medal of Honor, Silver Star, Navy Cross 276–277
DeFazio, Technical Sergeant, USMC, Amphibious Reconnaissance Company, Camp Pendleton, CA. 81
Delezen, John Edmund, USMC, member, 3rd Force Reconnaissance Company 146
Del Valle, Lt. Col. Pedro A., USMC 49; in Ethiopia 51
Democratic Republic of Korea (North) 69; North Korean People's Army 69–70
Democratic Republic of Vietnam (North Vietnam) 88; 17th Parallel 88, 126
DeSoto Patrol 88
Detachment 101 (OSS, China-Burma-India) 30
Development and Procurement of Special Landing Boats 16–18
Dewey, Commodore George, U.S. Navy 9
Dieppe Raid, August 1942, 2nd Canadian Division 264; British Commandos 264; U.S. Army Rangers 264
Dill, Gen. Sir John, Chief of the Imperial General Staff 25
Dixon, King, USMC **164**
Dobson, Corp. Clifford D., USMC, SCUBA Team 1,

Index

1st Force Reconnaissance Company 180–187, *182*
Dominican Republic, Marine Reconnaissance in 94
Donaldson, Gunnery Sgt. Billy M., USMC, on Operation "Jackstay" 122, 132
Donovan, "William J, and OSS 36–7
Dowd, 2nd Lt. Thomas, USMC, Platoon Commander, Company E, 2nd Bn, 1st Marine Regiment 164
DUKW (amphibious truck) 60
Dunkirk 25, 26
Dunford-Slater, Brig. John 26
Dupras, Col. Edward P., USMC 115
Dutch East Indies (Indonesia) 64

Easterday, Captain, U.S. Army 179
Edson, Lt. Col. Merritt "Red Mike," USMC 20, 37, 72
Egan, 1st Lt. James T., USMC, Team HATEFUL 127, 282–283
Eifler, Maj. Carl F., U.S. Army, Office of Strategic Services, Commander, Detachment 101 in Burma 261–262
Eighth Route Army, Chinese Communists 37
Ellis, Lt. Col. Earl H., USMC 10–12; *Advanced Bases Operations in Micronesia* (Ellis, 1921) 40, 49–51, 255
Ely, Lt. Col. Louis, USMC, Amphibious Corps, Atlantic 21
Emrick, Lance Corp. Steven E., USMC 202
Erskine, Lt. Gen. Graves B., USMC 19, 21

Fahlstrom, Corp. Steven, USMC 174, 195, *207*
Finlayson, Col. Andrew R., USMC, 1st Force Reconnaissance Company 102, 104, 105, 116, 119, 120, 139, 284–295, 298; on insertion of a Reconnaissance Patrol 140–142, 149, 152, 153, 154; KILLER KANE 139, 149, 178; on the NVA's counter-reconnaissance tactics 171, 172, 175, **242**; Provincial Reconnaissance Units (PRUs) 242, 276; SWIFT SCOUT 139, 178, 233; Team BRISBANE *154*, 155, 163 167, *164*

Fire Support 13
"Firecracker" Missions 209–210
Fleet exercises 1, 8, 14–16, 70
Fleet Training Publication (FTP 167) 12, 14, 23
France, Indo-China 285
Fuhrman, James, USMC **104**
Fulton, Robert E., Jr. (inventor, Fulton Sky Hook) 74
Fulton Aerial Retriever System 75

Gata, Col. Keishi Japanese Army 59
Gatlin, PFC Thomas, USMC: awarded Silver Star 113; Battle of An My (3) 111–113; Reasoner Patrol 111–113
Giap, Gen. Vo Nguyen: Commander in Chief of North Vietnamese (PAVN) and Viet Cong (NLF) forces 168–170; Mao-Giap Doctrine 170–171; mobile strategy 171; "The Red Napoleon" 170–171
Gilbert Islands 32, 48
Giraud, Gen. Henri (France) 32
Glenn, 1st Lt. Jimmie, USMC, Team Leader, 3rd Reconnaissance Battalion 177
Goettge, Lt. Col. Frank B., USMC, Goettge Mission 44–45
Goodrell, Capt. Mancil C., USMC 5–6, 49
Goolden, PFC Richard P., USMC 229
Grannis, Lt. David L., USMC, Platoon Commander, Sub Unit 1, 100
Graves, 2nd Lt. Terrance ("Terry"), USMC, Commanding Officer, TEAM BOX SCORE 201–203; awarded Medal of Honor posthumously 204
Gray, Gen. Alfred M. 71
Greene, Gen. Wallace M. 20, **21**
Gregory, 2nd Lt. Willis M., USMC, Commanding Officer, 3rd and 4th Platoon, 3rd Force Reconnaissance Company 196–198
Griffith, Capt. Samuel B., USMC 20
Grissett, Corp. Edwin R., USMC, Team HATEFUL, missing in action (MIA) 127, 283
Gruenler, Lt. Col. R.E., USMC, III MAF 100

Guadalcanal, (Solomon Islands) 41, 44–46
Gurkhas 88

Hackworth, Col. David, U.S. Army, 1st Brigade, 101st Airborne Division, Air Mobile 270
Hagen, Maj. Edward, USMC 50
Hager, Lance Corporal, USMC 109
Hahn, PFC, USMC, Reasoner Patrol 112
Hahn, Corp. John, USMC **250**
Haines, Lt. Gen. Ralph E., Jr., U.S. Army 266; The Haines Board 266–268
Halsey, Adm. William H., USN 46, 47
Hamblen, 1st Sgt. Donald, USMC 81–82; *One Tough Marine* 83–84; on Provincial Reconnaissance Units (PRUs) 242–243
Hard, Lt. Col. Albert E., Commanding Officer, BCT-17 43
Hard, George (Australian) 52
Harris, Lance Corp. Charles E., USMC, Team LAGUNA POINT 190–191; killed in action 191
Hartney, Capt. Alan A., USMC, Commanding Officer, Company L, 3rd Bn, 3rd Marine Regiment 158; Operation Prairie II 158–159
Hauxhurst, William, USMC, 1st Force Reconnaissance Company 191
Hawrlyak, Sgt. Nichols, USMC, Team LAGUNA POINT 190–191; wounded in action 191
Hazelbaker, Maj. Vincil, USMC 133–134; awarded Navy Cross 134
helicopters: AH-1 "Cobra" Gunship 141, 142, 194, 218; CH-46 140–141, 144, **145, 146**, 152, 162, 177, 192, 201–202, 207, 212, 231, 290, 293, 300, 301; CH-53 Huey (UH-1) 76; Forward Looking Infrared Radar (FLIR) 218; "Jolly Green Giant" 75, 90; Side-Looking Airborne Radar (SLAR) 215; "Slicks" 134, 141, 177, 192, 194, 218; UH-1E 131, 139, 194, 202, 215, 251, 290; UH-34 113, 134, 140, 202; UH-38 141

Henderson, Darryl (historian) 169

Henderson, 2nd Lt. William, USMC, Commanding Officer, 1st Platoon, Company A., 3rd Reconnaissance Bn. 110–113

Henry, Maj. R.T., USMC, Commanding Officer, 5th Force Reconnaissance Company 160

Hermle, Brig. Gen. Leo D., USMC, Assistant Division Commander, 2nd Marine Division 54

Hill, Adm. Harry, USN 60
Hmong Tribesmen 88
Ho Chi Minh, leader of DRV 89
Ho Chi Minh Sandals 248
Ho Chi Minh Trail 89, 229–230, 233, 247, 295–285
Hobbs, Lance Corp. M.A., USMC 245

Hodge, 1st Lt. T.S., USMC, Third Force Reconnaissance Company, deactivation at Las Flores, Camp Pendleton, CA 241

Holcomb, Maj. Gen. Commandant Thomas H., USMC 20, 29, 36, 37, 40, 57

Holmes, Corp. Harlan E., USMC, patrol leader with 3rd Force Reconnaissance Company 205–206

Holzmann, Corp. James C., USMC 245

Honeycutt, PFC James E., USMC 201–203; action with Team BOX SCORE, killed in action 203–204; awarded Navy Cross posthumously 203

Hopkins, Lt. Col. Joseph E., USMC, Commanding Officer, 2nd Battalion, 4th Marine Regiment 224–225

Houghton, Maj. Gen. Kenneth J., USMC **67**-68

House of Commons (UK) 26

Howard, 1st Sgt. Jimmy, USMC: 1st Reconnaissance Battalion 1/9; Medal of Honor 179; parachute jump during Operation Kansas, Hill 488 179

Howell, Maurice, USMC **228**

Huff, Capt. Timothy, USMC, Charlie Company, 3rd Reconnaissance Battalion 150–151; Operation Hastings 150–152, 155

Hughes, Sgt. R.L., USMC, SCUBA Team 1, 1st Force Reconnaissance Company 180–187, **182**

Hunter, Col. Charles N., U.S. Army 260; China-Burma-India Theater 260, principles of 260

Huntington, Robert W. 6–7

Hunt, Wilson, USMC, commander, 8th Base Defense Battalion 52

Hydrographic Reconnaissance 11, 12

I Corps, RVN 1, 3, 285
Indochina, (Vietnam), French 64
International Harvester Corporation (IHC) 19
Inverness, Scotland 29, 38
Irwin, Comdr. William D., USN 51
Ismay, Gen. Hastings L. 26

"J-Hook" 75
Jackson, John L., H.M. 2, USN, Corpsman, Team LAGUNA POINT 191; awarded Bronze Star 191

Jacques, Sgt. Maj. Maurice J., USMC 99, 124

Jans, Corp. Olaf L., USMC, 3rd Force Reconnaissance Company 199–200

Japan, Imperial Navy 43
Japanese Army: on Attu 42; *18th Imperial Division* (Northern Burma) 253, 260, 285

Johnson, Rear Adm. A.W., USN 14

Johnson, Gen. Harold K., Chief of Staff, U.S. Army (1964–1968) 266; Haines Board 265

Johnson, 1st Lt. Russell L., Platoon Commander, 1st Force Reconnaissance Company 191; Battle for Hue City 191; TASK FORCE X-RAY 191

Joint Army-Navy Board (1927) 13; *Joint Action of the Army and Navy 1927* 13

Jones, Capt. James Logan, Sr. 1; awarded Silver Star 62; biography 18–19; Commanding Officer, Amphibious Reconnaissance Company 22, 29, 32, 39–40, 41, 44, 48, 51–56, 59–62; Commanding Officer,

Observer Group 19–21, 23, 29–30, 32, 37–38

Jones, Lt. Gen. William K., USMC 19

"*Jungle Combat Principles*" (1925) 254–259; Brig. Gen. George S. Simonds, U.S. Army 254–259, **256**

"Jungle Penetrators" 77

Kachin Guerrillas, Burma, World War II, Detachment 101 261–262; Kachin "Rangers" 262

Kauffman, Lt. Cmdr. Draper, USN, Underwater Demolition Teams UDT) 54, 59; Fort Pierce, Florida 54

Kearney, Corp. W.D., USMC, Team COFFEE TIME II 213

Kelly, PFC Delbert, USMC **228**
Kelly, Francis J., Commanding Officer, 5th Special Forces Group, RECONDO School 270–271

Kelly, Sergeant, USMC, Team ROAD TEST 248–249
Kennedy, Pres. John F. (1961–1963) 82

Kent, Col. William D., Commanding Officer, 3rd Reconnaissance Battalion (June 1968) 194

Kern, Corp. Lou, USMC, member of 1st and 3rd Reconnaissance Companies 144, 149, 161

Kester, Staff Sgt. Larry, USMC 134

Keyes, Adm. Sir Roger, (UK Royal Navy) 27

KEYHOLE Operations 127, 136, 193–196, 204–205, 210, 214, 222, 223

King, Staff Sgt. Neal D., USMC, Amphibious Reconnaissance Platoon 71

Kington, PFC Randy, USMC, member of 3rd Bn, 7th Marines 145; Special Landing Force, USS *Iwo Jima* 145

Kinkaid, Comdr. Thomas, USN, 7th Fleet 43

Kiska 42
Klein, Lt. Lee, USMC, Intelligence Officer, 3rd Bn, 26th Marines 153; on Operation Prairie II 159

Knee, Staff Sergeant, USMC, Battle of An My (3), Reasoner Patrol 112

Koch, Gunnery Sgt. G.A.,

USMC, Team DATE PALM 212; Operation HOUSTON 212
Koehler, 1st Lt. Richard D., USMC, Commanding Officer, Company F, 2nd Bn, 3rd Marine Regiment 159
Korea, Republic of (South) 241; 2nd Division, Republic of Korea Marine Corps (KMC) 241, 286; South Korean Commandos 265, 271
Korea, War in (1950–1953) 50, 68–70, 265; first heliborne assault 70; 38th Parallel "Punchbowl" 70, 78–79
Koval, Lance Corporal, USMC *121*
Kraince, 1st Lt. Francis, USMC, Commanding Officer, Amphibious Reconnaissance Platoon 71
Krepinevich, Andrew (historian) 274
Krueger, Gen. Walter, U.S. Army, Commanding General, 6th Army (Southwest Pacific Theater of Operations—New Britain, Noemfoor, and Sansapor, Philippines 262
Krulak, Lt. Gen. Victor H., USMC: Commanding General, FMFPac 72–73, 81, 116; Commanding Officer, 2nd Parachute Bn 47; G-3, FMFPac 71

LaHue, Brig. Gen. Foster, U.S. Army, Commanding Officer, Task Force X-Ray 211–212
Lamontagne, Corp. Timothy, USMC 161
Landing Craft Utility (LCU) 140
Landing Vehicle Tracked (LVTs) 56, 60, 140
Lanning, Michel Lee 190
Laos 3, 90, 104, 156, 165, 172, 199, 229–230, 275
Leaker, Lt. J.C., USMC, Commanding Officer, 2nd Platoon, First Force Reconnaissance Company 123
Lee, Capt. Alex, USMC, Commanding Officer, 3rd Force Reconnaissance Company 235, 236, 295
Lee, Capt. Howard V., USMC, Commanding Officer, Company E, 2nd Bn, 4th Marines, "The Magnificent Bastards" 132–134; awarded Medal of Honor 134
Leinster, Colin (journalist on Combined Action Groups [CAGs] and Combined Action Companies [CACs] 155
Lewis, Doc," Navy Corpsman, Company A, 1st Platoon, 3rd Force Reconnaissance Battalion, Battle of An My (3) 113
Livingston, Staff Sergeant, USMC, 3rd Force Reconnaissance Company *206*
load bearing equipment (LBE) 76
Lopez, PFC Adrian S., USMC 202
Lownds, Col. David, USMC, Commanding Officer, 26th Marine Regiment at Khe Sahn 216
Lowrey, Maj. William B., USMC 135–136; Commanding Officer, 1st Reconnaissance Company 135; Operation Prairie 135–136, Provincial Reconnaissance Units (PRUs) 242–243
Lynch, Lt. Cmdr. Richard, USN 52

MAGIS (Marine Air Ground Intelligence System) 2, 217, 219
MAGTF (Marine Air-Ground Task Force) 217
Marshall, Gen. George C., U.S. Army, Chairman of the Joint Chiefs of Staff (1941–1945) 263
Marshall Islands 48–50
Martin, Corp. Paul, USMC 69, 78–79
Maupassant, Guy de 277
McCalla, Capt. Bowman, USN 5–6
McCarthy, Lance Corporal, USMC *121*
McCutcheon, Maj. Gen Keith B., Lieutenant General, III Marine Amphibious Force 118, 223, **224**
McGuire Rig 74, 76
McKenzie, Lance Corporal *12*
McKeon, Col. Donald M., USMC, Commanding Officer, 1st Reconnaissance Battalion 165
McMullen, Lance Corp. Charles, USMC, 3rd Force Reconnaissance Company **200**
McNamara, Robert S., Secretary of Defense (1963–1968) 87; "McNamara's Line" 210, 219; PLAN 34A 87, 89, 91
McWilliams, Corp. William, USMC, Operation Hastings, Team PRIMNESS" 130–131
Menary, Sgt. Gregory, USMC, Company C, 3rd Reconnaissance Bn. 152
Menning, George "Butch," USMC 250, **250**
Merrell, Corp. Lowell H., 3rd Reconnaissance Bn 93; Camp "Merrell" 93
Merrill, Brig. Gen. Frank D., U.S. Army, Commanding General, 5307th Composite (provisional) Unit, "Merrill's Marauders" 253; Col. Charles N. Hunter, U.S. Army 260; "Galahad" 259–261; Merrill's Marauders 259–261
Metz, Sgt. David, USMC 161, 198–200
Meyers, Col. Bruce F., USMC 17, 33–34, 41, 48, 52, 73–76, 79–82, 276
Michaux, Col. Alexander L., USMC, S-3, 3rd Marine Division, FMF, Operation "Dewey Canyon" 231
Miles, Capt. Milton Edward "Mary," USN 50
Military Assistance Command, Vietnam, MACV 89; USMACV 91, 268, 270–272
Miller, Corp. Joseph, USMC, Team PRIMNESS, Operation Hastings 130–131
Milleson, Corporal, USMC, Team DANNY BROOK 248
Momsen, Charles B. "Swede, USN, Momsen Lung 73–75
Momsen Lung 73–74
Monti, Lt. Col. Anthony A., USMC, Commanding Officer, 1st Bn, 26th Marnies 134–135; Special Landing Force, Operation DECKHOUSE IV 134–136
Moran, Corp. Thomas, USMC, TEAM PRIMNESS 130–131, 246
Moss, Corp. William, USMC, Team ATLAS **240**, **250**, 300–301
Moungs, tribesmen 88
Mountbatten, Lord Louis, head

of Combined Operations 27, 29
Murray, Sgt. Maj. Frederick, USMC 111–113
Mussolini, Benito 51

Nation, PFC Michael P., USMC, Team BOX SCORE 201–203
National Liberation Front (NLF), Viet Cong (VC) 87, 98–99, 110, 126–127, 149, 154, 156, 163–164, 169, 176, 211, 213, 216, 236, 245, 248, 250, 265, 269, 274, 281–283, 289–291; Main Force units 167–168; 3-by-3 Principle 168, 178–180, 210, 233
Natzke, Corp. Nicholas L., USMC, Operation GREAT DIVIDE II 163
Naval Reconnaissance: Instructions for the Reconnaissance of Bays, Harbors, and Adjacent Country 1906 (Williams) 1, 9–12
Naval War College (U.S. Navy) 1, 8
New Georgia 1
New Guinea, Hollandia 67
Newman, Capt. D.I., U.S. Army 51
Nickerson, Lt. Gen. Hermann, Jr., USMC, Commanding General, III MAF 220, **222**, 223, 241
Nimitz, Adm. Chester H. 41, 43, 56, 58
Nixon, Pres. Richard M. 222
Nixten, Corp. Robert, USMC 161, 198, ***199***, 200
North Vietnamese Army (PAVN; People's Army of Vietnam) 2, 102, 110, 127, 132–134, 141, 143, 150, 152, 154, 155, 157–159, 167, 169, 176–178, 183, 188, 191, 194, 201–202, 204–206, 211, 213, 216, 218, 221, 226–227, 229–230, 233, 236, 240, 245–248, 250, 265, 269, 274, 282–287, 291; 1st Regiment 239, 286; 21st Regiment 239; 2nd Division 284–287; 31st Regiment 234; 90th NVA Regiment 135; 304th Division 129; 324th Alpha Division 139, 206; 324th B Division 129, 130, 131, 135; 325th Division 124, 126; 368B Artillery Regiment (Rocket) 178; 402nd Sapper Battalion 288; 812th Regiment, 324D Division 157; Base Are 112, 220; "Cheiu Hoi!" ("Surrender") 248; counter-reconnaissance 167–176; counter-signals intelligence (SIGINT) 173; diagram of regiment 169; Giap, Vo Nguyen 168–170; Giap-Mao Doctrine 170–171; Group 44 Headquarters 239–240; infantry battalion 170; Lao Dong Party 284–285; Military Region V (NVA) 239–240; TET Offensive 153, 156, 229
Northern Solomon Islands 67
Norton, Bruce "Doc," USN, Navy Corpsman 109, 110
"Nungs" (ethnic Chinese) 87, 88, 94, 124

Oberhaus, Lance Corporal, USMC, Team HATEFUL, wounded in action 282
Observer Group, Quantico, VA. 18, 19–21
O'Connor, 1st Lt. Michael M., USMC, Commanding Officer, Team FLIGHT TIME 228
O'Darby, Brig. Gen. William, U.S. Army 263; "Darby's Rangers" 263, ***263***; 34th Infantry Division 263
Office of Strategic Services (OSS) 27, 29–30, 253; Detachment 101, 253
Ohanesian, Lt. Col. Victor, USMC, Commanding Officer, 2nd Bn, 3rd Marines, Operation Prairie II, (February–March 1967) 157–159; killed in action, 159
Okinawa, (Japan) 1
Olson, Private 14
Olson, Brig. Gen. Harry C., USMC, Assistant Division Commander, 1st Marine Division 161
operations (1919–1953): D-Day (Normandy) 264; Dynamo 25–26; Flintlock 55; Forager 58–60; Husky 264; Iceberg 62; Killer 70; Land Crab 42; Overlord 27, 264; Sundance 55; Torch 27–30, 40, 253, 264
operations (Vietnam War, 1965–1971): Allen Brook 211; Birdwatcher 123; Blue Marlin 72; Dagger Thrust 96, 101; Dagger Thrust I 98, 99; Dagger Thrust II 99; Dagger Thrust III 99; Deckhouse IV 134–136; Delaware 218; De Soto 156–157; Dewey Canyon 229–230; Double Eagle 113; Double Eagle I 126; Double Eagle II 127; Great Divide II 162; Hastings 100, 130–131, 136, 150, 152, 156; HMM-362 87; Houston 211–213; Imperial Lake 246; Jackstay 120–122, 180; Kansas 179; Knox 105, 178; Lancaster 139; Mameluke Thrust 211; Market Place II 176–178; Market Time 99; Neptune 225–226; Oklahoma Hills 233–235; Oregon 128; Pecos 163; Pegasus 127, 141, 191–194; Pirahna 99; Prairie 131–136, 138–139, 152; Prairie II 157–159; Red Snapper 94; Scotland II 195–199, 205–206, 220, 224; Shu Fly 87, 274; Sierra 136; Starlite 96, 13; Swift Saber 211; Texas 116; Trailblazer 122; Union 161–162; Upshur Stream 247; Wheeler/Wallowa 211
Ostrie, Capt. William, USMC, Company S-3, Operation "Hastings" 131

Panama, Isthmus of 8
Pannell, PFC Thorace L., USMC, Reasoner Patrol 111–113; Battle of An My (3) 113
"Paras" (British Airborne Troops) 20, 34
Parker, 1st Lt. R.F., USMC, Commanding Officer, Team HATEFUL 127, 282–283; wounded in action 282–283
Pathfinders 79–80; in Dominican Republic 94; 1st Lt. David Ramsay 79–80, 90–91
Patrol Seismic Intrusion Devices (PSID) 108, 236
Patton, Maj. Gen. George S., Jr., Commanding General, Western Task Force 27–28
Paull, Capt. Jerome T., USMC, Operation KANSAS 179
PBY (Navy Patrol Aircraft) 33
Pearcy, PFC Robert L., Team FLIGHT TIME 228
Pearl Harbor 18
Pearson, Brig. Ben. Willard, U.S. Army 270
Peatross, Maj. Gen. Oscar F., USMC, Commanding Officer, 7th Marine Regiment 72, 73, 96; Operation Starlite 96, 115, ***116***, 117
Peers, Lt. Col. William R., US Army, Commanding Officer,

Detachment 101, Burma, World War II 261–262
People's Liberation Army (PLA) (China) 50, 69-70
People's Republic of China, (PRC) 64
Perry, Lt. Col. Aydlette H., USMC, Commanding Officer, 3rd Reconnaissance Battalion 222–223
Petrus, Francis C., Platoon Sergeant, USMC 45
Philippines 7, 9, *9*, 64, 262
Photo Imagery Interpretation Center (PIIC) 216
Pike, Douglas 169
Pipes, USMC, Radio Operator, Reasoner Patrol, An Amy (3) 112
Plain, Lt. Col. Louis 29
plastic explosives (PE) 28
political warfare executive 29
Pratt, Lt. Comdr., USN, killed on Guadalcanal 45
Premel, Corp. Donald, USMC, Team ATLAS *221*
Price, Maj. Gen. Charles F.B., USMC, Commanding General, Department of the Pacific 37
Primaflex Camera 52
Prins, Lieutenant, USMC, team leader, Team HANSWORTH 245
Provincial Reconnaissance Units (PRUs) 242–243
PSID (handheld sensor) 219
PSR (handheld sensor) 219
Puerto Rico, Culebra and Fleet Exercises, 1, Vieques and FLEX 4, 14, 71
Puleston, Capt. William Dilworth, USN, head of Office of Naval Intelligence 50
Puller, Col. Lewis B. "Chesty," Commanding Officer, 1st Marine Regiment 69

radios: A Mark III 30; AN/GCR-9 80; AN/PRC-6 80; AN/PRC-10 80, 102; AN-PRC-25 80, 99, 102, 114, 138, 233, 288; AN-PRC-77 102, 138; B Mark II 29, 30; BA 386 Battery 114; MAY Radio 80; Morse WT Transmitter 29; MOS 2531 (Field Radio Operator) 161; PRC-47 (VHF/FM) 101–102, 114; PRC-93 138; receivers 29; SC-300 62
Ragan, PFC Ray *228*–229
Reasoner, 1st Lt. Frank, USMC, Commanding Officer,

Company A, 3rd Force Reconnaissance Battalion 110–111; An My (3) *111*–113; Camp Reasoner 113, 154, 165, 242, 252, 289, 290, 292; death 113; Medal of Honor citation 281; Reasoner Patrol 110–113, 115, 274
Reconnaissance Indoctrination Program (RIP) 247
Republic of China (Formosa or Taiwan) 50, 64
Republic of Vietnam (South) 1, 265; A Shau Valley 167, 169, 218, 222, 229–233, 235, 241, 243–244, 254, 261, 265, 272–275; An Giang 286; An Hoa 165, 172, 227, 233, 235–236, 292; An Hoa Basin 233, 286–287; An Tam (1) 209, 210; Annamite Mountains 144, 285; "Antenna Valley" 165, 226, 240; "Arizona Territory" 149, 209, 285; Ba Long Valley 193, 199; Ba Long Valley 228; Ba To 123, 125, 126, 127; Base Area 101 232; Base Area 112 165, 172, 286; Base Area 116 287; Base Area 611, Da Krong Valley 229; Ben Hai River 157, 162, 232; Ca Lu 193, 198–199; Cam Lo 132, 152, 208; "Charlie Ridge" 104, 126, 149, 165, 167, 194, 220, 246, 251, 286; Chu Lai 98, 126, 128, 156, 220, 234; The Citadel, Hue City *185*; Con Thien 156, 157, 188, 208, 213; Cua Viet 208, 225; Da Nang 1, 98, 100, 105, 110, 122, 126–129, 134, 149, 157, 164–165, 176, 178, 180, 190, 224, 229, 233, 234, 242, 245, 252, 281, 287–288, 295; Dai Loc 110–113, 274; De Kron River 232; Demilitarized Zone (DMZ) 2, 104, 129, 150, 155, 156, 157, 159, 178, 189, 208, 222, 235; Dong Ha 102, 129, 139, 152, 161, 194, 198, 225–226, 232, 277; Dong Ha Combat Base *197*, 200–202, *204*; Dong Ha River 295; "Elephant Valley" 98, 165, 235, 246, 247, 251, 252; "Enchanted Forest" 165; Go Noi Islands 209, 210, 287; Goi Linh 157; Happy Valley 122, 149, 163, 165, 167, 176, 211, 233, 234, 286, 288–291; Highway 1 ("Street Without Joy") 178, 252; Highway 9 153; Hill 124 158; Hill 174 162–163; Hill 327 110; Hill 372 288; Hill 471

227; Hill 487 245; Hill 488 179; Hill 537 288; Hill 582 289; HLZ X-Ray 246; Hoi An 241; Hon Coc Mountains 209; Hue City 128–129, 178, 181–187, 189, 191–193, 211, 222, 229, 232, 295; I Corps 86, 114, 127, 129, 137, 149, 150, 154, 156, 157, 162, 166, 173, 189, 190, 209, 216, 222, 226, 229, 231–233, 235, 237, 241–243, 246–247; II Corps 127; Khe Sanh 128, 135, 139, 153, 156, 188, 189, 193, 194, 198–200, 205–206, 211, 213, 216, 219, 227, 232, 235; Lang Vei I 142, 227; Lang Vei II 142; Leech Valley 246, 247, 251, 252; Liberty Bridge Road 287; Long Than Peninsula, Rung Sat ("Forest of Death"; RSSZ) 120–122; Mekong Delta 1, 180; "Monkey Mountain" 247; Nam Hoa 190; Nam Hoa Mountains 212; Nui Bai Cay 128; Oceanview 208; Ong Thu Slope 165; Phu Bai 128, 129, 190, 191, 211, 212, 238; Phu Gia Pass 178; Phu Loc 105, 178, 211; Phu-Loc-Hai Van 178; Qua Viet River 139; Quang Nam Province 172, 209, 221, 233, 235, 240, 241, 273, 284–287; Quang Ngai Province 123, 126; Quang Tin Province 221; Quang Tri 129, 139, 144, 208, 221, 227, 235, 301; Que Son Mountains 246, 247, 250, 286; Que Son Valley 211; Qui Nhon 145; Red Beach 12, 86, 252; The "Rockpile" 132, 151, 156, 189, 208; Route 1 178; Route 9 152; Route 548 229; Route 922 230, 231; Saigon 178; "Sherwood Forest" 246, 247, 252; Silver Bridge, Hue City 186; Soc Ta Trach Region 190; Song Cai River 286; Song Huong River 286; South China Sea 225; Sung Vu Gia 209; Tat Lay Mountains (ZC0266) 286; Thong Tra River 179; Thu Thien Province 178, 222, 286; Thung Doc River Valley 244–246, 248, 249; Thuong Duc Corridor 241; Tiger Tooth Mountain 232; "Yellow Brick Road" 172, 175–176
Reserve Officer Training Corps (ROTC) 267–268
Reserve Officers' Course (ROC), Quantico, Virginia (USMC) 19

Reynolds, Capt. Phillip F., USMC, Operation SCOTLAND II 195–196
Rhodes, Pvt. John R., USMC, team member, 3rd Reconnaissance Battalion, Market Place II 176–178
Riddick, 1st Lt. Morris E., USMC 162–163
Riddle, Lt. Col. William S. 22–25, "Planning and Execution of a Seaborne Raid" 22–25
Robertson, Maj. Gen. Donn, USMC, Commanding General, 1st Marine Division, FMF **164**
Robinson, Cmdr. James, USN, Operation "JACKSTAY" 120
Rockwell, Rear Adm., USN, Commander, Amphibious Task Force North 42
Rollings, 1st Lt. Wayne E., USMC 77, 179–180, 226–227
Roosevelt, Pres. Franklin D. 37
Roosevelt, Capt. James, USMC 36, 38
Roseneath, Scotland 38
Royal Marine Commandos (UK) 15, 19, 20, 22, 25; 41st Independent Commando 68, 263–264; independent companies 26–32, 37–38, 40; Lt. Col. Douglas Drysdale (Korea) 68
Royal Navy (UK) 27, 264
Royal Ordnance Corps 28
rubber rafts 15, 16
Russell, Lance Corporal, USMC, Team SWIFT SCOUT 289; wounded in action 290
Russell, Maj. Gen. Commandant John H., USMC 50

Saipan 1
Sang, Phan Van (Vietnamese tiger hunter) 229
SCAMP (Sensor Control and Management Platoons) 2, 219
Schank, First Lieutenant, USMC, Commanding Officer, Team PRIME CUT, Operation OKLAHOMA HILLS 234
Schemmel, Staff Sgt. Frank, USMC, Third Force Reconnaissance Company 241
Schmidt, Maj. Gen. Harry, USMC 60
Schmitt, Corp. R.E., USMC, SCUBA Team 1, 1st Force Reconnaissance Company 180, **182**
Schoelkopf, Robert "Doc," Navy Corpsman 109, 110; Hospital Corpsman, SCUBA Team 1, 1st Force Reconnaissance Company 180–187, **182**
SE-11 "Night Marker Lights" 8
Search and Rescue 77
SERE (Survival, Evasion, Rescue, and Escape) School 80
Sexton, Corp. Charles T., USMC, 3rd Force Reconnaissance Company, Navy Cross 243–244
Shainline, PFC Thomas, USMC, Team CENTIPEDE **228**–229
Shepherd, Brig. Gen. Lemuel C., USMC 60
Shinn, 1st Lt. Leo B., USMC 57, 59, 71
ships (U.S. Navy): USS *Cook* 91; USS *Diachenko* 98; USS *Epping Forest* 91; USS *Gilmer* 59; USS *Harris* 54; USS *Iwo Jima* 145; USS *Kane* 55; LST-272 55; USS *Maddox* 68, 88; USS *Maine* 8; USS *Marblehead* 5, 7, 40; USS *Nereus* 73; USS *New Jersey* 147; USS *New York* 6; USS *Oregon* 7, 40; USS *Orlech* 68; USS *Stringham* 59–60; USS *Warbler* (MSC-206) 91; USS *Weiss* 91
Shockley, Lance Corp. James, USMC, Reasoner Patrol 111–113; Battle of An My (3) 111–113; wounded 113
Silva, Lance Corp. Gilermo, USMC **221**
Silver Bridge, Hue City, RVN, SCUBA Team 1, 1st Force Reconnaissance Company 181–187
Silverthorn, Capt. Merwyn, Jr., USMC 57–59
Simmons, Maj. Roger E., USMC, Commanding Officer 1st Force Reconnaissance Company 220–221
"Simmons Ladder" **145**, 276
Simonds, Brig. Gen. George S., Commanding Officer, 20th Infantry Brigade, Panama Canal Zone 254–259, **258**; jungle combat principles 254–259
Simpson, Maj. Gen. Ormond R., USMC, Commanding General, 1st Marine Division 75–76
Sino-American Cooperative Organization (SACO) 50
Skaggs, PFT Harold A., Team FLIGHT TIME 228
Slim, Lt. Gen. William, Commanding Officer, British Army 14th Army 262
Slocum, Sgt. Danny, USMC, 3rd Force Reconnaissance Company 200–203; awarded Silver Star 203; Team BOX SCORE 201–203; wounded in action 203
Sloss, Lance Corp. Joseph, USMC, Operation NEPTUNE 225–226
Small Boat Squadrons (UK) 34
Smith, Lt. Gen. Holland M., USMC 19, 20–21, 37, 38, 43, 48
Smith, Maj. Gen. Oliver P., USMC 68
Snap-Hook D-Rings 141
Sniadeki, Lance Corp. Albert, USMC 81
Snyder, 1st Sgt. Robert F., USMC 81
Solomon Islands 41, 44–48; Northern Solomons (Maloelap, Mille) 67
Spain 5–8
Special Air Services (SAS) (UK) 34
Special Assistant for Counterinsurgency and Special Activities (SACSA) 89
Special Operating Forces (Vietnam) 2
Special Operations Executive (SOE) (UK) 2, 20, 25, 27, 28–31, 34–5, 38, 40
Special Purpose Insertion and Extraction (SPIE) 74, 76–77, 249, 276, 293
Special Service Battalions 27, 34
"Spider Holes" 162
STABO Rig (stabilized body) 74–77, 276
Steinke, Lt. Harris I., USN 74
Steinke Hood 74
Stilwell, Lt. Gen. Joseph W. "Vinegar Joe," U.S. Army, Commanding General, 10th U.S. Army 61–62, 262
Stinemetz, Lt. Col. Broman C., USMC, Commanding Officer, 3rd Reconnaissance Battalion 194–195
STINGRAY 100, 101, 120,

127–132, 136–137, 147, 149, 156, 161, 166, 193, 201, 208–210, 214, 220, 223–224, 232, 274, 293
Stubbe, Ray 15, 190
Studies and Observation Group (SOG), 1, 68, 76, 87, 88, 89, 92, 156, SOG Teams, 156, 167, 173, MACV-SOG Operations, 175–176; 242–243, 275
submarines (U.S. Navy): USS *Argonaut* (SM-1), 32, 34; USS *Grayling* (SS-209) 32, 34; *Guppy Class* 32; USS *Narwhal* (SSN-671) 34, **35**, 43; USS *Nautilus* (S-168; later AP-1), 32, 34, 43, 51–52; USS *Perch* (APSS-313) 32, 34, 68, 72, 74; *S-47* 14, 15; USS *Sea Lion* (APSS-315) 32, 34, **36**; use in reconnaissance 18, 29, 32
Surveillance and Reconnaissance Center (SRC) 217
Swiderski, Lance Corporal, USMC **103**, **221**

Tactical Group 1 56
tanks 69
Tarawa 12, 25, 32, 40, 41, 48–53
TET Nguyen Dan Truce 157
TET Offensive (1968) 2, 232, 234
Thompson, Corp. David, USMC, SCUBA Team 1, 1st Force Reconnaissance Company 180–187, **182**, **183**
Thompson, Stephen R., HM3, USN, Team BOX SCORE 201, 202
Thomson, Corp. Robert B., USMC, Team Box Score 201–203; awarded Silver Star 203
Tinian 59–60
T/O K-6623 71
Tollerson, Col. Frederick, USMC 72, 73
Trainor, Lt. Gen. Berand M., USMC **88**–89
Trevathan, Gunnery Sgt. Bruce D., USMC 162; Operation UNION 162, 163, 191
Trooper's Ladder 74, 75
Truman, Pres. Harry S. 64
Tulagi, Solomon Islands 41
Turner, Adm. Richmond Kelly, USN 51, 58–60

Underwood, Capt. David, USMC, pilot, CH-46, 202–204; awarded Navy Cross 203
Union of Soviet Socialist Republics (USSR) 64, 117, 179; "Soviet Army 254

United States Air Force (USAF) 2, 72, 89–90, 102, 131, 219; units (13th U. S. Air Force 90; 56th Air Commando Squadron 90; 606th Air Commando Squadron 90; Air Commando Teams 90; Col. Harry C. Aldershot 90; Combat Controller Teams 89–90; U.S. Seventh Air Force 215)
United States Army (USA) 2, 22, 25, 48, 82, 91, 127, 147, 188, 215, 219, 253, 265, 268–271; Brig. Gen. George S. Simonds 254, **258**; Cuba (1906) 254; FM 31–16 Counterguerrilla Operations 258; "Harassing" and "Bushwhacking" 255–256; Jungle Combat Principles (1925) 254–259; Lt. Col. Earl H. Ellis, USMC 255; Mexico (1914 and 1917) 254; Philippine Insurrection (1899–1903) 254; U.S. Army and Counterinsurgency, Seminole Wars 254; United States Military Advisory and Assistance Group (MAAG, Saigon; 1951) 260–261
United States Army (Units): 1st Air Commando Group—5318th Provisional Unit (Air), Project 9 262 ; 1st Armored Division (WWII) 263; 1st Battalion, 9th Cavalry (1/9) in the A Shau Valley 218; 1st Battalion, 17th Regiment 43; 1st Battalion, 327th Infantry 212; 1st Battalionn, U.S. Army Rangers 28; 1st Brigade, 101st Airborne (Air Mobile) 270; 1st Cavalry Division 150, 193, 210–211; 1st Engineer Amphibious Brigade 28; 1st Field Artillery Group (1st FAG) 212; 1st Infantry Division 21; 1st Ranger Battalion (WWII), Arzew, Algeria 264; 2nd Battalion, 17th Regiment 42–43, **143**; 2nd Battalion, 106th Infantry Regiment 55; 2nd Battalion, 327th Infantry 212; 2nd Battalion, 502nd Infantry 212; 2nd Squadron, 17th Cavalry Regiment 243–244; 3rd Battalion, 17th Regiment, 7th Infantry Division 42–3; 5th Special Forces Group 270–271; 6th Ranger Battalion (WWII) 264–265; 7th Infantry Division 41;

7th Scout Company 41–44; 7th Squadron, 17th Cavalry 211; 10th Airborne Division, XXIV Corps 243; 10th U.S. Army (Okinawa) 61–62; 11th Airborne Division; 17th Air Cavalry Regiment 210–211; 20th Infantry Brigade, Panama Canal Zone 254, 258; 23rd Infantry Division, "Americal" 150, 210. 211; 32nd Infantry Regiment 43; 101st Airborne (Air Mobile) Division 241, 254, 274; 173rd Airborne Brigade 270–272; 82nd Airborne Division 253; 85th Medical Evacuation Hospital 243; 5307th Composite Unit (Provisional), "Merrill's Marauders" 253, 259–262; 8240th U.S. Army Unit, 8th U.S. Army (Korea), United Nations Partisan Infantry Korea (UNPIK) 265; Airborne Course 267; Airborne School 160; Airmobile Divisions 267; "Alamo Scouts" 262; Alaska Scouts 43; Army Special Operations Group (SOG) 167; Army Valorous Unit Citation 243; BCT-17 43; Combat Platoon Leader's Course (CPLC), Fort Benning, Georgia 268; Company A, 17th Infantry 43; Continental Army Command (CONARC), Fort Monroe, VA 266; Darby's Rangers 26–27, 263, 264–265; Detachment 101 (OSS) 261–262; Fort Gordon, Georgia 266; Fort Knox, Kentucky, Reserve Officer Training Corps, (ROTC) 267–268; Fort Monroe, Virginia 266; "Galahad" 259–261, 271; "Green Berets" 254; Haines Board 266–267; Infantry School, Fort Benning, Georgia (USAIS) 266–268; John F. Kennedy Center for Special Warfare, Fort Bragg, NC 265–266; Joint Action of the Army and Navy 1927 13; Joint Army-Navy Board (1927) 13; Long Range Reconnaissance Patrols (LRRPs) 95, 167, 169, 173, 175, 216, 253, 254, 259–261, 265, 267, 271–276; LRRP Organization Diagram

Index

10-11, 272-273; Military Assistance Command Vietnam's Advisory Team/ Dong Ha Training Center 243; Officer Candidate School 267; Operation PEGASUS 193-194; Pathfinders, (U.S. Army) in World War II 253; Provisional LRRP detachment and units 272-274; Rangers 25, 27, 253, 267-268, 271; Rangers 253; Reaction Team "Bald Eagle" 147; Reaction Team "Sparrow Hawk" 147; RECONDO School, Nha Trang 237, 271; Reconnaissance Troop, 7th Infantry Division 42, 44; Small Unit Training, Fort Benning, Georgia 268; Special Forces 2, 75, 89, 90, 95, 122, 123, 125, 126, 189, 243, 254, 259, 276; "Task Force Yankee" 220; Thung Doc Special Forces Camp 244; U.S. 6th Army (WWII) 262, 264-265; U.S. Army Air Forces 58; U.S. Forces (USSF) "A" Caps (Combined Action Platoons) 100; U.S. Military Academy (West Point) 265, 267-268; United States Special Forces (USSF) Camp 282-283 ; Western Task Force 21; "White Tigers" 265; XXIV Corps 216, 241, 243

United States Marine Corps: Camp Elliott, CA. 37; Department of the Pacific 37; Headquarters Marine Corps (HQMC), 8, 18, 19, 20, 57, 63, 64, 65, 71, 91; Marine Barracks, Washington, D.C., 8; Marine Corps Schools (Quantico, VA) (MCS) 16, 18; Marine Corps Tactics Board 167

United States Marine Corps (bases): An Hoa Combat Base 165, 220, 284-287; Bogue Field, NC 71; Camp Carroll (RVN) 158, 189, 208; Camp Del Mar, Camp Pendleton, CA 71; Camp Elliot 37, 40; Camp Joseph H. Pendleton, California 64, 74, 95, 100, 160, 241, 246; Camp Lejeune, NC 71, 95, 160; Camp Reasoner 113, 154, 165, 242, 252; Con Thien Combat Outpost 213; Fire Support Base Alpine 228-229; Infantry Training Regiment (ITR) 300; Khe Sahn Fire Support Base 193, 206, 207, 208, 227; Las Flores, Camp Pendleton 241; Las Plugas, Camp Pendleton 81; Marine Barracks, Boston Navy Yard 8; Marine Corps Recruit Depot, San Diego, CA 71; Marine Corps Schools (MCS; Quantico, VA) 14; Reconnaissance School, Camp Pendleton, California 294; San Diego, CA 40, 42; Vandegrift, Combat Base 140, 208

United States Marine Corps (units): 1st Amphibious Reconnaissance Company 73; 1st Force Reconnaissance Battalion (1st Marine Division) 3, 76, 95, 126, 137, 157, 164, 165, 190, 210, 211, 222, 233, 235, 241, 244-247, 252, 294, 295; 1st Force Reconnaissance Company 3, 41, 70, 76-77, 81-83, 87, 93, 95-96, 98, 102, 103, 105-107, 116, 123, 126, 128-129, 131-132, 134-137, 144, 150-152, 154, 156, 164-165, 178-179, **188**, 190, 233, 238-241, 244-246, 252, 288-291, 293-294; 1st Marine Aircraft Wing (1st MAW) 143, 215, 239, 244; 1st Marine Brigade Headquarters 14; 1st Marine Division (FMF) 19, 21, 46, 61, 62, 69-70, 86, 95, 150, 157, 161, 190, 214, 215, 220, 245-247, 251-252, 292, 295; 1st Marine Raider Bn. 20, 45, 72; 1st Marine Regiment 69, 96, 164, 233, 251; 1st Platoon, VAC Reconnaissance Battalion 53-54, 58-63; 1st Provisional Marine Brigade 60; 1st Tank Battalion 69; 2nd Amphibious Reconnaissance Battalion 70-71, 74, 95; 2nd Force Reconnaissance Company 160, 161; 2nd Marine Division 52-53, 70, 71; 2nd Parachute Bn. 47; 2nd Platoon, VAC Reconnaissance Bn. 54-55, 59-60; 2nd Raider Battalion 32, 40, 50; 2nd Reconnaissance Bn. 71; 3rd Force Reconnaissance Company 3, 77, 87, 95, 96, 103-104, 110, 126, 135, 136, 138, 139, 143, 144, 146, 161-163, 190, 193, 196-198, 201-208, 212-214, 220-222, 224, 230, 232, 233, 235-238, 241, 243-244, 251-252, 277, 292, 298-299; 3rd Marine Amphibious Brigade (3rd MAB) 93, 97; 3rd Marine Division 3, 60, 70, 86-87, 93, 95-98, 100-101, 110-113, 116, 122, 123, 126, 128, 129, 135, 136, 137, 150, 156-159, 176, 190, 207-209, 215, 220-222, 224, 225, 227-229, 231-233, 235-237, 241, 245-246, 247, 274-275, 281, 2923rd Marine Regiment 94, 97, 101, 157-159, 178, 188; 4th Marine Division 56, 129, 132-**133**, 134, 224; 4th Marine Regiment 94, 97, 101, 128-129; 5th Force Reconnaissance Company 81, 159-160; 5th Marine Combat Operations Center (COC) 213; 5th Marine Expeditionary Brigade (5th MEB) 241; 5th Marine Regiment 14, 54, 213, 233, 246, 247, 251, 252; 5th Quick Reaction Force 247, 251; 5th Reconnaissance Battalion 95, 96; 7th Marine Regiment 72, 96, 123, 156, 178, 233; 8th Base Defense Battalion 52; 9th Marine Expeditionary Brigade 12, 91, 93, 95, 96, 97, 252; 9th Marine Regiment 91, 97, 229-231; 11th Marine Regiment (Artillery) 46, 239; 12th Marine (Artillery) Regiment 129, 166-167, 239; 26th Marine Regiment 95, 134-135, 150, 153, 216; 27th Marine Regiment 161; Alpha Company 249; Amphibious Corps, Atlantic Fleet 21-22; Amphibious Reconnaissance Battalion 48, 57, 59-62, 64, 74; Amphibious Reconnaissance Company 22, 25, 29, 38, 48, 68, 71, 72; Amphibious Reconnaissance Platoon 71; Anti-Aircraft Defense Battalions 19; Battalion Landing Team (BLT) 3rd Bn, 7th Marines 96, 98, 145; Battle for Hue City 191-193; Charlie Company 295; Combat Swimming Company, 1st Marine Division 62, 64, 68; Combined Action Company (CAC) 155; Combined Action Group (CAG) 155; Delta Company 161, 295; Division Reconnaissance Battalion 82, 83, 86; Division

Reconnaissance Company 69; Fleet Logistics Command 298; Fleet Marine Force 16, 64–65, 70, 86, 109, 216; Force Logistics Command 161; Force Reconnaissance Bn. 64–65, 159; Force Troops, FMFLant 71; HMM-161 134, 143–144; HMM-163 99; I Corps 67; I Marine Amphibious Corps (IMAC) 47; I Marine Amphibious Force 108; III Marine Amphibious Force (III MAF) 100, 122, 126, 129, 150–151, 153, 155, 159, 194, 214–217, 220–222, 235, 241, 274; Lima Company, 3rd Bn, 4th Marines 157; MAG-11 135; MAG-16 134; MAG-39 143; Marine Amphibious Force (MAF) 86, 153; Marine Composite Reconnaissance Squadron 1, 215; Marine Medium Helicopter Squadron-161 207; Marine Observation Squadron 2, 6, 215; Marine Observer Group 30; Marine Reconnaissance Test Unit 1, 74; MARS-16 87; NIGHT STICKER 129; Organizational Chart 58–60; Paratroops 19, 20, 26, 38; PRIMUS 129; Provisional Air Group 39; Provisional Reconnaissance Group (PRG) 126, 128; Raiders (Marine) Battalions (WWII) 19, 25, 29–30, 32, 38, 46, **65**, 115; Reconnaissance Group ALPHA 98; Reconnaissance Indoctrination Program (RIP), (Class 24-70) 247; Scout Companies 56, 57, 217; SCUBA Team 181–187 193, 222, 247, 252, 295; SPARROW HAWK, 3rd Marine Division Reaction Force 225; Special Landing Force 91, 96, 100, 145, 232; Special Operations Group 91; "Special Troops" Glider Troops 19, 20; Sub Unit 1, 91, 94, 96, 100, 101; Surveillance and Reconnaissance Center (SRC) 220; Surveillance and Target Acquisition teams (STA) 217, 295; T/O&E, 82–84; Task Force Bravo 129, 130; Task Force Charlie 129, 129; Task Force Delta 130; Task Force X-Ray 191, 192, 211–214, 220, 221, 226, 235; Team 51 179

180; V Amphibious Corps 25, 39, 41, 48; V Amphibious Reconnaissance Battalion, Fleet Marine Force, Pacific 57, 60–64; VAC Amphibious Reconnaissance Company 40, 41, 43–44, 48; Western Task Force 21; WestPAc 161; Zulu Relay 246
United States Marine Reconnaissance Teams: 2nd Platoon, 1st Force Reconnaissance Company PRIMUS 129; DOGMA 163; GROUCHO MARX 132–134; HATEFUL, 21–22, 128, 282–283; HAVEN 213; "Killer Kane" 119, 139, 152, 163–167, 172, 178, 188, 288–291; LAGUNA POINT 190–191; PRIMNESS 130–131; Provincial Reconnaissance Units (PRU) 242–243, 275; SWIFT SCOUT 139, 172, 178, 188, 233, 249; Task Force Hotel, 220; Team AMANDA 231–233; Team ARCTIC 243; Team ATLAS 105, 107, 114, 246, 300; Team BOX SCORE 200–202; Team BRISBANE **154**; Team CAYENNE 209; Team CENTIPEDE 228; Team COFFEE TIME II 213; Team CORAL BUSH 206–207; Team COUNTERSIGN 164–165; Team DATE PALM 212; Team DESKWORK 212, 213; Team ELF SKIN 209; Team FLIGHT TIME 227–228; Team GARLIC 243; Team HANSWORTH 245; Team MISTY CLOUD 244–245; Team Parallel Bars, 210; Team PONY 243; Team PRIME CUT 234; Team RECORD 213; Team REPORT CARD 226–227; Team ROAD TEST 247–248; Team TINNY 243; Team WAR CLOUD 249
United States Marine Reconnaissance Doctrine: FMFM-2-2, Amphibious Reconnaissance 118–119, 130; FMFM 6-1 Marine Division 118–119; FMFM 6-2, Marine Infantry Regiment 118–119; FMFM 8-1, Special Operations 119; FMFM 8-2, Counterinsurgency Operations 119
United States Navy 1, 2, 22, 23, 46, 126, 219, 225, 235; 95th

Construction Bn. (Seabees) 52; Amphibious Corps, Atlantic Fleet 21–22; Boston Navy Yard 8, 11; "Brown Water Fleet" 98; Bureau of Construction & Repair 17; Bureau of Engineering 17; Chief of Naval Operations 51; Commander-in-Chief, Pacific (CinCPac) 89; Field Medical Service School 109; Fleet Training Publication (FTP 167) 12, 23; Joint Action of the Army and Navy 1927 13; Joint Army-Navy Board (1927) 13; Mine Flotilla ONE (MSC) 91; Naval Advisory Detachment 87; Naval Amphibious Base 74; New London, CT 74; "New Steel Navy" 5; Office of Naval Intelligence (ONI) 49–51; Operation NEPTUNE 225–226; Pearl Harbor, HI 74; SCUBA School 160; SEALS (Sea, Air, Land) 12, 54, 89, 271; Seventh Fleet 90; Special Operations Group, CinCPac 89; Task Force 76, 94; UDT-1 91; UDT-11 91; UDT-12 91; Underwater Demolition Teams (UDT) 5, 13, 54, 59, 60, 68, 73, 98; U.S. Naval Hospital, Cam Ranh Bay, RVN 203
Unkel, Corp. E.J., USMC, SCUBA Team 1, 1st Force Reconnaissance Company, 180–187, **182**
Unsworth, Lt. USMC, Patrol Leader, Team PRIME CUT 234; in "Happy Valley," Operation OKLAHOMA 234

Vandergrift, Lt. Gen. Alexander A., USMC, Commandant of the Marine Corps 57
Van Drasek, Lance Corp. John, USMC 81, 161, 195, **204**
Vankat, 1st Lt. William, USMC 98
Van Ness, 1st Lt. C.P., USMC 16; *Development and Procurement of Special Landing Boats* 16–18
Vaughn, Lieutenant Colonel 29
Vaughn, Lance Corp. David, USMC, Team Coral Bush 206; Scotland II area 206
Vaughn, Corp. Donald W. 143; Door Gunner, HMM-161 143–144

Index

Vetter, Lt. Lawrence C., USMC 94, 104, 153
Vichy, France, North Africa 19, 35
Viet Cong (VC) 3, 91, 93, 96, 117, 120, 122, 124, 149, 150, 154, 155, 164, 166, 168, 249; Main Force units 167-168; 3-by-3 Principle, 168, 178-180, 210, 233, 245, 282-283
Vietnam War 1, 2; Vietnamization 247
Vietnamese Marine Corps, VNMC (South) 91
Vogel, Capt. Frederick J., USMC, Commanding Officer, SCUBA Team 1, 1st Force Reconnaissance Company 180-187, *182*, *184*; dive on the Silver Bridge 193, 210-211

Walt, Lt. Gen. Lewis W., Commanding General, III MAF 72, 73, 96, 97, 115, *117*; WWII Raider Commander 117-*118*, 120, 123, 130, 150-152, 154-155, 163
War Plan "Orange" 48-50
War with Spain (1898) 5-8
Watson, Brig. Gen. Thomas E., USMC, Commanding General, 4th Marine Division 56
weapons (North Vietnamese, Chinese, Viet Cong) 296-297; 82-mm Mortar (Soviet) 159, 170; 122mm Rockets 208; 300mm Rockets (Russian) 179; AK-47 87, 107, 109, 142, 170, 177, 205, 233, 248, 250; D30 122-mm Howitzer (Soviet) 229-230; French 7.5 Semiautomatic Rifle 170; Japanese 6.5 Semiautomatic Rifle 170; M1 Garand Rifle 170; NVA Anti-Aircraft Guns 230, 233; Rocket Propelled Grenades (RPG-2) 158, 170, 228; SKS 7.62mm Carbine 87, 170; Soviet 82mm Recoilless Rifle (B-10) 170; Soviet 107mm Mortar 170; Soviet 120mm Mortar 170; Soviet-Chinese 7.62mm Light Machine Gun (Chinese Type 56) 170; Type 50 Machine Gun (Chinese) 170; US M1 Carbine 170

weapons (United States) 279-280; 30 Caliber M1919A1 Machine Gun 80; .45 Caliber Pistol 29, 109, 138, 191; .50 Caliber Machine Gun 234; 57-mm Recoilless Rifle 87; 60-mm Mortar 235; 105-mm Howitzers 130, 135, 239; 155-mm Howitzer 135, 239; AR-15 98; Browning Automatic Rifle (BAR) 79, M-14, 79, 83, 107, 138, 145, 146, 234, 235, 288; C4 Explosives 147; Claymore Mines 147, 234, 235; CS Gas 147; CS Grenades 103, 108, 136, 138-139, 205, 228, 245, 289; "Howtars" 135; K-Bar Knife 103, 108, 138, 229; M-1 Carbine 77; M-1 Garand Rifle 77; M-16 79, 107, 138, 141, 152, 174, 272, 288, 289; M-18 Smoke Grenades 108; M-26 Grenade 108; M-26 Grenade Launcher 288; M-33 Shell-Fragmentation Grenades 209; M-60 Machine Gun 83, 109, 138, 234, 272; M-72 LAAW 108; M-79 "Blooper" Grenade Launcher 83, 138, 145, 146, 225, 288; M3A1 Machine Pistol "Grease Gun" 77, 80, 83, 108, 138, 282-283; M7A2 Gas Mask 139; Starlight Scope 146; Stoner, Light Machine Gun 109, 288, 289; TNT 147; Tommy Gun 26; .x750 Binoculars 288
Webb, Gunnery Sgt. Walter A., USMC 179
Wellman, Corp. William M., Jr., USMC, Team FLIGHT TIME 228
"Welman," One-man Submarine 34
West, Staff Sergeant, U.S. Army, U.S. Army Special Forces 124
West, Bing, Marine Officer, Operation Hastings 130
Westmoreland, Gen. William C., U.S. Army, Commanding General, US Military Assistance Command, Vietnam (ComGenUSMACV) 89, 128-129, 150, 154, 155, 266, 268-271; strategy 269-271

Whaling, Lt. Col. William J., USMC 46
Wheeler, Capt. Edward, B., USMC 46, 115, 118
Whittingham, Capt. David, USMC, Commanding Officer, Sub Unit 1, 91
Williams, Lance Corporal, USMC, wounded in action Team SWIFT SCOUT 289
Williams, Brig. Gen. Dion, USMC 1, 7-12, *9*, 17, 22, 32, 40, 255; *Naval Reconnaissance: Instructions for the Reconnaissance of Bays, Harbors, and Adjacent Country* (1907) 1, 10-12
Williamson, Brig. Gen. Ellis W., U.S. Army, Commanding General, 173rd Airborne Brigade 270
Williamson, 2nd Lt. Thomas W., USMC, Commanding Officer, TEAM DOGMA 163; Operation Pecos 163
Willoughby, William H., U.S. Army, Commander, 7th Scout Company, 42-3
Wills, HM2, Hospital Corpsman, Team SWIFT SCOUT, 290
Wingate, Orde, Brigadier General, 26, Chindits, 26, 259, 261-262, 265
Winston, Corp. Harry, USMC, 230, (photo of), Team ATLAS, 230
Woo, Corp. Donald M., USMC, 124-125
Worton, Maj. William A., USMC, 50

Yamazaki, Col. Yasuyo, Commander, Japanese Forces on Attu 42

Zais, Lt. Gen. Melvin, U.S. Army, Commanding General, XXIV Corps 241
Zedong, Mao 50-51, 168; Chinese Civil War 168-169; on counter-reconnaissance 171; Giap-Mao Doctrine 170-171; Maoist Model of Organization 168; Maoist tactics 269; military tactics 169-171

www.ingramcontent.com/pod-product-compliance
Lightning Source LLC
Chambersburg PA
CBHW060335010526
44117CB00017B/2835